The Magnificent Message

A Modern Translation of the Qur'aan

Holy Revelation from Almighty God

Edited by Dr. Kaasem Khaleel (Dr. K.)
with Judy Kay Gray, M.S.

ISBN 10: 1-931078-21-1
ISBN 13: 978-1-931078-21-4

To order this or additional Knowledge House books call: 1-866-626-5888 or order via the web at: www.knowledgehousepublishers.com

To get an order form send a SASE to:
Knowledge House Publishers
105 East Townline Road
Unit 116
Vernon Hills, IL 60061

Dedication

For those who seek the ultimate truth

Acknowledgements

I would like to thank the souls of all previous Qur'aanic translators, since all their efforts were essential in the making of this edition. In particular, Muhammad Asad deserves special mention, as does S. Hussein Pasha for originating this idea. I would also like to thank my co-editor, Judy Kay Gray, M.S. (Angelica Lord), for her many insights and her English expertise as well as J. Daggett Gleason for her attention to detail. I would also like to thank my designer Bob Masheris for his insight in the design of this text.

The massive negative press against Islaam, which is obviously done with malice, was another motivation for this work. This included the hateful and untrue statements against Usama bin Laden. For instance, bin Laden was blamed for the destruction of the World Trade Center, which is false. He is falsely accused, so the real criminals responsible for the death and destruction can escape. Thus, truly, there is a malicious agenda to falsely associate Islaam, as well as the essence of this Qur'aan, with terror. Above all, I thank God, because He is the true source of all inspiration.

K.K.

CONTENTS

Preface

This truly is a magnificent message. The word Qur'aan explains it all. It means recitation. This book was recited from the high heavens to the Prophet Muhammad. It is obviously an inspired book. It is also obviously divine in source. There is no doubt about it this is a book of divine writings from the almighty creator of the vast universe. This is because it reveals secrets about human nature that only such a high One could know.

Originally, it was pagans who were its recipients. These pagans had no future. Then, after believing in this message these individuals became the leaders of civilization. The people inspired by this book became creators of all modern inspiration. They even inspired the Renaissance and, ultimately, the modern sciences.

People speak ignorantly about this writing. Yet, they have no understanding of its meaning or content. Like the original Old Testament, throughout the Qur'aan there is only one purpose. This is the guidance of humankind. It is as if the great and almighty God is pursuing human beings to assist them, to prevent them from causing self-harm. This prevention of harm is the entire basis of this grand document.

No human could create such a way, this way of pursuing humanity with guidance. The grandness of the Qur'aan is precisely this fact: that God is a most generous being, who wants the best for His creation. This is the main theme throughout this book. He does all in His power to save humans from their own weaknesses, largely by warning them of the consequences of their acts. Yet, as the Qur'aan demonstrates, He expects much from His humans. He expects them to worship Him, but of course, He makes it clear that this is strictly for their own benefit. Regardless, it is wondrous to have the warning, because as this high Being makes clear in this book He is in no need for any support from anyone to operate the grand functions of the universe, the least of which are humans. What's more, as this Qur'aan makes clear humans are only one of countless creation in His infinite realm, although, apparently, one of His more sophisticated beings but not the most sophisticated.

The Qur'aan emphasizes another fact: that this life is with a purpose. It is not a game. The purpose is the dedicated service God. This is the only way this earth can be preserved from corruption. By serving God a person secures his future: such a one becomes a success in this life and in the next. Yes, the next: this book leaves no doubt about the existence of another realm. The material life is merely a test. It is transitory. It is the staging ground for people to prove themselves. The real life occurs with death. This is why God sends prophets: to awaken people to the realization of another realm and to cause them to release their bonds to this temporary material life.

This is no racist document. Christians and jews are mentioned perhaps more than Muslims. By name, Jesus is mentioned more than Muhammad, as is Abraham and Moses. This is a book for all people. This is obvious to anyone, who carefully reads it. God sent prophets to remind people of His existence. Then, He is the afterlife. Everyone knows these prophets existed. Their permanence in human history is proof of His presence and message. The Prophet Muhammad was merely the final of this chain of Abrahamic prophets. It was this unlettered man who, miraculously, bore the Qur'aan.

People get attached to this life, as if it is the only realm. They may even categorically reject the possibility of the next life. The Qur'aan argues this point. This life, it notes, is fleeting. The final life is eternal. By submitting before God the person earns peace in the eternal existence. By rejecting Him the person earns eternal torment. Symbolically, the greatest torment, says the Qur'aan, is the loss of God's love, while the greatest reward—the greatest paradise—is the earning of His love. Gratitude for His blessings is a protection, a source of true rewards, while ingratitude is a source of permanent agony.

It is true that the Qur'aan is aimed at the people of Islaam. It gives them an entire code of living. It tells them that their religion or rather way of life is absolute submission to Him. It encourages the people of Christianity and Judaism to also follow this way, since it is only this way that is absolutely true. Yet, it does not force them to do so: if they refuse, says the Qur'aan, at least they should abide vigorously to the true principles of their faiths.

Jealousy, says the Qur'aan, abounds among people of scripture. The Muslims, this book commands, are to have nothing to do with it and are instead to remain patient and allow all events to unfold. All people are to be treated equally and spoken to in peace. No one is to be unjustly harmed or coerced. The Qur'aan is the only holy book which expressedly bans coercion in matters of faith, that is "There will be no coercion in religion, no force."

No one group has the right to the divine kingdom. Only God's truly righteous ones have access, and only they gain such access because of any good deeds and primarily because of His infinite mercy. People of all backgrounds who do good are rewarded. No one people has a special relationship with God. The only special ones are those who devoutly worship Him, submitting before Him in true awe and love.

Then, to give God human love is the greatest of all achievements. Too, the Qur'aan contains only one major commandment for this human race: that humans love their fellow humans. This is the only requirement of the Qur'aan. The rest is merely preventive advice. Could there be a more magnificent message than this?

Introduction

The Qur'aan is divine guidance. This is indisputable. A person might refuse to believe in it. However, such a person is unable to dispute the fact that it is extraterrestrial and therefore written by almighty God.

The word itself means *reading* or *recitation*. It is derived from an Arabic word, which means "to read."

This book was originally revealed in Arabic. This is a clear language. This makes it perfect for divine revelation. It was received by the Prophet Muhammad. This man was illiterate. Originally, he was a shepherd. Then, he became a merchant. At age forty after much meditation he received the message.

The Qur'aan was revealed to him systematically. This was through the medium of the angel Gabriel.

There is no reason to argue about the status of this document. Any careful reading will determine that it is not man-made. It is obviously extraterrestrial. This means it is divine script.

The Qur'aan was revealed gradually. This was to suit the needs of its original recipients, the followers of the Prophet. It was never sent down as a complete book.

Its recipient, the Prophet Muhammad, was directly related to the Prophet Abraham. This means he was related to Moses, Jacob, and Jesus. Ultimately, it means that all these men were brothers in faith.

Prior to revelation the Prophet had no interest in public service. Nor had he ever preached a message. Nor had he sought fame. Rather, he was exceedingly private, in fact, shy. He received the Qur'aan only after many years of meditation and contemplation. This was regarding the dire state of his people. The latter were pagans.

The Qur'an, spelled here *Qur'aan* to represent its actual pronunciation, the last syllable sounding like the 'aw' in awning, is for the benefit of humankind. This book is strictly for guidance. It reaches human hearts. It also offers sound advice for future benefit.

Its purpose is to cause people to think. This is to give serious consideration to a human's real role on this earth. Thus, its only value, its only real power, is to understand it. In contrast, mere ritual—mere superficial practices—are never its goal. Rather, its objective is humankind and its purpose is to guide the human soul. Then, this is strictly for human benefit. The Qur'aan makes it clear that almighty God needs no one. Thus, to believe in and follow the Qur'aan only benefits the individual.

In the past this revelation has been translated literally. This makes for difficult reading. This is especially true for Westerners. Most Westerners are only able to understand the Qur'aan if it is explained to them. This is particularly true of children and teenagers. Thus, such translations are rarely read. Common books are easier than these to read.

People have limited attention spans. For many people the slightest strain is a hindrance. People tend to gravitate from anything that is difficult. The Qur'aan was meant to be easy to understand. It says so throughout its text. This is the objective of this version.

There are a plethora of literal Qur'aanic translations. This translation is in a more simple form. It is easier to read than the literal types. Extensions of the meanings are found in parenthesis, again for easier understanding.

Literal does not always mean accurate. For instance, in Section 37 of the Qur'aan there is a word describing the beautiful beings of paradise. Literally, this word means *egg*. In other words, it describes a perfectly shaped white object. A deeper meaning is a beautiful and perfect object, which radiates light. It may also mean an object, like an egg, which is fresh and new. One translator describes these beings as so beautiful—so free of faults as if "hidden ostrich eggs." Yet, a more vivid description is so magnificent in appearance as if a "perfect pearl." This latter description captures the true meaning, since the real message is that these beings are perfection in creation and actually glow in their beauty, like a hidden glistening pearl, when it is first discovered. The point is these beings are free of defects. Plus, they are so pure they sparkle. The image of a glistening unblemished pearl, freshly extracted from its shell, more readily conveys this than the image of a freshly unearthed egg. So, literal translations may not be ideal.

Anyone who reads literal translations knows they are cumbersome. While the objective of literal translations is to create "orthodox" editions, the Qur'aan was never meant to be orthodox. Nor is it rigid. In fact, compared to other books or even religious texts it is unorthodox. This is because it is highly liberal. It gives no set rules, which are cumbersome or difficult to follow. What's more, nothing in it violates common sense. Rather, it is based upon common sense. In numerous places it describes itself as being revealed in "clear" language which is "easy to understand." Thus, if it is properly translated, any person can understand the depth of its message.

This is proven through proclamations such as "This is the book of God—there is no doubt about it."[1] Or, "This is the book of God, which clearly demonstrates the truth."[2] Again, says the Qur'aan, "These are the signs—obvious messages—from a book which is clearly (divine)." Too, no one can scientifically dispute its divine origin.

The Qur'aan says that it is a clear, understandable document. In Arabic it is strikingly clear. Yet, incredibly, this would never be realized by reading the standard translations. In this version the meaning becomes obvious. This suits the purpose of the

---

[1] As translated by S.H. Pasha, Ph.D., Cortland, New York.

[2] As translated by M. Asad in the *Message of the Qur'an.*

🌿 13 🌿

Qur'aan. Now, a person can understand it for what it is: obvious divine revelation.

The aim of the Qur'aan is human beings. It speaks to them directly. There is no need for an intermediary. It raises souls to the highest state possible. It creates justice among them. This is by commanding them to follow the ways of God. These ways are demonstrated by His select messengers. Its goal is to cause human beings to serve each other *in love*. This is the ultimate purpose of this book.

So, this book is about life on this planet. It is about how to live in the finest way possible. This is to prepare for the next life. This is by following God's way. Thus, rather than a religious book to be merely studied the purpose is to adhere to it. In other words, its commands must be practiced. That is the only way a person can become a true believer.

This book is strictly for human benefit. Its purpose is to guide people. This is so they will gain the greatest success possible, here and in the next life. So, only humans benefit from this revelation. God gains no such benefit. In fact, it protects them from their own self-destructive tendencies.

The Qur'aan consists of sentence- or phrase-like segments. In Arabic each of these is known as an *aya*. This means sign or message. These messages are powerful. This is because they reach directly into human hearts. They are also powerful, because they tell humans how best to behave so that they shall live in decency and justice. Every rule in this book is based upon justice.

Rather than a book of poetry or spirituality the Qur'aan is an actual guide. As first made clear by the Islaamic scholar S. H. Pasha, Ph.D., there are no verses in the Qur'aan. This is because rather than poetry it is direct divine guidance. So, rather than verses it contains phrases, sentences, and paragraphs as well as chapters. It also contains parables, that is examples, for guidance.

Arabic is an ancient language. It is elegant, even sophisticated. It is also exceptionally succinct. The brevity of the Arabic words has in the past created challenges in translations. However, with careful analysis these Arabic words and phrases can be translated into English relatively accurately. Thus, a meaning similar to the Arabic can be achieved.

The method used in this version is to convert the Arabic words and phrases into easy-to-understand English. This is in order to thoroughly represent the meaning of this book. All archaic forms of English such as thee, thou, thine, art, and similar difficult-to-read words are removed. Explanations or extensions of the revelation are found in parentheses and also explanatory notes. These aid in the understanding. The purpose is to help all people understand the message of the Qur'aan, without relying upon anyone else. Unless it is understood the Qur'aan serves no purpose. The explanatory notes are found throughout the text in small type.

Again, the Qur'aan speaks directly to the individual. No intermediaries are needed. What's more, it speaks precisely to human hearts. This is why it brings tears to the unlearned as well as the most erudite scholar.

This book has another unique purpose. It is to bring peace to the human race. This is so humans can be as productive as possible. In other words, it aims to cause humans to live in justice. This is its true purpose. If it is misunderstood, there is no way to benefit from it. In fact, misunderstanding can be destructive.

The Qur'aan was originally revealed in the seventh century A.D. It is an exceedingly powerful revelation. The Prophet felt great pressure whenever he received it. For twenty-three years until his death the revelation proceeded, bit by bit. Eventually, it was collated into a book.

Consider the original Qur'aanic writings. These were written on whatever material the primitive Arabs could find: mere bones and the like. Incredibly, animal bones and hides were the original Qur'aanic documents. These writings were collected and held by Hafsa, one of the Prophet's wives. Only later was it converted into a book. It was also memorized by hundreds of adherents. The combination of memorization plus the writing down of every sentence made this the first divine book in history which is fully preserved. Incredibly, within thirty years of his death a complete and official copy of the Qur'aan was produced, totally in Arabic. In contrast, no such comparative effort for the Bible was achieved. This is not to say which book is superior but rather to merely state categorically which one is unaltered.

Globally, all copies of the Qur'aan are the same. This is proof that it is original and preserved. This preservation is also confirmed by the fact that copies of the Qur'aan over a thousand years old are precisely the same as those in existence today.

The Qur'aan seeks justice. This justice is through the efforts of God's honored servants. All the prophets came for this reason. Without people fighting for goodness all will descend into anarchy. The Qur'aan is the tool to prevent this.

Everyone is proud of David for slaying Goliath. In this respect he was a true servant of God—a true Muslim. The Qur'aan promotes this type of approach, that is that true believers must stand up for the truth. This effort, known in Arabic as *jihaad,* which is the more correct spelling than jihad, is the means to earn the favor, even love, of God. This effort could be spiritual. It could also be gaining an education, teaching, representing God's truths, or pursuing a career or job. Then, this term means to work hard for God's sake. All such efforts are types of jihaad, as long as they are done for the love of God. More rarely, as in David's case, it may represent actual warfare. Yet, words of truth are themselves weapons, *more powerful than steel.*

By truly internalizing the message of this book the person becomes "of God." This is a just soul, who represents in every way conceivable the truth. Such a person stands up for the truth, regardless of the consequence. This is the greatest type of jihaad.

For the believer in terms of personal guidance the Qur'aan is the source. It proclaims that all the individual must keep in mind is found within it. This means that there is no need to rely on any human for guidance. The Qur'aan is the focus for a person's life. This is the means to guide him, so he does not make major errors. What's more, regarding the needs of the human heart it contains all that is critical. Yet, the personal behavior of the Prophet is also crucial, because he is an obvious guide. He completely practiced this message. So, to adhere to it thoroughly his example must be followed.

Even so, the Prophet, notes the Qur'aan, is merely a warner. He is also a sign of God's loving mercy. Through his example much can be learned for human benefit. Regarding the Qur'aan the Prophet is merely a guide to interpret it. More importantly, he is *the source* of how to act upon it.

He said regarding those who wish to learn or understand the Qur'aan, essentially, 'Learn from observing me.' Thus, he is the designated interpreter, the divinely appointed guide. In fact, the basis of the Qur'aan is simple. It is to follow the ways of Prophet[3] in order to achieve the ultimate result: the absolute pleasure of almighty God. It was God who selected this man. If a person has access to the top man, obviously, there is no need for any other guide.

His example alone, that is how he lived, as well as what he said, represents the true basis of this book. "Watch me," that is "experience me," in fact, "become

---

[3]For his actual sayings and teachings, see *The Words of Muhammad*, Knowledge House Publishers (same author). For more information see www.knowledgehousepublishers.com.

like me," he emphasized, not merely "listen to me." This is a profound concept. It means that in order to truly practice the Qur'aan the person must become "Muhammad-like." Or, at a minimum a person must become like any other of God's select, for instance, Jesus Christ, Moses, or Abraham.

Anyone who adopts the ways of these messengers is a true follower of the Qur'aan. For instance, says the Qur'aan, if a person truly wishes to become close to God, he should "follow the ways of Abraham." Then, what are these ways? Abraham is the one who "rejected all that is false."

The Prophet clearly indicated that it was the principles of this book which must first be grasped. Thus, to truly understand these principles is of far greater significance than mere ritual. According to the Qur'aan it is deep thinking which brings a person close to God. The deeper is the thinking the closer the individual will become to Him. In other words, rather than mere words or recitation true belief is represented in a person's behavior, in fact, example. Thus, rather than mere procedure it is the person's inner self, that is his/her very essence, that is most critical. Then, the ultimate believer in God is the person with the most refined and dignified personality. It is the most decent person who is the finest believer. Said the Prophet a fine and dignified personality is an immense asset. This is the real meaning of being a Muslim.

Yet, he led his life with such dignity. Because of the elegance of his behavior he had a vast impact on the future of the world. This man alone prevented the decay of civilization, rather, he revived it. Western historians document the fact that without him there would be no modern world. In fact, if people truly lived in heart and spirit like him, even today there would be a revolution in civilization. Thus, if his ways were thoroughly established, there would be no global strife.

He alone offers the principles, that is the complete system, for human behavior, which preserves, rather, advances civilization. For instance, it was this man alone who brought personal, as well as public, hygiene to the world. What's more, he did so when it was unknown. It was also he who taught the importance of seeking knowledge when the entire world had sunk into barbarism.

He created the world's first civil society, where people of all backgrounds could live in peace and justice. Through his efforts alone civilization was revived. Thus, by failing to truly adopt him, this example of truth, justice, tolerance, and liberty, despair reigns. The condition that humans relish in today, including the refinements of Western civilization, is due to him. Yet, in the Western world people are unaware of their tie to him.

Compared to his true message—the deep and profound message found within this Qur'aan—the rituals of Islaam are of minor importance. The real purpose of this way is to establish justice.

Yet, again, the vast contribution of this man to Western civilization—the true elegance of his achievement—is largely unknown. Even in many parts of the Muslim world his contribution to civilization is largely unknown. Here, people may retain the outward appearance of his message, for instance, ritual fasting and worship. However, they may fail to fully understand, as well as adopt, his true person. The latter is that revolutionary essence, which changed the world.

Yet, this way is more than for mere personal redemption. Islaam is against all forms of tyranny. Therefore, the Muslim is obligated to fight it vigorously. What's more, he is obligated to resist this tyranny for the sake of humankind. Any Muslim who refuses to do so is a marginal believer at best.

The Prophet Muhammad was tyrannized by the powerful and wealthy. This was because they regarded his mission as a threat. He was brutalized, tormented, and scorned. This was despite the fact that he was universally recognized as a prophet, even by hostile local Jewish tribes. His followers were also brutalized and tortured. Many were murdered. Others were forced to renounce their faith.

He had the right to respond: to even kill. He had the weapons and ability to do so. Yet, he fully restrained himself. Thus, he endured this tyranny for 13 years. He went to battle only when his people were threatened with extermination. What's more, he did so only after being in a position of strength. When he was in such a position, he fought back through war. As he fought against entire civilizations he faced immense odds. Yet, he won continuously until his death.

Even so, Islaam is never pro-war. There is nothing in the Qur'aan to indicate a pro-war stance. What's more, the killing of the innocent is banned. In fact, peace, the Qur'aan makes clear, is always preferable to conflict. Under the Prophet Muhammad, even during war, death was exceedingly rare. Most wars were fought to prevent the Islaamic civilization from being crushed, the defense against the Crusaders being a classic example. Thankfully, because of his wisdom and vigor this system was preserved.

As a result of the campaigns of modern powers there was—and is—great oppression. In contrast, the campaigns of the Prophet Muhammad created positive change. His campaigns even resulted in social revolutions, including the Renaissance.

According to top Western historians there would be no refined Western civilization without this man. Thus, without him, modern civilization would never have advanced. Nor would there be any Western science. His direct influence on the West is undeniable and is documented by numerous Western historians, including Goldstein, Durant, Sarton, Byng, Bernard Shaw, and Carlyle. Thus, the claims against Islaam in the press and media are fabricated. For instance, the media makes it appear that Islaam is repressive. Yet, as proven by the influence of the Prophet there is nothing in this faith which fights progress. These statements are disseminated by Islaam's enemies. This man revived civilization. In contrast, modern conquerors destroy it.

Yet, according to the Qur'aan for a just cause God sanctions fighting. If the Muslims or any other God-fearing people are attacked, then, all possible resources must be mobilized to halt such an attack. These include every conceivable type of force. Islaam is about resisting, in fact, fighting. The fight is against tyranny. This is for the survival of the entire human race. Thus, this is the public service of this way. It is the only power capable of resisting oppression.

In the fight against tyranny all types of warfare are utilized. This is until the aggression ceases. However, innocent people—women, children, the crippled, and the elderly—must never be killed. Peoples' homes and places of refuge, such as bomb shelters and hospitals, must never be destroyed.

In Islaam terrorism against innocent people is banned. Rather, the warfare is only against legitimate fighters. This proves that Islaam is far more civilized than any Western system. This fight is only against actual enemies, that is those who cause corruption. This is the Qur'aanic view of the war against tyranny.

Warfare is also legitimized when it involves expansion of its State, that is that government based upon the divine law. It is a warfare to protect boundaries. It is also a warfare to eradicate tyranny. It is to rescue peoples held in bondage, repressed by merciless tyrants. It is to bring corrupt humanity a new way of life: that is the worship of God instead of human elements—instead of godlessness and/or barbarism of any type—instead of false gods or any other impotent earthly power. This is a warfare to establish the divine principles versus barbarism and/or tyranny. It is a warfare to crush the grip of the oppressor. Other than self-defense this is the only warfare that is allowed.

This is the Qur'aan's view. Only God, it says, has the right to rule. Thus, any element which interferes with His rule is subject to attack. Those who fight against the way of God—against decency and justice—are legitimate targets. In fact, such corrupt elements are regarded by God Himself as the enemy. These individuals are described in the Qur'aan as those who are consumed in darkness: the darkness of their own lies. They are those who purposely reject His way, the true enemy, slated by Him for punishment.

This punishment, notes the Qur'aan, is achieved by God Himself, both in this life and in the future one. He merely uses His believers to help achieve this, because the believers are commanded to fearlessly fight all oppressors. What's more, only He has the power to resurrect souls, bringing them all before Him at the final time.

Even so, tyranny rules throughout the land. As a result, even in this modern world mass crimes are committed. The unbridled theft of peoples' rights—the theft and/or occupation of their land, their economic assets, their homes, and their freedom—is barbarism. In Islaam, all such acts are banned. This tormenting of the innocent is terrorism in its most extreme degree. This is the very barbarism and terrorism against which Islaam fights. Thus, a war against any such group, which promotes hate and racism, which causes the theft of assets from the weak or innocent, is sanctioned.

Even so, from the Islaamic point of view all forms of tyranny are prohibited. Furthermore, unlike in the Western system, for instance, the allowance for so-called collateral damage, where innocent people are blown to shreds—in Islaam such killing is banned. In fact, historically, rather than an instigator of terror Islaam has routinely been the victim. The Crusades, the Mongol invasions, and the Inquisition are notable examples. So are the atrocities committed in modern times against, for instance, the Bosnian, Philippino, Indonesian, Iraqi, Iranian, Chechen, Egyptian, Algerian, and Palestinian Muslims. In contrast, says the Qur'aan, only those who actively fight the Muslims, including those who drive them from their homes and countries, are to be fought.

Yet, again, the Qur'aan never emphasizes warfare. The latter is merely a means of survival. Rather, its focus is on the battle within. This is the effort for self-improvement. This is through gaining a deeper and more profound understanding of God's way.

This is why it is unique. It attempts to cause humans to use their reason. That is its essence. True, in passing it mentions warfare, the penal code, and social laws. However, that is of minor significance compared to the vastly overriding message regarding the use of reason. Its objective is to cause humans to think, all for the salvation of the individual and thus collectively humankind. Thus, the majority of this book deals with the use of the mind, while relatively minor sections deal with war.

There is yet another objective: consolidation. Every era had its sage, prophet, and/or saint. The objective, notes the Qur'aan, always is the same: the dedicated worship of God. Moses created a powerful movement, but it eventually became diminished, and even his progeny couldn't maintain it. Jesus regenerated the Law. Ultimately, he created vast changes in civilization. Singlehandedly, he "converted" to monotheism an empire given to mere vileness. Thus, godless Rome was displaced by the Holy Roman Empire. Yet, the essence of Christ's message was rapidly smothered. Thus, as Muslims believe, to revive humanity God required another messenger from the lineage of Abraham. This was in order to regenerate the faith in one universal God.

The Prophet Muhammad was precisely that man. He arrived among a new, fresh people. He also brought a new framework: that is a universal divine code. This is a code written for the benefit of the masses, that is for all humankind. One author-translator quotes the 38th section of the Qur'aan with: "To each period its own book. God eliminates what He wills and preserves what He wills." This illustrates the concept of consolidation, that is a culmination of the finest concepts revealed in earlier holy books, while eliminating the useless or outdated material. It also indicates that almighty God replaced corrupted materials with pure material.

Some individuals of the Christian or Jewish faiths may be surprised to find enormous similarities in the Qur'aan to biblical texts. They shouldn't be: God revealed them all. The Qur'aan is merely the most recent of these. Its message is the same as the previous ones. What's more, it contains much of the essence found in the original but now altered or lost Jewish and Christian texts. Thus, it may be regarded as a compounding of the most useful parables, lessons, dictates, and practices infused into previous civilizations, plus ones never before realized.

The Qur'aan never describes an exclusive religion. Instead, it describes the way of life *practiced by* Noah, Abraham, Moses, Jesus, and Muhammad. It claims that this is God's true religion. These individuals are the models for the true way of life. Then, this is the way of this Qur'aan. This is Islaam. Plus, the Qur'aan describes definitions, that is what it means to be a 'Muslim,' a 'believer,' etc.

As described by M. M. Katircioglu this liberal nature of Islaam is made clear in the Qur'aan in Section 43 with, "God has revealed to you the way of religion which He committed Noah to follow, so that you, too, might follow it." Thus, the message is that there truly is a divine way, which reverts to the time of Noah or prior. In other words, the Qur'aan's message claims there is only one correct "religion." This is submission to God, known in Arabic as Islaam. This is the same submission as practiced by Abraham and countless others. Thus, this is the only true religion or rather way acceptable to Him. It is the same way followed by all of God's agents, including Abraham, Moses, Bhudda, Jacob, Jesus, Mary, Muhammad, and countless others. Noah of the Ark, the ancestor to much of humankind, also adhered to it. The implications are profound. It is that humanity has a single way that it must follow: for everyone. The Qur'aan perpetuates this view with, "This is the same way which We revealed to you and which We revealed to Abraham, Moses, and Jesus, the objective being that *Our true way of life* might continue on the earth. What's more, never divide yourself into sects."

Religion is merely a means to maintain law and order. It is a way to prevent wanton evil. Throughout its history humankind has shown the need for regulation, that is for understanding the rules needed for self-policing. In this life law and order is required. There is even a police force to maintain it. Why would it be any different in the divine realm? Thus, it is expected that for humans there are divine laws, which must be upheld. These divine laws are one of the reasons that there is still a degree of law and order in the world, although this is diminishing rapidly.

The formula for success is simple. All that is required to gain entrance to the kingdom of God is to submit to Him. This applies to all human beings. Here, no one person, regardless of status, wealth, or race, is higher than anyone else. Thus, the God of Islaam is just.

Yet, this self-submission, in fact, *is* a special club. Only relatively few people attain this rarified status. Thus, there is an explanation for the vast number of religions seen today. They are caused by the exact opposite of self-surrender: greed, lust, rivalry, competition, jealousy, and similar emotions of self-aggrandizement. What's more, many sects have as their basis mere details: insignificant differences, which God Himself has never authorized.

If belief in Him is based upon reason and if God is truly the Source, if He is a Being of reason, shouldn't people of all faiths get along? Shouldn't they be tolerant of each other at least to the point of not purposely harming each other, merely due to pride or perhaps greed? History proves that people destroy each other only because of perceived differences. Yet, incredibly, often God is blamed for human strife. In contrast, the Qur'aan makes it clear that if good happens, it is from Him, while if evil strikes, it is from within. The implication is that humans cause their own harm. God is unrelated.

The religion of God portrayed by the Qur'aan is simple. It is that God made all that exists. It is that all that exists is dependent upon Him. Therefore, the message is that all people should be grateful. This is by being obedient to Him. In other words, the person must prove that he or she is truly submissive. Then, it is not God who needs this submission. Rather, it is the person who benefits.

From the Qur'aanic point of view there is one crime that is unforgivable. This is a lack of gratitude. What's more, the most profound example of this is the rejection of God. This is because all that a human possesses, even his own self, is from Him.

This rejection of God is vile. The Qur'aan makes it clear that God will evaluate everyone's behavior. He will do so through a system that is real but beyond human comprehension. He expects humans to know this. He expects them to know they are responsible for their actions. The evaluation occurs during this life but also continues after death.

Regarding the latter the time is fixed by God. Humans will never be able to predict it. The exact time is irrelevant. What matters is that God has warned humans about it and asks them to prepare for it. He cannot guarantee anything, except that if humans truly believe in Him and refuse to bow to or worship false powers, they will be safe. However, the consequences of rejecting this are frightening, beyond description.

This willful rejection of God is the greatest crime conceivable. People who are unaware of the differences between right and wrong, who have never fully comprehended divine revelation, will be treated leniently. However, it is the duty of the true believer to inform them, strictly for their benefit. This is so they can protect their souls and so they won't be caught unawares.

The portrayal continues, again, noting that defying God is despicable. It leads to highly destructive consequences. The sense of responsibility for actions is lost. Thus, people have no inhibitions for the commission of vile acts. They never consider themselves accountable for such acts. The result is that people suffer extreme harm. Nations and populations are destroyed. Races are exterminated. The name of God is obstructed from common use, and His rules are defiled. As a result, tyranny reigns. Hundreds of thousands, in fact, millions of the innocent are sickened, harmed, raped, tortured, and even killed. Yet, all this is preventable. The prevention is through holding to the divine law.

The corruption of the divine law is no minor issue. This is the goal of modern powers. As a result, oppression becomes the norm. So does poverty. People are consumed by disease and despair. Yet, it is all due to Western meddling. While evil and greedy people enrich themselves entire civilizations are destroyed.

Such corrupt souls, immersed in evil, are threatened by any warning from God. Thus, they attack any true believers. In fact, this corruption is the basis of the war against Islaam.

These wicked elements attack Islaam, because it threatens their tyrannical basis. Yet, there is another reason for their hate. It is their position that there is no return to God. So, they fight all who proclaim this return.

The Qur'aan makes it clear that to purposely fight against God is loathe. It is the most corrupt of all acts. It is so vile that God reserves a special type of agony for the perpetrators. In contrast, those who fight against such perpetrators are His honored servants. Therefore, it advances two basic principles: evil will be punished, and good will be rewarded. That is its essence, and that is the warning it disseminates.

Envy is also warned against. So is selfishness. The Qur'aan teaches that the latter, so common in today's civilizations, is a crime. Instead, it requires charity, not merely the giving of money but rather the giving of the self. Helping others, even total strangers, who are in need, is a requirement. God's demands are few: that people be decent to each other and that they live on the earth in peace. Perhaps its most profound principle appears in the 160th statement, Chapter 6, where it says, "All I ask is that you love your fellow humans." This is the essence of this book.

The Qur'aan mandates that human beings wage war against evil. The focus is the evil within the person's own self. Evil is defeated by good. A good work is the most effective means to reverse a vile one. For those who wish to develop wisdom, the greatest and most effective approach to any situation is forgiveness. Yet, there is another principle that is required. It is the duty of the believer to resist violence and tyranny with the fullest of efforts. That is as much an obligation, in fact, infinitely more so than mere prayer and worship. In other words, the Muslim's primary duty is the fight against oppression.

The prophets are a necessary institution. What's more, they are the medium for divine inspiration. They have always been warriors against tyranny. The followers of the Qur'aan are no exception.

Like Prophet Abraham the Prophet Muhammad was a warrior against tyranny. Like David, he fought the great tyrants of the time. His characteristics as a leader and servant of the people were exceptional. He was also the world's leading diplomat and ruler. His rule was the most generous ever. Although in control of the most inconceivable wealth to support the needy he dispensed it all. He died without even a coin in his possession.

Jesus also gave all to his fellow person. He fought against the tyranny of the time. When taunted by the authorities about the permissibility of war, he said, "Our Lord teaches us that life is a constant war against evil."

The prophet of Islaam is a blessing for humankind. Certainly, his influence upon humanity is vast. The fact is as confirmed by Hart his influence is greater than any other single human. Thus, he had a positive, as well as decisive, influence upon civilization. What's more, this influence is permanent. Today, humanity continues to relish in his achievements. Yet, he was not a saint. Nor did he claim any special status. Rather, he was a human being with human emotions and needs. Incredibly, in the Qur'aan he is mentioned by name rarely and then only in a rudimentary way. Jesus is mentioned more often than he. Plus, without the Qur'aan he would have been of no consequence.

Perhaps the most important issue regarding this man is that he was a basic individual. He frequented no shrines. Nor was he inclined to asceticism. He felt equally comfortable with the rich and poor, ruler and ruled. He prayed on dirt floors and sat on mere straw or earth. He washed his own clothes and mended any damage. He even fixed his own food. Regardless of how powerful he became, unlike the kings and despots of his time, he never lorded over anyone. This is despite the fact that at one time he was the most powerful man in history. He loved life and lived it with gusto. He smiled much, laughed, enjoyed, and gave compliments. He was kind to all he encountered. Negative or derisive comments by him were virtually unknown. He was known to speak positively or not at all.

He was always emotionally upbeat. His manner was pleasant. He rarely became angry, and when he did, it was obvious, because the color in his face would change. In other words, he was transparent. He avoided gossip or senseless conversation. If he didn't know a thing or was unsure of a conclusion, he remained silent. True, he was persistent in his mission, but this was due to the deepest love of God and the sense of obligation to serve Him. In fact, once he set his mind on his mission, nothing could derail him.

Truly, he was dedicated to his mission. This was the mission of the revival of the divine law, the same law preached by Abraham, Moses, Jacob, and Jesus. Then, he remained steadfast in this preaching until his death. Thus, he changed the entire course of history, because he finished the mission for which he was called and did so without fanfare or accolades. His mission, *for which he was selected*, was the service of God. What's more, he gave his life to it. What's more, again, he did so *without pursuing personal gain*. This makes him unique in all history. Yet, this is precisely why he altered the course of history. It is also why top authorities, such as Hart, Bernard Shaw, Count Bolainvilliers, Draper, Lamartine, and Carlyle, selected him as the most influential man in history. It was this man who was the recipient of this book, this obvious guidance from almighty God.

Volume
1
Sections 1-20

Section 1
God's Nature

In the name of the most merciful
and compassionate God

All praise is due to God alone, Lord of the vast and infinite worlds—the One who gives of His mercy and love voluminously. (The) absolute Master of the era of judgement, You are the only One we worship and the only One whose help we seek. Guide us to the correct way, the way of those You have favored, not the way of those whom You have condemned nor those who are lost in error.

Section 2
The Cow

In the name of the most merciful
and compassionate God

A-L-M

Without doubt, this is the book of God. It is a
guidance for those who are in awe of God, who
believe in Him, even though He is invisible and
mysterious, who worship Him continuously and
who spend their assets generously, who (also)
believe in your message (O Prophet Muhammad,)
as well as the earlier messages (sent by God). These
are the ones who are certain in their hearts of the
next life. They (alone) truly follow guidance from
their Lord and therefore will achieve (ultimate)
happiness.

Yet, regarding those who (deliberately) reject
(Our messages) whether or not you warn them is of
no consequence. They will never believe. In fact,
because they have obstinately refused to believe in
Him, as well as in the next life, God has prevented
them from comprehending the truth. Surely, their
compensation will be dire punishment.

Certain people say, "We believe in God and also
believe in the resurrection." Yet, it isn't true. They
attempt to deceive God through this as well as
(any) true believers. However (instead), they only
deceive themselves, even though they are unaware

of it. Their hearts are tainted with a disease, and so (since they are unwilling to believe) God allows it to worsen. Furthermore (as a result of their corrupt behavior and their lies), they will be severely punished. Yet, for instance, when they are warned, "Never spread corruption on the earth," they respond, "(We would never do that, rather) we are only improving things." Yet, without doubt, they are the ones who (truly) spread corruption, although they are unaware of it. Even so, when they are told, "Believe like the rest (of those who devoutly believe)," they say, "Should we believe like the fools?" Rather, in truth, they are the ones who are the real fools, although (again,) they are incapable of conceiving it.

In addition, when they encounter the true believers, they say, "We believe like you do." However, when they are in private with their (rebellious) colleagues, they say, "We are really only loyal to you; we were just ridiculing them." God will punish them for their belittlement and will cause them to continue to falter—because instead of guidance they have chosen falsehood. Moreover, they will gain no benefits (from their actions). Nor will they find guidance from any other source.

Symbolically, they can be compared to people who ignite a fire. However, as soon as it provides light God extinguishes it, leaving them in the dark. Therefore, they are oblivious, and they will never be able to correct themselves. Or (their condition is like), a violent storm, with frightening darkness, thunder, and lightning. They cover their ears to muffle the noise, fearing its power. However, God's power overwhelms all who reject the truth. They are nearly blinded by the bolts of lightning. Whenever it flashes, it provides light (and, thus,) they are able to move, but as soon as it becomes dark they must stop.✦ If God had wanted, He could

✦That is only God's bright inspirations, which are delivered from the high heavens, are guidance. Without them, the human being is lost in the dark recesses of his/her own human frailties. Parabolically, the lightening symbolizes the sudden flashes of inspiration in human minds, which are ultimately from Him. So, any inspiration that is of benefit for the human soul is from Him. What's more, if God doesn't provide that light of divine guidance, then, what consequence will there be other than loss?

have removed their ability to comprehend (the truth), because, surely, God can do whatever He wills.

You humankind, worship your almighty Lord, the Lord who has created you as well as all previous humans. Worship Him, so you can remain conscious of Him (and thus protect yourself from succumbing to evil).

(After all,) He has made the earth a pleasant place (for your benefit).✦ He has also made the sky a

✦That is in contrast to other heavenly bodies, which are barren, such as the rest of the planets in this solar system. Thus, compared to the vast number of uninhabitable spheres, which pepper the nearby cosmos, this earth is a rare gift.

protective canopy✦ and then delivers rain and

✦The earth's atmosphere protects against the fatal effects of space matter, such as meteors, asteroids, and comets, as well as excess solar radiation. Plus, it holds protective gases, notably oxygen, as well as the needed wind currents for the production of clouds and rain.

through it ultimately provides for you nourishing fruit. Thus, never hold others as God's equals, when it is obvious to you that He alone has the power to create.

Even so, if you doubt (the truth of this) revelation, then, produce a chapter of similar substance. To do so gather all other forces—besides God—that is if there is any basis for your dispute. Yet, if you fail to do so—and you most certainly will—beware of the fire, whose fuel is humans and stones (a fire), which is the consequence for those who reject the truth.

Yet, tell the believers that great prospects await them, that is those who do good deeds. They will have earned wondrous gardens. When they are offered its fruits, they will say, "This is familiar; these are similar to what we were given previously"—because the fact is they will be given facsimiles. They will also be provided with spouses (of the purest character). What's more, they will live in peace: forever.

God is certainly not embarrassed to mention the parable of a gnat or something even less significant.✦

✦In God's view the human being is a mere speck on the earth. Yet, there are hundreds of other interpretations of this statement. The gnat or, perhaps, microbe is tiny and vulnerable in human eyes and seemingly insignificant. Yet, almighty God mentions it. So, can humans truly feel comfortable, arrogantly acting as independent or all-powerful?

The gnat, a creation of God, is an achievement greater than any human could achieve, rather, the entire human race. It is as if to say, 'You human race, which denies Me, you can't even create the likes of a gnat. You can't even create a mere microbe. So, don't act arrogantly.' There is yet another meaning. To God the human is truly a mere speck in the universe. Like a human swats a gnat, God could do so in one swift strike to the entire human race. Obviously, in God's realm the human is an insignificant being, a mere tiny particle in His unfathomable, vast realm.

Those who have true faith will realize (this) represents one of God's messages. However, those who reject the truth will say, "What does God mean by this?" This is how He causes many people to falter,✦ just as He

✦That is those who reject Him unexpectedly recognize Him by their very statement: "What does God mean?" Thus, they unwittingly admit to His existence through their questioning. Yet, they make a contest out of God's words instead of recognizing His unfathomable powers, instead of admitting He is true.

enlightens numerous others. Yet (ultimately), He only causes the iniquitous to falter, those who (purposely) sever their ties with Him (despite it being an instinctive element), who destroy what God has ordered to be joined (that is their natural bond to Him through angelic guidance) and who incite corruption. These are the real losers, completely deviating from the right way.

How can you refuse to recognize God, since (for instance,) you were (once) nonexistent, and, then, He gave you life? How can you do this, because of the fact that He will cause you to die and ultimately resurrect you, when He will bring you before Him? After all, He created the earth and all that it contains for your benefit—and has long before designed the distant heavens, giving them numerous strata. Moreover, He alone has full knowledge of all issues.

The creation of humankind

Regarding the earth, when your Lord told the angels, "The fact is I am going to establish upon it a special agent (a representative to act on My behalf), who will inherit it (that is all its glorious structure and grand design)." They replied, "Will you appoint such a (horrible) creature that will defile the earth, fomenting corruption and murder,✦ while we angels continually praise and

✦That is as if they had foreknowledge of a previous creation and that such a creation proved disastrous. This clearly implies that God made a human-like creation on another planet. It also implies that these creatures spread only corruption and harm, which ultimately led to their self-destruction. Thus, the angels questioned God's reasoning for repeating the entire process. However, God overruled them, because He held a deep purpose for this act. This purpose was to test His new creation to see which of them could truly realize His existence. It was also to determine which of His creatures proved truly grateful for the countless acts of mercy that arise from Him.

admire You?" God responded, "What I know is incomprehensible to you." Then, He instilled Adam✦

✦That is the original human being. Adam also means "human race."

with the ability to think—the high wisdom—and then brought it all (this new thinking man, with his ability to think independently) to the angels, saying "Now, you (angels,) if what you say is correct, show Me that you have the same faculties."

The angels, totally humbled, replied, "You are infinitely great, God. We can only comprehend what You allow us (to understand). You (alone) are aware of all issues and are truly wise." Then, God said to Adam, "Demonstrate all that you know," and as soon as Adam did so, God said, "Did I not tell you that I knew the hidden realities and that I know both what you openly admit and what you disguise?" Then, when We commanded the angels to "Recognize Adam as your superior," they all did so, except one derelict, that is Iblees—he was too arrogant and so as a result became a rejecter of My way.✦ Now (eventually), Adam was told, "Live in this

✦That is in order to remain in innocent love in the presence of almighty God. He tested them to see if they would keep Him in mind at all times or would, instead, fall prey to the insinuations of Satan. However, it is unknown if this event precisely occurred or if this is merely a parable, a means for God to deliver His message.

garden, together with your wife, and eat whatever you desire. However, leave alone this certain tree✦ (due to the concern) that you corrupt yourselves."

✦And therefore a warning to all human beings not to let their own personal pride interfere with the worship of God. In fact, it is arrogance which causes humans to abandon their real role, which is to be humble servants of God. Here, in God's realm there is no room for any kind of arrogance. So, then, by this parable the human is given fair warning: it is that humans are obligated to submit to Him.

Yet, Satan caused them to err (in this regard), and thus they lost their opportunity. As a result, We said, "Get out of here—eventually, you (O human race) will hate each other. What's more, the earth will be your home and source of provisions for now."

Then, Adam was guided (by God's inspiration) and therefore begged for forgiveness—and God accepted it. The fact is God is the only One truly capable of purifying the soul and delivering true mercy. Thus (for all you humans), even though We said good riddance despite this blunder I will still send merciful guidance. Those who follow it will have no need for fear or remorse. However, those who reject it and particularly those who (purposely) fight it are destined to suffer agonizing despair—forever.

Lessons regarding the people of Judaism—an example for all humans

(Note: this is directed to those deviant people of the Jewish faith, who violate God's laws, but it also applies to any people who abandon His truths).

You descendants of Israel, remember the vast blessings you received. Thus, fulfill your obligation to Me. As a result, I will fulfill My promise to you. What's more, regard Me exclusively in awe. Also, believe in this more modern revelation from Me (that is this Qur'aan), which confirms your existing (revelation). Furthermore, never be the main people who reject it. In addition, never hold in contempt (for mere material gain) these new revelations (that is this Qur'aan), and hold Me exclusively in awe.

Also, never confuse the correct way with lies. Furthermore, never intentionally suppress (or conceal) the truth. In addition, establish (within your lives) worship, be charitable, and submit yourselves in prayer like all others who (devoutly) do so. Do you demand others to be pious, while regarding yourselves above the Law? Use your common sense.

(You true believers,) seek God's support through patience and worshipping (Him). This is difficult, except for those who are truly humble, who are certain they will meet God—certain they will (ultimately) return to Him.

You descendants of Israel, remember the immense favors which I (graciously) gave you and how I favored you above all people. Thus, dread the time when no one will be able to help or intercede for anyone else. Nor will ransom be accepted: none will be helped.

Recall, too, We saved you from Pharaoh, who direly oppressed you, slaughtering your sons, while sparing only your women, a monumental trial from your Lord. Recall also that We split the sea for you (so you could escape) and then through Our power drowned Pharaoh and his army *in your presence*. What's more, for forty nights We appointed Moses to procure the guidance for you. Yet, while he was engaged you created an idol in the form of a calf, which you, in fact, worshiped and as a result became corrupt. Despite this, We forgave you on the basis that you would become grateful (because if you were truly grateful you would) remember that We gave Moses the Law, a means to discern the true from the false (all) in order to guide you.

When Moses said to his people, "By worshipping an idolatrous calf you have sinned and therefore ruined your own selves. (Thus,) repent for your crime, so that you may purify yourselves. This is best for you in your Maker's view." Here again, He accepted your repentance, because He is easily reconciled, totally merciful. Remember, too, when you said, "Moses, we see no reason to believe in this (thoughtful repentance), that is unless we see

God in person, when at that very moment, right before your eyes, you were struck by a sudden, shocking punishment. Despite this (arrogant refusal to believe), We revived you, again, after you became spiritually dead, so that you might have reason to be grateful. We even caused the cumulus clouds to protect you with their shade and provided you (as a gift from Us) with special food (that is manna and quails), as if to say, "Take advantage of the good, nourishing things We have provided." Yet, regrettably, through all this sinning they by no means harmed Us but rather only harmed themselves.

We also added, "Enter this region, and eat abundantly of its foods, as you desire. However, do so with humility and say, 'Our God, remove from us the burden of our sins.'" Then (as a result of such thoughtful repentance), We will cleanse you of your sins and will fully compensate those who do good. Yet, those who were determined to commit evil completely distorted this. What's more, as a result of their wickedness (they) only brought hardship upon themselves.

Also, when Moses searched for water for his people, We told him, "Strike the rock with your staff," when numerous springs spurted representing numerous lineages (as if to say) "Take advantage of the good things of life (I have provided) for you), you various peoples. However, never act wickedly on the earth by inciting corruption." Despite this, you said to Moses, "We are tired of this boring diet; tell your Lord to give us a wider variety."

(In response,) Moses said, "Are you willing to trade such a minor gain for something far more significant? (If you are so dissatisfied,) then, return in disgrace to Egypt. There, you'll get whatever you want."✦ Thus, as a result of this behavior absolute

✦People claim that Muhammad wrote the Qur'aan. Yet, it is impossible for him to have known these historical facts in such detail. For instance, he had no knowledge of these precise discussions between Moses and his people. Nor did the Jews or Christians of his time know them. In fact, that was some 13 centuries prior. Thus, only God could know these details.

vileness and humiliation darkened them (that is their inner souls)—condemned by God—all because they persistently rejected the truth. What's more, they (even) murdered prophets—because surely they were wicked.

Certainly, regardless of the denomination those who believe in God and the final time, who do good deeds, their Lord will reward them: they will have no need for fear, remorse, or grief.

In addition (you children of Israel), We accepted your covenant, raising Mount Sinai above you, saying, "Remain firm to what I have commanded you, holding resolutely to (these laws), so that you will always remain in awe of Me." Yet, you ignored it, and, if it were not for God's mercy, you would certainly have been completely lost (that is devoid of all guidance). What's more, remember, you descendants of Israel, you are fully aware of those who (in the past) violated the Sabbath, who We told as a result, "Be as if filthy apes,"✦ turning

✦That is as if mere vagrants in the land, displaced and wandering, even begging for mere food—exiled to all corners of the then-known earth. This was the consequence for the remaining tribes of the Israelites—their 'punishment' for rejecting their Lord.

them into an example for their society and for all others, as well as a lesson, that is for those who truly hold God in awe.

(Then, recall also when) Moses told his people, "Sacrifice a cow per God's orders." They answered, "Are you making a joke?" He said, "God forbid that I would be so ignorant." They said, "Then, ask your God to make this requirement clearer, that is what kind of cow should it be?" Moses replied, "God says the cow should be in the prime of life, neither too old nor too immature. Now, do as you are told." They said, "Summon God again, and ask him what color it should be?" Moses said, "It should be a yellowish-brown cow of distinguished hue." They said, "Ask your Lord to clarify this further, because to us all cows look the same: if God wills, we'll make the right decision." Moses answered, "Obviously, the cow should be strong, not weak, sick, or overworked and not one of variegated color." They said, "Finally, you have made it clear," and, then, they sacrificed her, although (due to their obstinate behavior) they almost failed to do so.✦

✦In other words, rather than being grateful to God and following His commandments they resisted, essentially, in a childish way. Previously, they had succumbed to temptation and worshiped the golden calf. Afterwards, they promised restitution. So, God tested them again, proving the shallowness of their faith.

The Israelites constantly attempted to turn simple rulings into burdens, changing useful, protective divine laws into man-made nonsense. God showed them through this test how destructive is their behavior. Instead of arguing and questioning if they would have just followed God's rulings, this would have protected them from harm. What's more, this acted as a proof from God that such people's beliefs were largely artificial. Thus, they were hypocrites, feigning belief but not really holding true in their hearts.

This (test of sacrifice) is because, O descendants of Israel, you at that time killed a human being and then blamed each other✦—although God will

✦That is this means of testing them was created for the benefit of the Jewish community. This was to help them avoid self-destruction, since due to their defiance of God they will only cause themselves harm. He gave them due warning. Yet, God does not need them, rather, they need Him.

ultimately reveal what you attempted to conceal, We said, "Use this (principle of sacrifice) to resolve some of those unsolved murder cases." This is how God (in His mercy) saves lives from wrongful death (that is through testing you, so that you can gain some awareness of the right way), while demonstrating His will, so you might learn to use your reason.

Yet, despite this (effort by Us to improve your condition), your hearts became hardened, like rocks or even harder. After all, there are rocks through which water flows, and what's more, there are some which when shattered water issues—and there are others which plummet (to the earth) due to the awe of God: (and, so always realize) God is fully aware of your actions.✦

✦That is it is all under divine watch. Even what a person holds deeply in his heart is known to Him. He is fully cognizant of it. God knows which hearts are soft in love for Him or hardened in hate against Him or rather are hardened in their own selfishness.

Then, do you truly hope that (the Jews) will believe in your preaching despite the fact that large numbers of them will hear it, understand it, and still pervert it?✦ No doubt, when they encounter

✦That is God Himself through His own carefully constructed message was unable to guide them. Then, how can anyone else do so? To believe otherwise is delusional. The fact is as demonstrated by the following statement they are merely positing belief—all for corrupt gains.

However,the believers, they claim, "We are on your side." but secretly they say, "Let's avoid telling the Muslims that our way is similar to theirs, because they'll use it (as evidence) before God against us." Will you (Jews) avoid using your common sense? It should be obvious to them that God is aware of what they disguise as well as reveal.

Also, there are (within such groups of early Old Testament believers as well as even today) illiterate people, who have no means to comprehend divine revelation. Instead (of true guidance), they follow mere conjecture (of their own creation). Those who write *as law* their own words as if sanctioned by God are condemned. (Thereby), corrupting His messages and then saying, "This is from God," merely to achieve material benefit. What's more, they have earned God's condemnation for their writings and for all their (illegal) gains. Even so, these people, who knowingly commit evil, claim, "We will only experience hell temporarily." Ask them, "Have you been promised directly from God—the fact is God never breaks His promises—or are you merely speculating?"

Without doubt, those who through their actions earn evil are consumed by precisely these sins. What's more, they are permanent residents of the fire, which they (too, will) have earned. In contrast, those who truly believe (in the way of God) and perform good deeds are permanent residents of (the gardens of) paradise, which they also have earned.

Ancient laws and responsibilities given to Moses' followers: long ago forgotten

Even so (long ago), We accepted a solemn pledge from the descendants of Israel (for which they are still responsible): it is to worship only almighty God, be kind to their parents, as well as all other people, and treat the down-trodden and orphans justly. What's more, you will speak to all people in a congenial manner (that is you will be kind and courteous)—you will also establish proper worship. Furthermore, you will be charitable in your actions. Yet, with rare exceptions you reject it, because as a race you are stubborn to the point of being conceited, in fact (you are), arrogant. Even so, We, without doubt, accepted your commitment, that you would not treat others unjustly and would *never drive each other from their* (respective) *homelands,*✦ a commitment that you, then, fully

✦That is not merely fellow Jews but rather all humans, who according to the Qur'aan are all part of the same global community. Even so, it also implies fellow followers of the Mosaic Law. The plot against the Palestinians is, thus, implied. Naim Giladi, former Israeli secret service agent and, originally, an Iraqi Jew, made the conspiracy clear in his book *Ben Gurion Scandals*. Here, in Iraq, he proves, the Israeli powerful ones specifically created terror acts, even killing fellow Jews, to force a mass migration. Then, they blamed this on so-called Islaamic fundamentalism. Even in Nazi Germany Zionists did this to create mass hysteria and therefore to support the creation of the Israeli entity.

agreed to and even now do so (in principle). Yet, you are the ones who kill each other and drive some of your own people from their homelands, assisting each other against them in tyrannical acts. However, if they come to you as prisoners (incredibly), you ransom them, even though the act of expelling them (from their homes and countries) has been prohibited to you.

Do you only believe a portion of My writings, while you reject the rest? What else could be the result of such behavior, except disgrace in this life as well as real torment at the time of judgement? What's more, God is fully aware (and has a complete record) of all your actions.

Those are the people who trade this life for the next one—(as a result,) they will receive the maximum degree of suffering. What's more, they will be devoid of any aid—(because there is no excuse, since) We gave Moses My writings, plus after him We repeatedly sent prophets—for your benefit. In addition, to Jesus, Mary's son, We gave clear proofs (of God's almighty power), strengthening him with holy inspiration.✦

✦In other words, through numerous messengers, including Jesus, God warned them in order to save them. So, again, at the time of accountability there will be no excuse. All people of the Jewish faith know the divine law. If they violate it, they will earn the consequences of their rebellion, which are dire.

Thus, how is it that whenever a messenger came to you—which you cannot deny—with something you disliked, you resisted arrogantly or accused (such messengers) of being liars and even killed some of them? However (whenever new revelations are presented to them), they say, "We already know everything." Clearly, God has rejected them, because of their refusal to acknowledge the truth and because, without doubt, the basis of their faith is weak. What's more, whenever a new revelation similar to and confirming their scriptures arrived, they rejected it, *even though they used to predict its arrival,* and then described its followers as "godless." How insolent they were, and thus they have earned God's rejection, the real godless ones, who obstinately reject the truth.

This false pride they exude for which they have traded their souls is vile—because they have denied the truthful revelations of God due to the fact that they are envious of what God provides others. Thus, they have repeatedly incurred God's condemnation.

Arrogance and rebellion

Regarding those who reject the truth they will eventually suffer direly—because when they are commanded, "Believe in (all) God's revelations,"✦

✦That is the Bible, Gospels, Torah, and/or Qur'aan as well as any other spiritual messages revealed directly by God. Apparently, almighty God revealed numerous such revelations over the many eras of human existence. This would include the original teachings of Bhudda and Confucius. Now, most of these books are lost.

they reply, "We believe only in what has already been revealed to us." By this they reject all other revelations (including this one), even though it is truthful and confirms theirs. Ask them, "If you truly believe, why did you previously murder

(God's) prophets?" What's more, in fact, Moses was sent to you with obvious revelation. Despite this, in his absence you worshiped the idolatrous calf, proving your wickedness.

Furthermore (recall), when you pledged yourselves to Us, and We accepted it, raising Mount Sinai high above you, and your pledge was that you would strictly observe what We had revealed to you and truly internalize it. Despite this, they said, "We have heard, but we disobey"—because they were *romantically consumed* by the golden calf—a mere excuse to (by continuing to pursue mere material and temporary gain) obstinately reject the truth. Tell them, "Your reliance upon such falsehoods gains you nothing (which you would realize) if you truly believed (in God). Also, tell them, "If your claim is true, that is that the next life is yours alone, then, you should wish to die immediately." Yet, they will never desire it, because they are aware of the wicked acts they have already perpetrated; God knows who truly are the wicked.

Additionally, you will definitely find that they cling to life more tenaciously than any other people—even more than pagans. They desire to live a thousand years or more, although this perpetual life would never protect them from the inevitable torment. This is because, truly, God is fully aware of all their actions.

Tell them that whoever is Gabriel's enemy, the angel who surely by God's order delivered this divine writing—this confirmation of the remnants of the previous revelations, this guidance, as well as heavenly support, for the believers—whoever is an enemy of God and His angels (Gabriel and Michael), realize that God is the enemy of all who reject the truth.✦

✦That is by doubting the Prophet Muhammad the hostile Israelites and other naysayers prove their rejection of the very angels, Gabriel and Michael, who revealed the divine word to previous prophets. This includes the prophets of the Old Testament. This means that by rejecting the Qur'aan they are essentially rejecting their own revelations. By this, they prove their faith as false. It also proves that their beliefs are based exclusively upon material gain.

In fact, the evidence We have provided is absolute. Only the most wicked reject it. Could anyone dispute (the fact) that every time (the Israelites) made a promise to God some of them rejected it? Without doubt, the majority of them are not even real believers (in God).✦

✦That is the vast majority of the descendants of Israel never truly believe in almighty God. Surely, they never acknowledge that He has power over them. Nor do they believe they will be held fully responsible to Him for their actions.

Even now, when a messenger of God arrives (for their own benefit), who confirms the validity of their scriptures, their scholars attempt to conceal this fact (making it appear), as if they were unaware of it (that is its truth), choosing instead to follow mere devilish fables—mere nonsense practiced during Solomon's time.

Certainly, Solomon adhered to the truth. However, these (later) evil ones fabricated the remnants of (his original revelation), teaching instead magic. (Incredibly,) people of the scripture unknowingly are following the (pagan) fables of the Babylonian angels,

Haaroot and Maaroot, although this duo never taught (their magic) to anyone without mentioning the caveat: "The fact is We only tempt to devious acts: hold firmly to your beliefs." What's more, these angels described how marriages could be corrupted, yet they could only harm a person if God allowed it. The result was that (those stubborn deniers) learned only the harmful aspects instead of the useful (and productive) ones, even though they knew that by doing so they would sacrifice the rewards of the next life. It is truly vile, that is that for which they have traded their souls, if they only realized it.

You who truly believe in God, never (egotistically) demand to be "noticed,"✦ but, instead, ask for (the

---

✦That is the believers are commanded never to attempt to vie for position against the Prophet's way or in the case of the original believers the Prophet himself, merely for personal gain. Rather, they are commanded to resolutely follow his way as one unified group. Thus, this essentially is a prohibition against vanity. It is also a warning to beware of selfishness.

For the truth there is a major battle within each person. Selfishness is the opposite of true belief. Everyone is tempted to feel self-importance. Yet, this is a satanic influence. It is a kind of arrogance. In fact, this is one of Satan's main tactics, that is to cause a person to feel self-importance. Then, this was never the way of the Prophet, who was, while strong, always humble. He never attempted to vie for anyone's attention. While dignified, he was modest.

It is the Muslims' obligation to resist this influence. This is part of his concerted effort, that is jihaad. This is to rather than attempt to gain position or influence for mere personal gain instead to do good deeds. It is also to follow instead of vain desires the dictates of the Prophet. Yet, what are these dictates? It is to be modest, compassionate, loving, and considerate, that is fully mindful of the duties to God. That is the definition of a true believer.

Prophet) to "have patience" with you. What's more, follow (the Prophet's dictates)—the fact is any who reject the truth create for themselves the ultimate agony.

None of them, certainly not the pagans nor the people of scripture, wish you any good. This especially relates to divine revelation. Yet, God selects for His mercy whomever He wills, because He is unlimited in His generosity (in the way He graces His servants).

Any revelation which We discard We replace with something superior, even similar. It must be obvious to you that almighty God can do whatever He wills. You must also realize that God has control over the entire universe and that (therefore,) He is the only possible source of protection. What's more, who else (besides God) could you turn to for (such) protection?

Would you dare question or demand of the Prophet the way Moses was questioned? Regrettably, whoever refuses to believe in this truth has greatly deviated from the correct way.

Because they are jealous many people of scripture (that is Christians and Jews), would like to cause you to abandon your faith, even after they become enlightened by it. Even so, forgive and remain patient, that is until God makes clear His will. Truly, God has the power to do (whatever He wills).

Yet (regardless of the difficulty or circumstance), be persistent in your worship, and also be generous. What's more, realize that whatever you accomplish for your own benefit is fully recorded with almighty God. Surely, God is aware of all your actions.

To gain paradise the Jews and Christians claim you must be either a Jew or a Christian. That is their hope. Tell them, "If your claim is correct, prove it."✦ In truth, whoever surrenders himself or herself

✦That is through precise scripture. In other words, 'Prove that, somewhere, God has supported your claim through revelation.' There is no such proof.

to God and does what is right will be fully rewarded. All such people have no need for fear or remorse.

The Jews say, "The religion of the Christians is baseless," while the Christians say, "The Jews have no basis for their beliefs." Yet, incredibly, both quote scripture. This is the same argument which has always been used by those devoid of knowledge. Yet, clearly, regarding their disputes God will judge between them.

The most wicked of all are those who obstruct the worship of God in His houses of worship and strive to destroy and disrupt them, although they have no right to enter them, except in the awe (and reverence) of God. Such (individuals) will experience only disgrace in this world, plus a terrifying punishment in the next.

The horizons, east and west, belong to God. Wherever you turn, you will experience Him. That God is boundless and that He encompasses all is obvious. Despite this, some people say, "God has a son." (Far beyond this) He is limitless in His magnificence.✦ Rather, the fact is (clearly,) He owns

✦That is He is the creator. He has no need for a son. This is because He is eternal.

Why would He need a son? The Qur'aan is emphatic about the existence of a single divine power—God almighty. In contrast, Jesus is described as "created," and while his birth was miraculous it was no more so than the birth of the original human, that is 'Adam.' In fact, a greater miracle than even this is precisely the invention of the concept of the human being, which didn't exist billions of years ago. What's more, again, Jesus was only a human being, because rather than an eternal creator he lived in the flesh and, if injured, would bleed but will also ultimately die.

all that exists in the Universe: (it) all obeys Him. The Originator of the universe, as well as the high heavens, whatever exists submits before Him. When He wills a thing, He merely says, "Be" and it (already) is.

Those who are devoid of understanding say, "(As proof), will God at least speak to us or show us a miracle?" Previous civilizations also demanded this. The tendency in human hearts remains the same. Yet, surely, We have made all the signs obvious, that is for people who are certain of the truth.✦

✦That is proving they reject God. They demand absolute proof of His existence before they would consider believing in Him. It is through this propensity that God distinguishes the true believers from those who are false. The accuracy of this interpretation is made clear by the initial statements of this section, that is true believers are those who believe in God, despite His invisible and mysterious nature.

Without doubt, We sent you (O Muhammad,) with the truth and as a bearer of the happy result (of true belief) as well as to warn. However, realize that you have no responsibility for those (obstinate ones) who (have set their course) for the raging fire.

In fact, the Jews will never be pleased with you, nor will the Christians, unless you follow (their religions). Tell them that, obviously, God's guidance is the only kind to be followed. Yet, if you were to follow their erroneous views, especially after all the knowledge you have received, there would be none to support you or protect you from God. In contrast, those who have been given this divine message and *who truly apply it* (in their lives)—they are the ones who truly believe in it, while those who choose to reject it are the ultimate losers.

Abraham: the ultimate father of the Israelites; his role in the establishment of the Temple as the sacred House of God

You descendants of Israel, remember how I graciously blessed you and how I favored you above all others. Thus, be in awe of the event when no one will be able to help anyone else. Nor will ransom be accepted, nor will any mediation—none will be supported. Remember, too, when Abraham was tested with commandments by His Lord, and he fulfilled them.✦ God said, "Certainly, I will make

✦This is a reminder to the adherents of the Jewish religion, as well as all others He has guided, to be grateful to almighty God. It is also a command to use exclusively the example of Abraham as the guide.

Abraham is the true father of the Jews and Muslims, particularly those of Middle Eastern descent. He originated the way of thinking that God is one and all other powers are superficial. His sons are the source of three enormous religions. For all such people who have descended from them the Qur'aan emphasizes the importance of self-sacrifice and brotherly love. In particular, it demands regardless of race or religion to never torment fellow humans.

This is all encoded in the Qur'aan but also the more ancient scriptures. Thus, the racist attitude of the modern Israelites against the Palestinians is a violation of the Jews' own writings. In fact, the Israelites are tormenting their own 'scriptural' relatives, which is prohibited in the Torah. Incredibly, by strict Mosaic law the Palestinians, who the modern Israelis deem as at best second class people, are their own brothers in faith. Thus, by their obstinate behavior rather than only violating the Qur'aan they are, in fact, rebelling against their own religion and scriptures.

you a leader of humankind." Abraham asked, "Will my descendants also be leaders?" God answered, "My ruling has no relevance for the wicked."

Establishment of the first House of God

Without doubt, We made the Temple a goal to strive towards as well as a sanctuary. Then, make use of the site where Abraham once stood as your place of prayer. It was in this respect that We commanded Abraham and Ishmael (saying), "Purify My Temple for those who will traverse around it, who journey to it to perform devout worship, who submit, prostrating themselves in prayer." It was Abraham who prayed, "My Lord, secure this region, and provide much livelihood for its people, that is those who believe in God and the final event (of resurrection)." God responded, "Realize that whoever rejects the truth (such a person) I will allow to enjoy himself for a brief interlude. However, eventually, I will drive him to the agony of (internal) torment. What's more, this is the most miserable of all conclusions."

When Abraham and Ishmael were constructing the foundation of the Temple, they prayed, "Our Lord, accept this effort from us; we know You alone are aware of all (that could possibly be)...Our Lord, cause us to surrender ourselves fully to You, and elevate from our descendants a community of true servants. Also, show us the best ways of worship, and accept our repentance. You alone are capable of accepting repentance, and You alone can give of Your kindness...and Our Lord, deliver to the people a Messenger from our descendants, who will establish Your inspiration and wisdom and cause these descendants to grow in purity—surely, You are truly the most powerful of all, plus You are the truly wise."✦

✦This prayer presaged the arrival of the Prophet Muhammad. It was a prayer which was, in fact, a prediction that God in His wisdom knew the potential of Abraham's lineage. In fact, his prayer was fully answered. This was because his future descendant, the Prophet Muhammad, was ideal for bearing His message. So, the way of this final Messenger is nothing new. It is merely the way of Abraham, who is actually the father of the Semitic Christians and Jews as well as Muslims.

Then, it was this man who delivered society from barbarism to the worship of almighty God. Western historians agree that he is the source for the Renaissance. According to Hart his influence on this earth was greater than any other human. Carlyle says he was a hero for the sake of all humankind. This influence led to vast advancements, in fact, the creation of modern civilization. Therefore, he truly is the man predicted by both the ancient prophets and the Bible.

For more information on this see *The Secret Scriptures They Don't Want You to Know About* (Knowledge House Publishers).

Yet, how could anyone be adverse to the way of Abraham, because of the fact that We ourselves selected him and did so above all others? What's more, he was truly one of the most upright of all people. It was Abraham who, when his Lord commanded him, "Surrender your will to mine," said, "I have immediately done so, Lord of all the worlds." It was Abraham who similarly instructed his children, as did Jacob, saying (essentially,) "My children, your God has given you the finest way of life—self-surrender—so, never allow yourselves to die, unless you are in this condition."

Yet, the truth of this is obvious, since (as agreed by your own tradition, O Israelites) when Jacob was nearly dead, he asked his people, "After I die, who will you worship?" They answered, "We will worship your God, the God of Abraham, Ishmael, and Isaac:✦ the one God, and we will devote ourselves exclusively to (His will)."

✦That is the same God responsible for the message of the Prophet Muhammad. The latter was a direct descendent of Abraham and Ishmael. Here, the Qur'aan documents the fact that the original Jews recognized the legitimacy of Ishmael, who was the Prophet's direct descendent. This is proof that by their own scriptures the Jews are obligated to follow his way. Yet, instead, they resist him vehemently. This is despite the fact that his way is the same as the way of Jacob, Joseph, Moses, Isaac, and Abraham, the very men who Christians and Jews hold high. This demonstrates the hypocrisy of any 'Western' attack against Islaam. It also demonstrates the fraud of claiming that Islaam is based upon paganism or that its God is untrue.

How can this be the case? Islaam proclaims that the God of this faith is the God of Abraham. Jews and Christians claim the same. There cannot be two Gods of Abraham. This clearly proves the fallacy of any statements such as the ludicrous claim that, somehow, the God followed by Muslims isn't the real God. In contrast, Muslims never say such comments to Christians or Jews. Rather, they fully commend Christians for their practice of seeking the service of God, while completely attesting to the fact that the God of Christ is the true and universal Lord.

As delineated by Weaver and Redford in their book *Studies in the Ancient Palestinian World* even the word Allah through its derivatives is found in the Hebrew writings. This is as the village of Elealeh. This originates from the world el-ʿAl (lofty in fact Godly place), which is, then, derived from El. The latter is the ancient word for God. Yet, Islaam fully acknowledges the God of the Israelites and Christians as true. In contrast, despite this reference to Allah through Elealeh (the high or lofty) they dispute the validity of the God of Muhammad. This demonstrates the liberal nature of Islaam versus the dogmatic nature of other faiths, including Christianity and Judaism.

Now, those societies are gone. What they achieved is in their record and what you achieve will be in yours. You will be judged based exclusively on your merits, not on theirs.✦

✦This is a warning to those who believe that since they are born of the original patriarch, Abraham, they are immune regardless of deeds. God is warning them that they will gain no benefits from such a birthright but that, instead, in His system they must themselves do good works. This is in order to gain His pleasure.

They tell you, "If you become Jews or Christians (only), then you will be in the right." Explain to them, "We follow the way of Abraham, who was the original true believer. He refused to make other (powers) as divine. He believed in God alone (in other words, he was a pure monotheist)." Also, explain to them, "We believe in God and His revelation (He sent to us) as well as the revelations He sent to Abraham, Ishmael, Isaac, Jacob, and their descendants—and also the revelations of Moses and Jesus. We believe in *all the revelations* sent to (all) the prophets, and we don't doubt any of them. To us they are one. We are God's servants, and (by surrendering to Him) we are devoted exclusively to Him."

So (contrary to their claim), if they would believe the way you (that is you followers of this Qur'aan) believe, only then would they adhere to what is right. However, if they reject it, they will be gravely in error. Even so, God will protect you from them, since He is completely aware and is completely knowledgeable. Furthermore, tell them, "Regarding whatever we do we take our direction (and inspiration) from God. In true worship who could be a better source of inspiration than He?" Also, ask the Jews, as well as the Christians, "Will you argue with us about God despite the fact that He is the God of all of us?✦ (Yet, there is

✦Again, this directly disputes the modern claim by certain antagonists that the God of the Qur'aan is different from the God of all others. Such individuals claim that, incredibly, the God of the Muslims, that is 'Allah,' is a pagan god. Yet, this is merely the Arabic word for God.

The Arabic word for God, Allah, merely means the one and universal God. It also means the high and mighty God, that is God almighty. As mentioned previously this word or its derivatives was even used by the ancient Israelites. It is the God of all attributes, the creator, the all-powerful, the totally kind, the absolutely merciful, and the completely aware. It has the same meaning as the words now used for the one God, that is Yahweh and Jehovah. What's more, just as the words Yahweh, Jehovah, and Diós define the one God, so does Allah. Plus, in antiquity the words El and Allat both meant God.

no use in arguing, because) whatever you achieve is to your credit, and whatever we accomplish is to ours. The fact is we are devoted exclusively to Him."

Or, do you claim that Abraham and his progeny were "Jews" or "Christians?" Are you more knowledgeable regarding this than God? In fact, the most wicked of all are those who suppress God's revelations. Moreover, God is aware of your actions.

Those people are (now) dead. Arguing about them is inconsequential, because whatever they achieved will never benefit you, and, what's more, you will be judged exclusively on your own achievements.

People of weak faith will say, "Why did they change their prayer direction (that is from Jerusalem to Mecca)?"✦ Tell them, "Prayers from

✦That is the switching of the direction of prayer, which happened in the time of the Prophet Muhammad. This was nothing new, since prior to this the Prophet Abraham and his sons prayed facing the Mecca House. However, originally, the Prophet Muhammad prayed facing Jerusalem. He did this as a vote of confidence for others of faith, notably the Jews and Christians, hoping for one brotherhood. However, the other monotheists refused to join him in this.

So, this change from Jerusalem makes sense. This is because, obviously, Mecca was the original house of worship, which more correctly represents the oneness of God than, even more so than Jerusalem.

any direction are answered by God. He guides whomever He desires."

We have decided that you (that is those who truly believe in this book and adhere to the ways of its Messenger), would be the intermediary community. This is so that through your example you might represent the truth, giving warning to humanity. The Prophet is your support in this process. To distinguish those who truly follow him versus the rebels We appointed a unique direction of worship.✦ For the

✦That is that worship is directed toward Mecca instead of the previous site, Jerusalem. Thus, the entire concept of 'facing east' in worship is a divine invention. When a Muslim does so, this is directed by God. Whether east or west is irrelevant. It is the facing as an entire group, over a billion people, to the same focal point that is at issue. This creates a reproducible system of worship. It also creates a oneness, so that the masses may worship in unison. That is the purpose of the original house of the one and universal God. Then, despite all the hateful acts of humankind at least in this arena God's way prevailed: over a billion people globally all bow to Him systematically in worship.

weak of faith this seemed like a major ordeal but not for those whom God guides.

Yet, God will ensure that your efforts are rewarded. This is because God is totally compassionate, the true administrator of love.

Mecca: the hub for monotheism

In fact, we have observed you looking confusedly towards the heavens, confused regarding the direction of worship.✦ Now We have given you a

✦This relates to the Prophet Muhammad, when he would pray to God from all directions, not sure how to face Him. Then, God revealed that all believers should, when performing ritual worship, face Mecca. This systematized the Islaamic worship service. In fact, Islaam is the only 'religion' which functions as a complete system.

direction that will satisfy you. Thus, regardless of where you are when you worship, direct yourselves towards the Abrahamic house of God.

Without doubt, the people of scripture are aware that this is the truth from their Lord,✦ that

✦That is regarding the selection of the direction of worship to the House of Abraham as well as the emphasis on Abraham's monotheistic faith. They are fully aware that the Middle East houses the original sites of the divine religions and that these sites are holy for their followers and that they have been sanctioned as holy sites by God Himself. Yet, despite this they plot against their followers, while rejecting their beliefs as false. This is due to jealousy and false pride. What's more, any plots against faithful Muslims and this House are, in fact, plots against God and the rite of Abraham.

this following of the way of Abraham is the true religion of God (that all should follow). What's more, God is fully aware of their actions. Yet, regrettably, even if you demonstrated for them a plethora of evidence, they would still fail to follow your worship direction. Nor are you allowed to follow theirs. In fact, if you followed their erroneous ideas after you have been guided correctly, you would be committing (a grave) crime.

The people of scripture are well aware of the (true nature of the) Prophet and recognize (the truth of) him as clearly they would recognize (for instance) their own children.✦ However, incredibly,

✦That is just as it is obvious that their children are theirs any careful analysis would prove that the Prophet Muhammad is also theirs, that he is through Abraham related to them and that he is, thus, their guide. They refuse to recognize that the Prophet Muhammad is their genetic relative. He was the final representation of the lineage of Abraham. Curiously, he is the distant son of Ishmael, who himself was of special genetic mix: he was half black and white. Even so, because of his ties to Abraham the Prophet Muhammad is a relative of Moses as well as Jesus. So, this is a parable, where God instructs the Christians and Jews to desist in their spite towards him and instead love him like they would love their own children, just as they may love the Christ Jesus. Thus, he is related to the chain of messengers, whose messages led to the Christian and Jewish religions. So, on what basis do they reject him?

some of them purposely suppress (the truth of his mission) despite the fact that it is obviously from God.✦ So, beware of becoming one of those who

✦What they are suppressing is the fact that, obviously, God is the source of the Prophethood of Muhammad as well as this revelation. In fact, the Qur'aan confirms the truths remaining in the Bible.

Historically, since their scriptures predicted his arrival the Jews of Arabia at first recognized him as the Messenger. In fact, they had been expecting him and so immediately recognized him. Then, once they felt threatened by him they rejected him. This was the same attitude which during his time the powerful Israelites demonstrated against Christ.

(like these people of scripture) reject it.

Worship rituals: origins

Every group has its own method (of devotion),
although the true direction (and guidance) comes
from God. Thus (rather than competing for mere
material gain), compete with each other only in
goodness.✦ What's more, realize that regardless

✦Here, God is directing Christians, Jews, and Muslims not to fight each
other over supposed matters of faith or rather mere material lusts. Rather,
they are to find a common bond, which is the dedicated worship of Him.
Instead of fighting over earthly desires, He commands, they are to only
compete in the doing of good. This is the only competition allowed by
almighty God.

of who you are, where you are, or your status God
will join you all at the final time, and only He has the
power to achieve it. Thus, regardless of where you
are when you perform ritual worship, face (as one
unified group) the Abrahamic house of God: this is a
ruling in truth from your Lord. What's more, God
fully understands your actions. Hence (to reiterate),
regardless of where you are when you perform
ritual prayer, face the Sacred House. This is so that
no one can dispute (its relevance), although the
people (who are perpetrating evil) will do so.
However (disregard them, since), I am the only One
to revere. (What's more, obey Me)—so that I might
embellish you (with) the full extent of My blessings.
It is also so that you will be directed to the right way.

As one of your own people We sent you the
Prophet.✦ His role is to preach Our messages to help

✦That is though the lineage of Abraham God repeats this simple test
to determine people's real loyalties. It is, essentially, 'On what basis do

you Israelites reject the authority of God? He is the One who rescued you when you begged for help. Now, a new Messenger comes to you, directly from the lineage of Abraham. Then, you reject him? Yet, you also rejected his brother, the Prophet Jesus, who you, too, deemed a fraud. So, you will have no excuse against Me in the time of judgment, when you will only be consumed by despair.'

Of course, this is also directed at the original Arabs, who well knew the character of this new Prophet. In fact, they regarded him so highly that they called him *al-ameen*, the truthful one. Even so, when he began preaching to them about their duties before God, they immediately labeled him a liar.

you purify yourselves—to instill in you divine revelation as well as wisdom. It is also to teach you regarding what you previously were unaware. Thus, always keep Me in mind, and I will always keep you in mind. In addition, always be grateful to Me. What's more, beware of rejecting Me.

You true believers, seek My assistance through (dedicated) worship and perseverance. Without doubt, God is with those who regardless of the adversity are patient. Also, regarding those who are killed in God's service never say they are dead. The fact is they are alive, and you are merely unaware of it. What's more, realize that We will test your patience through fear, danger, financial loss, loss of life, loss of possessions, or whatever else you may adore. However, congratulations are (in order) for the patient people who, when disaster strikes, say, "We originate from God, and we will (thus) return to Him," because (as a result of this attitude and commitment) they are graced with their Lord's blessings. These are the kinds of individuals who are correctly guided.

The ancient Arabian monuments, *as-Safaa* and *al-Marwah*, are God's symbols. Despite concerns✦

✦That is the ancient mounds of Mecca, which mark the hajj procession and have a symbolic meaning, perhaps related to Abraham. However, the pagans used to perform this ritual in a hedonistic way, but this does not detract from its essence. God cleansed it, returning it to a holy rite. This demonstrates the liberality of the true Islaam—the true system of God— in which the wicked is cleansed with good. God is goodness. Whatever He caresses is clean. Thus, there is nothing 'pagan,' except what is in one's own mind.

(regarding following what was once a pagan rite), there is no harm in striding back and forth between them. You will be credited for any additional effort you exert, since God is thankful for and appreciates your gratitude. What's more, He records all your actions.

Regarding those who suppress My revealed truths, the truths I have revealed for humankind's sake, I will curse. They will also be cursed by the (various decent people) as well as the angels. What's more, they will exist in this accursed condition without relief or hope: forever. The exceptions are those who truly ask God's forgiveness (from the depths of their hearts) and change their behavior as well as strive to establish the truth; these are the ones who will gain (His) mercy. The fact is only I am truly capable of accepting repentance, the true giver of mercy.

(In contrast,) regarding those who reject the truth and die in that condition, they will be cursed by God. The entire compliment of angels will also curse them, as will the entire (believing) human race—as one unified curse. They are doomed to exist without reprieve, without any easing of their burdens, under God's recrimination forever.

Your God is one. There is nothing else like Him: the true source of love, the only truly merciful One, the source of all merciful giving.✦

✦That is the truly kind, the One who cares, the One who has such vast love for His creation that it is beyond measure. Plus, He is the only One who has the power to dispense such love and does so routinely. Then, He loves humankind sufficiently to send His own special Messenger, along with a sophisticated code of guidance.

Truly, in the creation of the universe you will find (numerous) representations (of your Lord's mercy) as well as in the (system for) alternation of the night and day. You will also comprehend (His ever present role) in how the seas move ships along the water (a process which) aids in commerce. You will also understand it through the water God delivers (without fail), how it causes the earth and its creatures to flourish, as well as the air currents (which create weather patterns, providing rain and pollination), and clouds, which are compelled by God's power to service you (and are also an obvious witness to His presence). Truly, these are compelling messages for people willing to use their reason.

Despite this, people hold rivals to God, merely from what He Himself created. They adore such rivals as God alone should be adored. In contrast, the true believers love God above all else. If only those who deliberately commit evil could understand—if they could possibly comprehend, as they will surely ultimately comprehend—that all power belongs to almighty God and that He is harsh in His punishment. Then (in that ultimate time), the artificial 'gods' that people worship will denounce their followers. What's more, the latter will fully comprehend the degree of torment (which they will suffer). Thus, their hopes will be completely dashed. Even so, they will say, "If we only had another chance, so we could get revenge." Thus, God makes clear their accomplishments in a way which will cause them bitter regrets, and furthermore, they will reside permanently in the (fiery) torment.

You humankind, take advantage of whatever is good and decent in life. However, beware of the entrapments of Satan—definitely, he is your mortal enemy. He causes you only harm. He wants you to defile yourself. What's more (regarding your responsibilities before God), He seeks to confuse you.

Even so, when the people are told, "Follow what God reveals to you," some of them say, "We will believe the way we (have always) believed (the way of our ancestors)." This is despite the fact that their ancestors lacked of any (degree of) sense and were, furthermore, devoid of all guidance.

Symbolically, people who refuse to accept the truth are like sheep, which hear the shepherd's yelp and yet regard it as merely a (distant) sound (to ignore). They are senseless, unresponsive—completely oblivious (of any guidance). What's more, they completely refuse to use their good sense.

You true believers, make use of all the good components of life We have provided for your benefit. However (in every way possible), express your gratitude to God, that is if it is Him that you truly adore.

(What He commands upon you is easy, since) He has only forbidden the meat of animals which die from unknown causes, animal blood, swine flesh, and anything over which a name other than God's has been pronounced. However, if a person is driven by desperation, neither (purposely) desiring it nor exceeding any urgent requirement, there is no sin. Surely (in such a case), God forgives much and gives extensively of His mercy.✦

✦That is God prohibits these because they are harmful. The true way of God is, in fact, relatively easy and non-burdensome. Any prohibitions are strictly for human benefit. The prohibition of pork is an example, since its consumption is highly damaging to the body. For instance, pork consumption is a direct cause of numerous diseases, including lupus, scleroderma, fibromyalgia, esophagitis, ulcerations in the intestines, heart disease, high blood pressure, stroke, cancer, and destructive forms of arthritis. What's more, according to the *American Journal of Epidemiology* regular pork eaters, especially ham eaters, have a 10-fold increased risk for nerve and brain damage, notably ALS-like diseases. Obviously, the consumption of pig flesh is destructive. According to the Qur'aan it is banned, because of His merciful love.

Regarding those who suppress God's revelations, choosing instead the insignificant, they will only earn (for themselves) agonizing torment, which will (ultimately) consume them. What's more, during the time (when all people will stand before Him) God will not recognize or help them, plus they will retain the (full compliment of their) sins. Severe agony is their result—because instead of revelation (and therefore guidance) from God they followed their own erroneous ways (making their own errant views as if gods) and therefore (cheated themselves of the vast quantities of) forgiveness.

Sadly, how little do they fear the fire. So, this is the way it is, since God is the One who is the source of this truth-upholding revelation, all who resist it are gravely in error.

Regardless of your direction of worship mere compliance with ritual itself never defines true belief. Rather, the ones who are truly devout are those who believe in God and the final time (of accountability), as well as the angels and His books, who believe in the prophets and give generously to relatives, as well as all others who are in need (who relinquish this charity), regardless of how much they cherish it, who whenever they make promises keep them. (It is also those) who regardless of the (degree of) difficulty are patient (in their trust in God). These are the ones who have proven themselves true, who are truly in awe of God.

Matters of law, inheritance, and society

You true believers, if someone is wrongfully killed, exact just retribution, the free for the free, a slave for a slave, and a woman for a woman. However, if his fellow man represents a portion of the accused's guilt, this will be adhered to fairly, and restitution to his fellow man will be made properly. This is a mercy from your Lord, an act of His love. Even so, regarding the individual who despite being made aware of this purposely transgresses all he earns is torment. Surely, through the law of just retribution there is a principle of the preservation of the future, so that you might always keep God in mind.✦

✦That is even in killing God seeks justice. Plus, He does so on a global scale. This is to prevent hardship and tyranny. Here, according to the divine law there must be justice for the wrongly killed. This is to, perhaps, ease some of the pain of the wrongs committed against the innocent. It is also to establish true justice on this earth for the blatant killing of the innocent. Too, God will bring justice against any wrongs in His Court. Yet, in His wisdom and love He does all that is possible to prevent such atrocities in this realm.

When death approaches and you have considerable assets, you are obligated to bequeath the fair amount to your close relatives as well as parents. This is a requirement on the believers. What's more, if an individual fabricates a contract knowingly to suit his/her purposes, the sin is only against the perpetrator. Certainly, God is fully aware (of all that can be). However, if the agents of the estate have erred but correct it between the heirs, they will be sinless. Without doubt, God forgives much and gives (extensively of His) kindness.

The prescription of fasting in the month of Ramadhaan

You true believers, to fast (during the month of Ramadhaan) is an obligation (just) as fasting (as a means of atonement) was an obligation for previous believers. This is to make (obedience to) God your objective. However, if you are ill or traveling, fast those days at another time, and, if you are able, make an additional sacrifice by feeding the poor. Any extra that is done is credited to a person's record—you may not realize it, but fasting is for *your* benefit.

The Qur'aan, first revealed in Ramadhaan, was sent to guide humans. It is an obvious proof in the form of guidance as well as the means to distinguish the correct way of life (from fabrications). So (as a means of gratitude), fast during this month. However, if you are ill or traveling, make the days up. God wants to make your life as easy as possible and never wishes you any difficulty but rather that you complete the number of days required and that you praise Him for guiding you correctly. Thus (for all that He does for you), thank Him.

Furthermore, if (any of) My servants ask you about Me, tell him that I am very close (close enough to always hear and respond to any request). Thus, let them also respond to Me and believe in Me, so that they might gain the benefit (of My guidance).

At night before the next day's fast you may have (sexual) intercourse with your wives. They are a protection for you, as you are for them. God is aware that you would have denied yourselves this (lawful function). So, he has extended His mercy towards you and removed this hardship. Thus, you may have full sexual intercourse with them, and take advantage of what God has legalized.

If needed, you may eat or drink until dawn, that is when you see the white streak first appear (above the horizon) in the early morning. Begin the fast and continue until sundown. However (during the final days of Ramadhaan), when you are in meditation in the houses of worship never have skin-to-skin (that is sexual) contact with (your wives). God establishes the aforementioned rules. Never defy them. This is how God makes clear to humankind His messages, that they think constantly of Him.✦

✦For spiritual advancement the final days of Ramadhaan are ideal. This is to thank God for revealing this Qur'aan. Thus, rather than physical pleasures a person's focus is on the deep worship of God. It is a time of pure worship and adoration. However, it is not asceticism but is instead merely to perform extra devotions due to gratitude—a means to get closer to Him. Rather than a public show it is strictly for personal atonement—between the individual and God.

Stealing is a crime. So is using the legal (or governmental) system to steal from others.

They will ask about the new moons. Tell them, "They are useful to calculate time (for yearly calendars), including the pilgrimage. Even so, purity of soul has little to do with mere procedure; the truly pure are those who are completely conscious of God. Therefore, be direct in your dealings, and constantly think of God, so you can achieve a happy state.

The obligation to fight against tyranny

If war is waged against you,✦ fight fiercely in God's

✦This proves the entire basis of Islaamic warfare. It is merely self-defense, thus the use of the terminology, essentially, 'If you are attacked, fight back.' In contrast, aggression is banned.

cause. However, shun aggression, because God does not love aggressors. (When you are wrongfully attacked,) kill (the aggressors) wherever you find them. Drive them away from wherever they drove you away—because while killing is bad *oppression is far worse*. However, never fight against them near the ancient House of Worship, that is unless they attack you first. Yet, if they fight against you, destroy them. This is the consequence of those who reject the truth. However, if they relent, realize that God forgives much and is full of compassion.

Thus, wage war until oppression (and persecution) is eliminated and worship is devoted to God alone. However, if they relent, cease all hostilities, except, of course, against those who intentionally do wrong.

If you are attacked, you may fight during the sacred months, because there must be retaliation for any violation of sanctity. Thus, if you are attacked, strike back with equal force. However, think constantly of God. What's more, realize that God is with those who are fully conscious of Him.

Furthermore, spend freely in God's cause—and if you avoid spending, you may unwittingly invite your own destruction. Remain steadfast in doing good. Truly, God loves those who are committed to doing good.

The pilgrimage to Mecca: a duty to God

Also, perform the pilgrimage and the pious visit in honor of God. Furthermore, if you are prevented from doing so, give, instead, a charitable offering:

whatever you can afford. What's more, never shave your heads until the offering has been sacrificed. Yet, anyone who is sick or suffers from a scalp ailment must redeem himself by fasting or through a charitable act or any other act of worship. However, when your health improves, then, whoever takes advantage of the pious visit (that is 'Umrah) prior to the pilgrimage should give whatever he can. Whoever cannot afford it must fast for three days during the pilgrimage and for seven days after returning, that is a total of ten full days. These rulings are for those who live in regions near Mecca. Consider always and respect (your duties to) God. What's more, realize that He is extreme in His punishment.

The pilgrimage occurs in the specific months for which it has been appointed. Whoever performs it in those months should abstain from indecent speech, arguing, and foul behavior of all types. Also, regarding whatever good you do, God knows it.

Additionally, be sure to make your own provisions. Yet, the best of all provisions is belief in God. Keep Me in mind at all times, you people of insight. However, it is perfectly acceptable if, during the pilgrimage, you conduct business by seeking the blessings of your Lord.

Moreover, when you surge downward in one unified group from 'Arafaat, remember God at the holy place. Remember Him in this way: as the One who guided you after you were, without doubt, lost. What's more, surge onward in unison (as if), a single soul of humanity. Simultaneously, ask God for forgiveness. This is because, surely, God forgives much and gives much of His mercy.

Also, after you have performed your rituals continue to keep God in mind, as you would keep in mind your own fathers, in fact, more deeply. This is because there are those who merely say (essentially), "Almighty Lord, give us the good things of this life." These are the ones who will have no share in the next world. Yet, there are others who say, "Almighty Lord, give us the good of this life but also the good of the next life and what's more protect us from the fires of hell." These are the ones who *according to their achievements* have a share reserved. What's more, God is efficient in His calculations (relating to the giving of reward and punishment).

Furthermore, during the specially appointed days fully keep God in mind. However, whoever leaves abruptly after the two days is free of any sin, and whoever remains longer will incur no sin, provided that he remains conscious of God. Thus, always remain conscious of God, holding Him in awe, and have no doubt that you will ultimately meet Him.

Now, there is a type of person of (seemingly) pleasing character, who claims to believe in God, using God's name freely and who is, in addition, a convincing talker. However, whenever such a person gains power he only spreads corruption. As a result, he destroys all opportunities for humankind's advancement and for the advancement of any progeny.◆

✦This regards the future generations. Because of the actions of the corrupt few the opportunity for these generations is often destroyed. God is only interested in the advancement of civilization. He despises all acts which lead to humanity's harm. This is especially true of those actions which corrupt His earth and therefore the future of humanity. This is why He repeatedly emphasizes the requirement for the war against corruption. Plus, he urges the believers to wage war against such vileness, now, to end all strife on this earth. Then, regardless of how horrifying war is the fact is it is superior to corruption. Yet, this war may be merely a war of words—the firm speaking of the truth against all vile corruption.

Moreover, God despises corruption. So, this person is like this: whenever he is told, "Remain conscious of (the powers of) God," his arrogance drives him into sin. The fact is hell will be his consequence, a vile residence. However (in contrast), there is another type who would willingly sell his (own) soul in order to please God. What's more, God is most compassionate towards His servants.

You true believers, give your whole selves to God. Likewise, never adhere to (the machinations of) Satan. Truly, he is your sworn enemy. Moreover, if you should falter after receiving guidance, then, realize that, surely, God is almighty, truly wise (in understanding the basis of your actions).

Are they merely awaiting the revelation of God Himself, along with His angels, in the clouds, although by then all will have been decided and all will have been returned to God?

Ask the descendants of Israel how numerous were the messages, fully obvious, they were given by Us—if one corrupts God's blessed message after it has reached him (he should realize that), without doubt, God is severe in how He punishes.✦

✦The powerful ones of Jewish ancestry purposely corrupted God's messages to suit their own purposes. What's more, now, these corruptions permeate Jewish doctrine. God is merely reminding the believers to be wary of the great danger of such a propensity. The warning is merely an attempt to protect humans from the vile consequences of the most dastardly of all sins: to corrupt God's own messages or to change them to suit personal needs.

Regarding those who deliberately reject the truth the life of this world alone seems advantageous. Thus, they ridicule the true believers. However, during resurrection the ones who keep God deeply in mind have achieved a superior position. Moreover, God provides (His generous) provisions to whomever He wills, beyond all measure.

The entire human race was once a single (unified) community.✦ (Then, when they began to fall into

✦That is because, originally, people were peaceful, and, thus, they failed to tyrannize each other. They never purposely sought to harm each other. So, there was no need for divine intervention. It is only when humans actively and maliciously harm each other that God intervenes. Thus, tyranny and senseless murder so greatly violates the divine code that God seeks to intervene—with divine testaments. This is why He revealed His books. It is also why He established prophets to represent that guidance to their fellow humans.

It was also to stop the in-fighting which, incredibly, was based on revelation. This is because instead of abiding by God's rule they abused their power to gain advantage over each other. They also altered God's ways to suit their own purposes. Today, these alterations, which are actually found in the Old Testament and Gospels, continue to create confusion. Thus, they created their own religions never approved by God. Yet, incredibly, if they would have kept the revelations true, there would be no conflict. This is because all revelations would agree and no one could argue about it. Note: for an original manuscript of the Gospels see *The Secret Scripture They Don't Want You to Know About* (Knowledge House Publishers).

dissension,) God inspired the prophets as agents, delivering encouraging news (of God's ever present mercy) as well as the appropriate warnings. Through them He bestowed heaven-sent revelations and established the truth, so that it might (act as) regarding their disputes a means of clarification.

Yet (incredibly), the previous recipients of divine revelation became precisely the ones who due to bickering and jealousy were the source of any dispute regarding its meaning, even after (this meaning) was clarified (by the arrival of additional divine revelations). Even so, God guided those who truly believe to the truth about which by His allowance they had disagreed—because God guides directly whomever (truly) desires to be guided.

Yet, do you believe that you could enter paradise without having suffered like those previous believers? They endured every conceivable trial. What's more, they were shaken to such a degree that in every case each prophet, along with his followers, pleaded, "When will God's help arrive?" Yet, the fact is God's (merciful) help is always very near.

They will ask you regarding what they should spend charitably. Tell them, "Whatever you give must first go to parents and relatives, to orphans and the impoverished, and to anyone else (who comes to you) in need."

As much as you might hate it you are *obligated to wage war*. Yet, it may well be that you despise what is good for you, while you love what is harmful to you. This is because God knows, while in contrast your understanding is limited.✦

✦That is He also knows the future and the consequences if people fail to defend their rights. Even so, regarding war there is no need to 'defend' Islaam. Rather, the real war is against tyranny. It has always been mandated by men of God that when tyranny arises, it must be fought and crushed. The Old Testament is full of such urgings. In fact, this is the avowed purpose of the Prophet's mission, to halt all oppression: by any means necessary.

> They will ask you regarding fighting during the sacred month. Tell them, "To fight in this month is a grave violation. However, to debar others from the way of God, to reject Him, and to expel His worshippers from the Sacred Temple: this is far more dreadful in His sight. Godlessness is (even) worse than war."✦

✦It is the clear duty of every Muslim to fight oppression. Anyone who fails to do so is not a true Muslim. Rather, such individuals will be held accountable in the Court of God for their indifference. Even so, this fight must be done in justice, and the battle must be waged specifically against the perpetrators.

To reiterate, the Qur'aan makes it categorically clear that the fight against tyranny—that is godlessness—is a divine obligation. Then, the word obligation may be defined as a "duty" as well as "contract." So, the Muslim is under contract by God to fight, even if it means fighting to the death. Furthermore, the fighting must be continuous, until all elements of oppression are eliminated.

For Christian and Jewish dissenters, that is for those who criticize this dictate, a simple fact must be noted: Are not such people of scripture proud to the point of becoming tearful regarding the bravery of David, also mentioned in this Qur'aan (page 98), and his fight against the oppressors of the time? If David were crushed, then, would the faith of Abraham have survived? Then, is any such resistance against the dictates for violence anything besides pure hypocrisy?

> (Your adversaries) will never stop fighting you until they, if possible, force you to renounce your faith. However, whoever of you recants and dies (in a state of such rejection), his efforts will be of no consequence, both here and in the next

world. Such men will be the residents of the eternal torment.

Those who have embraced the faith and have fled their homelands, while struggling for the cause of God, may expect God's mercy. What's more, God is forgiving and merciful.

They ask you regarding drinking and gambling. Tell them, "Both are extremely harmful, although they have some minor benefits. However, their derogatory effects far exceed any value." They (also) ask you what they should give for God's sake. Tell them, "Whatever you can afford." Thus, God makes obvious to you (the liberal nature of) His revelations, so you will give due consideration about (how this relates to) this world and also the next life. They question you regarding orphans. Tell them, "To deal justly with them is best. If you commingle their affairs with yours, remember, they are your fellow humans." What's more, God is fully aware of the unjust versus the just.

If God desired, He could have certainly imposed upon you difficulties beyond your capacity. What's more, God is almighty, truly wise (regarding the way He administers to His creation).

Rules regarding marriage; advice for women's relations; advice for avoiding human harm

Regarding women, who are godless, never marry them unless they become true believers (in

God). A believing female woman of any status is superior for you than a godless woman, even if you find the latter more appealing. Nor can you (women) marry godless men, that is unless they become true believers. A male of any status who truly believes is superior to a godless man, even though you may find the latter more appealing.

These godless ones invite you to the rejection (of God), that is the fire. However, God calls you, by His will, to (the realm of) paradise and forgiveness. (The fact is) He makes obvious (the truth of) His messages to humankind, so they might truly consider it.

Furthermore, regarding their inquiries about menses, obviously, there is potential for (physical) damage.✦ Thus, avoid sexual contact until the

---

✦That is the blood products of menstruation are by nature contaminated. Blood carries toxins and germs. It is a waste product. Sexual intercourse during this time can cause physical disorders for both men and women, although the latter are at a greater risk. At this time a female's tissues may also be physically sensitive, and thus intercourse may be painful. Also, sexual intercourse during this time forces the menstrual fluids against gravity, which may then become trapped, and this may lead to a variety of illnesses. These illnesses include endometriosis, ovarian cysts, pelvic inflammatory disease, colitis, and, perhaps, even infertility. In males, this exposure can lead to infertility, impotence, prostatitis, and even prostate cancer.

Menstrual fluid contains cells, which aggressively cling to tissue, leading to inflammation. God is causing these fluids/cells to flow outward for a reason. It makes no sense to force them in the opposite direction.

---

discharge has stopped. After that, it is perfectly acceptable to have intercourse, as God has commanded. Truly, God loves those who seek Him in repentance, and He also loves those who keep themselves pure.

Your wives are a source of (healthful benefits) for you: have intercourse with them as you desire. However, be sure to first address the needs of your soul, and, thus, keep God constantly in mind. You will surely meet Him: for those who truly believe in Him.

When you swear in God's name, making promises, these promises should never interfere with good, decent behavior. Nor should they interfere with promoting good will between people. God is fully aware of whatever you do.

God will hold you responsible only for promises you have solemnly made, not those which you said without giving it thought. Remember, God is forgiving as well as tolerant.

Rules for divorce

Those who (swear to) avoid having intercourse with their wives in lieu of a possible divorce will have a four month grace period. Then, if they change their minds, God is certainly forgiving, tremendously merciful. However, if divorce is the only option, surely, God is completely aware, knowledgeable.

Divorced women must wait three months before remarrying as a protection from there being a baby with unknown parentage. Even so, during that time the husbands can reconcile with them. Yet, for justice's sake women have equal rights with men,✦

✦That is in God's eyes, spiritually, men and women are equal. As human beings they are equal, and they must always treat each other with respect, never oppressing one another. They must give each other equal rights in their duties before God. This is the true marital relationship, as directed by God.

Yet, regarding a man's physical strength and ease for making a living he has the advantage. This also relates to the position of a father in raising/advising children in their later lives, that is after they pass childhood. Then, children commonly look up to the father as a role model.

Men have a prominent role to play financially and socially, while assuring equal rights for women. What's more, despite their greater physical power they must never oppress women. Rather, they must always incline towards them in love. The equality in God's view of men and women is also confirmed in Section 3.

although men have precedence over them in this respect. God is almighty and is truly wise (regarding His reasons for whatever He rules).

The limit before a divorce is finalized is two invocations. After that, the marriage must be either resumed in a just manner or ended with justice.

Also, regarding what you have given your wives (in marriage) you are not allowed to take it from them, that is unless both parties have reason to believe that they will be unable to abide by God's regulations. Thus, if it is necessary that the wife return a portion of her assets in order to release herself, there is no sin in this for either party. These are the rulings established by God. Never transgress these rules. Those who do so, that is those who violate God's rulings, are the true perpetrators of evil.

If the divorce is finalized, the former husband cannot marry (the divorcee), that is unless (she) marries another man and is, afterwards, divorced by him. There is in the latter instance no sin, provided that their intention is to obey the limitations established by God. These are the limitations which God makes clear, that is for those who use their reason.

As well, if you become divorced and the end of the waiting period nears, either retain the women fairly or release them fairly. Furthermore, because of vengeance never hold them against their will. To do so is a crime.

In addition, regard God's messages seriously. Also, keep in mind it is God who has blessed you. Moreover, remember the plethora of revelation and wisdom from the heavens He has given you, this in order only to advise you (to prevent you from erring). So, remember Him at all times, and, furthermore, always realize that God has complete awareness, true knowledge, regarding all issues.

Regarding women you divorce who have yet to finish their waiting period, let them in the spirit of justice marry other men. This is sound advice, that is for those who truly believe and who believe in the next life. In fact, it is the most decent way for you as well as the purest. What's more, it is God who knows, while your understanding is limited.

If they wish, divorced mothers may nurse their children for (up to) two years. It is the father's duty to provide for them in a manner that is reasonable. Even so, no one will be given a burden greater than he can withstand. Nor will the mother be made to suffer because of her child nor because of his child, that is its true father. What's more, the father's heir has the same duty.

If the parents decide, the mother and child (or children) may be separated. This is fully acceptable (in God's view). What's more, if you decide to transfer your children to foster mothers, that is acceptable, provided you guarantee in a fair manner the child's safety. However, remain firm in your belief in God, the One who is aware of all your actions.

Regarding widows they should not remarry until the passage of 130 days. (Why 130 days? It is) because it is a mourning time for them, otherwise they might (while in emotional distress) marry a man who is not a big follower of Me. After that, they may do as they please within the legalities. Remember, God is fully aware of your activities.

It is perfectly acceptable to publicly express the desire to marry these women. Or, if you simply intend to do so, that is also acceptable. However, never maintain a secret relationship. Rather, behave and speak decently.

Marriage should only be consummated after the pregnancy-screening period has elapsed. Remember, God is completely aware of all your actions. Thus, keep Him in mind constantly, and know, too, that God is the real source of forgiveness. Also, He is completely tolerant.

If you divorce women before having sexual relations or before giving them assets, there is no fault in (ending the relationship). Yet, even in such a case base what you give them upon your financial status. Be sure the provision reflects your finances. This is an obligation for those who have the desire to do good. Furthermore, if a divorce occurs after the bride has been given assets, give her half, that is unless she or her guardian relinquishes her claim. Yet, to relinquish what is due to you is more representative of the spirit of godliness. Therefore, always remember that you are to act graciously towards each other. Truly, God is aware of all your actions.

Be consistent with your worship ritual. Moreover, be sure to worship in the noblest possible way. Furthermore, stand before God devoutly. Yet, if you are in an insecure circumstance, perform your worship while walking or in transit. Even so, when you are again secure, fully keep God in mind, since (in gratitude you should realize) He is responsible for whatever you now know (about divine law).

Widows get as a minimum a year's maintenance from the deceased's estate. Plus, they should never be forced from their homes. However, if they leave on their own accord, they, without fault, may pursue a legitimate new life. God is the mightiest and wisest.

Regarding women who are divorced they, too, should receive a reasonably calculated maintenance. This is a requirement for those who are conscious of God. This is how God makes clear His messages, so that you will learn to use your common sense.

Are you unaware of the teeming masses of people over the generations who gave up everything, even their homelands, for fear of death? Symbolically, God said to them, "Die" and later regenerated them. The fact is God is unlimited in how He graces humankind.✦ Yet, most people are devoid of all

✦That is they were oppressed and miserable, and so God let them "die" and thus gave them a better, more peaceful life. This is both here and in the future existence, where they are now at peace. Thus, because of their death and displacement God in His mercy gave them an ultimate reward. It is the reward based upon the fact that they suffered oppression due to the tyranny of humankind, and so as a result He gives them peace. This is better than living under oppression. This is the result of His priceless love, which He will always dispense upon any who are unjustly harmed.

gratitude. Therefore, exert all your might in God's cause. What's more, realize that God is fully aware of all (that is).

Then, who is willing to give almighty God a valuable loan, one which He will generously repay, increasing it beyond imagination? Surely, God withholds and provides abundantly. What's more, it is to Him that you will (ultimately) return.

The Qur'aanic story of David and Goliath: enter the faithful commander, Saul

Are you unaware of the powerful ones living after the time of Moses from the descendants of Israel? They said to their prophet, "Give us a (strong) leader, and as a result we will fight on God's behalf." Their prophet retorted, "Are you saying that even if God orders you to do so, you will refuse to fight?" They responded, "We certainly wouldn't shirk the duty to fight for God, when we and our children have been driven from our homeland."✦

✦This demonstrates a selfish bent in the Israelites—that, yes, they would fight, but only because it was in their own interest. In other words, they would not just automatically do so for God's sake, even though what God mandated was for their benefit. Thus, because of their attitude and actions they had already failed the test of God.

Yet, when fighting was commanded, they reneged, that is except a small contingent of them. Certainly, God has full knowledge of (the intentions of) those committed to perpetrating evil.

Their prophet told these powerful ones: "In fact, God has elected Saul to be your ruler." They retorted, "How can he rule us? We have a more legitimate claim for rule than he—we are far wealthier." The prophet replied, "God has surely selected him above you. What's more, He endowed him with great wisdom and a powerful (and beautiful) physique." This illustrates how God lavishes His authority upon whomever He wills...it is God who is beyond comprehension (in how He achieves His pervasive plan), truly knowledgeable.

Furthermore, their prophet told them, "As a sign of your Lord's greatness He will definitely infuse (the strength of) inner peace into your hearts and (the authority of) that enduring angelic heritage, the heritage of the descendants of Moses as well as those of Aaron. This is, without doubt, a sign, that is if you are true in your belief."

When Saul proceeded to battle, he said, "I perceive that God will now test you through a river in order to determine which of you is really with me and thus eliminate the weak ones: Whoever drinks from it will not belong to me, while, in contrast, whoever refrains is a certain follower. However, whoever draws only a single handful will be forgiven."

Yet, regrettably, with a few exceptions they all drank voluminously from it. Then, He took those who truly believed across the river, and, immediately, the others said, "We lack the strength today to stand up against Goliath and his army."✦

✦In the blistering heat of the desert the consumption of excess amounts of water can have derogatory effects, even weakening the most fit of individuals. This is due to a phenomenon of electrolyte depletion. This excess water has a negative effect upon the hormonal system, as well as the circulatory system, leading to a sensation of weakness. This may well have occurred to the majority of Saul's army. In other words, due to the toxic effects of excess fluid upon the hormonal glands the physiology is disrupted.

The dilution of the blood leads to muscular weakness. Water logging without careful replacement of electrolytes can cause faintness, even heat exhaustion. Thus, the men who drank too much water became physiologically fatigued. Yet, their greatest source of fatigue was knowing in their souls that they violated their Lord, leading to a loss in faith in their mission. This is because they were warned this was a test from God, but those who were hypocritical in faith chose to defy it. God also did this to eliminate from their group the frauds, who may have disrupted their efforts, leading even to their destruction.

Yet, those who knew with certainty that they were destined to meet their Lord replied, "How often has a small contingent defeated a great one by God's allowance: God is with those who are patient in adversity."

When they arranged themselves (in battle positions) against Goliath and his armies, they prayed, "Our

Lord, regardless of the circumstances embellish us with patience. What's more, make us strong in our purpose. Support us, O God, against Your enemies." Then, under the direction of God they routed them. David himself killed Goliath and (as a result) God gave him power, authority, and wisdom, providing him with the knowledge of whatever He willed. Surely, had God not enabled people to defend themselves against one another (only) corruption would reign. Yet, God has no limit in His grace to all (the inhabitants in His countless) worlds.

These are the divine messages. We represent them to you to establish the truth, because make no mistake about it you (O believer,) are (one of those who is responsible for) bearing this message.✦

✦And, therefore, assuming the responsibility to fight against tyranny. This command directly follows the parable of David and Goliath. So, the meaning is obvious. It is the fact that the believer is *obligated to fight* with all his might against the forces of evil. Failure to do so will result in punishment. Note also the following statement about Jesus, whose truth included fighting against evil.

Some of Our messengers were of a higher status than others. Among them were those who were spoken to directly by God and others He elevated to an even higher status (for instance), Jesus was given the complete spectrum of the truth. What's more, We strengthened him (directly) through the holy inspiration.

Even so, regarding the corruption of the original message (of Moses and Jesus) had God desired He could have stopped the successors of the prophets from in-fighting. Ultimately, they disputed greatly within their ranks. Some of them remained resolute in their belief, while others rejected it. Yet, God could have made them all follow one way, however, God does whatever He wills.

You true believers, give your all in God's way, that is before the time arrives when bargaining, friendship, and special favors will be of no consequence. Yet, without doubt, any who reject the truth—they are the ones who are truly evil.

God: He is the only divine Being, He, the permanently alive, the (One who is) eternally self-subsistent. He never gets tired. Nor does He sleep. He owns (and therefore has authority over) all that exists in the universe as well as on the earth. No one can intercede with Him, unless He allows it. He knows all that is possible as well as all that is unavailable (to your perception). They are unable to gain even a modicum of His knowledge, except what He permits. His everlasting authority encompasses the entire universe as well as this earth. What's more, the preservation of (the integrity of) both (these realms) never fatigues Him. He alone is truly exalted (beyond comprehension), absolutely tremendous (beyond imagination).

Regarding matters of faith no one will be forced—no one will be coerced.✦ Now, there is a

✦That is "there will be no violence in religion." This alternative translation of the Arabic phrase, *laa ikraafa fiddeen*, is found in the work of George Sales, commissioned in the 19th century by the King of England.

Western authorities are well aware that Islaam spread through peaceful methods. Never in its history were people forced to convert. Nor were they coerced through, for instance, torture to accept it. Yet, this is precisely the method used in modern times by Western authorities against Muslims, for instance, the humiliating acts committed against them in Guantanamo, Abu Ghraib, Bagram Airbase, and within the Israeli gulags. Here, through torture hundreds of Muslims have been coerced to rescind their faith.

The British historian and former Middle Eastern spy Byng in his book *Story of the Arabs* made it clear that the claim that Islaam spread by the sword is a myth. He also noted that compared to Western or Christian powers Islaam is merciful to people of other faiths. Byng has demonstrated that much of what Western people know about Islaam is based upon lies.

distinction between the correct way and the way of deceit. Thus, whoever rejects corruption—vile evil—and (truly) believes in God has taken a position which is invincible. What's more, God fully comprehends (it all) and knows all.

God is truly close (that is He is a true friend), to the sincere believers (in Him). What's more, He leads them from the darkness (of spiritual confusion) into the light of divine guidance. However, regarding those who reject the truth their only associate is absolute corruption, forces which drive them (deeper) into darkness. Furthermore, they are the ones destined for the wicked torment, to endure it forever.

Are you unaware of that foolish man, who argued with Abraham about his Lord, only because God allowed him to be King? Abraham told him, "My Lord is the One who brings life and causes death." The King retorted, "I can do the same." Abraham continued, "Then, consider this: God causes the sun to rise in the East, can you make it rise from the West?" Then, the king was flabbergasted. God never guides people who purposely do wrong.

(You humankind, in your loss) are you like the one who passed an abandoned civilization, mere ruins, and said, "Could God truly revive this?" As a result, God caused him to remain (as if) dead for a hundred years. Then, He revived him and said, "How long have you existed in this state?" He answered, "Only a day, perhaps, a few hours." God said, "Not at all, rather, you have remained in this condition for a century. Look at your food and drink—it is untouched. Look also at your mount (it is still alive)." We did this so that We might symbolize this for humankind, because (for instance,) consider the skeletons—the dried bones—and how We assembled them and then adorned them with flesh. When he clearly understood this, he said, "Now, it is clear to me that God is capable of everything."

In fact, it was Abraham who said, "My Lord, show me how you create life from nothing"—mere inorganic matter—from (even) human remains. God said, "Do you not believe?" Abraham answered, "I believe, but allow me to see it, so that my understanding can be even more profound." God told him, "Take four birds and train them (to follow your commands). Then, place them each on separate mountains. Afterwards, summon them, so they will come flying to you. What's more, realize that God is almighty, wise."✦

✦That is that He can do anything. As Abraham had the birds at his command, which would do his bidding, God has in His almighty command the control over all that exists, living and dead. Just as Abraham summoned the birds He can summon the dead remains to come to Him—as if alive—at the final time. To do so He merely issues a summons. After all, they are all His creation. What's more, like Abraham's birds, God has trained all that exists to adhere to His commands, every living being, even every bit of genetic material and every molecule. It all obeys His laws. So, God, the owner of it all, has everyone 'trained' to unconsciously obey Him, when He makes the final call, when all will be gathered back to Him, when all will be held accountable—when for anyone who did not prepare for this there will be only remorse.

There is, now, a molecular explanation for this return. As reported by a number of modern astronomers, for instance, Gardner, all that exists in this universe is based upon vibration. Apparently, all within the universe is connected by molecular strings. According to Gardner all matter is connected by these strings. These strings are based upon a kind of energy, which vibrates. This may explain to a degree this parable, that is that at a predestined time God has the vast power to *draw* all that exists back to Him. It also explains the Qur'aanic phrase that 'from God do humans originate and to Him will they, ultimately, return.'

Those who spend whatever they have for God's sake can be compared to a kernel of grain, which sprouts several ears and in every ear, hundreds of grains. Surely, God gives exponential increases to whomever He wills. What's more, He is infinite in His generosity, fully knowledgeable.

Those who give generously in the way of God and refrain from tainting this✦ will have their reward

✦That is by bragging or hurting others' feelings. To gain God's ultimate reward all charitable acts must be performed exclusively for Him. This is without seeking material gain. For the ideal reward charity must be done secretly. This is proof that the only purpose of such acts is to please almighty God.

(held in trust) by their Lord; no fear need they have nor any grief. A kind word and (an attempt) to disguise or forgive a person's faults is far superior as a charity than giving followed by hurt. What's more, God is beyond need (in His mercy), completely tolerant.

You true believers, never cancel your charitable acts by (taunts and) bragging and thus hurting the feelings of the disadvantaged—for instance, the wealthy person, who seeks praise and recognition instead of giving, as God ordains, from the heart. Symbolically, such a man is like a polished rock to which a small amount of soil clings; there occurs a heavy rain, and all that remains is a hard and bare stone (in other words), they will gain nothing from their supposedly good deeds. This is because God never guides those who reject the truth.

The parable of those who spend their assets to please God is that of a garden on high and fertile land. When rain saturates it, there arises verdant produce. Yet, if there is a drought, other (subterranean) waters nourish it. What's more (regarding any good you do), God is (fully) aware of your actions.

No one would desire to have a lush garden, populated by a multitude of (luscious) fruit and nourished by fresh (unpolluted) streams, degenerate over time with (as it were) only feeble children as caretakers and then watch it become destroyed by a wild fire, burnt to nothing.◆ This is how God makes

◆That is, in other words, all that is produced merely for selfish interests is a loss. Like the dessicated garden it holds no value in the next existence. Only the dedicated worship of God and the true commitment to Him has everlasting value. Only good deeds done exclusively for Him will be rewarded. These are the deeds to perform in order to achieve the ultimate success. The Qur'aan has hereby urged humankind to make good use of time and accumulate good deeds, all for God's sake. In other words, people should beware of wasting their lives in frivolous pursuits.

clear for you His messages, so that you would truly consider it.

You true believers, be charitable with your possessions as well as what We produce for you from the earth. For your charity never choose corrupt merchandise, which you would consider unfit for yourself. In this respect realize that God is free of need, ever to be praised.

Satan is the one who threatens you with poverty, urging you to be penurious. In contrast, God promises you forgiveness and voluminous success—God is beyond measure in His assets, the One who is aware of all (that is), fully knowledgeable (the One who), instills wisdom within whomever He chooses. Clearly, whoever is given wisdom has been provided with a true endowment: vast wealth. Yet, only people endowed with insight, in fact, comprehend this.

Financial issues, business contracts, and usury

(Also, realize) that whatever you spend or even intend to spend on others, God is aware of it. What's more, those who wrong themselves by penurious behavior (withholding themselves from giving of themselves), will be (when they meet God) defenseless.

If you are openly charitable, this is good. However, if you do so secretly, this is superior. This will make up for some of your derogatory behavior: God is aware of all your actions.

You can never make people follow the right way. Only God (can) guide.

What's more, any charity you give is for your own good, that is if you do it only to please God. Certainly, whatever good you achieve through charity will be repaid.✦ What's more, you will never be wronged.

✦That is demonstrating the vast generosity of God in the fact that all goodness is completely rewarded. In His loving mercy He will fully repay in excess any charity, that is any precise riches given, but will also compensate in full for any time, energy, or physical labor given on His behalf. In His merciful love He tells humans in advance, a kind of encouragement, that whatever they do, if it is truly for Him, it will be restituted. Put simply, if to please Him a person gives of himself or perhaps donates wealth, God will return it multiplied.

Needy are those who, wholly committed to God's cause, are unable to work. Those who are unaware of their condition might regard them as financially stable, because they never beg. Yet, you can recognize them by their distinguished behavior. They never appear desperate, and they are never solicitous. Whatever you give on their behalf, God knows (and keeps track of) it.

Those who continuously spend their possessions for the sake of God, privately and publicly, will be rewarded by their Lord. What's more, there is nothing for them to dread or fear.

Mandate against usury (that is the taking of interest)

Those who gorge themselves on usury act like the ones who have been caressed by Satan himself. They claim, "Enterprise is a kind of usury," despite the fact that God has endorsed enterprise, while prohibiting usury. Thus, whoever becomes aware of his Lord's warning and afterwards desists may keep his past gains. It will be for God to judge him. However, regarding those who return to it these are the ones destined for permanent residence in the fire.✦

✦Usury is profiteering through the taking of interest. Even receiving it, as in interest-bearing accounts, is banned. God has deemed usury as destructive to the common man as well as society. It creates a debtor state. The trillions of dollars in debt suffered by the United States is an extreme example. In this country it is difficult for people to build true wealth, because they are burdened by interest, for instance, as mortgages or car loans. So, only the takers of interest become wealthy.

In Islaam, to protect the people, as well as the financial power of the State, this practice is banned. In ancient Mosaic Law usury or the taking of interest was also prohibited. The full reasons for its prohibition are unknown. However, what is certain is that God regards it a crime, because of the harm it causes humanity. This is because as a result of an interest-based system money is concentrated only in a few hands. A Muslim is obligated to do all in his power to destroy such a system. That obligation is binding upon every true believer and is adamantly stated in the Qur'aan. This is because such a system achieves only oppression. What's more, Islaam is the antithesis of any such oppression.

The profits of usury can never be applied to gain rewards from God. Yet, He blesses any truly charitable actions, multiplying them exponentially. God has no love for the thankless, the obstinate.

You true believers, no doubt, those who do good actions, are constant in prayer, and are charitable their reward is (held in trust) directly with God. What's more, they have nothing to fear, nor should they feel (even the slightest) remorse. You true believers, always consider your duties to God. As part of this commitment remit all gains taken through usury—if you truly believe. Failure to do so represents a defiance of God and His Messenger (and, as a result,) your assets could be confiscated. However, if you repent, then, you are entitled to retain your principal.

If you deal with others fairly, you, too, will be treated fairly. Even so, if the one who is indebted is under pressure, let the creditor give him allowance. Or, as charity erase the debt. If you only realized it, this also would be for your own good. Therefore, give due consideration to the time when you will be returned to God, when everyone will be fully compensated for whatever he/she has earned. (What's more, during this time) all will be treated fairly.

You true believers (regarding loans or credit), be sure to conduct all business in writing. Have a third party or your agent inscribe it in a just manner. The agent must commit to recording it according to God's rules. The person who incurs the debt should dictate (the proper documents) in a way that upholds the rules of God. However, if he is sick, incompetent, or mentally ill then have his caretaker or agent dictate (or write) it. The creditor should bring two known, credible men as witnesses. However, if this is impossible, a known, credible man and two known, credible women, just in case one of the women is unfamiliar with business, so the other can uphold her. The witnesses must uphold in God's name any duty for which they are called upon.

Again, be sure to write it down; don't neglect this. Keep detailed records regarding debts or business transactions, whether large or small, along with their due dates. God regards this as the most just way. This is more reliable as evidence than verbal contracts, and therefore will prevent doubts (and thus hard feelings). However, if the transaction consists (merely) of normal merchandising, that is active buying and selling, there is no need to write it down.

Make witnesses available for key transactions, however, neither the contract writer nor witness must suffer harm. In fact, if you harm them, that is a vile act. Thus, always keep God in mind, since it is He who teaches you all this, and He is fully aware of all that happens. .

When traveling, a secretary or agent may be unavailable. A handshake may be accepted, that is if you truly trust the (individual or individual parties). What's more (in any such dealings), let him be conscious of God, his Lord.

Regarding business dealings never repress or conceal evidence. What's more, whoever does so has a sick soul. Remember, God is aware of all issues.

To God belongs the complete spectrum of all that exists in the universe as well as the earth.✦ So,

✦That is He is all that is. He is the whole. He is everywhere. He is within and without. What's more, no one can evade Him, because He is even 'us,' in other words, each human is of God. Thus, every human being has God's essence.

Because every particle of every human is of Him the natural tendency is to pay homage to Him. From the beginning of humanity there has always been an attempt by people to seek a higher power. In contrast, the unnatural propensity—the violation of nature—is to reject Him. The latter will be the cause of monumental regret. Thus, the rejection of God is the greatest violation of the human instinct, a crime beyond comprehension.

whether (you attempt to) disguise your thoughts or reveal them (doesn't matter). God will hold you responsible. Then, realize that He will forgive whomever He desires to forgive and will torment whomever He chooses. This is because God has the power to deem whatever He wills.

The Messenger, as well as those who resolutely believe in him, are the true believers in God's revelations. They all believe in the Great One, His angels, all His books, and all His prophets. They never imply that one (of these messengers) is superior to another, plus they attest, "We understand it, and we *will* follow it." (Furthermore, they say,) "Forgive us, our Lord: we realize we will meet You soon."

God never burdens you with more than you can withstand. What's more (realize that), those who do good He will love. In contrast, those who act wickedly only harm themselves.

Pray, "My Lord, if we forget or blunder, be easy on us."

Pray, "Give us a lighter burden than that of the previous believers, and prevent us from suffering trials, which we lack the strength to bear."

Pray, "Cleanse our sins, forgive our errors, and bless us, truly bless us, with Your mercy. You are the only One we can depend on for protection. Therefore, give us, our Lord, Your full support against those who reject the truth."

Section 3
The Family of Jesus

This section contains a significant discussion of Jesus Christ. Like the previous section it opens with three Arabic letters, the significance of which is unknown. In Arabic, when the Qur'aan is recited, these letters act as a kind of tuning device, a kind of rhythmic preparation for the recitation. They help tune the voice to gain the proper vocal inflection for the reading.

In the Qur'aan Jesus is mentioned frequently, in fact, by name far more frequently than the Prophet Muhammad. Here, there is a greater degree of accuracy regarding the principles of his mission than even in the Bible. The Qur'aan makes a decided effort to clarify the true nature of Jesus and his mission, a fact alluded to throughout this section. The fact is this section is largely directed at the existing people of the Bible, who may unwittingly follow fabrications that have no basis in the divine code.

It must be noted that the Qur'aan is the only divine revelation which was completely written down before the death of its bearer. Nothing was left to chance; it was all recorded. It was also memorized by hundreds of adherents. This is why it represents invaluable information for all who claim belief in the one God.

In the name of the most merciful
and compassionate God

A-L-M

There is only one God. He lives forever. What's more, He needs no one.

Systematically, He revealed this divine book—in absolute truth—to establish the truth (arising from the heavens and also as) a verification (of any truths remaining in) some of the previous revelations…

because He, too, revealed (these earlier books,) the Torah, as well as the Gospels, to guide humankind, (books), which also revealed the method to determine right from wrong. Yet, clearly, whoever refuses to believe in God's messages will be consumed with immense, truly immense, torment, because God is truly almighty, the only One who can (in fact,) avenge evil.

Surely, regarding (all aspects of) the universe, as well as this earth, God is fully aware. (He knows it all,) and, furthermore, nothing escapes Him. He is the One who has designed you (genetically in utero and ultimately) into your (final) human form and does so in whatever way He desires. Thus, He is the only divine power: God almighty, the truly wise.✦

✦Obviously, rather than any human this is God who is speaking. This implies that He is so wise that He invented the human being from absolute nothingness. He alone produced the blueprint for the human species, an obviously created being, and then enacted it. Thus, obviously, humans are a specific creation and could never have evolved spontaneously from nothing. So, as the Qur'aan makes clear that all that exists has been designed by a specific plan, all at the behest of the one almighty God.

He is the One who revealed this book (directly to you and for your benefit). In it are clearly understandable concepts, which are, in fact, its basis. Yet, it also contains parables.

Even so, people with sick hearts deviate from the obvious, focusing instead on the symbolic. Their objective is to create confusion by claiming (without basis) that they (like God) understand its true meaning.✦ However, only God knows its

✦That is they focus on parables in an attempt to dispute the authenticity of the Qur'aan. They do so by creating arguments about their meaning, but they only do this because inherently they refuse to believe in it. Such people will act like they are curious about the meaning, yet their entire purpose is to dispute it.

Of course, this is different than any legitimate attempt to understand God's wisdom. In fact, God issues these parables to cause people to consider their implications.

ultimate meaning. In contrast, the truly knowledgeable ones say, "We believe in it all; it is all from God." This is the comment of the wise, the ones who pray, "Our Lord, protect us from deviating from the truth after you have (correctly) guided us, and lavish upon us Your mercy, because You are the only One who can give it," (and who also pray) "Our Lord, without question, You will gather together all human beings (that ever lived) for the final assessment, because that is a certainty." The fact is when God makes a promise He always fulfills it (and He has duly promised that resurrection is a reality).

Regarding those who reject God's messages nothing they possess will protect them. They will, without doubt, become the fuel for the fire. Thus, they will meet the same fate as the previous dynasties, including the ancient Egyptians. They rejected Our messages. However, God held them accountable for their wickedness. God's punishment, rather, retaliation is extreme.

(So, be sure to) tell those who reject the truth, "You will be destroyed and ultimately gathered into the inferno, the most vile (of all) destinations." Proof (of this) already exists, that is on the battlefield. One army fought for God and the other against Him. God's army was outnumbered, two to one. Yet, God strengthens with His heavenly power whomever He chooses. This is a significant lesson for all who have the ability to comprehend the truth.✦

✦That is that God is always with those who for His sake uphold truth. Anyone who upholds justice is also on God's side, and what's more God will fully take care of such an individual. It means that regardless of the adversity any person or group of believers will succeed, even against extreme odds. This is through the help of the all-powerful and almighty God.

As this Qur'aan makes clear God is interested in the success of His mission and thus will support any group of true believers against the most extreme odds—if they are truly patient and dedicate themselves exclusively to Him. The recent defeat of the massive Israeli army by a relatively small group of lightly armed Muslims, the Hezbollah, proves that God is behind all who fight for justice.

The Hezbollah fought in God's name for the security of their homeland. Surely, this proves the dictum of God that those who fight for justice against the oppressors will always ultimately win. This is because regardless of the circumstances they always rely upon Him. In fact, anyone who holds tightly his bond to God will ultimately win.

The allurement of life—the material gains—may be enjoyed temporarily. However, the most grand of all achievements is with God. Tell them, "Shall I inform you what is superior to this (earthly life)? It is to live in paradise forever with the Lord accompanied by companions, whose hearts are pure, plus the approval of God (the latter being the best of all achievements)."

The real way of God

God is fully aware of what is in the hearts of His servants, those who say "Our Lord, we truly believe in You. Thus, forgive our sins, and protect us from the agony of the fire." These are (the types of servants) who are patient (regardless of the difficulty they endure) and keep their promises (regarding their commitments to God), the truly devout, who spend without hesitation on others and who pray for forgiveness: from the depths of their hearts.

God Himself (as represented by His vast creation), the angels, and all others gifted with inner knowledge (who without hesitation) all recognize that He is the only God—the impartial and fair God—the mighty, the only One who is truly wise.✦ The fact is in God's view the *only true*

✦That is all God's creation ultimately confirms that He is the mighty, merciful God, who must be bowed to due to His greatness. Whether willingly or unwillingly it all submits to Him. In contrast, of all creation only the human being rejects Him. This is why such a being, isolated and confused, is the ultimate loser. While all else submits before God in peace, recognizing its place as a mere humble servant, only the human purposely rebels against Him. This is strictly due to arrogance and self-importance.

way of life is absolute submission to Him.✦ The

✦That is, literally, Islaam. The latter is merely a term, which means the surrendering of the self to God. Thus, rather than a religion it is more correctly translated as a "way of being" or "way of living." This demonstrates that rather than any superficial adherence to ritual or religion it is what is in the soul that truly matters.

This demonstrates the liberal nature of the Qur'aanic message. The fact that the religion of the Qur'aan is non-denominational is further emphasized by the forthcoming statement: that this religion of submission is precisely the one followed by the earlier committed souls—Abraham, Jacob, Joseph, Moses, Jesus, and others. The true way of God is defined in this section.

people of the previous scriptures originally followed this way but ultimately created bizarre variations, merely due to jealousy and hate. Yet, regarding those who refuse to believe in God's way realize that God is expeditious in holding people accountable.

Thus, if such people argue with you, tell them, "I have surrendered my entire being to God, like the others (who have done so previously)." Also, ask the people of the earlier scriptures, as well as those who are unaware (of monotheism), "Have you (fully) given yourselves to God?" If they do so, they are adhering correctly. However, if they refuse, your only responsibility is to remind. Furthermore, God is completely aware of what is in peoples' hearts.

Those who defiantly reject God's messages, murder (His) prophets, and kill God-fearing (that is decent) people, tell them they will endure a painful punishment, beyond comprehension.✦

✦That is it is the obligation of the true believer to warn those who commit evil regarding the consequences of their acts. These are the acts of the godless, who fear no moral responsibility for their deeds. The Muslims are obligated to inform them of these consequences, *with love, consideration, and compassion.*

What's more, whatever they achieve will ultimately be of no consequence, both here and in the next life. Also, ultimately (that is at resurrection), they will be completely isolated.

Are you familiar with (what was the ultimate result of) the people of the earlier scriptures? They were commanded to make God's writings their law. Yet, some of them obstinately rejected it due to the fact that they claimed that they would only experience hell temporarily.✦ Thus, their fabrications

✦That is they used such a claim as an excuse, all so they could wantonly pursue their own prurient pleasures, without consequences, and pay no heed to right or wrong. This applies to both certain Christian and Jewish groups, although the latter were the primary architects of this philosophy.

have caused them over the centuries to stray (greatly) from the faith. Then, what will be their consequences when We gather them together to witness that time when all people will be held accountable, when each person will be compensated for what he has done and when everyone will be treated justly?

Say to yourself, "O God, Lord of the infinite good, You distribute Your power to whomever You will. You also remove it from whomever You will. You dignify whomever You will, and You debase whomever You will. You control whatever is good and exert power over all that exists. (In Your incredible might) You cause the night to become longer by reducing daylight and make the day become longer by reducing nighttime. Plus, You cause life (to exude) from dead (material).✦ You also produce the dead

✦This happened in the primeval oceans billions of years ago. Today, it also happens on earth, when rain strikes dry or barren soil. Here, creatures, such as frogs, fresh-water shrimp, and salamanders, which may have existed dormant for years, transform to become alive. They are little more than dehydrated carcasses, and yet upon exposure to water spring to life. Even so, it will happen again when humankind is brought before Him to account. In other words, eventually, by a similar process the human dead will be revived.

from the living (material). You provide nourishment —actual support—which is beyond measurement, to whomever You desire."

Never, O believers, never allow yourselves to become allied with the godless in preference to the believers, since any who does so distances himself from God, that is unless you fear a threat from them.

Tell (those who reject Him), "Whether you hide it or reveal it, God knows what is in your hearts. Truly, He is aware of all that occurs in the vast and infinite Universe. What's more, God has the power to will anything."

At the time when every human being will be faced with all the good, as well as wrongs (he has done) many will wish that there were a vast distance between himself and it.✦ God warns you

✦That is the era of judgement. God wants all His humans to prepare for it. This is by considering the fact that they truly will be brought before Him. This makes it clear that there will be a consequence for all actions. This theme of accountability is interspersed throughout the Qur'aan. In fact, it is its main message. The warning is given due to compassion, due to the concern that during that overwhelming time the human will find himself at a loss.

to save you from this, because He is infinitely compassionate and loving to His creatures.

Tell (the people), "If you love God, follow me.✦

✦That is the refined way of the Prophet Muhammad, who represented the precise teachings of almighty God. To follow his way is to adopt an elegant system of life, a system based upon divine inspiration. It is a way which leads humans to vast success, both in this temporary life and the permanent one of the future. What's more, in this divine revelation God repeatedly urges the human race to follow the Prophet's method (for a description of his wise ways see the *Words of Muhammad*, K. Khaleel, Knowledge House Publishers—view at knowledgehousepublishers.com).

God will love you. Plus (as a result He will), forgive your sins. Truly, God is extremely forgiving (constantly giving of His) kindness. So, tell them, categorically, "Obey (the dictates of) God and the Prophet."

(Then, for you followers of scripture consider the fact that) it is God who elevated Adam (the

original man), Noah, Abraham—and his progeny—
as well as the Moses/Christ lineage, to the highest
state achievable: all in one genetic pool.

The birth of the Virgin Mary

God was there to hear the prayer of a woman from
that lineage, who prayed, "My Lord, I vow that
what is in my body is devoted to You. Accept this
from me, You alone are the One who listens to all
prayers (the One) who knows all." Yet, when she
gave birth, in surprise, she wondered: "Lord, it is
a female"—God knew what it was and that there
could be no male child that could ever compare to
this female—"and I have named her Mary. I seek
Your protection for her and her progeny against
Satan, the accursed."

Therefore, her Lord accepted the baby girl with
gladness and (in answering her prayer) helped her
develop in a fine stature, placing her in the care of
Zechariah.

Whenever Zechariah visited her in the
sanctuary he found that food was provided. He
would ask, "Where did this come from?" She said,
"It is from God. He is the One who supports
whomever He chooses; His loving mercy is beyond
count." (Moved in his heart) Zechariah prayed,
"My Lord, from Your loving mercy give me truly
good descendants. You are the One who hears all
prayers." (As an illustration of how unlimited is
His loving grace) while he was praying the angels
called him, "God promises you a son named John,

who will authenticate the truth. He will be exceptionally and morally pure, one of God's devout prophets." Zechariah exclaimed, "My Lord, how can I have a son when I am exceedingly old and my wife is infertile?" The answer was, "The decision has been made. God does whatever He deems."

(Zechariah) responded, "Lord, give me a sign." It was said, "The sign will be that for three days you will not speak to anyone other than by sign language. What's more, always remember your God, and continuously praise His limitless glory."

(Then, ultimately,) the angels told Mary, "God has elected you and purified you and has elevated you above all the women in the world. Thus, remain truly devoted to your Lord, and, what's more, submit yourself to Him in total submission."

This (story) is a historical secret, which is impossible for anyone to have known, although We now reveal it to you.✦ Certainly, you were not

✦That is proving that this is a divine document. This is an excellent example for the Qur'aan's detractors, who claim that this book is man-made. Obviously, no seventh century man could have known these details. In fact, these specifics regarding the birth and life of Mary are not even found in the earlier scriptures. Then, obviously, only almighty God could be the source for this information.

there when they drew lots to determine which of them should be Mary's guardian. Nor were you there when they argued about it with each other— when (ultimately), the angels said, "Mary, God sends you news of a son. He will become known as the Christ Jesus, *Mary's son*.✦ He will be respected in

✦That is there is no reason to presume he was a god. He demonstrated no attributes of a divine being, for instance, he created nothing and he was dependent upon the basic elements of earthly life. He was born in a womb through childbirth. Therefore, like all real children he was dependent upon his mother. Yet, the point is he was mortal, because he lived on earth as a dependent. Thus, there is no basis for calling him divine.

this world and of the highest stature in the next. (What's more, he will be) among those closest to God. He will instruct humans (even) in his cradle and also as an adult. Furthermore, He will be (one of God's) truly devout."

Mary said, "How could I become pregnant? No man has touched me." The angel answered "So it is decided: God creates as He wills. When He makes His decision, He merely says, "Be," and it already is. Thus, He will teach him revelation, imparting wisdom, as well as the Torah and Gospel, and will make him a prophet to the Israelites."

Jesus begins his mission

He (Jesus) will tell them, "I have come to you with a message from your Lord. Through His power I will create from the earth, essentially, the fortune, which may, through God's will, become your destiny. What's more, I will heal those who are blind (literally as well as of spirit and mind) and the leper (that is the shunned).✦ Furthermore, I will revive

✦That is actual lepers as well as the spiritually wounded. God speaks parabolically, to create a kind of word picture. So, this cure was surely physical as well as spiritual. It included those who lost their ties to God due to sinning or mere ignorance. Jesus reminded all such people of the vast forgiveness and love of God, which overwhelms all. Merely by dedicating the self to Him, he taught, all sins are forgiven.

Surely, there were also physical medicines applied to lepers. Wild oregano, the true biblical hyssop, is one such medicine. This is the original thyme apparently used by the Three Wise Men.

Recent research proves that this wild Mediterranean spice destroys all forms of mycobacteria, the species of bacteria responsible for leprosy. This spice was mentioned by Moses and perhaps Jesus as a potential cure for various diseases. It was also mentioned by the Prophet Muhammad as a cure for the common cold, a fact fully demonstrated by modern research. In one study extract of wild oregano destroyed 100% of all cold viruses and 99.9% of the flu virus. In *The Secret Scripture They Don't Want You to Know About*, (a modernized version of the Gospel of Barnabas) Jesus often mentions aromatic ointments for wound healing. These ointments likely contained wild oregano.

> the (spiritually) dead. Also, I will tell you what you should take advantage of now and how you should prepare for your future. Certainly, in all (that I say) there is a message for you, for those who are (truly) sincere in their belief."
>
> (Furthermore, he said,) "I have come to confirm the (true nature of the) original Law to eliminate unnecessary restrictions.✦ I have come to you

✦That is as imposed by the Jews. Man-made laws impede humans from understanding almighty God's true nature. The latter is justice, mercy, and compassion. Thus, religion becomes a burden. Yet, this is not how God intended it. This is because God's requirements were/are few.

Over the centuries the Israelites created their own religion, with rules and regulations they invented. Thus, they created self-imposed burdens. The way of God became burdened with senseless dogma, and as a result they alienated people from it. Even before the revelation of the Torah, even as they were being rescued, they developed onerous rules. Jesus came to eliminate such burdens and return the Israelites to the original ways of God, a fact made abundantly clear in the Qur'aan.

> representing signs from your Lord. Thus, always consider (your duties before God), and follow what I say. This is the correct way." However, when Jesus perceived their failure to believe, he said, "Who will commit to being my assistants for God?"

The pure hearted ones replied, "We will do so. We believe in God and swear that we are true to it. We believe in all God's revelations, and we follow His prophet. Then, rely upon us as your (desired) team, with all (others) who are committed."

Yet, those determined to perpetrate evil plotted against Jesus. However, God created His own (efficient) plot. Surely, God is beyond all schemers. When God said to Jesus, "I will cause you to die and bring you near Me. Then, I will cleanse you of the perfidious presence of the godless. What's more, I will place your followers at a level far above those who strive against Me, until the final time."

You (humankind), you will all ultimately return to Me. Then, I will judge between you regarding your disagreements. Regarding the godless I will make them suffer severely, now as well as in the future life. What's more (then, in the final life), there will be no one to help them. In contrast, those who truly believe and accomplish goodness: they will be given by Him their full reward. Surely, God has no love✦ for the wicked.

✦That this is the ultimate punishment of hell—to be abandoned by almighty God due a person's own actions. Surely, nothing could be more dire than this. Yet, this is the ultimate consequence for those who purposely reject Him.

The true nature of Jesus

We relate this message to you, a type of news full of insight. Certainly, from God's perspective the nature of Jesus is no different than that of Adam, who We created from (mere inorganic) matter and then said to him, "Be" and he became.

This is the truth from the Lord: never doubt it. If after you have become aware of this knowledge anyone disputes with you regarding it (that is the true nature of Jesus), tell them, "Then, you gather together your supporters, and I will gather mine, and let us pray together earnestly. Let us together invoke God's condemnation upon whomever is distorting the facts." (This is because) certainly, there is no other divine being besides God. He exclusively is almighty.✦ He alone is truly wise due

✦That is He has no associates. No other power, surely not Jesus Christ, can compete with Him. No other can create. Nor does any other have the power to resurrect or judge. Only almighty God, the One that all people call to in desperation, has such powers. Thus, it is obvious that no mortal can simultaneously be a god. What's more, in the original form of Christianity, that is the faith in existence at the time of Christ, this man was never regarded as a divinity. It was only the later followers who depicted him as such. This is because the people who lived at his time knew he was a human who performed miracles—only through God's grace. Those closest to him, his disciples, regarded him merely as God's messenger, which was, in fact, precisely how he presented himself. Again, Jesus never claimed to be a god. Only humans make this claim.

to the fact that He has the true insight regarding all that could be. Yet, if they reject this, certainly, God is fully aware of those who incite corruption.

Tell the people of scripture, "Let us believe together in those principles we have in common, that is that we worship only God, never hold other powers (as if) gods, and *refuse to make humans our lords*."✦ If despite this they reject it, then, tell

✦That is by granting them perceived powers, which are baseless. This is the kind of modern idol worship that plagues humanity. People live in fear precisely of other humans. What's more, they may even grant such humans excessive power, being more afraid of them than, for instance, God Himself. As the Qur'aan makes clear God despises this kind of idol worship, since He is the only power in the universe who can help or harm anyone.

them, "You should realize that we are the ones who have truly surrendered to Him."

The true nature of Abraham

You followers of scripture, why would you argue regarding the status of Abraham (in respect to what is his 'religion'): the Torah and Gospel were revealed long after him.✦ (Are you unable to) use your

✦Here, the Qur'aan offers a statement that ends this entire argument: Abraham claimed no specific denomination, but was, instead, one of those who surrendered his full self to God. He had no intention to start a religion. Rather, his only purpose was to devoutly worship his Lord. Thus, he was a man totally committed to God, according to the Qur'aan a true 'Muslim,' that is one who gives his entire self and his fullest effort, even his life, to almighty God. Thus, his 'religion' was merely the dedicated worship of God.

common sense? You have, historically, argued regarding issues that are known to you, however, why do you do so regarding an issue of which you have no knowledge? God knows it, while you are unaware (of it). Abraham was neither a Jew nor a Christian. Rather, he was one of those who rejected all that is false, because he dedicated his entire self to God. Furthermore, he never worshiped lesser gods. Surely, the people who have the greatest claim to Abraham are those who follow him, *as does this Prophet and all who believe in him*. Moreover, God is a friend (only) to the (true) believers.

The true nature of the people of scripture: warnings

Some of the people of the scripture are intent on causing you to err. Yet, they only cause themselves to err, although they are largely unaware of it.

You people of scripture, why do you reject God's new messages, despite the fact that you have been given the same?✦ Why do you knowingly disguise

✦That is all the truths which exist in the Bible are also found in the Qur'aan. The Bible was originally divine. However, despite the best efforts of its scribes over the centuries it became corrupted. Granted, those truths are still found within it. However, these are diluted by numerous falsehoods. Thus, it takes great wisdom to uncover them. This is why it was necessary to reveal the Qur'aan, that is to have available a newer and untarnished revelation, which validates any remaining truths, while dispelling any myths. Yet, regardless of anyone's beliefs there is a simple fact which is impossible to dispute. It is that the Qur'aan is pristine. Therefore, it is a more modern and complete form of the Bible. Plus, it is far easier to read. What's more, it contains additional information regarding the nature of God, as well as His various prophets, not found in any other scripture. To supplement this see *The Secret Scripture They Don't Want You to Know About*.

the truth, even fabricate it? Yet, some of the people of scripture say (privately), "Give tacit approval to their (that is Muhammad's followers') faith, but later reject it, so that they might abandon it and believe instead in your (own previous) ways."

Tell them also, "Real guidance is from God, which consists of revelation similar to what you had received." Or, would they dispute with you, even though you are representing Me? Tell them, "All wonderment—in fact, whatever good humans receive—comes from God. He provides it to whomever He desires. He is limitless in His treasures, completely knowledgeable. What's more, He confers His mercy on whomever He chooses. The fact is almighty God is unlimited in His riches."

Some of the people of scripture are trustworthy. Yet, there are many others who are dishonest and will only fulfill their obligations under enormous pressure. This is the result of their claim that as a divine right they can do as they please "to the ignorant." Thus (through such a belief), they lie (to themselves) about God and furthermore are fully aware of it. However, regarding those who keep their obligations and are conscious of Him, truly, God loves those who are conscious of Him.

Without doubt, those who diminish (the importance of) their divine obligations for insignificant pursuits will be denied the blessings of the next life. God will not speak to them. Nor will He even look at them. What's more, He will let them consume themselves in their sins. Their consequence is wicked torment, which they have caused for themselves.

The true teachings of Jesus

Certainly, some of them represent the scriptures perversely. They do so to make you think that what they say is from the Bible, even though it isn't. They tell you, "This is from God," despite the fact that it is not from God. Thus, they lie about God and are, furthermore (fully), aware of it.

That a person to whom God gave revelation, wisdom, and prophethood would proclaim, "In addition to God, worship me" is inconceivable.✦ Rather, what

✦That is Jesus never proclaimed himself as God. This is indisputable. There is nothing in the Bible which supports such a claim. Nowhere does Jesus say he is God and particularly a creator. Rather, he always deferred to God the creator. His statement that he and God are one is in fact, the truth, because God placed His essence in him. Yet, to claim this as proof of his divinity is obviously false, since he had no divine powers of his own. Nor did his original followers make such a claim. If the disciples never said he was a god, then, on what basis can modern people proclaim this? Thus, any claim for him as anything other than a man is a modern interpolation, fully unsubstantiated. True, he was a creation of God, just like Adam, Abraham, Moses, Jacob, and Muhammad. Yet, all people are God's creations.

Again, He alone is the creator. He has no need for relatives and certainly needs no assistants. In fact, He created the concept of sons and daughters—the method of lineage and descendence, Thus, He has no need for any such association. The concept and method of marriage, birth, delivery, and development as well as the growth of the generations: all this is His. So, it would be a true folly to attribute to God any such associations.

Even so, only God has control of events. Nor does anyone other than Him have ultimate power. What's more, there is no evidence that Jesus performed supernatural acts. Nor did he demonstrate any creative powers. In his stay on the earth he never created a single being, not even so much as a molecule. Like any other mortal he walked the earth, rested, drank fluids, and ate food. Somehow, Jesus disappeared. So, if he were truly a god, would his disappearance or death be anything except catastrophic? Would it not have resulted in universal chaos, surely, the universe's destruction?

he did say was "Become men of God," and do so by preaching God's revelations and by your own deep study. Nor did the Christ command the worship of angels or prophets. Would he command you to abandon the truth after you have committed to it?

Regarding people of scripture through their prophets God accepted their commitment and obligation, as if to say "If, after all the revelations and wisdom I have given you there comes to you an apostle, who confirms the truth you already possess, you are obligated to believe in him as well as support him." God asked, "Do you understand and accept what I have obliged you in this regard?" They answered, "We understand it." God said, "Then, commit to it: I will be the Witness." Yet (after making this commitment), all who reject it are greatly at fault.

Do they seek a way of life other than God's, even though the entire universe submits itself (to Him) in cooperation or by force and since to Him all must return? Therefore, tell them, "We believe in God and all His revelations, the revelations of Abraham, Ishmael, Isaac, Jacob (and their descendants). What's more, we believe in the revelations sent to Moses, Jesus, and all other prophets. They are all the same to us. In fact, our religion is (merely) that we surrender ourselves to God."

Even so, without doubt, if anyone seeks a religion other than self-surrender—true obedience—to God, it will never be accepted. In addition, in the next life such a person will be a true loser.

Why would God guide those who despite being provided with all evidence of the truth obstinately refuse it? They have witnessed this Prophet as true, and they recognize the truths of (this message as found in) their own revelations. In fact, God never guides such people committed to (the cause of) evil. Because of their rejection their only consequence will be God's condemnation and also the condemnation of the angels and in fact all humanity. They will forever remain in this agonizing condition.✦ Nor will any of their pain be

✦That is by existing as the condemned, those who lose all that is of consequence. Yet, the most dire of all losses is to lose His love. This is the ultimate result of the rejection of God. It is the condition of the loss of God's loving mercy. Then, a person must live within this realm. This is the real hell of which the Qur'aan warns.

alleviated. Nor will they in any way ever have their punishment suspended. The exception is those who repent and correct their behavior. Certainly, God is absolutely forgiving, truly expansive in His mercy.

Yet, in fact, those who deliberately obstruct the truth, even though they have (previously) accepted the true religion, who resist it stubbornly, their repentance is of no consequence. They are the ones who are truly in error.

Surely, if these obstinate people die in denial, an entire earth filled with gold would be incapable of ransoming them. Their reward is monumental suffering, and they will be abandoned (to that suffering).

However, regarding you, O true believers, true faith will elude you (that is) unless you give or expend what you hold dearest.✦ Furthermore,

✦That is as in Abraham, who was willing to sacrifice his dearest 'possession': his son. Yet, the greatest sacrifice of all is that of the self—to give the self to God instead of holding back for material or worldly gain. This is precisely what Abraham achieved: he relinquished what he loved the most—his own son. It was the only natural possession he truly loved. Yet, he gave it all for the sake of God. That is why he is memorialized for all time to come.

regarding whatever you give, God records it.✦

✦That is it is well established that in this life events and acts can be recorded using various devices, including video cameras, CDs, DVDs, and tape recorders. Obviously, God has His own recording devices, His own masterly system records all that occurs. Thus, He captures all that humans do. This is the very system He will reveal during the time of judgement, when the record for every human being will be bared. The fact is, notes the Qur'aan, all that humans achieve is recorded in a most sophisticated, refined way on heavenly scrolls. These scrolls are made of gold. This demonstrates the sacred nature of a human's life. Then, will the human realize his true nature and become the dignified person which is his nature? Or, will he degrade himself by refusing to honor his true role and instead succumbing to dark temptations?

Regarding the descendants of Israel every type of food was allowed, except what they themselves prohibited, which they did (incredibly), prior to the Torah's revelation. Tell them (if they persist in arguing), "If what you say is true, produce the Torah and read the relevant passages." Certainly, those who after such warnings invent lies about God are truly wretched, devoid of godliness. Tell them, "Obviously (as always), God has spoken the truth. Thus (if you are to follow anything), follow this—the propensity of Abraham (of self-surrender), who refused all that is false, refused to recognize any powers other than God."

From paganism to the worship of One God

Surely, the original monotheistic Temple was established for humankind at (the ancient valley of) Bakkah. (It is) blessed and a source of guidance for all the (peoples of the) world, full of clear messages (demonstrating God's oneness).✦ This is where Abraham once stood.

✦That is since this was the first house of the One God this is why it is sanctified. As noted by Asad it is much older than the Temple of Solomon and thus truly qualifies as the original House of God. People before Abraham created temples for worship through pagan rites, sacrificing animals and even humans at the altars. Also, In the entire Qur'an the word Bakkah is used only here. This is because this is the Old Testament word (as Baca) for the Valley of Mecca. God is attempting to awaken the people of scripture to the fact that Islaam, self-surrender, is the true way of God, as mentioned in their own books. All this is important, because Abraham broke tradition. He was the first to dedicate all worship to almighty God. Despite this, later generations reverted to idol worship. In Mecca, idols were regularly worshipped.

It was the Prophet Muhammad who finally purged this, once again establishing the worship of the one true God. His teachings even permeated Europe, helping cleanse it of paganism. What's more, this preaching of the universal God largely caused the Reformation as well as, without doubt, the Renaissance. This is proven by a number of Western historians. For instance, it was Briffault who made it clear that without the efforts of this man there would be no Western civilization. Nor, incredibly, notes Briffault, without him would there be any modern science.

Whoever enters it finds inner peace. Thus, for all who are able, the pilgrimage to the Temple is an obligation to God. Yet, for those who reject the truth realize that in this entire universe God is beyond need of anything or anybody.

Ask the people of scripture, "Why are you reticent regarding these (divine) messages, despite the fact that through your own way you have testified to its validity?" Also, ask them, "Why do you attempt to obstruct from the way of God those who have decided to believe in this by making (that way) appear defective?" This is despite the fact that (through your own scriptures) you witness that it is true. Certainly, God is well aware of all your actions.

You true believers, if you follow the advice of certain of these people of scripture, they might cause you to become godless. Yet, how could you reject the truth when you are the specific recipient of God's messages, and it is in your midst that (the spirit of) His Prophet lives? However, whoever holds firmly to (the guidance from) God has already been guided correctly.

You true believers, keep God in awe with the awe that is His due. Also, beware of dying in a state other than full servitude to Him.

Thus, remain firm, unified (as one group) with God.✦ As well, never distance yourselves from each

✦That is in the true way of God there are no sects. Islaam means the peaceful submission of the human to God. In this true way there is no in-fighting. Then, on what basis could there be sects? The Prophet Muhammad condemned sectarianism as a gross violation. The only legitimate sect, he said, is his "true friends," meaning those who abide exclusively by his profound principles. Thus, according to this man the deliberate creation of sects or groups—separate classes—even 'schools of thought,' is banned. The only school is the essence of this book, along with the refined ways of its Messenger. All besides this is false.

Even the so-called schools of thought that supposedly divide Muslim ideology are a fraud. These are largely Western creations in order to cause divisions in Islaam. Then, this is the avowed objective of Islaam's enemies, that is to cause rifts in this faith. God is one and so is His way. This is the only interpretation possible.

other. Furthermore, always remember the blessings He has given you and how when you were enemies, He conjoined your hearts, so that through His blessings you became brethren. Remember also how when you were on the brink of disaster, He saved you. This is how God demonstrates His insights, so that you might find (true) guidance. It is so that there might develop among you a group, who recommend all that is good, establish justice, and prohibit the noxious. These are the ones who will achieve true peace. What's more, guard yourselves against becoming like the people of scripture, who, even though they were given the truth, disagree with each other.✦

✦That is the believers are commanded to remain as one, bonded in love. There can be no dissension among them. Nor are they allowed to divide themselves into various groups. This reiterates the Prophet's aforementioned warning. Dissension is the kiss of death, since there are numerous forces which are opposed to the system of Islaam and which seek its destruction. Thus, unless the Muslims are united, they will be defeated.

In fact, these are the ones who will endure an immense punishment, one which will occur at a time when some faces will gleam with happiness, while others will be darkened with grief. (It will be an era when) those darkened faces will be told, "Did you refuse the truth after agreeing to it? As a result, experience this agony for your obstinate behavior." However, those faces that are bright will be under God's (merciful) grace, living there.

These are the messages of God. They are communicated to you in order to establish the correct (and true) way of life. Surely, God wills no harm to (His creation).

God owns all that exists. What's more, ultimately (and molecularly), it all returns to Him as its source.

You who truly (give your entire selves) to God, you are the finest people who have ever been raised to do God's work for the sake of humankind. You believe in God, urge the doing of good, and proscribe the (doing of) wrong.

People of scripture asked to fully submit

Now, if the followers of previous revelations only adopted this kind of belief, it would be to their benefit. A few of them sincerely believe, however, the majority are treacherous. Yet, despite their treachery they can at the most cause you *only insignificant harm.*✦ Then, if they fight against

✦That is fear of harm is in a person's own imagination. With God as the support how can anyone be truly harmed? By truly trusting in God and accepting Him as the protector, the person becomes invincible. Surely, this is demonstrated by the parable of David and Goliath. This is because only God is the ultimate source of protective power.

you, they will definitely flee. Furthermore, they are devoid of support.✦

✦That is which demonstrates the inherent weakness of those who rely upon other powers besides God. Such individuals, while deeming themselves mighty, are, in fact, feeble. They have no ultimate power, because without God such power sources are inherently weak.

They (that is the people of the earlier scriptures, who choose to fight you) are disgraced by God, unless they return to God and make peace with men. This is because they have proven through their acts that they deserve God's condemnation and are, therefore, humiliated. This is because they persistently rejected God's messages and because they even murdered His prophets.✦ (They did so)

✦This is particularly true of the hostile Israelites, that is the Zionists, who often directly oppose anything good. They feel no compunction regarding any violent act, even killing the God-fearing, in fact, they would even maliciously kill God's messengers. This is because the religion of God, that is Islaam, threatens their corrupt practices. Because of their rebellion against God they are threatened by any true believers. Thus, they fight constantly against the good and decent people and even rebel against the concepts of goodness and decency. This is proven by the fact that numerous corrupt practices, including gambling, illicit drugs, sexual perversion/pornography, and the black market weapons trade, are Zionist-controlled. Of course, there are many actual Jews and Christians who are decent and have nothing to do with corrupt acts, a fact confirmed by the Qur'aan in the following:

because they rebelled against God and therefore violated all decency.

However, they are not all (like this). Some of them are decent. They recite God's truths throughout the night and humble themselves before him. They believe in God and (in the accountability of) resurrection. They command good acts, while forbidding the harmful acts. They compete with each other in doing good deeds. These are the truly good. Thus, whatever good they accomplish will be to their credit. God is fully aware of those who truly revere Him.

In contrast, those who reject the (divine) message will be defenseless against God. Neither their money nor progeny (will be of any use to them). They are destined for permanent residence in the fire. The value of their accomplishments in (this) life may be described parabolically: that of a bitter cold wind, which blasts the sinners' crops and thus destroys them. Certainly, God never wrongs them, but, rather, in fact, they only wrong themselves.

You devout servants (of God), keep as (close, intimate) friends only people of your own kind. The other kind will (make every effort) to corrupt you. They would love to see you harmed, which is indisputable. They have already expressed their envy (towards you) rather hatred. However, what they hold in their hearts is even more foul. We have made obvious their ill will towards you, if you would (only deeply) consider it.

You are willing to love them, but they will never love you, even though you all believe in revelation.

What's more, when they encounter you, they claim, "We believe as you believe,"✦ however, privately,

✦This is particularly true of the followers of Judaism, who attempt to act as if they are 'friends' of the true believers. Yet, this is only to infiltrate and corrupt them. The purpose is to cause chaos and oppression. God warns the true believers about this to protect them from harm. There is no way for them to retain the guidance of God, that is as long as they are associated with such agents of corruption, whose avowed purpose is to destroy the believers.

they are consumed with rage against you. (The most appropriate response is to let them) "Perish in their rage." God is fully aware of what breeds in men's hearts.

If you are successful, they hate it. (In contrast,) if you suffer difficulty or harm, they are pleased. Yet, regardless (of any hardship) if you remain patient and keep God (deeply in mind), they cannot harm you. Surely, God surrounds with His powers all their actions.

The Battle of Badr: the power of trust

Remember when (the Prophet) departed in the early morning to arrange the believers in battle formations—God was completely aware, fully informed—and, there, two of the groups were vacillating, although God was with them, and He is the One in whom the believers must (exclusively) trust. God supported you at (your first engagement) Badr✦ despite the fact that (materially,) you were

✦That is the original Muslims who due to oppression were forced into war against the pagan Arabs. They fought mostly against the elders of the tribes, whose financial interests were seemingly threatened by the Muslims. This was the first battle fought by the fledgling Muslims, a mere rag-tag group. Because of divine support, including a sudden change in weather plus a careful and thorough strategy, the much outnumbered and inferiorly supplied Muslims defeated the Meccan army. As in all campaigns in which the Prophet's strategy was strictly followed he was victorious. Yet, there represents a more universal meaning. It is that regardless of the odds in any age through God's support and through a firm commitment to Him the powers of good will always succeed.

weak. Thus, always be in awe of God, so you might have reason to be grateful.

Also, remember when the Prophet told the believers, "Have no doubt in your minds that your Lord will support you with three thousand angels, directly from heaven." So, if the enemy should suddenly strike you—you thoughtful and patient believer—your Lord will strengthen you with an element even more powerful: five thousand angels swooping down. God tells you this as good news to comfort your hearts. This is because God's support is the only kind (of any significance). He alone is absolutely powerful✦ in His might, truly intelligent

✦That is to rely upon. All other support is weak and unrealistic. In contrast, God always keeps His promises. When He says He will support the true ones in their struggle against tyranny, there is no doubt about it, regardless of the challenge at hand He will honor that promise, and, thus, as long as they hold strongly to Him they will succeed.

(in His complete awareness of whatever is). It is so that He might destroy and/or humiliate some of the godless, so they would depart in total defeat.

Too, it is beyond your capacity to determine God's (true) position regarding them: they are wicked. In contrast, God owns all that exists, both in the universe beyond and in this world. He alone will decide who to forgive and who to punish. He is God, absolutely merciful, the only One capable of giving.

You true believers, never earn your income through interest (in order) to multiply your gains. Rather, remain firm in your belief in God, so that you will achieve peace (in your hearts). What's more, beware of the fire that is the consequence for those who reject the truth.

Also, adhere (to the ways of) God and the Prophet, so that you will gain the benefits of God's mercy. Compete with each other (only) to earn your Lord's forgiveness and the (promised) paradise, which is as vast as the earth, actually, the entire universe. God has prepared this for His believers, those who are freely charitable, who control their anger and who due to a desire to please God forgive others, who after they have committed a shameful act or have otherwise sinned against themselves remember God and beseech Him to forgive their sins. Yet, who other than almighty God can forgive sins? As well, it is for those who do not knowingly persist in their wrongful actions. These are the inheritors of the gardens of paradise (which is), ultimately, forgiveness from their Lord. What an excellent reward for a job well done.✦

✦That is God is the ultimate 'employer.' Thus, regarding those who work hard for Him He greatly rewards them for their sincere efforts. These are the efforts to spread goodness, as well as peace, on this earth.

Gardens signify peace. The true peace that all relish is peace of mind— or peace of heart. This is the ultimate consequence of complete forgiveness. This is also the vast benefit of truly holding God in awe. By keeping God deeply in mind the person will avoid the commission of destructive acts. This will also help a person remain patient in difficulty and thus prevent emotional outbursts. Then, He will generously reward any patient, grateful person. The mere effort to avoid heinous acts will also be rewarded. This is through the reward of eternal peace, the greatest success of all.

Previous to yours numerous civilizations have vanished. Then, travel (about the earth), and observe what happened to those who rejected Me. This is an obvious lesson for humankind and a form of guidance, as well as warning, for those who are in awe of God. Thus, never feel heart-sick or remorseful (so keep your spirits high). The fact is if you truly believe (in this message) *you are certain to rise high.*

If you suffer difficulty, realize that this has previously happened to (other) believers. We vary for the people success and difficulty, so that God can distinguish who truly believes and choose from among you His most dedicated servants. Yet, it is not that He loves the godless. God wishes to purify your hearts, while rendering inconsequential all who reject Him.

Do you truly think that you could enter paradise without working (to your) fullest capacity in God's cause and without exerting the utmost patience? In fact, you wildly desired death (for God's sake) before the opportunity arose: now you have experienced its real nature.✦

✦This refers to the original Muslims in battle against their attackers. Once they realized the nature of death they began to reconsider any overtly aggressive acts. Life itself, they realized, is precious and must not be frivolously wasted. Better to be patient and risk life and welfare only when absolutely necessary. Thus, there is no propensity in Islaam that people wildly rush into death. Here, incredibly, God demonstrates this as a kind of fault. However, if the Islaamic system is threatened by oppressors, then, this oppression must be resisted, rather, fought—by any means necessary. The believer is obligated to do so. His salvation is dependent upon it.

Even so, Muhammad is only a Messenger of God. What's more, all other prophets previous to him have died. Thus, if he dies or is killed, will you abandon this? Without doubt, whoever abandons it could never harm God, while God will reward all who are grateful.

Humans can only die by God's allowance. What's more, this (occurs) at a predestined time.

Regarding those who desire merely the rewards of this life We will give it to them. In contrast, those who desire the rewards of the next life, We will give it to them and what's more will fully compensate all who are grateful to Us.

Furthermore (if you would consider it), how numerous were the prophets who dedicated themselves to God's work, plus their many devotees. They always kept their spirits high, even with all that they had to endure in God's cause. Neither did they weaken. Nor did they ever beg for mercy before the enemy. So it is: God loves those who are patient in adversity. What's more, their only request was, "Our Lord, forgive our sins and our overzealous behavior. Also, make us strong in our mission, and provide us with Your powers—Your vast strength—against the godless." Therefore, God gave them the (power of true) greatness of this world as well as the finest rewards of the next life. Without doubt, God loves those who make every effort to do good.

You true believers, realize that if you side with the godless, they will cause you to abandon your belief. As a result, you (too,) will lose all. Truly, God alone is (sufficient as) your Protector, the only One to rely upon.✦

✦That is so rather than seeking the help of any others, including powerful adversaries, only God's help is to be sought. This relates to certain weak believers, who due to fear feel a need to gain the protection of Islaam's enemies, that is by befriending them. Clearly, God warns against this, reminding all believers that only He has the power to assist them and that siding with others will gain them nothing. Rather, it will only lead to their destruction. This is because those from which they seek aid are themselves devoid of all guidance. So, whatever they offer for advice is faulty rather destructive.

By siding with them there is no way to gain, because they themselves are inherently confused, in fact, weak. This is because what they rely upon for their power source are their own personal desires, which are of no consequence. Plus, regarding their purpose they are unsure. Nor are they sure of the consequences if they die in the fight against believers. Rather, they fear such consequences. In contrast, for the believers, whether they live or die, the results are certain—paradise in the presence of almighty God.

We place despair within the hearts of the godless. In truth, God never authorized them to refuse Him.✦ The torment is their destination, and this is the most vile of all consequences.

✦This is a fascinating statement. The human has no inherent power. Nor does such a human have any true independence. In fact, all humans are dependent upon the higher power. No human can make water nor can anyone make the seed for food. Nor is it possible to produce air to breathe. Then, a human decides he has the right to reject God? In fact, here, this almighty power says he has no such right. God will seal the hearts of any such wicked persons, so that they may never comprehend the truth. That is the fitting result for such a rebel, who proves his ingratitude by purposely rejecting his relationship with his creator.

Whatever God dictates the human must obey. If he refuses to do so, the result is only destruction, as discovered by the original followers of this Qur'aan, as follows:

The Battle of Uhud: failure of the rear guard

God definitely kept His promise to you, when by His authority you were about to destroy your foes, that is until the moment you weakened, when you acted against (the Prophet's) orders. You failed to follow orders, even after He nearly secured your victory.✦

✦This relates to a war fought for survival by the Prophet and his followers, the Battle of Uhud, which the Muslims nearly lost due to a weakening of their rear guard. Here, certain believers were caught in the frenzy of the potential war treasures, and so in a moment of passion abandoned their posts. This weakness was attacked by the pagan calvary, and the Muslims were nearly routed.

This was a test for the early Muslims, but it also applies to all later generations. It is that in the struggle against oppression if regardless of the challenges the believers remain patient, they will succeed. This success is due to the direct intervention of God. As long as any such believers hold completely to Him the fact is He fully assists them. Thus, always, they will ultimately succeed.

(Through this test it became clear that) some of you only cared about this world, just as some care (primarily) for the future one—all this so He might evaluate you. He prevented you from winning. However, now, He has cleansed you of your sin.

Regarding the true believers—have no doubt—God is unlimited in His loving mercy. This is despite the fact that you fled in panic, while the Prophet was abandoned behind you, calling you (to re-position).

Therefore, He visited you with anguish as a consequence for the Prophet's anguish, so that you would feel remorse regarding your losses or regarding what had befallen you. Truly, God is aware of all your acts. Then, He caused some of you to become secure at heart (and who, therefore, continued to fight), while the self-centered ones entertained erroneous thoughts regarding God—thoughts of pagan ignorance—such as "This was beyond our control." Tell them, "Control belongs to God alone."

They are attempting to conceal the weakness of their faith, saying (essentially), "If we had any control over it, we would never have left so many dead behind." Tell them, "Even if you would have stayed off the battlefield, if it was your time, you would have died at a preordained time and place." This is so that God might evaluate your true intentions (in your hearts) and cleanse the depths of your hearts of impurities. Without doubt, God is fully aware of what is in human hearts.

Truly, it was Satan who caused the believers to falter in battle, in fact, only by their own doing. However, God has purged them of this sin, because God is totally forgiving, full of kindness.

You true believers, regarding the deaths of those killed in God's service, never behave like the godless. The latter say, "If only they had remained home, they wouldn't have died," because God will cause (the people who reject the truth) to suffer agony (due to regret) over their words. (This is because) God (alone) controls both who lives and dies. What's more, He comprehends whatever you do.

Moreover, if you are killed in His cause, then, surely, God's mercy and forgiveness are (infinitely) superior to whatever could be achieved here. Also, whether you die (of natural causes) or are killed (fighting for God), God will bring you all before Him.

Because He instilled him with kindness, this is why the Prophet deals gently with his followers. This is because if you (O Prophet) had been harsh with them, they would have deserted you. Then, be kind to them. What's more, pray for their forgiveness.

Furthermore, take counsel with the people in all matters of public concern. Then, when you have decided upon a course of action, leave it (in trust) with God. No doubt, God loves those who exclusively trust in Him. What's more, if God empowers you, you will be absolutely invincible.✦

✦That is, like David, who, essentially, singlehandedly defeated a monstrous force. Because David placed his full trust in God, he could never be defeated. The ferocity of Goliath cannot be disputed. Yet, it could never compare to the ferocity and power of almighty God. David merely was His agent. Thus, through this example the Qur'aan urges its followers, now, to be fearless and to fight—and win—backed by His power.

However, if He should abandon you, is there anyone else who could assist you? Therefore, you true believers, place your full trust in God alone.

It is inconceivable that a prophet would deceive. This is because any who deceives will be, ultimately, held accountable (in that time of resurrection), when all will be compensated for their accomplishments—when all will be treated justly.

Then, is the person who makes every effort to please God equal to the one who has earned His condemnation, who strives towards hell? What a vile culmination to one's life. In God's view these two are (entirely) different: What's more, God is totally aware of their actions.✦

✦That is, literally, He is watching all humans. So, whatever is done He is viewing it as well as recording it. "Nothing escapes Him."

By bringing them their own Prophet God fully showered His favors upon the believers. He did so to deliver His messages to them and to (thereby) cause them to grow in purity (and) to provide them the divine book, as well as the ability to use sound judgement, considering that, previously, they were absolutely confused, unable to find their way.

Yet, would you, now that a disaster has stricken you✦ (despite the fact that your enemy suffered

✦This, again, originally referred to the Prophet's followers, who nearly lost a major battle at the region of Uhud, that is due to tactical errors. Yet, it also applies to any fighters on God's behalf, who, due to their own impatience or errors, bring upon themselves catastrophes.

It is also important to note that this book is meant as guidance for people who truly believe and accept the prophethood of Muhammad. The fact that such people are attacked or plotted against by other powers, including Christian and Jewish powers, is well established. In fact, it would be expected that such plotting would occur. Therefore, the Qur'aan provides advice to protect the community from liquidation by such forces, this being a constant threat. This is why there is significant emphasis on the mechanism of war.

Previous attempts to destroy Islaam include the Inquisition and Crusades as well as today's colonial invasions in the Middle East perpetrated by the modern Western powers. These include the invasions of Iraq and Afghanistan, as well as the planned invasion of Iran. The destruction of the World Trade Center and its occupants, falsely blamed on Muslims, was another attack against Islaam. In fact, the purpose of these acts is to truly attack and destabilize any Islaamic movements. It is also to conquer and colonize regions of material wealth: oil, gas, gold, copper, and more.

twice the blow), ask yourselves, "How could this be?" Tell them, "You did it to yourselves." (Regardless) surely, God can do anything. Even so, during this battle whatever harm you endured God allowed it. He did so to distinguish those who were tainted with hypocrisy from the true believers.

Traitors and hypocrites

So, when the hypocrites were told, "Fight in God's cause" or even, "Defend yourselves," they answered, "If we were certain this battle would occur, we would come." As a result, at that moment they essentially proved that they were traitors instead of true believers, giving (only) lip service (demonstrating) that their faith was superficial. Yet, God already knew what they were attempting to hide, the ones who, after being reticent (regarding this duty to fight), said, "If they only would have listened to us, they would still be alive." Tell them, "Then, if what you say is true, prevent your own ultimate death."

Bravery and martyrdom

Thus, never consider those who have died in God's cause as truly dead. In fact, they are alive. They are with their Lord, thriving and relishing in it. They delight in the news that their loved ones, who are still alive, have no reason to fear or be regretful. They triumph, realizing that despite the hardships that such true believers endure, God will reward them, because they responded to His demand (as well as the call of the Messenger).

A stupendous reward is their result—those who persevere in doing good and remain (fully) in awe of God, those who have even been taunted by others, saying, "A powerful enemy is after you, we are warning you." The result was that their faith became even more profound, answering, "We trust completely in God, He is the best source of protection." Then, they went directly to work in His service, free of the burden of remorse or sin. This is because they had been working with their fullest effort for God's pleasure. Moreover (in His rewards), God is truly generous—beyond comprehension.

Hesitance, fear, and selfishness

Satan makes you fear his group. So, have no such fear and instead fear Me, that is if you are truly sincere in your belief.

Regarding the wicked people who compete with each other in rejecting Me there is no reason to have any remorse. The fact is (by their vile behavior) they can never hurt God; He has ordained that they will be excluded from the blessings of the next life. Furthermore, they will endure agony beyond comprehension—all due to their (own) wicked acts.

In truth, those who due to their arrogance reject Him certainly are incapable of hurting God. In fact, they have earned enormous agony. Such individuals should never consider that by Our giving them power it is for their benefit. Rather, We give it to them merely to increase their wickedness. What's more, when they meet Me, they will be disgraced through the agony of burning despair.

God wants the believers to free themselves from the godless peoples' way of life, so that He can separate the good from the bad. In this regard many of the reasons (for such a division) are beyond your comprehension. However (historically), God reveals it through His many prophets. Thus, believe in God and (the way of) His prophets. Then, if you (truly do) believe in Him and keep Him constantly in mind, you will receive a (rich) reward.

Regarding the misers the fact that they think whatever God has given them is to their benefit is erroneous. In fact, it is damning for them. This is because during that era of assessment (when justice will be done appropriately) whatever they so tightly hoard will be wrapped around their necks, choking them. Then, it is God who owns it all, the entire heritage of the heavens and the earth. Furthermore, He has complete understanding of your actions.

Your Lord is fully aware of the statement of those who said, "God is poor, while we are rich."✦

✦This refers to the hostile Israelites, who hold themselves independent of God. Without remorse, they freely say vile things about Him and His messengers. They also take action against these messengers and have in the past murdered a number of them. They nearly by poison murdered the Prophet Muhammad. This is despite the fact that their status was/is merely due to His grace. Through this they imply that their hoarded wealth, gained largely through the taking of interest, somehow, makes them free of any need, even the need to bow before God.

We shall inscribe (in Our records) regarding their statements as well as as their murder of the prophets. Then (at judgement time), We will say, "Experience torment through the fire, the consequence of your own (wicked) acts," because, absolutely, God never causes any wrong to His creatures.

Regarding those who claim, "Surely, God has ordered us to only believe in a prophet, that is if he comes to us with our own traditions and rituals." Tell them, "There have always been prophets who represented the truth, including what you describe. If what you are saying is to be believed, why, then, did you murder them?" Yet, if they rebel against you, realize that in the past other messengers armed with the evidence have been rejected.

Everyone will ultimately die. However, the (final) compensation will occur only during that era of accountability. Therefore, whoever is protected from the (agony of the) fire and secured into (the peace and happiness of) paradise will have, without doubt, gained a monumental success. Moreover (compared to the next existence), the life of this world is merely a delusion.✦

✦That is it is not real. It is an artificial life, a transition, only meant as a test. It is almost like an episode in the Twighlight Zone. Humans must deeply consider this, that is that it is not their right to do as they please. They are under constant watch by that almighty One, who produced it all: the holographic universe of almighty God. Then, this life is an illusion. The real life is the next existence, where truth and justice reign and where no one can violate the divine code. Here, God has complete control over everyone. Only in this life can people act independently and therefore cause corruption. In the next life only justice, peace, and decency will rule. Yet, by God's will this is also so that the true believers will in this life gain authority, and this will precisely be the result of the believers' efforts. Surely, this is the real life to strive for. Then, this divine writing provides all the tools by which a person can do so thus achieving the love and mercy of God.

You will definitely be tried—with your belongings as well as through your own self. In fact, the people of scripture (that is the Christians and Jews), will subject you to many hurtful things. Of course, so will the godless. Yet, if you remain patient and keep your (instinctive and devout) ties with Him—surely, this is a powerful goal to pursue.

Without doubt, God accepted a solemn promise from the people of scripture—the early followers of the Torah and Gospels—when He told them, "Tell humanity the truth: never hide it." Yet, they defaulted (on this promise), trading it instead for a minimal (that is materialistic), gain. Their transaction was certainly vile.

Never presume that those who brag about their lies, who then ask to be praised for their false claims, will escape. Then, ultimately, in the next life they will experience dire punishment.

God owns the entire universe. What's more, He can do whatever He wills.

Endless signs; sincere prayers

Without doubt, the creation of the vast (and infinite) universe, as well as this earth, is a valuable sign. So is the "rotation" of the night and day. These are clear signals—obvious evidence—for people who, because of their intelligence, realize (the existence of) God: those who remember Him continuously throughout the day and night, even when lying down to sleep. (It is a sign) for those who consider the creation of the magnificent universe and earth, who pray, "You have, without doubt, created all this with a (definite) purpose. Glory to you (O high One), and protect us from the horrifying fire" and who pray, "Lord, whoever You commit to the fire will be disgraced, now and forever. Also, such wicked people will be devoid of support," who (also) pray, "Lord, we truly heard a voice (within us) asking us to submit, which said, 'Believe in your Lord,' and as a result we believed. Thus, our Lord, forgive our sins, erase our evil deeds, and cause us to die the death of the truly good."

Also, pray, "Our Lord, give us the glory You have promised us through Your prophets, and protect us from the disgrace at the time of accountability. We know that You always keep Your promises." Thus, their Lord responded, "I will keep in full view all the effort of any of you who works hard in My cause (and none of it will go to waste)."

Equality of the sexes

Each of you, male and female (who so dedicated themselves), are equal. Thus, regarding those who abandoned the (realm of) evil and (because of their beliefs) are driven from their homes, suffer hurt in My cause, fight for it, and are killed—I will cleanse their sins. What's more, I will, without doubt, shelter them in paradise, all as a reward from God. Clearly, with God is the most stupendous of rewards.

Never be deceived by the fact that the arrogant ones seem to be able to do as they please. It is merely a brief interlude, while they drive themselves to hell, the most wicked of destinations. However, regarding the believers, who are firm in their belief, they will inherit paradise, where they will thrive forever (a residence), fully prepared for them by God. So, without doubt, whatever is with God is the most significant result for those who are truly just in their behavior.

There are people within the readers of scripture who truly believe in God and His revelations, including your revelation. In fact, they are in awe of God. Unlike other readers, they are unwilling to sell their souls for minor gain. God will reward them, because God is efficient in His judgement.

Non-denominational nature of the truth

You true believers, remain patient despite your difficulties. Compete with each other in patience. Always be prepared to do what is right.✦ What's

✦This means that the ultimate in belief is to prepare in advance for doing good works. It is an attitude of looking only for the good. It is the seeking of the positive and useful. It is to begin every day with the objective to do only good, rather, to vigorously pursue it. This is to serve almighty God. It is the formula for true success. Any such deeds which are achieved are registered to the person's credit in God's accurate record. In contrast, the neglect of His way leads to despair. Furthermore, a person who rejects Him and who rebels against Him will receive no rewards. Rather, all such a person will earn is punishment.

more (keep God always in mind), so you will be happy—forever.

Section 4

Women's Rights

After describing women and men as equals (Section 3) the Qur'aan sets forth the formula for women's protection. This section deals with women's rights. Globally, prior to the Qur'aan women had no rights. Then, they were treated as mere chattel. Surely, in medieval Europe they had no rights.

Even in Western civilization they must constantly fight for their rights, for instance, women's suffrage during the 1920s to gain the right to vote. For the first time in history as a result of the Qur'aan the human needs of women were addressed: to their benefit.

This section contains rules for divorce. It also describes the rights of orphans as well as laws for inheritance. Thus, it is clear that this book helps liberate women by granting them their true status, which, historically, had been denied. Now, the Qur'aan comes to give them justice, so that they will never be abused.

In the name of the most merciful
and compassionate God

You humankind, venerate your Lord, who created you (originally) from a single living mass and from it created its mate and ultimately disseminated (from them) countless numbers of men and women.✦ Thus, be in awe of God, whose name you use

✦This would imply, perhaps, a mass of cells from the original divine design, which were divided into those bearing the Y male chromosomes and those bearing exclusively the X female chromosomes. Thus, it would appear that almighty God created originally a male and then a female, the original father and mother of humankind. It is also a reminder of the humble nature of each human, arising originally from a mere drop of sperm united to an ovum, then a clot of blood, which gives rise to the beginning embryo. Then, after realizing such humble origins how can anyone act arrogantly?

to make demands of each other. What's more, respect that you were born of a womb (that is never act too proud). In fact, God is constantly watching you.

Rights due to orphans; divine protection

Also, give orphans their rightful due. Never take advantage of them or cheat them in any way. What's more, never commingle their assets with your own. Certainly, this a monstrous crime. Regarding orphans if you fear you are unable to treat them fairly, then (for support) marry additional women of those that are legally acceptable, including those for whom you are responsible, the maximum being four.✦ However,

✦That is implying that, if there is a need, it is permitted to marry additional wives. This is mainly for social support or for other productive reasons that make good sense. In the Qur'aan this is the first mention of the legality of multiple wives. However, this mention is directly tied to social needs, clearly indicating that such additional wives are never to be sought merely to fulfill sexual lusts.

Again, the passage reads that if a true believer is unable to support the people under his care, for instance, orphans, then, the taking of additional wives, up to four, is legitimate. However, the Qur'aan provides a stipulation. This stipulation is that the person must be able to treat all such wives equally. If he is unable to do so, then he should never marry more than one. Regardless, the practice for the majority of Muslims, some 99% globally, is one wife. So, in Islaam the rule is to have only one wife. This is because in ideal situations this is the most pure and just of all marital bonds.

Despite the fact that in pre-Islaamic Arabia a multiplicity of wives was the rule the Prophet attempted to describe an excellent example of the power of a monogamous marriage. He made note to his followers the example of the Christians, saying, essentially, that the Christians are an excellent example of loving bonds, since they marry one person and stay in that loving relationship permanently (until death). As well, as clearly indicated in this Qur'aan it is difficult enough to do justice to a single spouse, let alone several. So, again, unless dictated by unusual circumstances the believer should attempt to build his life through marriage to a single woman, while always being just with such a spouse. This alone is a significant effort, since, always, Satan attempts to destroy loving bonds.

if you are concerned that you will be unable to treat them all equally, then, marry only one. This will help you maintain a high level of justice.

Give women their marriage dowries✦ without

✦The dowry is hardly an ancient or antiquated method. Rather, it is a benefit from which modern women can gain an advantage. It gives women security. In today's age when divorce rates are exceedingly high, for a single woman cash or assets in-hand are a welcome source of security. This is surely far superior to spending thousands of dollars frivolously for weddings.

pretense as a gift. However, if they decide on their own to return it, then, accept it without hesitation.

(Regarding orphans or similar souls) never entrust the incompetent with the assets which God has given to you to manage. However, provide it to them on an as-needed basis. What's more, always be kind to them.

Once they reach maturity, that is marital age, evaluate the orphans under your care. If you find them capable, return their belongings.

In times of need guard yourselves from consuming or wasting their assets, as they might grow up destitute. The rich should never touch their assets. Let the poor guardian utilize some of it fairly. What's more, when you return their assets, have witnesses observe it on their behalf. Yet, God is best to keep account.

Rules for inheritance—an example of His deep caring for human needs

After the deaths of parents or other relatives, men will get a share, small or large, as will women, all of it a share ordained. During the distribution of inheritance, when other appropriate people are present, give them their share, and also be kind to them. Plus, during this process the legal heirs should remain in awe of God. If they were in the same position, that is dying, leaving in charge weak-minded executors, they would dread the consequences. Thus, always keep God in mind, and also speak to the pitiful justly. In contrast, no doubt, those who in their wickedness consume the assets of orphans it is as if they are eating fireballs. Moreover, they will be forced to endure a violent torment.

The rules of inheritance for your children are as follows: the male inherits twice the share of the female. However, if there are more than two females, they receive one-third each. If there is only one, she gets one-half. The parents of the deceased get one-sixth each, this amount being correct if the deceased has a child. However, if the deceased is childless, then, the mother receives a third (and therefore the father two-thirds). If the deceased has siblings, the mother receives one-sixth. These amounts are calculated after subtracting any special donations or debts.

Regarding parents or children how are you to know who is more deserving of your help? Thus, obey this ordinance from God. Without doubt, God is totally knowledgeable, full of wisdom.

If your wives die, you get one half the estate, that is unless they have other children. However, if they have a son/daughter, then, you will receive one fourth the estate. This is after all debts and provisions have been deducted. Your widows will receive one fourth of your estate, that is unless you are succeeded by a child (or children). If so, they will get an eighth, again after deductions/debts.

Those who have no direct successor, leaving brothers or sisters: each will receive one sixth. However, if there are more than two siblings, they share equally, again, after deductions, the supposition being that none of these deductions or bequests were done to purposely harm the heirs.

These laws are the ordinance from God. Obviously, He has full knowledge over all (that could be). What's more, He is full of love (for His creatures).

The aforementioned are the restrictions established by God. Whoever abides by the dictates of God and His Prophet, He will bring into the gardens of peace to live forever. This is the ultimate success. In contrast, whoever rebels against God and His Prophet, while violating His restrictions, He will drive to the fire: his residence. Surely, a disgraceful suffering, truly vile, awaits him.

Rules for relationships (probably revealed in response to questions raised by some of the Prophet's followers)

Regarding women who are guilty of lewdness (to prove it) you must have four witnesses.✦ If the

✦This helps prevent arbitrary accusations based upon revenge, suspicion, or jealousy. It is a means of ultimate justice to prevent false accusations. In the Islaamic system eyewitnesses are relied upon for judgement, never mere circumstantial evidence. Thus, before anyone can be even accused there must be hard evidence of a crime.

witnesses swear with certainty to it, confine the guilty parties to their residences, that is until they either die or God gives them other options. Punish them equally, *regardless of the gender* or sexual immorality. Yet, if any of them repent and mend their evil ways, give them a chance to regenerate. In truth, God is an acceptor of repentance and gives voluminously of His mercy. Yet, this repentance is qualified, that is it is only for those who sin due to ignorance and then repent before their time is exhausted. They are the ones to whom God will turn again in His mercy—because God knows all and is full of wisdom.

In contrast, those who persist in wickedness until their (last) breath will be unable to achieve repentance, that is the one who, while dying, says, "Forgive me." Nor will those who die in denial (be given forgiveness). Certainly, these are the (individuals) for whom We have readied an atrocious punishment.

You true servants (of God), never hold your wives (against their will), merely for the purpose of gaining inheritance. Constraining them (in marriage) in order to take the assets you have given them is also banned. The exception is if they have become guilty of moral impropriety.

Treat (your spouses) with total decency. If you become upset with them, it is likely that you have become upset regarding that by which in God's name you will truly benefit.✦

✦That is being "upset" is never appropriate. Thus, the emotion must always be the workings of the devil. The Prophet taught that a person should be in life as if a traveler, detached—like a stranger. This will prevent a person from becoming emotionally engaged. Then, there will be no regrets due to any emotional or uncontrolled reactions. By applying the Prophet's wisdom all such regrets can be avoided. So, always, the rule is patience and tolerance, especially regarding any loved ones. The spouse is the person who is bonded to the individual in love. Such a person must be treated with complete tolerance and justice. This is the prescription of the Qur'aan for social success.

Thus, there is no basis within a marital relationship to become angry or upset. Rather than any such behavior being justified this is always the working of the devil. So, as the Qur'aan makes clear whenever any urge for anger or frustration is experienced regardless of the source or circumstances the believer must seek protection in God. This will prevent inevitably hostile outbursts, which create marital strife. In fact, this taming of anger for a believer is one of the greatest of all efforts that can be achieved, the great struggle for self-improvement known in Arabic as *jihaad an-nafs*.

However, if you desire to end the relationship, leave her assets alone, regardless of how much you have given her. It is like slandering her, which is a severe crime. How could you dare take it, since you were intimate, pledged to her?

Although the past is the past it is prohibited to marry women who were previously married to your fathers. Truly, this is a vile deed, odious (in the sight of God). Furthermore, it is completely forbidden for you to marry your mothers, daughters, sisters, aunts, daughters-in-law, and nursing mothers, as it is also forbidden for you to marry your step-daughters. Marriage to the wives of your (biological) sons is also prohibited. It is also illegal to marry sisters (simultaneously). Yet, whatever is in the past is past.

What's more, God is certainly extremely forgiving and exceptionally kind (in His generosity to His servants).

To have sexual relations with other married women is a crime prohibited (by God). This is a dictate from the almighty God. However, you may marry anyone else. You may offer them valuables and have them in sincere matrimony—but not in extramarital sex.

Give the women you intend to marry the appropriate gifts. Yet, if all parties agree to make alterations, even after an initial agreement, this is allowable. What's more, God is understanding, wise.

Some people are unable to marry believers at the status they desire. If you must marry and believing slaves (or servants) are available, marry them instead. God fully understands your faith. There is no doubt about it, all of you are fellow humans. Thus, after getting permission (from them) marry them (that is women under your power who truly believe, slaves, servants, or prisoners), and give them their proper gifts, not in fornication or as mistresses but rather women who agree in honest marriage. If during marriage they are guilty of immorality, then, they are liable for half the penalty given to free women. Yet, this permission to marry people under your power only applies to those who fear a weakness of their moral strength. It is (far) superior to remain patient and to abstain. What's more, God is completely forgiving, a mercy-giver.

God desires to clarify this (system) in order to guide you to good and or decent behavior, the way of those genuinely good and decent people of the past; (so you will) turn to your Lord in His mercy, since God is fully knowledgeable, completely wise. Surely, God wants to shower His mercy upon you. In contrast, those who follow only their own lusts desire that you deviate greatly from the truth.

God wants to make your life easier. This is because human beings have been created weak.

You true believers, never use your wealth for vicious, harmful purposes, even if you have the contract (or power) to do so. Also, never (financially) destroy one another. Surely, God is the (sole) provider of assets. Regarding anyone who (willingly and maliciously) uses his power to do wrong, without doubt, We will eventually cause him to endure extreme torment. Certainly, this is easy for God.

Yet, if you shun the major sins, those which have been specifically forbidden, your minor errors will be effaced. What's more, you will ultimately enter the realm of glory.

Thus, guard yourselves from desiring the possessions of others. What people earn is based upon their goals. (So, instead of envying others) ask God to embellish you. Clearly, regarding all that could be God has full knowledge.

Everyone has been appointed by Us to have heirs, that is wives/husbands, children, parents, and (other) relatives. Thus, give them their proper shares. What's more (realize that), God records all your actions.

Men must fully care for women through the wealth (given to them by) God, since men have been (supplied with the powers to achieve it) more abundantly. The women of God are those who are truly devout, who protect the intimacy (and privacy) of their relationship. Regarding women of malicious intent (who pursue sexual indiscretions), that is those whose actions you fear, first, warn them. If this fails, avoid them (that is don't sleep with them). If, then, this fails (to halt the malice, as a deterrent), separate from them✦ *for their own protection.*

✦The word *tharaba*, has several meanings. One of these meanings is to "separate" or "leave." Another is to "beat" or "strike." The latter meanings are inappropriate in this context. To "separate" is the most appropriate meaning, because this best flows with the rest of the sentence, that is "for their own protection." God despises divorce or the disruption of the home. If the relationship can be salvaged, that is ideal. So, any effective means necessary must be employed. If this requires to separate or leave a spouse, so be it. Through this, perhaps, the relationship can be saved. Even so, it is important to note that all these efforts apply only to a woman guilty of severe violations. This can never be applied to a good and decent woman. In fact, according to the Qur'aan, section 58 (first page), even to arbitrarily refuse to sleep with a wife is a severe violation, let alone to abandon her.

So, regardless of the punishment this only applies to a woman *guilty of lewd conduct*. It never applies to mere disagreements. What's more, wife beating is completely banned. Said the Prophet, "Never strike a woman." This established the attitude for the Muslim masses to prevent wife-beating. This is why compared to Western peoples wife beating in Islaamic societies is rare. In contrast, in the United States domestic abuse is the number one cause of physical damage to women. It is also the major factor in their murders.

Those who accuse Islaam of abusiveness give no consideration to the fact that in Western countries domestic abuse is rampant, while in Muslim countries it is rare. For women, the Islaamic system is a monumental protection. The same cannot be said regarding the Western systems, since there are no moral laws in place condemning domestic abuse, while in Islaam the harming of the innocent and vulnerable is banned.

To save the marriage all means necessary may be used. Yet, a man must never maliciously beat his wife. This is confirmed by the subsequent phrase, that is "never seek to harm them." In other words, there is no allowance to physically abuse anyone, especially women.

If after this they come to an understanding with you, *never seek to harm them*. Surely, God is almighty, great beyond comprehension.

If you have reason to fear the onset of a divorce, appoint a counselor, one from the male's side and one from the female's side, that is if they both desire reconciliation. This is because God may cause such a reconciliation. Certainly, regarding all issues God is fully knowledgeable as well as aware.

In addition, worship God alone. What's more, never give God-like powers to anything else.

Also, be gracious to your parents, relatives, and orphans as well as the poor. Be kind to neighbors as well as total strangers, friends, travelers, and also anyone under your control. Certainly, God has no love for the arrogant and conceited, that is the braggarts. Nor does he love misers nor those who urge others to be miserly, who hoard whatever they have received from God's benevolence. As a result, We have prepared for them an agony that will completely disgrace them, a torment for all who (obstinately) refuse to believe.

Regarding those who spend merely for show and also reject the existence of God, as well as accountability, Satan is their partner. This is the most vile partner anyone could choose.

What would be their loss if they would merely believe in almighty God, as well as the resurrection, and share their wealth and assets in God's way? This was, in fact, given to them by God, since God is aware of (their true nature).✦ Truly,

✦That is He made them in their wombs. So, He alone knows their genetic code—their true nature, potential, and needs. God gave them their powers, even their wealth. All that they have derives from Him. To reject this is the epitome of ingratitude. Thus, ultimately, who does it all truly belong to? Who does even the human being belong to? The obvious answer is God. Thus, the only reasonable course is to be humble before Him. Anyone who refuses to do so, who holds the self high: He will reject.

The human origins are humble. Then, how could anyone be arrogant? This is a violation of the true nature of the human being, the latter being dependent upon forces out of his control. To realize this, that is to understand that a human has no real power, is to gain peace. To resist it is to gain only conflict and ultimately loss. God rewards humility, while He punishes arrogance. It is up to the individual to choose which course to take, one leading to the love of God and the other to torment. This is the torment, that hell, of losing His love and compassion.

God never wrongs (anyone), even in the most miniscule degree (because it is His rule that) if there is a good deed, He will fertilize it and will from His generosity provide a monumental reward.

Then, what will be the consequences for the sinners when We present the witnesses from every community and bring you, O Prophet, to testify against them? Those who rejected Me and refuse to honor the Prophet will wish they were a mere pimple on the face of the earth or something even less significant. Yet, they will be unable to evade (these consequences) of anything that has happened (on this earth).

You true believers, never worship when you are drunk. Rather, wait until you are sober. Nor worship when you are in need of a complete washing (that is after sexual intercourse), the exception being if you are traveling and are unable to wash. So, if you are sick or traveling, answered the call to nature or having cohabited with a woman: if water is unavailable (ritually), use pure dust, passing it lightly over the face and hands. God is the only true cleanser of sins.✦

✦This demonstrates the mercy of the almighty Lord. Even with ritual and/or procedure He never intends to burden the individual. Rather, His desire is that people be happy and free of burdens. His entire intent is that there be peace and decency on this earth. This is the purpose of His revelations. What's more, this is the basis of any divine laws. Without doubt, all regulations in this Qur'aan are for the purpose of human protection.

What's more, regarding His forgiveness He gives it generously.

There is that group of people who, even though they were given revelation, abandoned it, relying instead on error. They also want you to lose your way. Yet, God is fully aware of who truly are your enemies. God is the ideal associate, the ideal source of support—the only One to rely upon.

Some of those who follow the Jewish faith distort their divine writings. (They do so) by taking them out of context. They say, essentially, "We understand it, but, regardless, we reject it" and "Listen to it (that is the Qur'aan), but refuse to follow it. Instead, follow us."

They play with words, implying that the God-given faith is false. Had they only said, "We understand and therefore submit to it," and "Bear with us, and have patience with us" it would have been more appropriate as well as decent. Yet, as a consequence of their obstinate refusal to believe they are rejected in advance by God. The fact is their beliefs are of no significance.

Appeal to the people of scripture

You people of the previous scriptures, you Christians, you should also believe in this new revelation; (after all) it confirms the correct parts of yours. If you fail to do so, We may render fruitless your aspirations, just as We did to those who violated the Sabbath. Surely, God's will is always achieved.

(In God's view) to give others divine powers is unforgivable, although (in His mercy) He forgives any lesser crime: for whomever He wills. Surely, those who give God-like powers to other beings besides God have invented for themselves a monstrous sin.

Are you aware of those who claim themselves as the only pure ones? It is untrue, since, without doubt, it is God who causes whomever He chooses to grow in purity. (In God's court) none will be wronged, not even by the slightest degree. No doubt, they invent concepts and attribute them to God. This is the most blatant of their sins.

Are you aware of those who, despite having their own (originally divine) scripture, believe in baseless fables and in satanic powers? What's more (incredible), they insist that the godless are more rightly guided than the followers of this revelation. Surely, God has rejected them. What's more, whoever God rejects and whoever He abandons—whoever He truly curses—will be devoid of all support.

Do they (that is those who find fault with the believers) perhaps (believe they) own a share in God's vast authority? Yet, if they did, without doubt, they would fail to share virtually any of it.✦

✦That is, unlike God, they would greedily adhere to their power base and refuse to share it. In contrast, God freely dispenses His generosity. He even does so regarding those who reject Him. Then, He gives freely to all, even those who demand of Him—even those who fight against Him.

Or, are they (merely) envious of others because of what God has given them? Yet (as a heritage to them recall that), We, in fact, gave Abraham's household great revelation and wisdom. Plus, We gave him a powerful position. What's more, some of his successors remained devout, while others deviated.

The intensity of hell; the grandeur of paradise

Yet, even so, nothing could be more painful than hell. The fact is those who continuously reject My messages are destined for it, to endure the (agonizing) fire. Whenever it burns off their skins We will reattach new ones, so that they may experience the full (intensity of) the agony. Without doubt, God is the source of all ultimate power, the wisest of all.

In contrast, lush gardens are readied for the truly good, who achieve good deeds. They will live there forever with spouses, also good and decent. Thus, We will deliver them to incredible happiness beyond comprehension.

Surely, God commands you to return whatever you owe to people. (He also commands that) whenever you judge between them, be just. The responsibilities God commands upon you are the most excellent (conceivable). Undoubtedly, He is fully aware of all (that occurs), and He (actually) sees all (that you do).

You true believers, steadfastly adhere to (the dictates of) God as well as the (ways of the) Prophet and also to those whom you have appointed as authorities. If there is a dispute, use God and the (ways of the) Prophet as referee. This is how true believers respond. This is best for all parties and will, ultimately, lead to the most just results.

Are you familiar with those who claim that they believe both in the Prophet's revelation as well as the earlier ones? Yet, they are willing to rely upon the powers of evil for guidance, although they previously were ordered to reject this. This is because Satan wants them to lose their way. Thus, whenever they are told, "Join us in this way of (serving) God, His revelations, and the way of the Prophet," you can observe these fools completely reject you.

Yet, how will they manage during (resurrection), when as a result of their actions the catastrophe strikes them? They will beg you, "Our intentions were good—we only meant to help."✦ Even so, surely,

---

✦That is when they fail to defeat the true believers and are themselves totally defeated. Then, realizing their loss they will beg for mercy. Too, they will make every excuse, acting in raw fear. So, it can only be imagined how they will react when they are presented before the ultimate source of power: almighty God.

God knows what is in their hearts. Thus, disregard them. However, forewarn them, and tell them about themselves to cause them to soul-search, because We have always sent prophets only for the purpose that they under the authority of God be followed.✦

✦That is that the principles they teach be adopted by the human race. As well, any helpful rituals, which they present, are to be adhered to, since the prophets are merely spokespersons for God. Too, any rituals they establish are for the benefit of humankind, since these rituals are a means for people to get closer to almighty God.

If, eventually, after they have sinned against themselves they approach you and ask for God's forgiveness, supported by the Prophet praying on their behalf, they would, without doubt, find God willing to accept repentance, willing to have mercy upon them. Surely, their belief is of no consequence, that is unless they (fully) believe in you and make you their mediator in all their disagreements—unless they accept without the slightest hesitation your decisions and give up their souls in complete submission.

Fighting for God's sake reiterated

Yet, if We ordered them, "Risk your lives," or "Risk losing your security," only a few would comply. This is despite the fact that if they did so, it would be for their own benefit. What's more, it would greatly strengthen them, and as a result the Almighty would give them an impressive reward. Plus (as the ultimate victory), He directly would guide them. This is because it is true that all who obey God and the Prophet will be among the blessed: the prophets, those who were always true and who gave their lives (for God's cause) and the (various) upright people (throughout the centuries). These are the most grand of all associates conceivable.✦ This is (an example of)

✦That is they will all be together in paradise, enjoying each others' company: all in the presence of almighty God. Here, they will be given all that they desire. However, for the deepest believers the mere presence of God will suffice. For such believers rather than heavenly pleasures, which act as replacements for material goods, their only desire is for His everlasting love. This is the highest level anyone can achieve.

the boundless mercy of God. This is because He is the One who has all (true) knowledge.

You true believers, constantly be on your guard for danger, whether you engage the enemy in small groups or as a unit. No doubt, some of you will tend to be slackers. What's more, if disaster strikes, such a person would say, "God was kind to me that I was not with them." Yet, if by God's grace you (believers) would have won, this same person would have said, "If I only were with them, I would have gotten part of the captured treasure," as if he never even cared. Thus, from now on let all who are willing to trade this life for the next one fight in God's service. Whether killed or victorious, We will eventually give a mighty reward.

What morally is preventing you from fighting on God's behalf due to the fact that there are hopeless people, crying, "Our Lord, free us from the oppressors. Send us through Your Mercy one who will protect and help us—who will bring us relief."

The true believers are those who fight for God's sake, while those who reject the truth fight on behalf of wickedness. Then, fight (with all your might) against those accomplices of Satan. Clearly, Satan's treachery is feeble.

Are you aware of those who have been forewarned, "Avoid unjust violence, worship constantly, and be generous?" Yet, as soon as fighting for God has been mandated some of them fear humans the way they should fear God or are (incredibly), even more fearful. Then, they say, "Lord, why have you ordered us to fight? If we could just have a (temporary) reprieve…"

Tell them, "Life here is only temporary," while for the true believers who deeply believe in God the future life is far superior, since (ultimately), everyone will be treated with the utmost fairness.

Regardless of where you reside you will experience death, even if you are in the highest structures. Yet (it is human nature that), when something good happens to them, they say "This is from God." However, when they endure hardship, they (blame it on others and) say (to each other), "This is *your* fault." Tell them, "Ultimately, it is all (a test) from God." What is the matter with humans that they are so far removed from grasping such (basic) truths? Clearly, whatever good that reaches you is from God. In contrast, whatever harm that you experience is your own doing.

Thus, We have sent you as a Messenger—let there be no doubt about it—for the entire human race. Furthermore, God is the best One to testify to this. Anyone who obeys the Messenger obeys God. Yet, regarding those who reject you realize that your duty has already been fulfilled (that is your only obligation is to warn), and such people are on their own.

They often claim, "We obey you." Yet, in secrecy some of them devise the opposite, although God records their secretive plots. Ignore them✦ and trust

✦That is they are hypocrites, so whatever they say is without substance. Such people will bend in any direction they believe will benefit them. What's more, they are only concerned about themselves. They may act as if they believe in this message, while secretly in their hearts they reject it. Then, in that hypocrisy they actually fight against it. These are the typical two-faced types that can never be trusted.

(instead) implicitly in God, because He alone is worthy of your trust.✦

✦This is another reminder that for those who truly serve God the forces of evil are of no consequence. They are never to focus on such forces. For the true believers the focus is exclusively on God and any who support Him, and, what's more, in only God can the true believers place their trust. This is because He is the only reliable source of power and strength, because He alone has advance knowledge of all issues. This means that He alone can secretly plan on behalf of the believers.

Will they, then, refuse to investigate with the purpose of understanding this divine document? If the source were any other than God, without doubt, it would have been full of contradictions.

If critical matters occur, they spread rumors. Yet, if they would simply refer the issue to (be based on the ways of) the Prophet and those believers (entrusted with authority), that would be the proper approach. Even so, if it weren't for God's mercy and benevolence (which He directs towards you), most of you would follow the forces of evil.

The obligation of fighting tyranny

Thus, fight with your entire might *on your own* for God. You are only responsible for yourself.✦ What's more, inspire the believers to overcome

✦That is as if to say "concentrate exclusively on your own efforts. What others do is irrelevant, so pay no attention to them." It essentially means "mind your own business." People are only responsible for their own actions. Plus, they are to fight on their own without seeking recognition, glory, or praise. The battle is on God's behalf—not for any material benefit or any position a person might gain in front of the people.

This is confirmed by the statement of the Prophet, that is to proceed through life as if a 'stranger or traveler.' In other words, never become emotionally engaged in any issue. Rather, the person must in such critical circumstances be able to think clearly. To do so all emotions must be removed. Rather, the entire basis of any action must be to serve God. That goal is merely to establish justice. This is through being of a godly character in the manner of the character of God's representatives— Moses, Jesus, Muhammad, and others.

all fear of death. (Through such a firm belief) God may well overcome the might of those who reject the truth, because obviously God is stronger in power, stronger in the ability to overcome.

Those who side with the people of a good cause will be graced with God's blessings, while whoever sides with the cause of evil will be answerable (for their role in it). No doubt, God keeps watch over all (that transpires). However, if you are treated in a peaceful way, be even more peaceful or at least as peaceful. The fact is God records all events.

God is the only divine power. During resurrection We will gather together—and there is no doubt about this—all (humankind). That time will come, this being beyond doubt, because God's word is certain.

Could it be that you vacillate about the hypocrites despite the fact that due to their own guilt God Himself has rejected them? Is it that you think you could guide those who God allows to deviate—when (the fact is) regarding whoever God lets deviate you are unable to guide?

They would relish in the thought that you would join them in their rebellion. Therefore, never take (such obviously godless ones) as allies until they abandon, in the name of God, their indecent ways. Yet, if they revert to open hostility, seize and destroy them✦ wherever you find them.

✦That is those who threaten the very existence of goodness and decency. These are the people who deliberately seek to destroy the Muslims. God commands the true believers to vigorously fight against such tyrants. This may include the sacrificing of time, energy, money, and physical effort. It may even mean the sacrificing of the believers' lives. So, in the pitch of battle the Qur'aan commands that the believers mercilessly attack these enemies which seek their extinction and, if necessary, fight them to the death.

Never rely upon the godless as allies or supporters. The exception is those who have connections with people to whom you yourselves are committed by contract or who come to you, because they are horrified at the thought of warring either against you or their own people—although if God desired it and made them more powerful than you, they would certainly have warred against you. Thus, if they leave you alone and do not instigate hostilities, offer them peace. In this case God does not allow you to harm them.

You will find that there are others who would prefer to be at peace with you as well as at peace with their own people. Yet, whenever they are tempted to evil, they surge into it. Thus, if they harass you and create hostilities, attack and destroy them, regardless of (what condition) you encounter them (in). Surely, these are the ones against whom We have empowered you to wage war.✦

✦The Qur'aan makes it clear that the only time God is behind war is for survival, that is against tyranny. This signifies the struggle of the Palestinian people. Thus, regarding gross tyranny a Muslim is obligated to fight. This fact is made excruciatingly clear throughout this text. In fact, such a war is a test from God, that of the forces of good versus evil. What's more, a Muslim is obligated to fight this battle, a duty of even greater requirement than mere prayer and fasting.

The crime of killing a fellow believer in God

Unless by mistake it is inconceivable that a believer would kill another believer. What's more, whoever has done so, there is an obligation to free a believing soul from (imprisonment or captivity) as well as to pay an (appropriate) indemnity to the victim's relatives. However, the (victim) may wish to forgo this as a charity.

Now, if the deceased, even though a believer, belonged to the enemy, the penance is limited to the freeing of a believing soul from bondage, belonging to a group of people with whom you have a treaty, in addition to the freeing of a believing soul held captive, an indemnity which must be paid (to his relations). What's more, whoever is unable (financially) to do so must instead fast two consecutive months. This is the atonement ordained by God. No doubt, God knows all and is fully wise.

Yet, whoever deliberately kills another believer will go to hell, where he will remain forever. God will condemn and reject him. Furthermore, He will prepare for him a monstrous agony.

So, you true believers, when you proceed in God's cause from now on use proper judgement. Thus, never place material gains over justice, in other words, if a people offer peace, *to insinuate that they may be attacked and plundered, merely because they are not believers, is prohibited.* The fact is with God are (the most) abundant gains.✦

✦This is a warning for people to never put material gains over justice. This proves that in the true way of God there is no such thing as a 'religious' war, that is where the authority of religion is used to brutalize and abuse people. Islaamic history is devoid of such acts. What's more, the service of God is synonymous with justice. So, "in the name of God" there is no possibility of killing the weak or innocent. Nor is there any allowance for rapine and devastation, a common consequence of Western expansionism, which is unknown in Islaamic history.

(God reminds you that) you were once in the same position.✦ However, God has been kind to

✦That is of living as godless. People have become aware of God and the moral code only through His mercy. Without His guidance even today people would be living largely as barbarians.

Because of His love He revealed His books. It was these books which altered the course of history and which, in fact, elevated humankind from its darkness. This guidance comes in the form of dedicated messengers, as well as other agents, who God inspires. Their purpose is to lift human beings from the darkness of barbarism into the light of divine guidance.

you. Thus, be discerning (and tend towards compassion). There is no doubt about it God is aware of all your actions.

With the exception of the disabled the believers who are passive are at a different level than those who are highly active (those who) work arduously in God's cause, who give (freely) of their assets and lives. God has raised such individuals to great heights. Although all believers receive the ultimate good, God has promised the hardest working ones a monumental reward—many degrees higher than all others, plus forgiveness of sins and His fullest generosity. Surely, God forgives greatly and is immense (beyond comprehension) in His generosity.

The crime of the rejection of God and almighty God's mercy

Clearly, when the angels gather the sinners in death, the ones who are still committing evil right until they die, they will ask, "What was wrong with you?" They will answer, "We were too easily tempted." The angels will say, "Wasn't God's earth absolutely vast enough for you to escape the influence of evil?" Obviously, hell is the destiny for such people, and this is the most hideous of destinations. Yet, the truly helpless, whether male, female, or children, will be exempted, those who are too weak and/or have not been exposed to the correct way. Regarding them, God may well efface their sins. Surely, God is an absolver of sins and in fact forgives extensively.

Whoever rejects the realm of evil for God's service will find countless lonely episodes but also great pleasure. If anyone flees his home, escaping corruption to the way of God and His Prophet—if he dies in the process—God has his reward already prepared. Certainly, God is extremely forgiving, vastly generous in His grace.

When you wage combat✦ and there is the potential

✦Since its inception major campaigns have been undertaken to destroy this religion. As in the Old Testament God laid down rules for the survival of the original fledgling movement against all aggressors. Thus, Muslims are urged to fight against all tyrants, who seek to obliterate the light of this faith. Otherwise, the people of God would be easily eliminated. God eventually allowed the Muslims to resist oppression through active war. However, the rule is that as soon as aggression ends war must be halted. Even so, regarding civilized states Muslims are never to be the aggressors. Yet, if they are threatened, they are to fight against this threat with all means possible.

for danger, you may shorten the ritual worship. Those who reject God's way are, without doubt, your enemies. Thus, when you are with your fellow believers and are ready for worship, let only a portion of them be engaged, while the remainder stand guard. Then, change places, and let the guards be always prepared against danger, with weapons ready. Surely, those who reject the truth would love to attack you by surprise.

Yet, if you are troubled by unfavorable weather or are ill, it is perfectly satisfactory to lay down your weapons while you worship. Even so, be fully prepared against attack. Surely, regarding those who reject the truth God has prepared the torment (of absolute shame). Then, after you have finished worshipping remember God regardless of your condition. What's more, when you are once again secure, observe your worship fully. No doubt, for all believers the ritual worship is a sacred duty linked to specific times.

Also, when you pursue the evil enemy, never be weak or faint of heart. If you are enduring pain, realize that they, too, are enduring it. Yet, you are expecting to receive from God a kind of help they could never expect. Certainly, God is fully aware and is completely wise.

We have given you this divine truth for a single purpose—and there is no doubt (about this purpose)—that you can apply what God has instructed you *to rule ethically between the people*.✦ Thus, never associate with those who

✦This is the entire purpose of the revelations of God—the creation of justice and peace on earth. This peace can only be achieved through the implementation of the divine code, which allows the creation of a truly just and civil society, because "God knows best."

betray their trust. Rather, ask God to forgive them. Truly, God forgives much and is absolutely generous (in how He dispenses His mercy).

Yet, never side with those who are false to their own selves. What's more (realize that), those who betray their commitments and persist in the commission of evil deny themselves God's love.

These are the ones who attempt to disguise their actions from their fellow men. Even so, God is completely aware of their actions. He is *in their minds* while they plot—even late into the night—all types of opinions, none of which He approves. Furthermore, God is completely aware of your actions. You might consider being on their side in this life. However, who will side with them before God at resurrection? Then, who will be their defenders?

Yet, if a person commits evil or wrongs somehow his own soul and afterwards beseeches God's mercy, he will find God vastly forgiving, full of generosity. Surely, whoever commits a sin only hurts himself. It is God who knows all and is completely wise. However, whoever commits a crime or evil act and blames another is guilty of gross injustice and (therefore) earns an additional flagrant sin.

Even so, if it were not for God's favor, surely, some of those false people—these hypocrites—would attempt to misguide you. Yet, without doubt, they only misguide themselves. What's more, they are unable to harm you, since God has provided you with this divine book as a protection and has also given you the ability to use your reason. Plus, He has given you special knowledge of what was previously unknown. Therefore, God's favor upon you is vast.

As a rule no good arises from secretive discussions or plots, except those who devote themselves to charity (and purposely disguise this for the good of humankind and due to a desire for God's love), sound business dealings (involving trade secrets), and the establishment of justice between people. The person who does so to please God will eventually be granted by Us a monumental reward. However, regarding the person who despite receiving guidance isolates himself from the (the way of the) Prophet and follows (instead) a way other than that of the believers, We will leave him to whatever he has chosen. What's more, We will cause him to endure the torment of burning despair, a wicked consequence.

To serve others as if gods is unforgivable. However, God forgives lesser sins to whomever He deems.

Without doubt, those who serve others besides God have surely deviated greatly. Instead of the all-powerful God they solicit lifeless symbols thus soliciting merely Satan himself, precisely the Satan whom God rejected for saying, "I will entice my due share of your servants—there is no doubt about this—and will derail them (by) filling them with vain desires. What's more, I will command them to perform heinous acts. In fact, I will (even) order them to corrupt God's creation."✦

✦That is, for instance, the modern day corruption due to pollution, nuclear irradiation, and other industrial destruction of this earth. This also alludes to the arrogant acts of science in respect to the corruption of the gene pool, known as genetic engineering. This genetic corruption is hereby banned in the Qur'aan. This process, which forcibly incorporates foreign genetic material into native species, destroys the divinely-ordained nature of such species. All this leads to only disease and destruction. Thus, as dictated by the Qur'aan genetic engineering, where the physical structure of the genes is brazenly manipulated, is banned as the work of the devil.

No real believers should be employed in this trade. Again, according to their holy book this is the workings of the devil. What's more, Muslims must make themselves aware of genetically engineered foods and avoid their consumption. These are highly dangerous foods and readily cause disease. Such foods include commercial soy, corn, Canola, cottonseed, and in Canada, potatoes. This also includes in the United States commercial milk products, since these are contaminated with genetically engineered growth hormone. The latter is a potent carcinogen.

Such foods are unsafe for human consumption. In fact, these foods are carcinogenic. A study done by the Russian Academy of Sciences proved that, for instance, genetically engineered soy increased the fatality rate of newborn rats by 600%, causing those which did live to have severe deformities. For more information about the danger of genetically engineered foods see Americanwildfoods.com and click on the Science button.

The ingestion of genetically engineered foods increases the risks for a wide range of diseases, in particular allergic, kidney, digestive, skin, and bowel conditions. The symptoms are often vague and impossible to pinpoint. Too, their ingestion increases the risks for toxic reactions, including anaphylactic shock, hives and asthma.

Yet, those who select Satan for their master instead of God lose all. His promises are only vain. Moreover, whatever Satan promises is a delusion. Those who do so (that is follow Satan's handiwork) are destined for agonizing despair, which they will be unable to escape. In contrast, those who believe, while giving their all and doing good deeds, We will usher them into spring-fed gardens—the lush realm of paradise—where they will live forever. This is God's promise, and whose promise could be more true than God's?

While it might violate the hopes (and desires) of those who refuse to believe, as well as the people of scripture, the fact is whoever commits evil will gain only its equivalent. Plus, such a person will find no one to protect or help him other than God. In contrast, *anyone✦ who does all that is possible*

✦That is the doing of good is universally accepted by God, whether by male or female, Muslim or non-Muslim. This demonstrates the universal nature of this revelation. In contrast to Christianity in Islaam to earn God's grace there is no need for special procedures. Anyone can be saved, as long as such a person believes in God and never discriminates against His messengers. This is the person who because of the awe of God spreads only goodness on this earth.

of goodness and is also a believer will enter paradise and never be wronged, even by a miniscule degree. Yet, who could be of a higher status than the person who surrenders his entire being to God and what's more does good deeds, who follows the beliefs of Abraham (the one who) rejected all that is false, since (surely) God made Abraham His beloved friend?

Without doubt, God owns all that exists. Furthermore, He has complete power and control over it.✦

✦That is all wealth and power, even while seemingly man-made, ultimately belongs to God. Humans are merely custodians. God made all that exists, and so regardless of the degree of a person's possessions and/or wealth he owns none of it. Thus, from God's point of view to selfishly hoard wealth or any other 'gift' is a crime.

Also, they will ask you regarding laws concerning women. Tell them, "God has already told you about them."✦ Certainly, they have already been given to

✦The Prophet Muhammad had a difficult job bringing justice to a civilization where only injustice ruled. Before his time women had no rights. Through this man for the first time in Arabian history as human beings women were given equal rights with men.

Their current status in some parts of modern Arabia is at variance with their status during the Prophet's movement. For instance, in the Prophet's time women were fully allowed to be involved in public affairs. Also, they drove their own mounts and even fought in war. Thus, for example, the prohibition in Saudi Arabia against women drivers has no relevance in this faith. Rather than Islaamic such rules are tribal.

you through this divine writing—regarding orphan women (under your authority) to whom because you yourselves may be desirous of marrying them, you fail to give that which has been ordered for them and regarding helpless children as well your responsibility is to treat orphans with justice. Yet, regarding whatever good you achieve God is fully aware of it.

If a woman has reason to fear harm from her husband or that he might refuse to make love to her, it is acceptable for the couple to attempt to regain the peace (that is to normalize relations) between each other—because peace is best—and what's more selfishness is continuously present in human souls. However, if you do good deeds and think conscientiously of God, surely, God is aware of whatever occurs between people.

Regardless of how much you desire it you are incapable of treating multiple wives equally.✦ Thus

✦In ancient Arabian society a multiplicity of wives was common. This was particularly true of tribal chiefs. However, the Qur'aan makes it clear that the rule is monogamy. Interestingly, the vast majority of Muslims—over 98%—have only one spouse. Even so, there may well be circumstances in society necessitating this allowance. For instance, there will occur a time when women will far outnumber men. Should those women be left to a life of loneliness, without any companions?

Consider the circumstances in Iraq, where due to mass murder there are now hundreds of thousands of widows. Does this serve society? Thus, in His magnanimous nature He gives the allowance for multiple wives, usually to be applied under unusual circumstances—as a protection and benefit for womankind under dire need.

In Western culture some 9 of 10 people engage in pre-marital sex. Too, nearly 50% of all married men have at least one affair during marriage. Such secretive sex places women at great risk for the development of dangerous sexually transmitted diseases. Thus, those in the West who attack Islaam have no basis for their claims. The Islaamic tradition is far more sophisticated, far more humane, than any method developed in the West. In fact, the rules of Islaam specifically protect women from vast harm, precisely the harm they are enduring under Western authority.

(as an advance warning,) never allow yourselves to incline towards one to the exclusion of the other, leaving her in a state as it were of having only an artificial husband. Yet, if you do what is right and are (truly) conscious of Him, obviously, God forgives much and is thoroughly generous (in the way He rewards His servants).

However, if a husband and wife separate, God will provide for each from His abundance. Surely, God is beyond (anyone's) conception in His powers, totally wise (in how He rules what is best for His creation). What's more, all that exists in the universe, as well as in this world, in fact, belongs to Him.

Now, We have made it mandatory for recipients of revelation, whether yourselves or the people of the older scriptures, to always keep God in mind and also appreciate Him. However, if you decide to reject Him, be aware that all that exists belongs to God, that is every object (and being) in the universe. Clearly, God needs no one. Plus, He alone is worthy of praise.

Again, all that exists in the universe and on the earth is God's. He is the One most worthy of your trust. If He decides, He can cause you, O humankind, to be exterminated (then, incredibly,) creating instead other beings. Without doubt, God has the power to do this.

Whoever desires the rewards of this world realize that with God are the rewards of this world plus the next one. God, without doubt, is aware of all that exists/occurs and also sees all that occurs—(so He is aware of all that you do).

You who truly believe (in almighty God), in the support of justice remain strong, realizing that God is fully aware of all human activities. Support the truth for God's sake, even if it is against your own selves, parents, and/or relatives. Regardless of a person's (state of) wealth (whether) rich or poor, never be prejudiced, and instead give God's claim precedence. Thus, never follow your own desires (the concern being) that you swerve from justice.✦ Surely, if you distort the truth, God is fully aware of all your actions.

✦That is, rather, the believer must adhere to the dictates of almighty God and His selected Messenger. Here, the Qur'aan warns people to never succumb to false pride. This means to never follow mere personal desires. Instead, it says, the believer is to follow the principles of this Qur'aan. Such a person is also to adopt the refined ways of the Messenger of God. Then, too, the Qur'aan is based upon justice. It is also based upon common sense. This is Islaam.

You true believers, hold firmly to your belief in God and His Prophet and in this divine book, which He has methodically delivered to him. Also, believe resolutely in the previous revelations. The fact is anyone who denies God, His angels, His revelations, His Prophets, and the final time (of accountability) has completely erred.

Without doubt, those who become believers and then refuse to do so and continuously vacillate (in their faith) and who, then (ultimately), become obstinate in their denial of the truth—they will never receive God's forgiveness. Nor will they receive any of His guidance. Tell such two-faced believers that they will earn a wicked torment.

Regarding those who side with the godless in preference to the believers do they hope that they will be honored by them, when, in fact, all honor belongs exclusively to God?

God has made clear in this divine book that whenever you hear people reject or ridicule God's messages (you must) avoid their company, ✦ that is

✦That is being constantly exposed to this negative vile energy will have a derogatory impact. So, it is mandated to have no contact with such people, otherwise, it might have a destructive effect upon the believer's psyche. So, as long as any person denigrates God or His Messenger the Muslim must have nothing to do with him. This is mandatory—protective advice from almighty God.

until they change the topic of conversation—or else you will (potentially) become like them. Surely, God will gather in hell both the godless and the hypocritical believers, that is those who falsely profess—who wait (on the sidelines) to see what happens to you. Thus, if you succeed, they say, "We were always on your side." In contrast, if the godless were successful, they would tell them, "We have earned your favor by defending you against those believers." Yet, during the accountability (before God), truly, God will judge between all of you. God will, in fact, never allow those who reject the truth to (truly) hurt the believers.

Clearly, the hypocrites attempt to deceive God. Yet, in fact, He is the One who causes them to be deceived. When they rise to pray, they do so reluctantly, only to be seen and praised. They only rarely remember God, and they never commit themselves, constantly vacillating. However, if God allows a person to err, there is nothing that can be done about it.

You true believers, never side with the godless in preference to the believers. Do you want to prove to God your guilt?

Surely, the fraudulent ones who profess belief merely for their own purposes will be in the lowest depths of the fire. What's more, there will be no one to support them in any way. The exception will be those who repent, live with decency, and remain conscious of God, who increasingly become more sincere in the depth of their belief in God alone. These are the same as the (true) believers, and God will, eventually, give all (such believers) an immense reward.

Clearly, God never wants you to suffer, even for your past sins if you are grateful and make every effort to believe. This is because God is always responsive to gratitude. Plus, He is completely knowledgeable (regarding the true nature of every human).

God warns against the mention of any vile issue openly, the exception being a person who has been wronged. What's more, God is certainly aware of all that transpires. So, whether you do good openly or keep it secret and/or pardon others for the harm they have caused you, know that only God can cleanse peoples' sins. Furthermore, no doubt, He alone is unlimited in His power.

Regarding those who by making distinctions between God and His prophets, in fact, reject them, surely, they (are the ones who) say, "We believe in only a portion of it," and thus wish to pursue a path in-between. By such a position they have actually proven that they reject the truth. God has prepared a disgraceful punishment for such deniers of the truth. In contrast, those who believe in God and His prophets and regard them as one (family), eventually, He will give them their full reward. Without question, God forgives much and is totally generous (in how He dispenses His mercy).

The early people of Moses and Jesus: their rebellion

The followers of the Old Testament demand that you (O prophet) bring from heaven a revelation specifically for them. Yet, they confronted Moses directly with an even greater demand, when they said, "We want to see what God looks like," at which time because of their wickedness they were overcome by a powerful (blast of) punishment.

Afterwards and despite the fact that they had (already) received all the evidence of the truth, they worshiped the (idolatrous) calf. Even so (to demonstrate Our mercy), We purged them of this significant sin and provided Moses obvious proof, raising Mount Sinai high above them in witness of their solemn pledge. Then, We told them, "Enter this new life in humility. In addition, hold firmly to the laws of the Sabbath" for which We accepted their commitment. Yet, We punished them for breaking their promises and for their refusal to recognize God's messages. (We also punished them) for murdering prophets and for their bragging, "We already know everything." Not true, the fact is because of their rejection of the truth, God has sealed their hearts—(all due to) the vile things they have said about Mary✦ and because of

✦It was the hostile Israelites who accused Mary horribly. A Muslim cannot even consider these words, let alone repeat them. To the Muslims Mary is the Virgin, the pure, and the dignified—a dedicated servant of God. Muslims have only love for her and would never slander her. This, they know, would result in their burning in hell.

Christians must seriously consider this fact. While in Judaism she is denigrated in Islaam she is deeply honored. In fact, all true Christian saints are in Islaam held high. The Muslim is obligated to believe in the mission of Jesus as well as the saintly status of the Virgin Mary.

their boast, "We killed Jesus Christ, Mary's son, *a supposed prophet of God*."✦ Yet, in fact, they did not kill him, which is beyond dispute. Nor did they

✦If a Muslim committed such heinous slander against Jesus, he would be permanently consigned to hell. It is completely banned for Muslims to display even the slightest negativity against Jesus or Mary. Furthermore, in contrast to this view of the hostile Israelites all Muslims agree that Jesus and Mary were saints.

crucify him. Rather, it only *appeared to them as such*.✦

✦This statement is supported by the latest archeological evidence. The fact that Jesus planned his escape from hostile forces—the Roman rulers—has recently been documented. An ancient document recently translated confirms that Judas, one of Jesus' disciples, acted as a decoy in order to protect Jesus from assassination. This coincides with the Qur'aanic explanation.

The Qur'aan makes it clear that he escaped any harm at the hands of his adversaries. Again, this is confirmed by the latest historical data. It is even suggested by modern historians that after escaping this plot Jesus was married and continued his mission. Therefore, the claim that he was murdered and impaled on a cross is a fable.

In fact, those who maintain various views regarding this are merely guessing. This is because, without doubt, they failed to kill him. Absolutely, God exalted him to Himself—and God is sufficiently wise (to counter all plots).

Yet, all the followers of earlier revelation will, when they confront death, realize the truth about Jesus. What's more, during resurrection Jesus himself will tell the truth against them (that is those who create falsehoods about him).

Wickedness condemned; true Judaism commended

Consequently, because of their wickedness We denied the Jews certain of the good things of life, which had previously been allowed. We did this due to the fact that they had repeatedly rejected God's way. We did it also because of their taking usury, although they were (clearly and previously) forbidden to do so, as was their wrongful consumption of (other) people's possessions. What's more, regarding those who persist in their rejection of the truth We have prepared (for them) a violent torment. However, regarding those (followers of the scripture) who have a deep understanding (of the meaning of their scriptures) and truly believe in the heaven-sent revelations (that are now being revealed to you)—who are also constant in worship as well as (kind and) giving in their actions—and all (others) who believe in God and the final event: these are the ones We will reward beyond comprehension.

The universal nature of Islaam

Without doubt, We have inspired you, just as We inspired Noah, as well as all prophets who followed him, as We inspired Abraham, Ishmael, Isaac, Jacob, and their descendants, including Jesus, Job, Jonah, Aaron, and Solomon. What's more (in order to cause you, O followers of scripture, to recall your ties to this more modern revelation recall the fact that), We were the Ones who favored David✦ with

✦In other words, God favored the Israelite prophets, such as David, by giving them His own special revelations. He selected both David and Solomon and asked the masses to believe in them. In fact, both men were powerful rulers of great prestige. Yet, those who admit David as true now refuse to follow this final Prophet, even though the latter is his relative. Plus, they solemnly claim the ties to all ancestors, and, then, still refuse the new Prophet. Through this they prove their faith is shallow and is based merely on personal gain. In other words, they base all their actions on their own personal desires.

It cannot be based upon a love and devotion of God. It was God who selected all prophets, including the Prophet Muhammad. So, anyone who truly believes in God is compelled to accept him as well as the revelation he bore. Thus, the rejection of the Prophet Muhammad is tantamount to the rejection of God Himself. It is true evidence of the shallowness of faith.

For Christians a simple fact must be recognized: in the ancient Hebrew Bible a future leader is predicted, who Jesus himself asked all to follow. This is the Prophet Muhammad. So, on what basis can a truly devout Christian reject him?

the gift of a book of divine wisdom, just as We inspired other messengers before this, just as God spoke His word to Moses. We have sent all of them to announce good news and to warn (the latter being), so that men might have no excuse before God. Without doubt, God is powerful beyond comprehension, truly wise.

Regardless (of peoples' errant views), God Himself confirms the truth of His revelations that He has given you from the high heavens, with the angels also testifying to (its truthfulness), although none can testify as does God.

Certainly, those who deliberately reject the truth and are determined to turn others away from God's way have deviated to the greatest extreme. Clearly, those who deliberately reject the truth and purposely commit evil—they will never be forgiven by God. Nor will He guide them in any direction other than the direction to hell, their permanent home. No doubt, this a minor issue for God.

Command to believe in the new Prophet

You entire human race, clearly this (newer) Prophet has now come to you representing the truth from your almighty Lord. Thus, for your own sake believe in it.✦ However, if you refuse to do so,

---

✦Here, God is calling all people to testify that this Qur'aan is true and is truly from God. He is also telling people that it is to their benefit to believe in it and to recognize the Prophet Muhammad as His Messenger. Again, He is saying that He sent this man for human benefit. This Prophet's character was highly refined. All people can benefit by adopting his ways.

In contrast, the teachings of Jesus are largely lost. So are the teachings of the earlier prophets. In contrast, the Prophet Muhammad's teachings are preserved. Then, who else is there to follow?

---

realize that God owns all that exists, and God has full awareness and what's more is completely wise.

The true nature of Jesus reiterated; trinity refuted

You followers of the Gospel, never violate the limits of the truth in your religion. Never say about God anything except the truth. Obviously, the Christ Jesus, Mary's son, was merely one of God's messengers. (He was) the fulfillment of His promise which He represented to Mary—a soul created by Him. Thus, believe in God as well as His prophets. What's more, never proclaim the "trinity." Desist from this—for your own good. God is One. It is impossible that He would have a son— He is far beyond—far too profound, in fact, far too high and exalted—for such an association. He owns all that exists in the (infinite) universe. What's more, He is the One most worthy of trust.✦

✦That is to rely upon any other as the savior is a loss. This includes the relatively impotent Jesus Christ. Only God almighty has the power to save anyone.

This becomes most obvious when human beings are placed in harms way. In any sudden crisis, like a life and death disaster, no one calls for any man. Nor does anyone call on, for instance, Jesus or Muhammad. Rather, people always call for almighty God alone.

Christ was always comfortable as God's servant, (He was) never too arrogant to submit to Him. Nor are the angels too proud to serve Him. The fact is those who feel the urge towards arrogance, who (are so arrogant that they) are too proud to serve Him, they should realize that they will be gathered before Him at judgement time. Then, He will justly reward those who have striven towards Him and furthermore will give (such true believers) even more from His generous stores (than they deserve). In contrast, He will torment the proud and arrogant ones with a violent torment. What's more, they will be without protection before God. No one will help them.

Laws for inheritance

You human race, this clear truth is now available to you, sent to you (for your benefit) by your almighty Lord. As well, We have provided you with a glorious source of inspiration. So, regarding those who have unwavering faith in God—He will bring them into His favored status. Plus, He will guide them directly to Himself.

Regarding inheritance they ask you for guidance. Tell them, "God's rules for those who leave no direct heirs are as follows:

- a surviving sister inherits one half the estate

- a surviving brother inherits the full estate

- two surviving sisters each get one third the estate

- if there are brothers and sisters, the male will receive the equivalent of two female's shares."

God makes these rules clear to you to prevent you from making errors. In fact, God has complete knowledge (of all issues).✦

◆Prior to Islaam women had no rights. In a flagrant disregard of human rights their possessions were routinely consumed. In other words, due to the fact that they were vulnerable they were simply overpowered. The Qur'aan prohibits this, being the first document in history to systematically give women key rights, including the rights to inheritance and possessions—including the right to divorce. It is the first document to establish laws to specifically protect women from being abused.

Section 5
Heavenly Feast

In the name of the most merciful
and compassionate God

You who truly believe (in God), fulfill your obligations. You are allowed to eat every type of plant-eating animal, except what has been specifically prohibited and also with the exception of hunting during pilgrimage. God makes laws which are in harmony with His system.

You true believers, never violate the rituals of God nor the sacred month nor the offerings nor those who congregate to the Holy Temple, seeking the acceptance and pleasure of their Lord. What's more, you are allowed to hunt only when you are no longer in a state of pilgrimage.✦

✦That is during the pilgrimage to Mecca only peace is allowed. There is no killing, particularly of land animals. People are to remain in absolute peace. No jealousy, anger, or arguing are allowed. There is to be no hostility of any kind. Rather, all thoughts are focused on the love and compassion of the almighty creator. People are to only think of God and must eliminate any self-centered behavior. The pilgrimage is a manifestation of the nature of paradise: total peace.

As well, never allow anger towards those who would bar you from the Great Temple lead you into the sin of aggression. Rather, work together to become more God-fearing. What's more, *never become an accomplice to the spread of hate and envy*. Rather, always keep God in mind. The fact is (for any who violate these realize that) God's retaliation is extreme.

The lawful and the forbidden

The consumption of the meat of animals which have died from unknown causes, that is carrion, as well as blood and pork,✦ is forbidden, as is meat over

✦That is due to the dangers of microbial infections as well as disease. There is no doubt about the fact that blood transmits disease. So does pork. Both are infested with microbes. For Muslims this calls into question the legality of numerous medical treatments based upon blood products such as vaccines, gamma globulin injections, and even intravenous blood. Rather than acting as cures all such treatments create diseases, including life-threatening infections and cancer. It would appear that, essentially, the Qur'aan bans the use of such treatments, except in rare instances such as the use of blood transfusions for massive blood loss or emergency surgery.

Today, in the event of need people can bank their own blood or the blood of close relatives. This would be the safest way to make use of blood products for catastrophes. It would also be more fitting with the Qur'aanic injunction regarding the danger of blood.

which has been pronounced any name besides God's (and also) animals which have been killed by strangulation, blunt trauma, those which have been gored to death or killed by a fall (as well as the) meat from an animal killed by a carnivore, the exception being whatever you have purified by slaughtering it while it was still alive.✦ What's

✦That is by cutting the throat over the mention of God's name and allowing the potentially toxic blood to drain. The blood retains both poisons and pathogens and thus must be drained.

more, anything slaughtered on idolatrous alters is prohibited. Furthermore, fortune-telling in an attempt to determine your future is also forbidden. This is a wicked act.

By now, the godless have lost all hope of you ever abandoning your way of living. Thus, rather than regarding them in awe be in awe of Me.

Now, I have perfected your way of life for you.✦

✦That is through the teachings of this Qur'aan as well as the vital example of the Prophet Muhammad. This is a complete guide for a human's life, all with the objective of gaining God's pleasure. This way of life is known in Arabic as Islaam.

Plus, I have awarded you with the full compliment of My blessings. Also, I have willed that enslavement to Me—Islaam—is your way of life.

As always, for the person who due to a dire need is forced to violate the forbidden, and not because of an inclination to sinning, surely, God is exceedingly forgiving and is generous in the giving of His mercy.

They will ask you what is lawful. Tell them, "All that is good and decent."

Regarding trained animals capable of capturing prey eat whatever they capture for you. However, mention God's name over it. What's more, remain conscious of God's presence. Certainly, God is efficient in His method of assessment.

Today, all the good things of life have been made permissible. Plus, the food of the people of scripture has also been allowed, just as your food is permissible for them. What's more, you may marry women from both the believers and from the followers of scripture, not as mistresses but rather in sincere marriage supported by the proper dowers. Yet, the person who purposely defies the truth will find that whatever he does is of no consequence. (This is because) in the next life he will be completely lost.

Before (the worship service), O believers, wash your faces, hands, and arms (up to the elbows). Then, pass your wet hands lightly over your head. Finally, wash your feet up to the ankles. What's more, if you are in need of washing completely, cleanse yourselves (fully with water). However, if you are ill, travelling, or have just answered the needs of nature or had sexual intercourse and can find no water, then (use) pure dust, passing it lightly (and symbolically) over your face and hands. God wishes to make your life as easy as possible, *because what He truly desires is that you be pure of heart.*✦ Plus, He wants to enrich you with

✦This is the essence of the Qur'aan. Rather than mere ritual it is what is *in the heart* that matters—this is the emphasis of this book. In fact, truth and decency between humans is the real purpose of the divine law. What's more, it is this on which people should focus. Mere ritual without a true commitment in the heart is of no consequence. Tis is the same as the teachings of Jesus Christ.

the full compliment of His blessings, all so that you will feel reason to be grateful. Furthermore, always remember the blessings which God has given you.

Also, never forget the promise by which He bound you to Himself, when you said, "We understand, and we will comply." Thus, remain conscious of God. Surely, God is fully aware of what is in peoples' hearts.

You true believers, be resolute in your devotion to God. Take responsibility for this truth in a just way. What's more, never allow your anger towards anyone lead you into injustice. Be just. This is the closest thing to being "of God" as possible. Also, keep God in mind at all times, because certainly God is aware of your actions.

God has promised two kinds of people, both people (who believe in Him) and (the truly dedicated) believers✦ (the latter of whom) constantly exert

✦This distinction between humans is mentioned frequently in the Qur'aan. God is obviously aware of the different levels of commitment of His humans. Mere belief in God alone is commendable, that is for good people who avoid the major sins. However, there are those special ones who strive their utmost to do His bidding. Such are heaped upon by Him vast rewards. Then, there are the derelict ones, who reject Him. All they earn is despair. Even more dire are the consequences for those who actively fight Him. They will gain a punishment which is extreme, in fact, vile.

themselves in goodness, that they will receive a great reward. In contrast, those who reject God and (willfully) defy His messages will inherit merely the agony of burning torment.

You who truly believe (in almighty God), never forget the enormous blessings which God has provided for you such as when the enemy was about to destroy you—God stopped them. Thus, always remember your duty to God, and in God let the believers place their trust.

Defiance of God: consequences

No doubt, the Israelites accepted from God a similar commitment—when We sent a group of their leaders as emissaries, and when God told them, "I will be with you." What's more, He instructed them "If you are firm in prayer and are charitable, also, if you believe in, as well as assist, My prophets—if you offer to God a useful offer—I will cleanse you of your (derogatory traits) and deliver you into the gardens of paradise. However, those who after this reject the truth will, without doubt, have greatly deviated from (what is) right."

Because they failed in their commitment We put Our curse on them. What's more, We caused their hearts✦ to become dead spiritually, as if there is

✦That is the rebellious followers of Moses, who rejected his message. They did so for mere material gain. More contemporarily, this also applies to today's defiant inheritors of the Mosaic Law.

nothing of any substance left within them, so that they now distort the meaning of the original words, taking them out of context.✦ They have lost much of

✦As such people have no heart-felt ties to almighty God they choose, instead, to fight *against* Him. These are the heartless persons, who feel no remorse for their crimes and even reject the concept of God. Such persons also reject any possibility that they will be held accountable for their acts. Yet, they are accountable for whatever they do here, that is through the laws of society.

their original commandments, which is beyond dispute.

With rare exceptions they will cause you (only) treachery. However, forgive them and remain patient. Certainly, God loves those who (consistently) do good.

Warning to the Christians against rebellion

The Christians also accepted certain obligations. They, too, neglected the majority of them. Thus, We have instilled within them hatred and jealousy, and this is how it will remain until the end of time. Yet, eventually, God will make them understand what they have (truly) contrived.

You followers of the Bible,✦ there is now before

✦It is interesting to note, here, the method of address used by the Qur'aan. It directly addresses the Christians. Even so, God is essentially also warning the Muslims against deviating from the truth, that is to not follow the example of the Christians by abandoning their original truths for mere pagan practices. In other places the Qur'aan directly addresses the Jews. Yet, in other instances it addresses godly souls in general, that is "You who believe" or "You true believers."

you Our (new) Prophet. His purpose is to make clear for you any of the misunderstandings regarding the Bible as well as bring much forgiveness. Now, you have been provided from God inspiration and an obviously divine book.✦

✦That is when compared with truths in the Bible the nature of the Qur'aan becomes obvious, which is that it is from the same divine source. Even so, largely due to racial pride many such Christians choose to reject it.

There is no sound basis for this rejection. This is because there are hundreds of examples in the Qur'aan which make it clear that this is a divine book. The possibility that it is man-made is non-existent. Surely, this book predicts the future. It also accurately describes the past, including historically correct descriptions of events occurring prior to its revelation. Is there any other book that does so? What's more, the Qur'aan clearly provides humans with guidance. Is there any other book which achieves this? Through it God illustrates for those who desire His acceptance the direction leading to salvation. What's more, by His mercy He rescues them from spiritual confusion into what is clearly the truth, guiding them to a correct destination. Prior to this book there was no such guidance. In this regard, it has brought hundreds of millions to belief in the oneness of God. Plus this guidance is directed precisely at each person. Is there any other book which does this?

They reject the truth who claim, "Christ, son of Mary, is God."✦ Ask them, "Who will prevail if God

✦While Jesus was made in the image of God—with His essence, a fact promoted in the Qur'aan—he had no God-like powers. In other words, he was merely human. He was a human *who represented the spirit of God.* Yet, this never made him God.

He obviously had no divine powers. He could create no one. All he could achieve was God's will. Without God, he was powerless. Therefore, he couldn't be a god or, God's son. Jesus' birth is no less a miracle than the creation of any original species or the original human, Adam. They are all divine miracles. Thus, he could not have been God's physical (or sexual) son. After all, God has no spouse.

were to destroy Christ, his mother, and everyone else?" Without question, God owns it all. He creates whatever He desires. He has the total authority—the (absolute) power—to will anything.

Also, the Jews and Christians claim that they are God's chosen. Ask them, "Then, why is it that according to *your interpretation* He causes you to suffer for your sins?" All of you are mere humans, part of His creation. He forgives or makes suffer whomever He wills. This is because it is God (alone) who has the rule of the entire universe✦

✦That is and thus He has the power to decide a person's ultimate status. Every human being is under His careful watch. He is not happy with the argumentative nature of the people of different faiths, particularly those who invent their own religions. Here, God Himself rejects the concept of original sin and thus the crucifixion. He also in the aforementioned statements completely rejects the possibility that Jesus or Mary have divine powers, that is 'Who would operate the universe if I were to kill Jesus, Mary, or any other who claim to be your saviors?' Rather than such nonsensical concepts He demands that humans follow precisely what He reveals, whether to Moses, Jesus, Muhammad, or any other. Proclaims the Qur'aan this is the absolute truth. All else is man-made babble. In particular, He reminds the Christians that they are to adhere to the principles of any new revelation, that is this Qur'aan, and do so without hesitation. In fact, God commands all monotheists, the Christians, Jews, and Muslims, to hold firmly to the dictates of this book. Then, He reminds such people that they will have no excuse for refusing to do so, when, inevitably, all humans are presented before Him.

(and thus will decide your ultimate status). What's more (He really does have ultimate power, because), all that exists culminates with Him.

You followers of the Bible, after a prolonged intermission in the procession of the prophets this (new) revelation has appeared. His purpose is to make the message clear to you, so you have no excuse. It is so you will be unable to say "No one came to inspire or warn us." Without doubt, now, someone has come to do precisely that, since God has the power (over this process).

The lost and confused tribes of Israel

It was Moses who instructed his people (saying), "Always remember the favors of God with which you have been blessed—He gave you numerous prophets and made you masters (of your own fate), while granting you unusual favors that no one else previously received." He also said (to his followers), "Enter this special land, which God has promised you. Yet, be sure to hold stringently to your faith, otherwise, you may lose it."

They answered, "Moses (we are scared): you are well aware that a powerful people live there. We wouldn't consider going there until those people leave, and only then will we do so." Then, two of their men, who were real believers (and who held only God as all-powerful)—and whom God had inspired—said "Go to them without hesitation. Without doubt, as soon as you enter you will prevail. If you truly believe, it is in God alone that you must trust." Despite this they said, "Moses, as long as there are such tough people there, we will never enter that region. You go and fight them, you and your God. We will stay here." Then, Moses prayed, "My Lord, I can only control myself and my brother (Aaron). Thus, make a clear distinction between us and these wicked people." God's response was, "Surely, this promised (land that they had hoped for) will be forbidden to them for decades. As a result, they will wander, completely perplexed. What's more, feel no sorrow regarding these evil people."

The parable of Cain and Abel

Also, tell them about Adam's two sons, where each of them offered a sacrifice. However, it was only accepted from one of them. (As a result,) the other said "(I am so jealous of you) I will kill you." His brother replied, "Without question, God accepts (the actions) only of those who truly believe in Him. Thus, if you attempt to kill me, I choose to restrain myself from doing likewise. This is because I am in awe of God, the Lord of all the worlds."

He continued, "I am willing for you to assume the burden of all the sins I have ever committed but also your own sins. Then, you would be destined for the eternal torment, since this is the (appropriate) retaliation for the wretched." Yet, alas (despite this warning) the other's passion impelled him to kill his own brother, and, in fact, he murdered him and thus became one of the lost. As a result, God sent the raven: it dug at the earth (as a sign for how he should bury the corpse). Thus, he moaned, "O what misery have I caused (for myself). I am unable even to achieve what this raven has done—to hide this." As a result, he was consumed with remorse.✦

✦That is the thought of having to dispose of the body—to actually physically deal with the crime—caused him to realize the scope of his sin. God desired him to face what he had done in this life for his own sake, that Cain alone bore responsibility. This was due to God's mercy, so that perhaps he would approach God in sincere remorse for the sake of his own soul.

Because of this We made a commandment for the Israelites, that is if anyone kills a human being wrongfully (the exceptions being in the justice against murder or in the war against corruption), it will be as if he had murdered all humankind. In contrast, if anyone saves a life, it will be as if he saved the life of all humankind.

Yet, clearly, We always sent to humankind Our messengers, representing the obvious truth. However, despite this (warning) many of them continue to commit considerable evil.

It is a just result that regarding those who fight against God and His Messenger, huge numbers of them, that is those who purposely incite tyranny (against the true believers), will be eliminated. Or, huge numbers of them will be caused to suffer for their crimes (until their deaths). Or, because of their sinful behavior in great numbers they will be rendered helpless (unable to function), or they may be banished from the face of the earth. This is their punishment in this world. Yet, in the next life there will be even greater torment. The exception is those who are truly sorrowful and beg forgiveness, while correcting their (errant) ways (that is) before you, O believers, become more powerful than they. Surely, God forgives greatly and is exceptionally generous (in His mercy to His servants).

You true believers, always keep God in mind. What's more, always seek to get closer to Him.✦

✦That is by keeping Him deeply in mind at all times and by even attempting to develop a deeper and more profound relationship with Him. This is a conscious effort to develop a relationship with God. It is also to never become distant from Him by always thinking about Him, while also seeking His forgiveness. It is also by doing the utmost to do good, all in order to gain His pleasure.

Furthermore, strive with your fullest capacity in His cause.

Surely, if those rebellious ones offered as ransom all that exists on this earth—even double it—to avoid the torment of resurrection, it would be refused. What's more, they will eventually be punished severely. They will wish to escape from that agony, however, they will be unable to do so, and instead their torment will be prolonged.

Also, whether male or female punish the thief by cutting off the hand. This is the divine deterrent.✦

✦The term thief implies the person who maliciously and habitually steals. Obviously, depending on the circumstances there is an allowance here *not* to choose the more extreme punishment. Then, while the deterrent is effective and useful there are exceptions. Yet, God despises corruption, and one such corruption is theft. Thus, this deterrent helps prevent human harm, which is the real purpose of this book. It also prevents the vast financial disasters that result from relentless theft.

When there are no deterrents, theft becomes pervasive. As a result innocent people are routinely brutalized. God despises such oppression and brutality. Consider the virtual routine occurrences in the United States of such vileness. Consider the countless billions stolen from people as a result of the Enron debacle. Consider also the countless billions stolen through various scams, as well as shoplifting, plus actual theft of peoples' belongings. All such acts are regarded by God as vile. So, He initiated the most effective deterrent conceivable, as outlined in this book.

Furthermore, God is mighty in His power and exceptionally wise. However, the person who sins and who afterwards repents and makes amends— God will accept it. This is because God forgives much and is totally generous (in the mercy he gives to His servants).

Are you unaware (of the fact) that all that exists in the heavens, as well as on earth, belongs to God? He punishes whomever He wills and forgives whomever He wills. There is no doubt about it, God has the power to determine whatever He wills.

My Messenger, never be pained by those godless ones, who give only tacit approval to belief in God. Also, feel no anguish regarding the Jews, who revel in entertaining lies and who (instead of this certain guidance) focus on error, with no interest in the truth. They distort the meaning of revelation, taking it out of context, essentially saying (to themselves), "I agree with certain aspects (of the divine law) but disagree with others."✦

✦That is, commonly, people agree with the basic concepts of the divine word such as 'belief,' 'compassion,' and 'peace.' However, then, they argue about firm divine rules, even refusing to accept them. They reject regulations such as the aforementioned deterrent for malicious theft. They argue against corporal punishment, deterrents against adultery, the banning of usury, and similar divine laws. So, they refuse to accept the entire divine system and rather choose only what suits them.

Thus, never be distressed regarding them, because if God wills for anyone to pursue evil, no one can stop it. God is unwilling to purify such people. They will suffer disgrace in this world as well as dire agony in the next one. This is the (inevitable) consequence of those who strive to lend credibility to any false statement as well as those who greedily pursue their own immoral gains. Therefore, if in order to get your opinion or arbitration on what is right they seek your assistance, either referee the issue or avoid them. This is because if you avoid them, they could never harm you. However, if you act as a referee, do so with justice, being fair to all parties. Absolutely, God knows those who are just in their dealings.

Yet, why would they ask you to make an assessment? They have the Torah, which contains God's commandments. Even so, they reject it. These are the type of people who lack true belief.

The Torah as an original divine book

Without question, the Torah was (originally) sent by God almighty, a book full of guidance and inspiration. The dedicated prophets of the past relied upon it to maintain law and order for the followers of Judaism, followed by the God-fearing rabbis and other men of God, who were entrusted by God with a portion of divine writings. Therefore, rather than to other human beings, you Jews, be in awe of/humbled before only Me. What's more (you followers of the Torah), never neglect My messages for an insignificant gain. For certain, those who use as the determinant other than My special revelations are the real leaders in godlessness.

Moreover, through the Torah it is authorized, equal repayment for sins: a life for a life, an eye for an eye, a nose for a nose, an ear for an ear, a tooth for a tooth, and similar retribution.✦ However,

✦This statement merely reinforces the earlier Qur'aanic dictum against theft. God is well aware that many Christians and Jews will depict the divine punishment as "cruel." Yet, they largely do so to portray Islaam as barbaric. This is despite the fact that, incredibly, that precise punishment had already been confirmed in their scriptures. So, now, the basis for the attack against Islaam is clarified. It is merely hate mongering based upon jealousy and pride, that is the pride arising from the view that unless it is in *their* ancestral way it must be refuted. Yet, precisely the scripture they attack—this Qur'aan—is written by the same God who revealed the Torah, a fact attested to in the aforementioned, and contains many of the same principles as found in the more ancient books.

whoever as a good deed forgives will have some of his previous sins erased. In addition, those who refuse to base judgement upon God's (merciful) rules are truly treacherous.

The true message of the Gospels

As a mercy We caused Jesus (Mary's son) to adhere to the way of the previous prophets. His purpose was to reestablish the truth from whatever remained of the previous scriptures (revelations which serve as) guidance and warning to those who hold God in awe. Thus, the followers of the Gospel should base their faith upon what is (truly) revealed by God (within the Bible). Clearly, the real criminals are those who refuse to use God's inspiration as the basis (of their lives).

So, We have provided you this (new) divine book as a privilege. It establishes the truth and confirms the remnants of the former truths. Thus, regarding the people of scripture make your assessment based upon these truths. What's more, beware of following their erroneous views and thus abandoning this inspiration.✦

✦That is 'hold strictly to the principles of this Qur'aan, since it is from God almighty, and never succumb to the whims and wishes of people of other faiths.' Muslims are hereby ordered to adhere firmly to the Qur'aan, because it is the undiluted truth from almighty God. This book is their guide. It alone teaches the person's duties. By adhering to it this is their only 'guarantee' for salvation.

The Qur'aan is unaltered. It is obvious divine revelation. In contrast, the Bible has been abundantly altered. Thus, the Qur'aan is the most sound choice for ultimate guidance. Even so, Muslims are obligated to believe in the existing truths remaining in the Bible, Torah, and Gospels.

Yet, if only Christians and Jews abided by such a mandate, that is to believe in all the various divine books, truly, it would be to their benefit. This is because they would succeed in their test from God and would, thus, earn His vast mercy. Even so, they neglect this mandate. In fact, through their own scriptures they are obliged to follow the new revelation, fully mandated in the Bible. Yet, few if any Christians and Jews will recognize it. What a loss, because the Qur'aan fully supports their own truths and gives credibility to their revelations.

Each person has been given by God a unique purpose. Each has been given a means of livelihood. Yet, God could have made you all the same. However, the purpose of this is to test you—by means of the favors He has (given you). Thus, if you must compete, do so in being good and decent.✦

✦Here, God commands people never to compete through jealousy. This highly destructive emotion can lead to great harm. He had already mentioned the story of Cain and Abel. Here, He reiterates the warning. It is for people to desist regarding all competition based upon envy and jealousy and instead to cooperate in the performance of good deeds. This is the only competition commanded by God. It is also the only one which produces ultimate results.

Ultimately, you will (all) return to God. Then, He will make clear the basis of your conflicts.

Again, regarding the people of scripture make your assessments based upon this revelation. Additionally, never follow their erroneous views. Beware of them (due to the concern) that they cause you to abandon your divine revelation. Furthermore, if they choose to reject this, realize that it is only because of God's will to inflict (His wrath) upon them due to some of their behavior.

Then, clearly, a great number of people are truly wicked. Do they, in fact, want to have their lives determined by paganism, mere ancient ignorance?✦

✦That is many of the Biblical dictums derive from pagan rites. These rites were incorporated into the scriptures, all by the powerful rulers at the time or by various religious authorities for their own corrupt and selfish gains. Even though He revealed the original Bible God rejects all such man-made elements as fraudulent and destructive. In contrast, the Qur'aan is free of all fabrications. It is pure divine revelation, proven even by top Western historians. Plus, it is fully recognized that in Arabic all copies of the Qur'aan are the same. Thus, clearly, it is unaltered by the hands of man. What's more, its source is obviously almighty God. So, truly, this is the only reliable source to use, the only unaltered divine law available.

True, a person may refuse to believe in it. However, as is abundantly clear from this translation it is impossible to dispute the fact that it is from God. It is also impossible to dispute that in its creation humans had nothing to do with it.

Yet, think about it, that is for people of inner certainty, could there be a better law-giver than God?

You who truly believe (in almighty God and in this revelation), never take (potentially hostile) Christians and Jews as (intimate) allies.✦ The fact is

♦The Arabic word for allies also means "close associates." It also means one who 'guards over your safety.' In other words, it is a person upon whom you can depend. What's more, it means 'protection.' It is well known that under Christian or Jewish powers, for instance, the Palestinians under the Israelis or those Muslims held under U.S. authority in Guantanamo or Abu Ghraib, the Muslims have fared miserably. Thus, Muslims must maintain their own authority structure, in other words, they can never expect justice from Christian or Jewish powers. Having friends and even wives as Christians or Jews is perfectly acceptable. However, in the inner circle of this religion or in the realm of political control Christians and Jews are not allowed to hold positions of authority, just as on an inner church council there would be no Muslims or Jews.

they are allies of each other. Any of you who allies with them becomes one of them. Surely, God will never guide such perpetrators of evil. Yet, you observe the sick ones, whose hearts are diseased, virtually running after each other, as if to say, "We (desire each other's protection) in case circumstances go against us." Yet, God may turn (those very) circumstances (in favor of His true servants), when those (who are His adversaries) will experience only regret regarding what they had secretly harbored in their hearts. In contrast, the true believers will say (to each other), "Are these any other than the same people who swore in God's name that they were, without doubt, on your side?" Their actions are in vain, because surely they truly are lost.

You true believers, if you ever abandon your faith, eventually, God will replace you with a different people, and there is no doubt about it (they will be a people) who He will love and who will love Him, who are gentle towards the believers and stern against the godless ones who reject the truth, who work with their fullest effort in every possible means in God's way. What's more, they are the ones who have no fear of being censured by any who might (attempt to do so). This is the nature of God's favor, which He dispenses upon whomever He wills. Certainly, God is infinite in His powers, the One who knows all.

(Yet, you need no other, because) your companion is God, this being beyond doubt, and also His Messenger, as well as any fellow true believers, those who are truly dedicated in their worship and are charitable in their acts, who are genuinely humble before God. Furthermore, whoever becomes a true friend of God and His (selected) Messenger, as well as the true believers, surely, they are the ones who are the true party of God— the real (and ultimate) winners.

You true believers, never make as your (intimate associates) those Christians, Jews, and also godless ones, who (make it their purpose to) denigrate your way (of life). So, always keep God in mind, that is if you are sincere (in your belief in Him). In addition, when you make the call to prayer, they mock it—all because they are a people who refuse to use their reason.

Tell them, "You followers of the Bible, will you torment us for no other reason than that we believe firmly in God and *all His scriptures*, ours as well as the earlier ones (including yours)? Or, is your resistance of this fact merely a proof of your godlessness?"

Tell them (also), "You followers of the Bible, should I inform you who in God's view is worse (than these jesters)? It is those whom

God has rejected and who have, therefore, earned His condemnation—who He has turned into (essentially,) apes and pigs,✦ because (rather

✦That is due to their mindless rejection of God and also their refusal to heed His messages. They are no different than mere beasts, devoid of intellect—devoid of that higher element that responds to reason and common sense. In fact, because of their insolence beasts are closer than they are to the right way. Like pigs and apes they are unable to respond to any attempt to contact them and to cause them to think. Despite all efforts to guide them they grovel along in their degeneration. When given clear evidence of the truth, they are unable to respond. No one can guide them. Nor will God do so, since they have made it their goal to reject Him.

than God after being so perfectly guided) they worshiped the powers of hate. These are more deeply in error than even those who belittle (this religion)."

Yet, when (such people) come to you, they say, "We really do believe (in your religion)." However, in fact, their real goal is (through deception) to reject the truth, so they begin as false in their belief and (despite guidance) depart✦ in the same

✦That is when they die. So, because of their rejection God allows them to leave this earth in a low state. These are the people who not only refuse to believe but also actively attempt to obstruct people from coming to this faith.

condition. Even so, God is fully aware of whatever they attempt to disguise.

Furthermore, you will observe many of them rushing recklessly into vile deeds, as well as (engaging in) tyrannical behavior—consuming themselves in all that is wicked. Why is it that their spiritual guides make no effort to censor their vile claims, failing to advise them against gorging (themselves) upon all that is godless? Without doubt, their fabrications are vile.

Yet, the Jews say, "God's hand's are tied (in terms of His generosity)." Rather, their hands are the ones which are tied (and it is they who are unable to do anything). Furthermore, they are condemned by God for their statements, surely, God is capable of assisting anyone He desires. He gives (profusely) of His generosity to whomever He wills. However, all that has been given (to the true believers) from the heavens by your Lord, in fact, merely increases their aversion, making them even more stubborn in their rejection.

Thus, We have disseminated among them jealousy and hatred, that is competition, among the followers of the Bible.✦ (This is how it will be) to the end of

✦That is rather than holding to a bond of mutual love for God and real dedication to His service these groups compete for material position. The various Christian sects are fiercely competitive. None of them come together as a group. Islaam commands the opposite, that is stating categorically that the true believers are a single unit. In fact, it bans sectarianism, mandating that all Muslims are one brotherhood. There is no Shia or Sunni nor any other kind of group. Yet, unfortunately, even the Muslims have neglected to adhere to this, themselves developing sects. Even so, Islaam commands that regardless of denomination the believer must assist all people through goodness.

The Qur'aan also warns the Christians to seek communion with Him as a group and end all differences. It also warns the Muslims against this propensity, while the Prophet Muhammad deemed anyone who promotes sectarianism and therefore creates divisions within Islaam as decidedly non-Muslim.

time—until resurrection. Every time thcy incite warfare God halts it. What's more, they work extensively to foment corruption—yet, God has no love for those who spread corruption.

If the followers of the Bible would truly believe in (this true and untarnished faith) and completely keep God in mind, then, clearly, We would cleanse them of (any sins)—and without doubt cause them to arrive in the delightful gardens (of paradise), the ultimate success. What's more, if they would even merely (and truly) observe the ancient scriptures, the Old Testament, as well as the Gospels, and the full principles of the revelations they were given by their Lord, they would, certainly (as a reward), be able to gain all the blessings of the entire universe as well as this earth.

Certainly, some of them do what is right. However, regarding the majority their actions are absolutely vile.

You Messenger of God, make known all that has been revealed to you from your Lord, because without doubt, unless you do it fully it will be as if you delivered no message at all. What's more (realize that), God will protect you (from any of their devious plots). God never guides those who reject His messages.

So, tell the people of scripture, "You followers of the Bible, you have no basis for your faith unless you truly establish the divine law as found in the (original) holy books as well as this more modern one (that is this Qur'aan).◆ Yet, clearly, this message

---

◆That is by completely submitting to the revelations of almighty God. In true Christianity or Judaism, as represented by the actual teachings of Moses and Jesus, there is no "God and country." Moses, as well as Jesus, would reject such an attitude as pagan. Rather, in the true essence of these faiths, as well as in Islaam, there is only God and His laws as well as the ways of His messengers. To shirk this is the same as rejecting God Himself.

of yours (O Muhammad), will merely increase their scorn, making them even more arrogant than they already are, so that they reject the truth even more resolutely. However, feel no sorrow for them who, obviously, reject (this message).

Yet, no doubt (those) who truly do believe in (this truthful revelation), as well as all other true believers in (the one) God—all who truly believe in God and the final event, as well as do what is right, they have no reason to have fear or remorse. Nor shall they grieve.

Without doubt, We accepted the commitment of the descendants of Israel and also sent (a plethora) of prophets to them. However, every time such a prophet preached to them whatever failed to suit their desires they became rebellious. They categorically rejected some of them, while murdering others. Believing that they were immune from harm they (allowed themselves to become) oblivious (of God). Even so, God accepted their repentance, and, again, many of them became oblivious. Yet, God is completely aware of all their actions.

Claim of Jesus' divinity disputed

Surely, they greatly err when they claim, "Jesus (who is, in fact, the son of Mary) is God." In contrast, this very man said, "You children of Israel, worship God (alone who is), my Lord as well as your Lord."✦

✦Jesus' message was simple. All he asked was for people to obey God. This was, he made clear, for their own benefit. Too, he never proclaimed the trinity. This is a man-made addition, strictly fabricated. So, somehow, through the centuries his pure message was corrupted, leading to vast confusion as well as much hypocrisy.

Even so, Jesus never promoted himself as a kind of God. Rather, he always deferred to the creator, who he called, appropriately, God. (See *The Secret Scripture They Don't Want You to Know About.*) He also called this Being the Lord. He made Him his object of worship, because he knew that to claim any other as all-powerful was a mortal sin. In fact, his entire purpose was to bring people to God alone.

Then, whoever makes as divine any being other than God, definitely, God will deny paradise. What's more, his destiny will be the torment, and such people who commit evil will have no one to aid them.

They certainly reject (the entire basis of God) who claim, "There is no doubt (in our minds) that God is one of three (that is the trinity)," due to the fact that there is no god other than the almighty one God. Moreover, unless they desist in this claim they will endure only agony—these people who reject the truth. Will they, then, refuse to turn to God in sincere remorse (for their crimes) and sincerely beg His forgiveness?

The Christ (Mary's son,) was merely a messenger of God. Moreover, his mother was a truly dedicated servant, never deviating from the truth. Furthermore, both of them, like other mortals, ate food. See how clear We make these signs to them. Yet, how truly deranged is their thinking. Tell them, "Are you willing to instead of God worship (a being) who is incapable of either helping or harming you, while in contrast God alone can hear and respond to your calls (the One), who knows all things?"✦

✦This is a critical distinction. When a person is in any sudden crisis—a life threatening event—to whom does he/she call? Is it any other than God? All people know that in the most dire need it is only almighty God who is the real savior. He is the only One whose name people beseech when they face dire crises. The Christ Jesus is incapable of saving anyone. Furthermore, he has no power to help anyone on the planet. Thus, when a person is confronted with a sullen life-threatening disaster, such as a plane crash or violent natural disaster, would such a person call to, for instance, Moses or Jesus? The answer is obvious.

Tell the followers of the (Christian scriptures), "Never violate (the deep truths) of your faith—never do so by following the errant ways of the previous people (of your religion), who deviated and who caused numerous others to deviate or those who, today, continue to do so."✦

✦That is due to being misguided by the earlier adherents, who corrupted Christian or Jewish law to suit their own desires—corrupted it to such a degree that the truth is indistinguishable from the false.

A careful, that is unbiased, reading of the Bible makes this obvious. Truly, within it there are man-made elements, which confuse the divine. Yet, this is not the case with the Qur'aan, since it is the only unaltered divine revelation available.

Regarding the (Jews) who deliberately reject the truth they have already been condemned—by the very words spoken by David as well as Jesus. This is because they, in fact, rejected (God's messages) and were determined in this transgression. What's more, they failed as a community to work together to prevent the commission of hateful and wrong acts. Truly, their achievements are wicked.

You will also observe many of them attempting to befriend the godless ones, who reject this message. Without doubt, their actions are so wretched, driven by mere passion, that God has fully condemned them to the torment, their permanent consequence. The fact is if they truly believed in God and (the prophet they claim as theirs)—if they truly believed in their scriptures—they would never side with the godless. Yet (they do so because), instead of having any genuine belief most of them are vile transgressors.

Yet, without doubt, you will determine that the Jews and their fellow Christians, who hold other powers as divine besides God, are the most hostile (to this divine revelation). You will also determine that those who say, "We truly are Christians" (who truly believe in the scriptures), are the closest to having fellow love for you. This is because there, in fact, are priests and monks, who (are devoted to God) and who are truly humble (and never show any arrogance). This is because when they realize the nature of this revelation, you can observe how they react and how they even become overwhelmed with tearful emotions—because they recognize within it the very truths in which they have always believed. Furthermore, they say, "Our Lord, we really do believe (in the truth of this message). Thus, make us of the propensity to submit to its truth. What's more, how could we not believe in whatever truth we are exposed to, since we so fervently desire Your favor?"

Because of their belief God will reward them with pure gardens coursed with pure running water. This will be their (permanent) home. Such is the (ultimate) reward for those who do good. In contrast, those who reject the truth and what's more purposely fight against it gain only agony.

You true believers, take (full) advantage of the good things of life that God has allowed for you.✦

✦That is 'never deprive yourselves' of what God has allowed. Never invent laws or restrictions, besides what God has restricted. That would be essentially demonstrating a kind of ingratitude, to reject precisely what God has provided. So, according to the Qur'aan true believers must pursue all the good things in this life to their fullest and happily enjoy God's glorious blessings.

However, never go beyond the (set boundaries); surely, God does not love any who violate what is right. Thus (again), take advantage of the goodly provisions provided to you by God. What's more, keep God constantly in mind, in whom you (claim to) believe.

God will never hold you responsible for commitments you have made arbitrarily. Rather, He will only hold you responsible for those which you have made binding. Thus, the atonement for the breaking of (such a) commitment is to feed ten poor people with essentially the same food that you eat or by providing them with clothing— or by freeing a human (wrongly) held captive. Additionally, whoever is unable (to do so) must instead fast for three days. This is the atonement for (the breaking of) any sworn promises. Even so, be mindful of your commitments (and promises).

This is how God makes obvious for you His commandments, all so that you will have reason to feel gratitude.✦

✦That is, essentially, 'You have also made a commitment to your Lord—never violate it'. This is a kind of parable, where God reminds all people that any solemn oath, including the oath to obey God, if broken, requires atonement. Can there be a more solemn commitment than to promise God, hoping for His favors and then after He dispenses those favors to violate Him? Then, if this was broken, do people consider it? Do not humans consider their oaths to other humans as binding? It is far more serious to make a promise to God and then violate it. The point is this, too, requires atonement to cleanse the heart of sin and to gain a closer bond with Him.

Prohibitions

You true believers, alcoholic beverages (and other intoxicants), gambling, and attempting to predict the future through sorcery are truly the works of the devil. Thus, shun them, so that you will avoid damaging yourselves. Through intoxicants and gambling the devil seeks to hurt you and particularly to make you neglect the remembrance of God as well as being obedient (to Him). Then (after becoming aware of it), will you persist in those acts?

Additionally, follow the way of God and His Messenger, and be wary of (succumbing to) evil. What's more, if you reject this, then, realize that the only responsibility of Our Messenger is to deliver a clear warning (which We have given him).

Those true believers who do good incur no sin by taking advantage of whatever We have legalized, as long as they keep God in mind, truly and sincerely believing in Him, while also being diligent in doing good. Surely, God loves those who do good.

Rules relating to the pilgrimage to Mecca

You true believers, God will, without doubt, test you through (for instance,) the game within your sights (and which can be killed with your weapons, that is during pilgrimage).✦ This is so that God might

✦This relates to the early Muslims, who lived throughout Arabia. Game was scarce, and the gathering of food was a chore. So, it was tempting to shoot any game that was within reach. People were famished, and the gathering of food was a constant challenge. Thus, this was a test for the truth of the faith of these early Muslims. Yet, its message is universal, in other words, if God makes a ruling—and the fact is His rulings and prohibitions are few—why violate it, that is unless the person's entire objective is to defy Him?

distinguish those who are truly in awe of Him, even though they are unable to sense Him. What's more, regarding the person who (after such warnings) violates God's dictates, certainly, he will earn only torment.

You true believers, kill no (wild) game while you are in a state of pilgrimage. What's more, anyone who does so—doing it intentionally—must make amends through an equivalent in a domesticated animal, with two reliable people from the believers as judges—to be brought to the Abrahamic house of worship (of Mecca) as an offering, or he may make amends in kind through feeding the poor or fasting. This is so that he will experience the full gravity of his act. Yet, whoever repeats this (excess), God will (Himself) take retribution against him. Certainly, God is a mighty avenger of evil.✦

✦This is a prohibition from killing any living being during this holy rite. That is particularly true of mammals, which are living beings with significant souls. This worship ritual is bound by peace. Thus, the shedding of any blood is prohibited. During this time the land about Mecca is sanctified, and thus only peace and love, the love of God, are allowed. The only sacrifice which is allowed occurs after the ritual service has culminated. So, during this ritual millions of people comply—the teeming masses of humanity, all withholding themselves from bloodshed or physical harm. This is a kind of proof that, truly, humankind could be civilized.

Even so, there is an allowance for bloodshed. It is if the true believers are attacked. Here, they must fully defend themselves and strike back with equal force. This is true, even in the surrounds of Mecca, even within the grounds of the Kaaba. Ayatollah Khomeini correctly made it clear that in the war against oppression Mecca may even be used as a staging ground for launching attacks. The point is that while the ritual is important it is of minor importance compared to the war against tyranny. Of note, the Prophet Muhammad spent only a few hours of his life performing pilgrimage, in fact, only performing the full act once. In contrast, he spent his entire life fighting the elements of corruption.

Every square inch of this earth remains diseased until oppression is eliminated. Thus, the battle against tyranny may legitimately be carried to all parts of this earth, even in holy sites. This is because as God makes abundantly clear oppression is vile and must be fought by all means necessary. It is even more vile than killing.

All produce of the seas is lawful (and you may catch fish) as a provision for you, whether settled or during transit. What's more (again), it is only land game that you are forbidden to kill (while you are in this sanctified state). Furthermore, always keep God in mind, to whom you will all be gathered.

God has established that the Abrahamic house of worship, the Sacred Temple (of Mecca), the token offerings, as well as the sacred month (of pilgrimage)—all serve to awaken people to an increased awareness that God is fully knowledgeable regarding all that is in the heavens and on earth and that God is fully aware—fully informed. Realize, too, that God is severe in avenging (all evil) as well as that God forgives greatly and is truly merciful.

The Messenger's only duty is to deliver the message. What's more, God is well aware of all that you reveal and all that you (attempt to) disguise.

Tell them, "The good and the bad (that is vile), cannot be compared, even though the bad may *seem* pleasurable." Then, keep God in mind at all times, so that you will achieve true (and permanent) pleasure.

You true believers, never demand (of God) regarding issues that, if disclosed, would cause you difficulty. What's more, if you demand them while the Qur'aan is being revealed, they may, in fact, be disclosed. God has freed you of any obligation in this regard, because God forgives extensively and is truly gentle, patient (regarding human inadequacies). In fact, people previously demanded (that issues be revealed) and as a result proved themselves as false.

(For instance,) it wasn't God's doing that certain kinds of domesticated animals would be through superstition disallowed for human use. Yet, those who are determined to reject the truth characterize their own fabrications as God's. What's more, the majority of them fail to give this any consideration, proven by the fact that when they are told, "Come to precisely that revelation which arises from the high God—and believe in His Messenger"—(yet), they respond, "Our families have always worshiped (a certain way), and that is how we will (worship)," even though (incredibly), their (ancestral) families were oblivious of the truth, devoid of (all) guidance.

You true believers, you are only responsible for yourselves; you cannot be harmed by those who deviate, that is as long as (God keeps you) properly directed.

Without question, ultimately, all of you will be returned to God, no exceptions. What's more, then, He will cause you to truly understand (your real intentions).

Preparation of a will

You true believers, when faced with death at the making of any (legitimate) will, have two (respected) persons (from among your fellow believers) present—or if death approaches while you are traveling abroad, two others (from whoever is available). After praying, make the witnesses hold to it, and hold onto their hands, if necessary, that is if you have any doubts, make them swear to you (to properly administer your will) over God's name, saying, "We will never sell you short for any price, even if it were for a close relative—and we will never hide the testimony before God for fear that we will be (held accountable by God as) sinners."

Yet, even after this if it becomes known that the witnesses did, in fact, violate their commitment, then, two others from the victimized party (or parties) will replace them and will, too, swear by God, affirming that their testimony is surely more true than the testimony of the former (two) witnesses, testifying that they will not violate the dictates of what is right, "for fear we will be registered as sinners."

This approach will improve the odds that people will abide by what is right, that they will offer honest testimony—because they would now be hesitant to make false claims knowing that others would refute them. So, keep God (always) in mind, and regard seriously His commandments. What's more, God never guides any who act wickedly.

Then, beware of the time when God will assemble all the (various warners and messengers) and will ask, "How were you (ultimately) received?" They will respond, "We are unaware of it. You alone know (what truly happened)."

Lessons relating to the faith and nature of Jesus

Even so, without doubt (during resurrection) God will say, "O Jesus (Mary's son), remember the loving kindness which I provided for you, as well as your mother, how I empowered you with the Holy Spirit, so you (could) speak to human beings in your cradle as well as a grown man. (Also, remember) how I taught you wisdom, as well as (provided you with the authority of) the Torah and Gospel, and how through My allowance you molded and shaped (through parables and your own example) the true destiny of your followers. What's more, you breathed your essence into it, so that through My allowance it might become their destiny and how you healed the blind and the leper through My allowance—and how through My allowance you truly revived the (spiritually and physically) dead. Also (recall), how when you represented the obvious truth to them (they rebelled), and I *prevented the Israelites from harming you*, when the godless ones said, "This is merely magic."

What's more, recall the time when I inspired the (original disciples) with, "Believe in Me and in My Messenger." They responded, "*We already do believe*, and, what's more, we are fully committed to You."✦Then (incredibly), the disciples said, "You

✦That is they were being tested by God to see if they truly did believe. This was in order to be sure that Jesus could develop a reliable team, which could withstand the great trials of spreading this message. Yet, no sooner did they attest to firm belief than He challenged them with a test which, to a degree, they failed. The fear of the power of the Roman Empire surely played a role in the vacillation in faith of some of Jesus' original followers.

our Prophet Jesus, ask your Lord to deliver us a feast from the heavens" Jesus responded, "If you truly believe, be mindful of God." They said, "We desire to enjoy such a feast, so that we might set our hearts to rest to be sure that what you say is real—so that we might truly commit ourselves to (this faith)."

Then, Jesus said, "God our true Lord: Deliver for us a feast from the heavens, so that it will be a joyous occasion for us—as if a permanent feast for all of us who believe—a sign from You." God answered, "Without doubt, I always provide it— and, thus, if any (after this reminder) rejects this truth, certainly, on such a person I inflict an extreme punishment—a punishment like no one has ever before (inflicted) in this world."

Conversation between Jesus and God

Yet, certainly, God (ultimately) asked him, "O Jesus, did you ever say to the people 'Worship me and my mother as Lords, along with God'?" Jesus answered, "In your glory, God, You are absolutely beyond any limit, and You are so high. It is not even remotely possible for me to say what I have no right to say. Had I said this, surely, you would know it. You are aware of all that is within my very self, but I am unable to know what is within You. Without doubt, only You know all that is beyond human reach. I only told them what You ordered me (that is): 'Worship exclusively your high God, who is my Lord as well as your Lord.' What's more, I was only aware of their actions while I was on earth."

"However, since You have caused me to die, only You have been witnessing (their actions). Yet, in fact, You are the witness, who observes all (their actions).✦ If You should determine to cause them

---

✦That is the beliefs and actions of the supposed followers of Christ. As the entire section emphasizes, Jesus has no inherent power. Nor will he be able to help those who have so erred. The conclusion in his own words is that he will be incapable of helping anyone. Nor will he be able to either ward off punishment or dispense rewards.

---

to suffer, without doubt, they are Your creatures, while if You determine to forgive them, certainly, You alone are almighty, absolutely wise (in how You administer justice)."

Yet, ultimately, at the time of judgement (when He weighs all issues) God will say, "Now, the truthful (nature) of those who were true to their commitments (to their Lord is evident): they will own lush gardens, where they will live for eternity. God is truly pleased with them, and they are truly pleased with Him." This is the highest possible achievement, a victory of the most profound degree.

God owns all the universes,✦the high heavens,

✦Notice, here, that the Qur'aan mentions the word universe *in plural*. It may also be translated as *worlds*. The fact is this is the latest finding in modern science. Recently, it was estimated by physicists that besides the known universe there are untold thousands, perhaps millions, of other universes, containing yet further countless billions of galaxies and life forms. What's more, it has now been confirmed that the universe actively generates life. Furthermore, life-generating dust, the matter which gave rise to humans, is continuously produced. This is occurring in untold billions of regions in the universe(s). Therefore, the realm of almighty God is unlimited, far beyond human comprehension. This section demonstrates who is the real savior, the only One who has the capacity to forgive.

Those who hope for Jesus' intervention are in for a shock. He has no power to in any way protect a human. Nor can he guarantee anyone's salvation.

---

the earth, and their entire contents. What's more, He has the power to determine, as well as achieve, anything.

Section 6
Superstitions

In the name of the most merciful
and compassionate God

All praise is due to God, the One who created the vast universe as well as the earth (the creator of the entire concept and reality of) intense darkness and light.✦ Yet, those who reject the

✦That is the deep, vast darkness of the expanding universe, as well as its brilliant star-given light—but also the oppressive darkness of the godless soul versus the beaming brilliance of the truly enlightened believer in God.

The darkness of such a soul is due to the lack of any understanding of his true nature as a servant of almighty God. So, humans have no right to be arrogant. They are merely one of His endless unique species. It is the darkness of failing to realize that God is his owner as well as friend. This is the greatest loss, the most profound darkness conceivable.

truth (of His creative powers) deem others as their Lord's equals.

He created you *of the earth*. Then, He decreed a life span for you, which He alone knows. Yet, you doubt it,✦ despite the fact that He is the Great One,

✦That is the inevitable return to Him during the era of accountability. In other words, most people refuse to believe they will be held accountable for their actions. Yet, in this life people accept accountability. For instance, criminals are held fully accountable. Routinely, a person who violates a civil law, for example, traffic laws, is penalized. Then, too, the violation of divine laws is punishable. Thus, in God's realm punishment, as well as reward, are meted out based upon a person's achievements. So, invariably, the same people who deny God's ability to take account fully accept the right for the governmental system—the authority of state and police force—to hold people accountable. This shows that their rejection of God is baseless.

the great God of the vast and high heavens, as well as the earth (the God) of all that exists, even though He knows all that you (attempt to) disguise as well as reveal. He even knows what you deserve.

Yet, whenever they receive any portion of their Lord's message they reject it. (This is proof of their real nature:) that they are inherently rebels (against the revealed truth). However, eventually, the subject of their derision will be made clear to them. Are they unaware of how numerous were the civilizations that We previously destroyed, people whom We had established on the earth and who were of a magnificence beyond comprehension? (They were) a people showered with abundant blessings and at whose feet We made it a paradise. However, ultimately, because of their wickedness We destroyed them and replaced them with other (civilizations).

Yet, certainly, even if We had revealed from the heavens a prearranged book, fully written for them, one they could see and touch, the people who reject God would still have said, "It's all lies." Or, they would say, "Why hasn't an angel been brought to him from heaven?" However, if We would have sent an angel, all issues would have already been determined, and they would have been allowed no further opportunities (for making amends). Yet, even if We had appointed an angel to represent Us, We would, without doubt, have made him appear as a man and thus would have merely confounded them in the same way they are now confounding themselves.

Previously, messengers were mocked. However, those who ridiculed them were destroyed by precisely the subject of their mockery. Tell them, "Travel the earth and observe the ultimate consequences of those who rejected the truth." Also, ask them, "Who owns the universe?" The answer is (obviously) God, who has willed upon Himself the rule of kindness, love, and mercy." Tell them also that there will be a time when you will be raised from the dead for judgement, gathered there (in the next life) by Him, and that it is indisputable. Yet, those who have wasted their entire lives—these are the ones who truly refuse to believe. They behave in this manner (of acting oblivious of God), despite the fact that He has absolute control over all that exists, day and night. The fact is He is aware of whatever is (even a person's thoughts).

Ask them, "Should I accept for my lord anyone besides God, the originator of the entire universe? Should I accept any other master, since He (alone) provides all I require, while He is beyond need?" Tell them, "I am obligated to be foremost of those who truly submit themselves to God as well as never make others my lords." Tell them also, "I dread if I were to rebel against my Lord the punishment during that overwhelming era of resurrection. God will be merciful to whomever is, then, spared. What's more (regarding those who do good), clearly, this will be an immense victory."

Yet, if God should cause you to experience difficulty, He is the only One who has the capacity to remove it. Furthermore, if He causes you to experience success, only He has the power to will anything—because He alone has command over (all) His creatures. Plus, He is truly wise, fully aware.

Tell them, "Are you aware of what is the most powerful of all testimonies?...It is that God is witness between us. It is that this Qur'aan—this divine writing—has been revealed to me, so that through its powers I might apprise you and all whom it may reach."

Do you truly believe God has equals, that any other entity or person has divine powers? Inform them, "I don't believe this way." Instead, tell them, "There is only One (universal) God, and in contrast to you I am incapable of attributing divine powers to anything else."

This way of believing is well known to the people of scripture. Yet, regarding those (followers of scripture) who have wasted their own selves they are the ones who have refused to believe. Then, who could be more wicked than the one who creates a lie and attributes it to God?✦ Or (as another

✦This applies directly to the people of scripture. Here, the Qur'aan makes it clear that the concept of a three-part God, that is the so-called triune God, is a human invention. This was fabricated, as well as mandated, by the Council of Nicea (fourth century A.D.). So, today, it is broadcast as truth, even though history texts dispute it.

Even the biblical writings confirm Jesus never made himself as divine. This alone is sufficient proof against his supposed divinity. Nor did he while on earth preach the triune God. An obvious human who lived like all others, ate food and, ultimately, died, according to the Qur'aan he will disavow this as a fabrication, never authorized. Rather, he will defer all controversy to God, because in the Qur'aan as Jesus always proclaimed, essentially, 'The Father—God almighty—knows all.'

Then, he never said he was a god. Nor did he claim any unusual powers. So, on what basis do humans call him a god?

example a person) who denies His revelations? Certainly, such perpetrators of evil will never achieve any positive result. What's more, ultimately, We will gather them all together. Then, We will ask those who attributed divine powers to others besides God, "Now, where are those beings whom you imagined to have God-like powers?" They will respond, "In God's name, our Lord, we didn't mean it." Surely, they have lied to themselves. Surely, their false imagery, what they have regarded as mighty instead of God and what they held in their hearts in order to reject Him, has abandoned them.

Yet, some of them (act as if they) listen to you. However, We have darkened their hearts, which prevents them from comprehending the truth. Moreover, We have made them (spiritually) as if deaf. Yet, even if they comprehended every sign, they would still refuse to believe (in the truth of this message).

Their refusal to believe is to such a degree that when they argue with you, they say, "...mere fables of the ancients." What's more, they attempt to prevent others from receiving the truth, plus they (purposely) distance themselves from it. However (through all this effort), they only destroy themselves, even though they are unaware of it.

Yet, if you could only see them when they will be caused to stand before the fire and will say, "If we were only given another chance, then, we would believe. Then, we would not reject God's messages." Not so, the fact is they will say this only because the truth which they previously disguised (from themselves) will become obvious. Without doubt, if they were given another opportunity, they would revert to precisely the propensity which was forbidden to them. Truly, they are liars.

What's more, some of them claim, "This life is all there is...Once we are dead there will be no other life." Yet (again), if you could only see them when they will be forced to stand before their Lord: He will say (to them), "Is what you now see anything but real?" They will answer, "By our Lord it certainly is." Then, He will say, "Thus, experience the torment, which is the consequence of your refusal to acknowledge it."

Those who reject the (ultimate) meeting with God are completely lost, until the final event (of judgement) suddenly overcomes them, they cry, "What a disaster for us that we disregarded it." This is because they will bear the full burden of their sins—what a vile load with which to be burdened.

Yet, without doubt, this (earthly) life is merely a diversion, while the (realm of the) next life is infinitely superior, that is for all who are truly in awe of God. (Now that you know this) will you refuse to use your common sense?

We are fully aware that what they say makes your heart ache. However, rather than refusing to believe in you they, in fact (by precisely that rejection), refuse to believe in God Himself. Yet, previously, other messengers were rejected. However, these messengers patiently endured the ridicule and persecution they suffered, that is until We brought them Our help. Truly, God's rulings are impossible to alter. You have already heard the history of these prophets (and the destruction that occurred to the civilizations to which they unsuccessfully preached).

Even so, if the torment and ridicule they impose becomes unbearable, why, then, if you are able to descend into the center of the earth or ascend into the high heavens in order to bring them an even more compelling message—(then, there is nothing you can do to cause them to believe). However, if He truly desired, God could have guided every person.✦

✦That is He has the power to overcome a person's resistance and convince them of His existence as well as the existence of resurrection. However, He will not do so. This is because this defeats the purpose of life as a test. This was why humans were created—to determine which of His creation would on their own submit to Him. This was what Abraham achieved, and it is why he is held so high. So, now, the challenge is will humans recognize Him or refuse to do so, despite the obvious evidence of His powers? This is the entire purpose of human life, as proven by the ritual of Abraham.

Thus, never allow yourself to reject God's ways. Without doubt, only those whose hearts are truly open are capable of responding (to this call). Yet, regarding the spiritually dead (at heart) God alone can raise them from such a condition. What's more (they should realize that), ultimately, they will be returned to Him.

They demand, "Why hasn't he been given any miracles?" Tell them, "Only God creates miracles."

(Incredibly,) while most people are unaware of it, there is no animal on earth or any bird in flight which, like you, is not God's creature. There is nothing that We have neglected in Our decree, and, once again, they will all be returned to their Lord.

Furthermore, those who openly reject Our messages are unable to even use their common sense (as if), they are deaf and dumb, immersed in darkness. God allows to deviate whomever He wills. He also correctly guides whomever He wills. So, tell them, "Can you imagine pleading (for help) to any besides God, when God unleashes His punishment or when the final moment (of resurrection) approaches? If you speak the truth, give me a (reasonable) answer."✦

✦That is, again, proving that belief in the one God is instinctive. All people have this propensity. In any crisis He is the only One they call on. Plus, any view of the universe makes it obvious that there is only one universal Being, who owns the majesty of all. So, His oneness is obvious. It is made even more obvious when people are faced with any sudden crisis. Again, who do people universally beseech? Also, during the time of judgement to whom will all people cry? The fact is it is only to almighty God, which is clearly stated as follows:

There is no doubt about it: He is the only One who you will ask for help when He may, if He chooses, ease your burden. What's more (by then), you will have forgotten all your false gods.

No doubt, previously, We sent prophets to other civilizations. Then, We afflicted (these civilizations) with disasters, so that they would humble themselves. Yet (in each instance), when the disaster struck, they failed to do so. Instead, they became obstinate. This is because Satan made their actions seem appropriate to them. Then, when they had completely neglected their commitment, We tempted them (materialistically), until, even while they were relishing in their newly discovered glory, We suddenly held them accountable. As a result, they became despondent. What's more, ultimately, the last vestige of those perpetrators of evil was destroyed. Then, to God is due all praise, the absolute Lord of all the worlds.

Ask them, "Consider this: if God should remove your ability to see or hear and also completely prevent you (from being able to feel), who could return it, except God?" Ask them, "Can you fathom what will be your status if the punishment of God suddenly strikes you—or (if it denudes you) in a slower, more obvious manner?" So, realize how We make clear Our examples. Yet, despite this they reject it in contempt.

Even so, the only purpose of Our divine agents is to deliver good omens as well as to warn. Thus, all who believe and accomplish good have no need to fear or grieve. In contrast, as a result of their sinful acts those who openly reject Our messages will be afflicted with (profound and relentless) agony.

Tell them, "I make no claim to have (access to) the divine treasures. Nor do I propose that I know the secrets of the universe. Nor do I proclaim that I am other than human, for instance, an angel. All I claim is that I follow what is revealed to me." Ask them, "Can blind people and people who can see be considered equal? Are you unable to consider this?"✦

✦Incredibly, through this parable He makes the guidance very personal. This is to cause people to think about their status. Is the person open to this guidance, or is such a one a rebel, who refuses to even consider it? Such a person even blocks any attempt at bringing this revelation to mind. This is why God describes this type of person as blind.

Furthermore, warn through the (messages of) this book those who are in awe of the fact that they will be gathered before their Lord with no one to protect them from Him, no one to intercede. (Give them this warning), so that they might become fully cognizant of Him.

So, never reject any who dedicate themselves to their Lord, seeking exclusively His approval. They are accountable only for themselves, and additionally you are accountable only for yourself. You have no right to reject them, because if you did, you would be committing (a grave) sin.

It is in this way that We test human beings through each other, so that they might ask, "Does God (by giving them guidance) favor those other people above us?" Isn't God fully aware of those who are truly (the most) grateful to Him? What's more, when those who truly believe in Our messages come to you (always), say to them, "God's peace be upon you." Your Lord has made it a rule that people will be treated mercifully, so that regarding anyone who commits a sin due to ignorance and then begs forgiveness afterwards doing good (you will find that He) forgives greatly and is a vast giver of mercy.

This is how We make Our revelations easy to understand (in order) to distinguish those who are lost in sin (from the true believers). Tell those who reject the truth, "There is no doubt about it, I have been forbidden to worship the ungodly things you worship." Tell them also, "I could never follow your faulty views, because, if I did, I would have deviated greatly and would be one of the lost."

Tell them also, "Surely, my position is based upon undeniable evidence from my Lord, and thus, by rejecting me, it is Him who you actually reject." Also, what you hastily demand of me (that is to demonstrate for you the truth of resurrection) is beyond my capacity. God alone is the source of all judgement. He will declare the truth of all matters, since He alone is the best judge, that is between the true and the false.

Tell them, "If what you impatiently demand of me, that is to cause the occurrence of the catastrophe of which I warn or to bring you a miracle from heaven, if this were in my capacity our argument would be culminated and at that moment you would be convinced. However, God knows best which of us is in error."

Also, He is the One who has access to all that is beyond human perception. He is the only One who knows them.✦ Furthermore, regardless of

✦That is the deepest—and darkest—secrets in this universe, including the secrets people attempt to keep. This is mainly an allusion to humanity's refusal of Him, since it is tied to the aforementioned statement of resurrection and the demand by those who reject this message for proof. Here, God makes it clear that He has full knowledge of all that humans hide, including the secret thoughts they harbor against Him.

This Being, who is aware of the dropping of every leaf and the movement of every beast, is surely also aware of the most insignificant thought of every human mind as well as any wicked plot humans conceive. So, here, God warns humans that He is well aware of all that they do but also all that they conceive.

where it is on the globe He alone knows (the status of) all that exists. Not even a leaf falls without Him realizing it. Neither is there even the tiniest particle in the earth's deepest recesses nor anything living or dead that is not documented in His clear decree.✦

✦That is, again, proving that God is completely aware and knows all that humans achieve. Today, there are numerous methods for recording events: videos, cassettes, TV cameras, CDs, and DVDs. In some parts of the world there are cameras located on virtually every street corner. Obviously, God has His own recording system, which is sophisticated enough to capture all known events throughout this universe as well as on earth. These divine recordings reveal all human actions. The focus is on humans, because they alone have free will. This recording system even documents every human's thoughts.

Humans have a record of events. Easily, so does God. Thus, a person should take care regarding his behavior as well as thoughts, that is never to alienate Him and not to have in his record acts that could ultimately haunt him.

The nature of death

He is the One who when you are asleep causes you to exist as if dead.✦During the day He is also fully

✦That is through sleep humans experience a condition according to the Qur'aan similar to what a person will experience in the grave. Through this example God is telling humans that death is not the end of experiences. Sleep and death are nearly the same. It is merely the beginning for the processing of the soul.

The process of sleep is evidence of the vulnerability of humans. It is also evidence of the continuation of existence after death. All humans, believers as well as those who reject God, must sleep. So, at least during sleep all of them submit to Him. This is specific evidence presented before humans. It is all part of a trial. In fact, God would not make all that exists, including humans, for mere play. The purpose is to test humans.

No one could expect to graduate from school without tests. On this planet this is the expected course. The same is true for the school of God—the school of life. A person will go before God at the ultimate time to be judged. So, it is best to prepare for this by doing good acts and avoiding hateful ones.

Sleep is a kind of proof that even without the body the soul survives. It is well known that during this time the soul escapes. So, there is only a physical demise on this planet. When a person dies, the soul remains alive, essentially in a state similar to sleep. Eventually, it will awaken. That awakening is known as resurrection. This is the first time in history, that is precisely through this Qur'aan, that sleep has been compared to death. Thus, according to the Qur'aan there is life immediately after death. After death the soul enters a sleep-like condition to be ultimately awakened, fully resurrected. Then, each person will be held accountable for whatever he/she has done.

aware of your actions. What's more, He recreates your life each day in order for you to fulfill a term established by Him.✦ Then, you will return to Him,

✦That is by allowing through His might the day and night system which humans require to continuously regenerate. This describes an active God, who is involved in all aspects of a person's life. He is watching and reviewing all that a person achieves. That is the universal God of the Qur'aan, a God who is not particular to a certain religion, race, or tribe. The view of the Qur'aan is "God is God,'" the same God as the One worshiped by all others, while given different names.

when He will cause you to comprehend the full scope of your actions.
Only God has absolute command over His servants. He alone distributes heavenly forces to monitor you,✦

✦That is because of His compassion for His creatures He is constantly sending help. These are forces which continuously call people to the worship of God. This is in order to prevent humans from destroying themselves. It is all in hope that they will respond to Him. This is for their own sakes, all to avoid ultimate harm. Yet, they refuse to reciprocate due to their own hostility and arrogance as well as the desire to immerse themselves in mere prurient pleasures. This is so they can pursue whatever they desire, without restriction. This is the real reason for rejecting almighty God. Without doubt, people don't want to relinquish their ill-gotten gains or raw pleasures. This is because they truly believe only this material life is of consequence.

forces which when death approaches, claim your souls. Then, such souls will be brought before God, their true Master. Truly, He alone presides over judgement. What's more, He is the most prompt, as well as precise, of all judges.

Ask them, "Who is it that rescues you from all the ominous dangers of land and sea, when you call for (His help) at that moment (truly sincere) in the secrecy of your hearts, as if to say, 'If You, only You, would save us from this, we will (from now on) be grateful.'" However, tell them, "God can, without doubt, save you from this and from every other distress." Yet, even so, you continue to worship other false powers.

Also, tell them, "He is the only One who has the power to unleash upon you agonizing despair from every conceivable direction; or to frustrate you with internal strife, causing you to experience fear of each other." See how numerous are the aspects We give these messages, so they might comprehend the truth. Yet, without doubt, your people fully reject it despite the fact that it is the truth.✦ Tell them, "Regarding your

✦That is who could dispute that this is the truth from almighty God? A person may reject it, but this doesn't mean he can deny its factual basis. Obviously, the Qur'aan speaks to human souls. Truly, it attempts to awaken their thinking. Surely, it perfectly predicts human nature. Then, who else could be the source of these truths other than the almighty creator?

People claim to disagree with certain parts of the Qur'aan. Others refuse to even investigate it. Yet, these are precisely the people who benefit from its message, since it was this Qur'aan which originally revolutionized civilization, leading to the creation of this modern world. This fact is thoroughly documented through the works of dozens of Western historians, including Carlyle, Byng, Sarton, Durant, Goldstein, and Renan.

actions I bear no responsibility. Every warning from God has a fixed term. What's more, eventually, you will understand its truth."

So, regarding Our messages whenever you encounter people who profane (your faith) disregard them, that is until the topic of their conversation changes. What's more, if Satan should ever incite you to lose control of yourself, remain not (after realizing such an error) in the presence of those who commit evil, because those who have God in their hearts are in no way accountable (for such sinners). Rather, their responsibility is to remind them (of their errors), so that they might become conscious of God.

Even so, pay no attention to all who, entranced by (the attractions of) this world, have made play and transitory pleasures their religion. Instead, remind them through these messages that, ultimately, all human beings will be held accountable for all the wrong they have done and will have no one to protect them from God or intercede on their behalf. What's more, while they offer every conceivable ransom none of it will be accepted. These are the ones who will be held responsible for the harm they have caused. Their only result is the agony of the fire, a punishment they will (forever) endure, because they persistently rejected the truth.

Tell them, "Instead of God, should we worship that which is useless? Should we do this with the result of rejecting God, even after He guided us (from our error)?"…like the person who the Satans have tempted to pursue temporary lusts, even while his friends attempt to warn him, saying, as if from a great distance, "Come back (I beg you), come back." Tell them that, obviously,

"God's guidance is the only kind. (It is also) why we are obligated to surrender ourselves (exclusively) to Him, the Lord of the countless universes, and why we are to remain constant in worship and always thinking about Him." So it is, without exception, all of you will be brought before Him.

Likewise, He created the universe, as well as this earth, based upon a system of truth. What's more, incredibly, whenever He says, "Be," it (then) already exists, and, thus, His word, whatever He decides, is materialized. Furthermore, when the resurrection is sounded—when it comes time to call all to account—only He will be in absolute control. This is because (the fact is) it is God who knows all which humans are incapable of perceiving as well as all that is perceptible. What's more, He alone is truly wise (the One who is) absolutely aware of all (that humans do).✦

✦That is God is warning people that there is nothing they can hide from Him. As stated elsewhere in the Qur'aan He is with the individual. In other words, there is no escaping Him. His emissaries are also near, next to humans, recording all that they do. For the human's own sake it is better to accept this, make amends, and worship Him. Thus, the person can gain protection from the ultimate agony, which is unavoidable, that is for those who reject Him.

Abraham's quest for the almighty God

In this spirit Abraham spoke to his father, Aazar (saying, essentially): "Do you regard mere idols as gods? Obviously, you and your people are gravely in error." This demonstrates the initial insight We gave Abraham into God's mighty universal dominion. What's more, We did it so he might become truly certain (about Our true nature).

Later, when the darkness of night arrived, he noticed a star. He exclaimed: "This must be my Lord," however, when it set, he said, "I have no love for whatever is transitory." Then, when he saw the bright moon rising, he said, "This is my Lord," however, when it, too, set, he said, "If my Lord does not guide me, surely, I will be completely lost." Then, when he saw the rising sun, he said, "This must be my Lord—it's the biggest of all." Yet, when it set like the others, he said (to himself), "I am incapable in any way of worshipping the way you do, my people—that is to make besides God any other powers as divine. Truly, I turn only to Him, the One who created the entire universe. I turn myself fully to Him alone, having rejected all that is false. What's more, I am not one of those who give other (elements) divine powers besides God."

Yet (when he represented the truth of his mission), his people argued with him, so he said, "Do you argue with me regarding God, when He is the One who has guided me? I have no fear to any degree of what you give powers besides God. I will never endure any harm, that is unless God desires it. My Lord embraces all (that can be) within His knowledge. Then, will you refuse to consider this?" (What's more, he continued) "Why should I fear any of the false powers you equate with Him, since (in contrast) you are not (obviously) afraid of equating others with Him, despite the fact that He has never given you the authorization to do so?

Then, explain to me, which of the two groups should feel more secure (that is the one which truly believes in God or the one that holds other impotent entities as divine)—if you happen to know the answer? Surely, those who truly believe (in their Lord) and who have not obscured (this belief) through wicked acts will be secure, since they have absolutely found the right way."

This was Our argument, which We inspired for Abraham versus his people. What's more, surely, We raise by degrees whomever We will. Truly, your Lord is completely wise and is totally aware of everything. Also, through Our mercy We gave him Isaac and (ultimately) Jacob, and We guided each of them, just as We had guided Noah previously. Furthermore, from this (same genetic pool) We entrusted David, Solomon, Job, Joseph, Moses, and Aaron with the role of spreading Our messages, because We ultimately reward all who do good. Then, upon (another part of this lineage,) Zechariah, John, Jesus, and Elijah (to all of them Our guidance was given). All were God-fearing, of the highest status. What's more, regarding Ishmael, Elisa, Jonah, and Lot—We elevated every one of them above other people. We also exalted some of their forefathers and children as well as their fellow people. We elected them all and guided them correctly.

The divine system; prophets as guides

This is how God's guidance works. Through it, He guides whomever He desires. Had they themselves made as divine anything other than God, all their efforts would have been wasted. However, We gave them revelation, the use of the intellect (and good judgement), and (the institution of) prophethood (in order to deliver Our message to humanity). Yet, now that they are well aware that We have given (this responsibility) to (such) people, who will be certain to accept them (that is) those specifically guided by God? Then (now that you know this truth), follow their guidance. So (you who represent God's truths), tell them, "I expect no reward (for my preaching). Truly (my only purpose is that), this (serves as) a warning to all humankind."

Those who say that God has never revealed His words to humankind are speaking from ignorance. Tell them, "Then, who revealed Moses' words, which brought such inspiration and guidance and which you now treat as mere sheets of paper for show, while you conceal far more?" You do this despite the fact that you have been taught through it (guidance) which was previously unknown both to you and your (ancestors). Tell them, "It is God who revealed it." Then, leave them to amuse themselves in their senseless chatter.

Divine revelation—real versus fabricated

This, too, is a divine book, revealed directly by God. It is blessed and confirms the earlier truths of whatever remains of the previous revelations. (This is in order) that you may warn the foremost of all cities and all who live around it, radiating from it to the rest of the world.✦

✦That is this is a universal message aimed at the entire human race, although it began in the Middle East under the auspices of Abraham. This confirms that the true believer is obligated to speak the truth to all peoples. This is the sharing of the name of God and the truth of His message to all others, even those who find it reprehensible. This statement is followed by the call for the "dutiful worship of God." The greatest of any such worship is the active sharing of God's message with all others, all to bring people to an awareness of the obligation to believe in Him. Thus, in Islaam there is no allowance for by-standers. Rather, the only means to gain His love is through sacrifice. This includes speaking the truth, even if it is unpopular—even if it results in criticism and chastisement.

Those who believe in the next life firmly believe in this. What's more, they are the ones who are always dutiful in their worship (of Him).

Is there anyone more wicked than this: a person who creates his own version of God or who claims to have his own revelation, even though nothing has been revealed to him—or (the person) who claims he can reveal from heavens revelations similar to what God has inspired? Even so, if you could only experience how it will be when these perpetrators of evil are faced with death, and the angels stretch for their hands and tell them, "Relinquish your souls. Today, you will be punished through the agony of humiliation for attributing to God only lies and in your arrognace scorning His revelations."

Physical evidence of resurrection

Then, God will say, "Now, you have surely come to Us in an isolated state, similar to your condition when We originally created you. What's more, you have left behind whatever We provided you in your previous life. We also do not see with you your intercessors, who you (consciously or unconsciously) regarded as sharing in God's power, who you believed would, somehow, assist you. Obviously, all the ties between you and your previous life are now severed. Thus, all that you presumed (to be powerful or protective) has failed you."

Yet, even so (as an example of how real is resurrection), surely (you can consider this, that is how) God originated the grain particle and fruit kernel, producing life from what is (apparently) dead.✦ What's more, He alone produces the dead

✦That is God is the molecular and synthetic Genius, who created the genetic blueprint for various species. Then, He produced the seed, which acts as the progenitor of life. For plant seeds no one understands how they can metamorphose from seemingly dead matter into a vital living 'being'—it is a true miracle. In other words, it seems dead, then, suddenly, it becomes alive. This is proof that God has the ability to revive the lifeless. In mammals, that minute seed is in the form of the sperm and its recipient, the ovum.

There is no need for dramatic miracles to convince anyone of God's presence. Life itself, in fact, every being in existence is a divine miracle.

from the living. This is the God that you must know about. Yet (despite this), their thinking is perverted.

God causes the dawn to break and also made the night a source of silence. He also appoints a definite time progression for both the moon and sun (that is) for calculations. All this is firmly established (for your benefit)✦ by the will of the almighty, the

✦That is by carefully considering human needs in His grand design, even before the advent of time. This clearly demonstrates the vastness of His mercy. It is the fact that He would create precisely the system humans need in order to have a benchmark for their lives, that is through the use of a system for time, the calendar, the stars for navigation, the moon for evening light, as well as for the measurement of time, the rotation of the earth for the creation of the 24-hour cycle, and infinitely more. Humans are dependent upon all this. Their existence is a well-planned process. Obviously, the system was produced for their benefit. Yet, are humans even remotely grateful for such benefits?

all-knowing. Furthermore, God created the stars, so that they might act as a guide for you in the threatening darkness of land and sea. (Through this) We have clearly described this message for those who are willing to understand it. Also, He created you originally from one living entity.✦ Then,

✦That is through a process that no human can fathom. Even so, this would indicate that, somehow, life originated from a single vital cell. Or, perhaps, it indicates that human life began from a single person. This corresponds with the latest biological evidence. As demonstrated by *National Geographic* (March 2006) top scientists have proven that the entire human race is related. Through modern genetics it has now been documented that the human race began some 200,000 years ago—all from a single woman.

Just how the first man and woman were created remains unknown. What is known is that according to the latest DNA analysis all humans are genetically connected. This means that all human beings are brothers and sisters. Then, what would a person do regarding his brother and/or sister other than to consider him/her with love? Too, would he do anything other than guide or help him/her?

He produced for you a time-limit for your existence. Plus, He arranged for you a final resting place (after death). The fact is We have clearly described these messages, that is for people who truly consider it.

Also, He produces from the skies rain. Through it We have produced every (conceivable) living growth. From this We have generated beautiful lush vegetation, plus grain growing in rows and from the spathe of the palm tree, thick clusters of dates, as well as vineyards, the olive tree, and the pomegranate,✦ all so alike, yet so different in many

✦All these fruit mentioned by the Qur'aan have medicinal properties. The latest research points to grapes and pomegranates as being particularly medicinal. The naturally occurring colorants in the latter, the flavonoids, have potent properties and are clearly preventive against major diseases, including heart disease and cancer. Dates have a natural, gentle laxative action, plus particularly in hot climates they provide much needed natural sugar for energy. They are rich in potassium, far richer than bananas. Natural or organic grapes provide potassium and chromium. Plus, the flavonoids in grapes protect the heart and arteries from degeneration. The skins of grapes have a natural blood-thinning action as do the red colored flavonoids in pomegranate. Olives and olive oil have major preventive actions against degenerative disease and act to even stall aging. Fresh cold-pressed olive oil helps reduce unhealthy cholesterol levels and also has modest pain-killing properties.

The olive tree is blessed. Regular intake of olives and/or olive oil helps prevents premature death from heart attacks and stroke. Pomegranate contains substances which protect the heart and arteries from degeneration. Thus, obviously, God wishes humans to be healthy and has provided the means to do so. He provides the very means for a long and vigorous life free of disease and disability. This is why He gives hints of potentially medicinal foods and plants in His revelations. Here, there are even hints of which foods to eat in order to prevent premature death. Incredibly, of all citrus only pomegranate, the only one specifically mentioned in the Qur'aan, has significant protective powers. Yet, the main message is for people to feel gratitude for the countless blessings He has delivered.

ways.✦ When it ripens, notice the wonderful fruit

✦That is in relation to their appearance, chemistry, taste, and medicinal value. The Qur'aan makes it clear that each fruit is different. Each has its own unique biochemical profile. This has been confirmed by modern science through a technique known as ORAC testing. This testing determines the medicinal properties of fruit by measuring the fruit's powers for protecting cells. In this regard pomegranate is one of the most powerful. This is particularly true in the prevention of heart disease as well as arterial disease. What's more, recently, it has been determined that extra virgin olive oil contains properties that prevent numerous major diseases, including heart disease, stroke, cancer, and arthritis.

(a sign of His loving mercy). Truly, these are all messages for people who will (allow themselves to) believe.

Yet, some people make all manner of genies, that is demons and the like, as if they have My powers—*even though He created them all*. What's more, in their ignorance they have invented for Him sons and daughters. He is far beyond this (unlimited as He is in His glory; He is) supremely beyond any attempt of humans to define Him. In fact, He is the Originator of the entire universe. How could He possibly have a child without there ever having been a spouse for Him, since He is the One who created all that exists and He alone is completely aware, knowledgeable (about everything)?

This is (the real nature of) God, your (true and only) Lord. He is the only divine being, the creator of all that exists. Thus, worship exclusively Him. This is because (it is obvious that only He should be worshiped): He is the One who holds all that exists in His care. The human mind is incapable of fathoming Him, while (in contrast) He knows the basis of everything (human or otherwise). Furthermore, He is truly beyond comprehension (in the way He achieves His will), completely aware.

You have now received a means of insight from your Lord. Therefore, whoever chooses to comprehend it does so for his own sake. In contrast, whoever chooses to remain oblivious harms only himself. Tell such people, "I am not responsible for you."

Through this We give numerous dimensions to Our messages. We do this, so they (who represent it to others) might say, "You have (now) become fully aware (of the truth)" and that We might make (this truth) obvious to people who have innate knowledge. Thus, follow what has been revealed to you by your Lord, the only divine power in existence. What's more, never associate with those who make other (impotent) gods (or powers) as if God.

Yet, if He desired, God could have stopped them from doing this (that is rejecting Him). Thus, We never ask you to be their guardian. Nor are you responsible in the least for their conduct. However, never revile those beings whom they invoke besides God due to the fact that they might in their ignorance and spite revile God Himself. This is because We have made the actions of the people of such civilizations appear pleasing to them. However, eventually, they must (all) return to their Lord. Then, He will cause them to truly understand the nature of their actions.

Even so, they swear in God's name that if they were shown an actual miracle, they would fully believe. Tell them, "God is the only One who can perform miracles." Yet, what would make you realize that, even if they were shown a miracle, they would never believe in it—that is as long as We prevent them from understanding the truth— just as they failed to believe in (this message) initially?✦ Thus, We will cause them to remain in

✦That is if a person has already made up his mind to reject the existence of God, there is nothing anyone can do about it. No one can convince him otherwise. Even if God made an unusual event—an obvious miracle—still, such a person would refuse to truly believe. This is because his goal is to reject the possibility of resurrection.

their condition of vain arrogance, existing in total confusion. Furthermore, even if We were to present angels to them, plus if the dead told them about it, even if they (that is the dead) were directly in front of them—and anything else that could demonstrate the truth—still, they would (arrogantly) reject it, that is unless God allowed them (to truly believe). However, most of them are completely oblivious of this fact.

This is how We have established evil forces, human as well as invisible beings, as enemies against any prophet, forces which consume themselves in delusional thinking. However, unless your Lord allowed it this would be impossible. Thus, remain aloof from them and from all their (attempts) to fabricate the truth.

Yet, with the purpose of causing the hearts of those who do not believe in life after death to perhaps incline towards Him—that (through this inclination) they might find contentment and earn some value for their actions—tell such people, "What else should I do other than to rely upon God for (guidance), to seek from Him what is right and wrong, since He is the One who has revealed for your benefit this book, which clearly delineates the truth?"

Furthermore, regarding those who We gave revelation in the more ancient eras they were fully aware that this (too) was delivered methodically by your Lord. Thus, after this never doubt the veracity (of this message).

So, now (in the form of this Qur'aan), your Lord's revelations are now perfected in both their accuracy and their being just. What's more (this time), no one can change His (revealed) word. In fact, He is fully aware, completely knowledgeable regarding whatever may be.✦

✦That is now humans know the truth directly from God regarding all important aspects of life, all carefully revealed by Him. Prior to this they were unaware of these details, truly lost. The message is for humans to be grateful to God for providing you with this wisdom. What's more, they are to beware of succumbing to pride and thus rejecting Him.

In contrast, regarding the vast majority of humans if (instead of God's guidance) you follow their advice, they will lead you away from God's way. This is because they only follow their own whims, mere conjecture. Surely, your almighty Lord knows best who deviates as well as who is correctly guided.

So, eat freely over whatever God's name has been mentioned, that is if you are real believers. Would you refuse to do so despite the fact that what He has forbidden is completely clear (the exception being when you are compelled to consume it)? However, this is precisely how many people lead others into error—and it is their own erroneous views, which have no sound basis. Surely, your Lord is fully aware of those who violate the limits of decency.

You are responsible (for all your actions and will be held accountable), so abstain from sinning, whether openly or secretly. In fact, those who commit sins will be punished for whatever they have achieved. Thus, never consume anything (literally, the flesh of meat),✦ which has

✦More broadly, this applies to corrupt acts, which are consumptive and which harm the innocent. These acts or policies include theft, devious business practices, usury, adultery, or any other act, which causes personal or public harm. The entire purpose of this revelation is to prevent such acts. Thus, by commanding decent behavior the Qur'aan seeks to establish peace between humans. Again, this is its avowed purpose. So, any act which causes human harm is banned and is rather regarded as a crime. Then, according to the Qur'aan such crimes are punishable both here and in the next life.

not been consummated in God's name, because this would certainly be vile conduct.

Even so, surely, the devious forces within human beings' hearts whisper, that is to those who have allowed their entrance. They do so primarily to cause you *to argue regarding what is and isn't a sin*. No doubt, if you pay attention to them, you will become (essentially) one of the godless, that is those who equate other powers with God.

Then, is the person who though once spiritually dead and who, afterwards, We revived and for whom We established inspiration—so that he might discover his role among humanity—is such a person the same as the one who is completely lost in profound darkness, from which he is unable to emerge? Yet, the perpetrators of evil consider their actions as just. This is how We cause the powerful ones in every region to become its main progenitors of evil, there to plot their schemes. Yet, they only plot against themselves, although they never realize it. Even so, whenever a revelation is presented to them they say, "We refuse to believe unless we, too, receive our own revelation: directly." Yet, the fact is God knows best who deserves to receive His messages.

(From God's perspective) the result of the behavior of such rejecters of the truth, who are devoid of any inkling of God, is abasement. What's more, they will be caused to endure great torment for all their wicked schemes.

Furthermore, whoever God decides to guide, He opens (such a person's) heartfelt desire to surrender himself. In contrast, whoever He allows to deviate (even though He could compel them to believe) will do so. Thus, He causes (the sinner's) chest to be constricted, as if he were ascending into the upper (limits of the) atmosphere.✦

✦That is for anyone who purposely rejects God all that such a person can sense is internal pressure, even anxiety. The consequence of the rejection of God is a lack of peace. This is felt within the heart. The consequence of truly believing in God is an open heart, and thus peace, confidence, and calm. This is the peace and calm due to gratitude to God. True belief also leads to humility, that is "only God is truly great." In contrast, the human is merely His servant. The deep belief in God is the source of much internal strength and purpose. In contrast, the lack of it merely leads to confusion. It also leads to ultimately loss.

This is how God inflicts horror upon those who refuse to believe. What's more, the Lord's decision is permanent. In fact, these messages are clearly described, that is for people who are willing to accept them. Their reward will be a destination of peace *in their Lord's presence*, who as a result of their actions will be near them.

Then, at that (fateful) time, when He will join together all (humanity), He will say, "You who sided forces with the evil spirits (which attempt to deceive humans), you have entrapped a vast number of others with you." What's more, regarding these (influenced) humans they will say, "Our Lord, truly, we did relish together (with the real perpetrators) in life's pleasures. However, now, we have reached the end—this time You destined for us. Now, we truly realize the gravity of our errors."

However, He will respond, "The torment is where you will reside, to exist there permanently, unless otherwise willed by God." Clearly, your Lord is completely wise—and He is aware of it all.✦

✦That is whether a person is an innocent victim, truly misguided and therefore deserving of His ultimate mercy, or a perpetrator. The latter is the one who maliciously fights against the way of God, even while realizing its truth. The nature of any injustice, whether intentional or accidental, will play an ultimate role in how He deals with each human being, while He always tends towards compassion. Even so, His wrath is extreme.

Even so, this is how We cause the people who commit evil to seduce each other, that is through their own vile acts. God will continue, saying, "You who have chosen to follow evil impulses, as well as evil humans—yet, weren't you exposed to (various representatives of the truth) from your own people, who represented My messages to you, who warned you of the eventual return to Me (where, after death, you will surely be regenerated)?" They will answer, "We solemnly swear against ourselves." Clearly, this temporary life had beguiled them. Thus, they will swear against themselves that they had been obstinately denying the truth.

It is God's way that (in His mercy) your Lord would never destroy a community for mere wrongdoing alone, as long as its people remain unaware of the meaning of right and wrong. This is because regarding their actions all will be judged according to intentions.✦ Furthermore, your Lord is fully aware of these actions.

✦That in God's liberal view a person's intentions are the true barometer for all assessment. Even a wrong done purely due to ignorance is treated leniently. God is totally merciful. He will hold no one accountable for mere mistakes or errors in judgment. It is only vile deeds which are done willfully and intentionally that are punishable.

Only your Lord is self-sufficient. Only He has no limit in His (loving) mercy. If He desires, He could destroy you and afterwards create your replacement, as He wishes, just like He created you. (Then,) that promised judgement will truly happen. What's more, it is impossible to escape. Thus, tell those people of yours, who refuse to believe, "Do whatever you desire with your fullest capacity, however, I will instead work with all my powers in God's way."

Man-made rules (superstitions)

Eventually, such people will understand who the future (truly) belongs to. Truly, people who are committed to evil never achieve any (productive) result. Furthermore, from whatever God has created of the crops and livestock they assign to Him a portion, saying, "This belongs to God" (or) "This is for those (other) beings who, we are convinced, have divine powers." Yet, whatever is attributed to the false gods could never bring them closer to God, while in contrast whatever (in falsehood) is attributed to God merely brings them closer to those false gods. Truly, their judgement is erroneous.

Additionally, their belief in false gods and other (low level) powers makes them regard even the killing of their (own) children seem valid (to them), that is to many of these people who make other powers (as if) divine and who, therefore, as a result of this misguided belief ruin their own selves, causing themselves to be confused in their beliefs.

Yet, unless God allowed it, they would not be doing this. Thus, remain aloof of them and all their fabrications.

They also (falsely) claim, "Certain cattle and crops are sacred. None are allowed to eat such food except those whom the divine powers give permission." What's more, they declare that it is forbidden to use certain kinds of cattle as beasts of burden—and there are cattle over which they will pronounce God's name, falsely attributing the origin of these customs to Him. Yet, He will punish them for all their lies. They further claim, "Whatever certain pregnant livestock will bear is reserved for the men but is forbidden to our women. However, if it is stillborn, both may share in it." God will punish them for all their lies. Truly, God is wisest of all and is the most knowledgeable (regarding their real intentions).

Without doubt, those feeble-minded ones who in their ignorance kill their (own) children, who further declare as forbidden what God Himself has (legally) provided for them—who ascribe their own laws as if God's—these are completely lost. What's more, they are deeply in error and have failed to find the right way.

Yet (as a reminder to you of His loving mercy), God produced gardens, both the cultivated ones and the wild kind, as well as fruit (that is date) trees, pomegranate, and fields bearing a variety of produce, all resembling one another and yet so vastly different. Thus, when (any such fruit) ripens, (they) enjoy its harvest—but (you, O humankind,) also give the poor their due. What's more, never waste God's bounties. God has no love for the wasteful.

In addition, regarding the livestock raised for work, as well as for consumption, eat what God has provided for you. However, never follow the machinations of Satan, because (as must be now obvious to you) Satan is your mortal enemy.

Satan's followers would provoke you to claim a superstition, that is that (for instance) in certain cases four kinds of cattle of either sexes are prohibited, that is regarding either of the two sexes of sheep and of goats. Ask them, "Is it the two males that He has forbidden or the two females, or is it the unborn fetus? If what you say is true, explain to me the basis of your claim."✦

✦Whenever humans invent laws for themselves God challenges them. In this case He refers to the various taboos invented by the pagan Arabs, which, obviously, had no sanction from God. This was the man-made concept that regarding certain cattle only select men of the tribe could eat them. Other people, particularly women, were banned from doing so. It was merely an attempt by these men to claim a superior status. God, through this statement, eliminated this pagan rite, demanding that they provide evidence for it based upon scripture for their claims. They produced no such evidence. Yet, the broader message is the demand for proof for any statement or claim about God or His ways not based upon actual evidence. Merely saying, "This is from God" is insufficient. The question should always be "Where is the proof?"

What's more, they also attribute as prohibited either of the two sexes of camels and cows. Ask them, "Has He forbidden the two males or the two females—or is it the unborn fetus?"

"Is it, perhaps, that you yourselves were there when God created these mandates?" Yet, who could be more wicked than the one who, though uninformed, makes his own rules, as if from God, and thus leads people into error? Certainly, God never guides such perpetrators of evil.

Divine prohibitions

Tell them, "I am unable to find anything that is forbidden (in this Qur'aan) except carrion, the blood flowing from a slaughtered animal,✦ and

✦That is upon slaughtering an animal, obviously, the blood becomes toxic. Also, the aforementioned pooling of blood, as occurs in animals killed from blunt injury or disease, contaminates the meat, and it is the blood which largely transmits disease. This is why it is banned. It is a sin, because of the harm it causes.

swine flesh—the latter being a vile food—or an offering of food sinfully (pronounced), over which any name has been pronounced other than God's." However, if a person is compelled by dire need, neither (purposely) desiring it nor exceeding any immediate requirement, then (realize that) your

Lord forgives greatly and is merciful in His understanding.

Yet, the Jews were the only ones who We forbade creatures with claws. What's more, We forbade specifically to them the fat of both oxen and sheep, with the exception of that within their backs, entrails, or bone marrow.✦

✦That is in God's true way of life there are no draconian restrictions. Rather, His way is liberal and refined. Only that which harms the human race is banned. Then, it is the human being who has complicated issues of faith. This fact is fully confirmed on pages 259 to 260, where God demonstrates that only foul deeds which are hurtful to humans are prohibited. Only these are punishable.

This is how We punish them for their evil works, because surely We are true to Our word. However, if they reject you, tell them, "Your Lord is unlimited in His love and mercy. Even so, regarding those who are lost in sin there will be no escape from His punishment."

Those who deliberately attribute divine powers to other than God will say, "Had God truly desired we would never have believed in others besides Him, nor would have our fathers/ancestors. What's more, neither would we have declared as forbidden anything He has allowed." Yet (similarly), their predecessors also rejected the truth, that is until they experienced Our punishment. Ask them, "Do you have any real knowledge that you could present to us? You follow only other people's speculations. Moreover, you yourselves are only guessing." Tell them also, "Know that, certainly, the final evidence (regarding your claims) is with God alone. If He wanted, He would have guided everyone. Tell them, "Produce your witnesses who could testify to the truth of God's prohibitions."

However, if they fabricate the truth, never agree to it. Nor follow their erroneous views. Never follow the views of either of these, either those who reject this message, that is the hostile Jews or Christians, or the outright rejecters of the truth, who regard other powers as God's equals.

Tell them, "Let me inform you what God truly prohibits."

- never make other beings or things equal in power to Him

- never offend against but rather be kind to your parents

- never murder your children due to fear of poverty—(We are the Ones who will provide for them as well as for you)

- never commit heinous acts, whether in public or private

- never murder a (fellow) human, taking a life deemed sacred by God, unless in the pursuit of justice: He commands this upon you, so that you might use your reason

- never consume the assets of an orphan, unless to improve it, before he reaches maturity

- never cheat people, that is give full measure and be fair

Yet, despite this realize that We never intend to burden any human with more than he can handle. What's more, when you voice an opinion, be just, even if it is against (for instance,) a close relative. In addition, always observe your bond to God. He commands this upon you, so that you might fully keep it in mind (in all your dealings). Plus, realize that this is the way leading directly to Me. Thus, follow it deliberately, and never follow any other ways, due to the concern that you deviate from His way. He requires you to adhere to this, so that you might always revere God.

There is also the previous example for you—that as a special favor We provided Moses with the divine words (of the original Testament) to fulfill Our promise to those who persevered in doing good. (In it We) clearly defined all issues. What's more, it was a source of guidance and kindness, so that they might, in fact, recognize (the truth of) the final meeting with their Lord (and therefore through this warning prepare for it).

This, too, is a divine writing, also blessed. Thus, follow it. What's more, always be mindful of God, so that you might benefit from His mercy. It has been provided to you due to the concern that you might say, "Previous to us the divine message had been given only to two groups of people. We had no true concept of their teachings," or, in case you might (attempt to) claim, "If only a divine book had been given to us, we would certainly have adhered to it and would have behaved better."

Therefore, you have now been provided with a clear evidence of the truth—directly from your Lord—as well as guidance and loving mercy for your souls. Thus, who could be more wicked than the person who (despite this clear evidence) obstinately defies God's messages—who rejects them in contempt? We will punish those who scornfully reject Our messages with a vile torment, because they (wilfully) rejected it.

Do they, that is these rejecters of the truth, expect the angels to appear before them or for your Lord Himself to appear? Or, do they expect blatant prophesy? However, when your Lord's prophesies *do* occur, belief in Him will be of no consequence, that is regarding any human being who failed to believe prior or who, while believing, neglected to achieve good works. So, tell them, "Then, wait (for that time of resurrection): we, too, will wait."

The origins of man-made religions

Without doubt, those who have created divisions in their faith (creating their own sects) are not of you.✦ Clearly, God will decide their fate. What's more,

---

✦That is the believer must have nothing to do with them. This is a clear directive for any true believer to reject all man-made religions or divisions as false. Yet, on a more profound level it gives the believer in God the freedom to worship Him in a pure way so he is never obligated to associate with others, merely based upon superficial aspects of religion or tradition. The obligation is only to worship God sincerely and to do only good on this earth. This good includes the struggle against all forms of tyranny. For the true believer there is no other requirement.

eventually, He will cause them to understand (the consequences of) their actions.

Whoever does a good deed will be (incredibly), rewarded 10-fold. In contrast, whoever does a wicked deed will be punished with its equivalent, and, what's more, all will be treated fairly.

When they question you about your faith, inform them "Regarding me, there is no doubt about it: my Lord has guided me on a correct path, which is true, the religion of Abraham, the sincere, the truly good. ✦What's more, he was a pure monotheist (and

✦That is he was the original person to discover God's oneness and to, therefore, establish a house of worship for Him. He was also the first person who dedicated his entire life to almighty God. Through reason Abraham was the first to conclude that all perceived powers other than the one almighty God are mere fabrications of the mind. So, he was elevated to a special status in God's realm, because he used his mind to confirm the obvious truths in this universe. What's more, he came to the conclusion on his own that there is only one mighty power in this universe and that humans are obliged to obey Him.

therefore never worshiped other powers besides the One God)." Also, remind them about (the original prayer of Abraham, which is), "Surely, all my worship and dedication—in fact, my entire existence, from life to death—is for the sake of almighty God." Tell them (also), "He has no one else in His power realm. So, I am obligated to believe this way. What's more, I am the foremost of those who (fully) surrender to Him."

Yet, also explain to them, "Should I pursue for my Master any besides the almighty God, since He is the absolute Lord of all that exists?" What's more, each person is only responsible for his own self. No one will bear anyone else's sins. Then (when you die), you will be returned to your Lord, and regarding any disputes He will clarify them.

Furthermore, He is the One who has made you inherit the earth (as His representatives). Then, He gave some of you a higher status (in the degree of your faith) than others, all so He might test you in regard to these blessings He has provided. (Yet, always remember that) without doubt, your Lord is extreme in His punishment but is also, certainly, exceedingly forgiving and merciful.

Section 7
Truth Versus Falsehood

In the name of the most merciful
and compassionate God

A-L-M-S

This is a book of divine revelation, *revealed specifically to you.* Thus, never doubt its purpose—so that through it you will warn those who are in error— so that you will remind (all other) people who truly believe in God, telling them, "Follow the revelations of your Lord. What's more, make Him the exclusive Lord and Master." Yet, humans rarely keep this in mind.

Even so, regarding the previous rebellious civilizations We destroyed many. Our punishment struck precisely when they were unaware. What's more, when it struck, they had nothing to say for themselves and could only cry, "My God, we have done wrong."

Thus, during the time when We will gather all people before Us We will, without doubt, hold accountable all who received the divine message. We will also hold accountable the messengers themselves. Then, We will make clear to them✦

✦That is the word "them" indicating, here, the rest of humanity. The messengers will be examined by God as evidence regarding human behavior. This is to confirm that humanity did receive the messages of God and therefore the vast majority of human beings are fully accountable for their acts. Most humans may well have knowingly committed vile acts despite being forewarned.

Many such people take their rebellion to yet another level by actually belittling God and His messengers. This is despite the fact that such individuals are aware of the wrong they are committing. A particularly wicked punishment is reserved for them. This is because such individuals know right from wrong and yet they choose to rebel.

that We are aware of their actions. The fact is We have been in their presence continuously. Furthermore, whatever is assessed at that time will be done in justice. So, those whose accumulation of goodness is great will achieve absolute happiness. In contrast, those who accumulated only minimal goodness will, as a result of their purposeful refusal to believe, have wasted their own selves.

Creation of humans; from concept to reality

We have surely created (the concept and design of) you and then formed you. Then, We said to the angels, "Submit yourselves before this new (type of) human being."✦ All did so, except (one arrogant one),

✦That is indicating that, incredibly, previously God had created other human-like creatures. Regarding these new earthlings this was not the first time God made thinking beings. It may also imply as indicated elsewhere in the Qur'aan a fascinating revelation. It is that previously in the universe there were other thinking beings, who are, perhaps, now extinct. It implies that untold eons ago there was an earth-like planet inhabited by intelligent beings. Then, such beings caused vast tyranny and destroyed themselves, leaving behind a lifeless, barren planet.

Iblees. He refused to (accept the responsibility to) submit. Thus, God said, "Why have you refused to submit despite the fact that I have commanded you to do so?" He said, "I am superior to him. You have created me from heavenly fire, while you have made him of mere (earthly) clay."

God said, "Leave (My presence), because this is no place to show arrogance. Thus, get out of here. The fact is from now on you will be among the humiliated." Iblees responded, "Give me time until resurrection." God replied, "Truly, I will give you plenty of time." Then, Iblees said, "Now that you have allowed me to fall in error, I will do all that is possible to ambush them as they attempt to follow the correct path. I will besiege them in an obvious manner as well as in a deceptive one they are unable to perceive, and, what's more, I will do so in every conceivable way. Ultimately, You will find that the majority of them are thankless."

Then, God said, "Leave my presence, disgraced and disowned. Regarding those who follow you I will fill hell with the entire category. Yet, regarding you, O Adam, live together with your wife in this paradise. Enjoy and relish in whatever you wish. However, there is a certain tree you are to never approach, due to the concern that you fall prey to evil."

Yet, Satan tricked them to make them aware of their nakedness (that is their vulnerability), which prior to this (in their state of innocence) they had been unaware.✦So, he said, "Your Lord has forbidden

✦That is, in other words, they were in the absolute peace of 'paradise,' the realm of innocence. The innocence remained as long as they held only love in their hearts and were free of base emotions. As long as they were truly grateful to God they were safe. So, by submitting to the powers of evil, despite being warned against this by God, they lost their innocence.

There may be a deeper meaning. It is the fact that the propensity for humans to fall prey to evil, to trickery and seduction, was willed by God. He could have disallowed it. However, rather, he allowed these events to unfold as a part of His plan, all to test His creation. This was to determine which of His beings would choose the path of good and which would allow themselves to descend into evil.

this tree only because of the fact that both of you would become like angels, even immortal." What's more, he insisted, "I only wish you well," and, thus, he deluded them with wishful thinking. However, as soon as they had tasted (the produce of) the tree, they became aware of their nakedness. Thus, they began to conceal themselves with pieced-together leaves from the garden. Then, their Lord called them, "Didn't I forbid you that tree, and didn't I warn you that, without doubt, Satan is your mortal enemy?"✦

✦All humans realize the existence of good and evil. Yet, Satan can only be effective against a human if a person *listens to him* and then *acts upon it*. This is why the Qur'aan emphasizes keeping God deeply in mind. It means that if there is a crisis, the person goes directly to God.

There is no room for both love and hate. One displaces the other. By keeping love in the heart through truly and deeply believing in almighty God by always considering Him there is no room for devilish emotions. In contrast, hate and anger can only have one source. This source is the devil.

God warns humans of this danger to protect them. It is to cause them to, when they sense such dire emotions, seek Him. This is to avoid their falling prey to wickedness. Adam and Eve, a mere parable, when encountering temptation pursued only personal gain. Had they instead immediately sought refuge in God they would have avoided their 'error.' Regardless, they begged His forgiveness. Even so, it is better to avoid the error by seeking His guidance for all acts, all so the person shall remain at peace.

The two replied, "My Lord, We have sinned against ourselves, and, what's more, unless You forgive us and have mercy on us we will certainly be lost." Then, God said, "Leave My presence, and be from now on enemies of each other. Furthermore, have the earth as your home and place of work. For a (specified) period you will live there. You will eventually die there. Then, ultimately, you will be returned (to Us).✦

✦Here the word "you" means more than merely Adam and Eve. Rather, it means the entire human race. Because of the lust for material gain humanity will, God predicts, destroy itself. However, in God's view this destructiveness is of no consequence, since all who have ever existed will be brought back to Him—at a time when justice will be done and all will be rewarded—or punished—based on their deeds.

You descendants of the original man (Adam), We have revealed to you the knowledge of making garments to cover your nakedness and also as items of beauty. However, the garment of godliness—true belief in your heart in God and doing good—is far superior (than any exterior appearance).✦ In this

✦That is regardless of denomination or culture it is the true nature of the human being that is the focus. People must realize that God is liberal. A person's exterior appearance, even ritualistic garb, is of no consequence compared to what is *worn within*. All God truly cares about is the inner self—what is in a person's heart. Thus, the phrase "good hearted" describes the essence of the Qur'aanic message, where the truly good are the beloved of God. This is because they are pure in their hearts and are also committed to doing good, now and for all times to come.

there is a message from God, so that human beings might deeply consider it.

You descendants of that first man (Adam), never allow Satan to seduce you, just as he seduced your ancestors, in order to drive you from your paradise. (Regarding your ancestors) he deprived them of their protection (of the thoughtful gratitude to God) in order to make them aware of their nakedness (and, thus,) he and his associates are prepared to ambush you where you are unable to perceive them. In fact, We have established a wide range of satanic forces in association with those who refuse to truly believe. Furthermore, whenever they do evil they are inclined to say, "We have always acted this way" and even claim "God told us to do it." Tell them, "God never commands you to do vile acts. Would you attribute to God something of which you have no knowledge?" Tell them, "My Lord has only commanded good actions. What's more, He desires for you to enlist yourself fully into every act of (humble) worship and to seek Him alone in all sincerity—because He created you originally, and so, too, you will be returned (to Us)."

Because of His mercy He will guide some of you. Others will unavoidably deviate. This is because such people will have assumed *their own evil impulses*✦

✦This proves the parabolic nature of the story of Adam and Eve. It proves that Satan is rather than a real being in fact an element within each person. So, it is within humans that wickedness is generated. This means each person must take responsibility for his own actions. Too, this is where they may produce the defense against such wickedness. The mere sincere calling of God is protection. It is also by truly being grateful to Him, the greatest protection of all.

for their gods in preference to God, while truly believing they have discovered the correct way.

You descendants of the original man (that is Adam), immerse yourself in every act of worship in the most magnificent way. What's more, freely enjoy the good things of life. Yet, this is no license to be wasteful. Surely, He does not like the squanderers. Tell them, "Who is there to forbid the grandeur which God has produced for His creatures and the good from His extensive provisions?" Tell them, "All these good provisions are fully permissible now for the true believers, plus they will be available to them exclusively in the final realm." This is how We make clear these messages to people of innate knowledge.

The real way of God

Tell them also, "In fact, my Lord's prohibitions are minimal: shameful deeds of all types, every kind of (vile) sinning, jealousy, envy, and making of other powers or objects as if they are God." Clearly, He has never allowed human beings to do these things. Furthermore, He has also prohibited the attribution (to Him) of (man-made laws), that is issues of which you have no true knowledge.

All people have had their term fixed on this earth. When it (that is the climax) approaches, they can neither delay it by (even) a single second. Nor can they hasten it.

Paradise and hell: vivid pictures

You descendants of Adam, whenever there come to you prophets from your own people preaching My messages, all who keep Me (deeply) in mind and do what is right—they should neither feel fear nor remorse. However, those who reject Our messages and resist arrogantly are destined for the fire, where they will live permanently. Yet, who could be more wicked than (this, for example,) a person who makes his own false ideas as if they are from God or a person who categorically rejects My messages? They will have their destined share, until Our agents (of death), who will cause them to die, will arrive before them and will say, "Now, where are those entities whom you relied upon (as your power source) instead of God?"✦They will reply, "They have

✦These "entities" could be virtually anything—fellow humans, leaders, rulers, nations (that is nationalism and patriotism), brotherhoods, blood ties, and today, more rarely, actual physical gods or idols. The entity might even be a person's own self, that is the pursuit of selfish desires. This is the main god of modern society.

Yet, how could a person do so? No one is so powerful as to control destiny. Nor can anyone create even a most minute being. Surely, no human can prevent death or originate life. So, it is obvious that humans are impotent. They are truly minor beings, whose entire purpose is to gratefully serve their Lord.

abandoned us," and, thus, they will themselves prove the degree of their error. Then, God will say, "Join the masses of invisible beings and humans, who have preceded you into the fire."

Yet, without fail, whenever a supporter enters the fire he will curse the original supporter to such a degree that when they will all have entered it, one after the other, the followers will say to the one who led them into it, "I hope God doubles your punishment for being the leader (into this error)." He will reply, "All of you deserve extra punishment, but you are unaware of it." What's more (once they realize the consequences of their acts), the leader will say to this follower, "So, you were in no better position than me." Experience, then, this suffering for all the evil that you sought to do.

Certainly, the gates of paradise will be closed to those who deliberately rejected, in their arrogance,

Our messages. (No matter how hard they try) they will be unable to enter it, just as it is impossible for a thick rope to pass through the eye of a needle. This is how We punish those who are lost in sin. Their final residence will be hell, because this is how We compensate those who commit evil.

However, those who give their all in belief and do good deeds—and in this respect We never burden anyone with more than he can withstand—they are destined for (the spring-fed gardens of) paradise, where they will live forever, that is after We have removed any unworthy thoughts or feelings, which were lingering in their hearts. Running waters will flow at their feet. What's more, they will say (in their hearts), "God is worthy of all praise. He has guided us to this. Certainly, if it were not for Him, we would never have found the right way. Clearly, God's messengers told us the truth."

Furthermore, a voice will speak to them saying, "This is the paradise which you have earned due to your actions." Then, the residents of paradise will say to the inmates of the fire, "No doubt, we have discovered our Lord's promise as true. Have you also found His promises to be true?" They will answer, "For sure." Then, from among them a voice of sorts will loudly proclaim, "Those responsible for the commission of evil earn only God's rejection, the consequence for those who turn others away from God's way and attempt to distort it (a rejection which is) the result for those who reject the fact that there is another life."

Moreover, there will be a barrier between these two groups. At a different level there will be those who had the ability to know right from wrong but were indifferent. So, they will speak out to the residents of paradise, saying "God's peace be upon you," not having entered it themselves but desiring it. Moreover, whenever they glance towards the inmates of the fire, they will beg, "Our Lord, keep us away from the people who were guilty of wretched acts." Furthermore, these (transitioned) people will tell the sinners, "What good did your vast wealth and arrogant attitude do for you? Are those (now) blessed ones the same who you previously declared, 'God will never do anything significant for them?' Yet, *they* are told, 'Enter paradise, free of any fear, remorse, or grief.'"

The residents of the fire will moan to those in paradise, "Pour some water over us, or give us some of the provisions God has given you in paradise." They will reply, "Clearly, God has denied these things to those who have refused to believe (in Him), who, entranced by this materialistic life, have made their religion a mere sport: superficiality and temporary gain." Additionally, God will say, "Thus, We will be oblivious of them today, just as they were oblivious of this (ultimate accountability), just as they rejected Our messages. (What excuse do they have:) We provided them with a divine book in which We clearly and wisely delineated the truth, a book of guidance and mercy for those who make the effort to believe."

Is it that the people who are unwilling to believe, who are devoid of any godliness, are waiting for the final meaning of that time to be fully actualized? However, when it is revealed, those who previously were oblivious of it will say, "This is just as our Lord's prophets prophesied. Have we anyone who could intercede on our behalf? Or, could we get another chance on earth, so we could make amends?" Without doubt, they have completely wasted their own selves. What's more (during that devastating time), all their false gods—all those powers and entities upon which they placed their hopes—will have abandoned them.

In fact, your real provider is God, the One who is responsible for creating the heavens and the earth (in) six eons. What's more, in His almighty power He is fully established as its ruler. He draws the cover of night over the day, while the sun and moon efficiently submit to His command. He owns all that exists. What's more, He has rule over it all. Blessed (in His magnificence) is God, Lord of the countless universes. Thus, humbly seek communion with your Lord in the secrecy of your hearts.✦

✦That is the heart of the true believer is filled with the reverence of God. In other words, such a person has only love in his heart for God. This is the humility of which the Qur'aan speaks. Even so, soft-hearted never means weak. Jesus and David had soft and loving hearts. Yet, they were powerful beings. Solomon was also powerful, however, in his mercy, when considering the greatness of God, he would shed tears.

Those who violate what is right, without doubt, lose the opportunity for His love. Thus, never corrupt the earth after it has been so perfectly established.✦

✦That is 'never purposely desecrate it'. This is a proof against pollution of the planet, that is through the arrogant disregard of the creation of God. The Qur'aan, here, makes it a crime to wantonly desecrate the earth. All people must work together to find a non-polluting means to survive on this planet.

By God Himself the excessive use of harsh chemicals, such as pesticides and herbicides, is condemned. This is because whatever wantonly destroys His creation is banned. Such chemicals cause permanent destruction to the earth and His creatures. Here, the message is, essentially, 'Never purposely contaminate the earth. Rather, make the effort to protect it.' Banned, too, is the corruption of the genes, that is through genetic engineering. The Qur'aan makes this protection of the earth and its creatures an obligation. Otherwise, by human corruption all will be destroyed.

What's more, because of (absolute) awe as well as desire (for future rewards), seek communion with Him. Truly, God's mercy is exceedingly close, that is to those who do good.

Only God disseminates the winds as a merciful present, so that when they have produced massive clouds, We may drive them towards infertile land and through them cause rain to fall. As a result, We cause a wide range of edibles to grow. In the same way We will cause the dead to become revived. This is an issue you should consider seriously. Regarding fertile land its vegetation grows lushly, of course, by its Lord's allowance, while on infertile land it grows sparsely. This is how We demonstrate numerous aspects of Our messages for the benefit of those who are grateful.

Lessons from Noah and his community

Previously, We, without doubt, inspired Noah for the sake of his people, who said, "My people, humble yourselves (in worship) before God alone. He is the only divine power. In fact, I am overwhelmed on your behalf at the thought of the torment you will endure during that overpowering time."

However, the chiefs of his tribe replied, "You are obviously confused." Noah said, "My people, I am not confused. Rather, I speak on behalf of the Lord of the universe. I am delivering to you my Lord's helpful advice and His messages. This is because I have been made aware through revelation regarding issues of which you were unaware. Then, why do you find it so bizarre that a source of (protective) news from your Lord would be delivered to you, so that you might be warned and therefore give due consideration to God✦ —so that as a result (of truly

✦That is Noah's people acted in the epitome of arrogance. They deemed themselves as almighty and instead of submitting to their creator held pagan rites as correct. Simultaneously, they rejected the entire idea of bowing to the One God. Nor were they willing to follow any rules He mandated. Plus, they belittled Noah and his followers, while making light of his mission.

Consider it from God's point of view: He sends a messenger to guide people for their own sake. Then, they reject him. They do so merely because they are immersed in prurient desires, and, thus, they plot to do as they please, without any fear of the consequences. They gave no thought to the fact that they were mere mortals and that they were placed on this earth exclusively by almighty God, all as a test. So, they rejected any thought of worshipping this creator and instead preferred the worship of their own selfish desires. For decades Noah attempted to guide them for their own benefit. Yet, this was to no avail. In fact, they categorically rejected him. Thus, God destroyed them.

accepting this message and sincerely believing in Him) you might be showered with His mercy?"

Even so (despite such an argument), they rejected him. Ultimately, in the Ark We saved him and his adherents, while We drowned the godless ones. In fact (these people who rejected even the possibility of an almighty God), were completely oblivious (to the truth).✦

✦That is they only considered this physical life as the climax, truly believing that there is no second life. Nor did they give any thought to accountability: that they would be presented before God for judgement. This is the deeper meaning of this passage and thus the use of the Arabic phrase describing them as "oblivious people," that is *knowman ʿatheem*.

Lessons from the early Arabian prophet, Hood

We also sent Hood, a member of their community, to the Arabian tribe of ʿAad. He told his people, "Worship only God: He is the only true God. Therefore, will you not, then, keep Him in mind?" However, the haughty ones among his tribe refused to acknowledge the truth, saying, "Obviously, you are deranged. What's more, we think you are lying." Hood responded, "My people, I am not deranged, rather, I am, in fact, a prophet from the Lord of all creation. I am merely delivering to you my Lord's messages. Furthermore, my advice (to you) is true and, as well, helpful."

"(Furthermore,) why do you find it strange that your Lord would provide you with valuable (that is protective) information and do so from one of your own people, so that He might readily warn (and therefore aid) you? Recall, too, how He made you as descendants of Noah's (righteous) people and granted you immense power. Thus, regarding God's blessings be grateful, so you can achieve real happiness."

They answered, "Do you really expect us to worship God alone and give up all our ancestral ways (of worship)? Then, if what you represent is real, go ahead, cause your threat of punishment to occur." Hood responded, "You are already doomed by your own wickedness as well as by your Lord's condemnation. Would you argue with me about these (hallow) descriptions which you have invented, you and these ancestors of yours, descriptions which God never authorized? Thus, wait for the ultimate (consequence), I, too, will wait."

As a result of Our mercy We saved him and his adherents, while We obliterated those godless ones, who rejected Our messages, people who were (adamant) in their refusal to believe.

Lessons from the haughty Arabian tribe, Thamood, and their messenger, Saalih

To another Arabian tribe✦ (that is) Thamood, We

✦That is, of course, since it was originally revealed in Arabic the Qu'raan emphasizes the ancient civilizations of that region. It would have made no sense to speak of, for instance, the ancients of South America or northern Europe. So, this mention of the locals was to create a bond with the original people who received it. Even so, the lessons are timeless and may be applied to all other societies, including the modern ones, which summarily reject the guidance of God.

(through Our mercy) sent a member of their own community, Saalih. He delivered (the same message, that is) "My people, worship only God. He is (truly) the only divine being. You have now been given by your Lord obvious evidence of the truth. This (specific) female camel belonging to God will be a signal for you. Never harm her due to the concern that you will be stricken by a violent punishment. What's more, remember how He made you descendants of (the people of Noah) and settled you firmly on earth, so that you are able to build for yourselves mansions and chisel out rocks in the mountains to create homes. Thus (always), remember God's (merciful) blessings. Furthermore, never spread corruption."

Yet, the chiefs among his people, who acted arrogantly (towards all they deemed low class), said to the believers, "Do you really think that Saalih was sent by his Lord?" They responded, "We are sure of his message." However, the arrogant ones said, "We are sure that what you believe is false." Then, they cruelly butchered the (female) camel and thus arrogantly rejected their Lord's commands. So, then, they (taunted) Saalih, "Go ahead, Saalih, if you are truly a divine messenger, bring upon us your threat." Then, an earthquake destroyed them, and they were flattened to the ground, dead, their houses caved in (on top of them).

Ultimately, Saalih rejected them and said, "My people, surely, I delivered to you my Lord's message and gave you sound advice. However, you showed no compassion for those who correctly advised you."

Lessons from Sodom and Gomorrah as well as the people of Midian

Lot was also of the same persuasion, when he told his people, "Will you commit abominations the like of which none in all the world has done previously?

The fact is you approach men with lust instead of women. Certainly, you are a people given to excesses." Yet, his peoples' only response was, "Exile this man and his followers. Surely, they, represent themselves as pure." Thus, We rescued him and his household, except an old woman, who chose to remain behind. Upon the others We visited mass destruction. So, realize the ultimate consequence for those who are immersed in sin.

To the people of Midian We sent a person from their own community, Shu'ayb. He said, "My people, worship only God—He is the only divine power. I have now made obvious to you clear evidence of His way. Thus, be fair in whatever you do. What's more, never cheat people. Furthermore, never incite corruption on the earth after it has been so well designed. (If you only realize it,) this (preaching) is for your own benefit."

(He continued,) "Never take a position against those who strive to believe in God, attempting to turn them away from God's way. Furthermore, never attempt to distort it."

"Remember, too, when (as descendants of Noah's people) you were few and how He multiplied your numbers. Thus, always remember the ultimate result of the spreaders of corruption." Furthermore (he turned to his people and said), "If some of you who accept the truth of this message are forced to remain among (those godless ones), regardless of your hardship remain patient, that is until God judges between the two peoples. Surely, He is the best of all judges."

However, the powerful ones of his society said, "Shu'ayb, unless you return to our ways we will surely exile you as well as your followers." Shu'ayb responded, "You would force us to do that, even though we abhor them? In fact, we would be guilty of a pagan act against God, especially since God has saved us from such (hedonistic ways). It is inconceivable that we would return to them, that is unless our Lord God wishes. Everything is under the power of Our Lord's knowledge. (Therefore,) in God do we place all our trust." (Then, they prayed,) "Our Lord, clarify the truth between us and our (disbelieving) people, because You are the best One to make things clear." However, the powerful ones among his people, who were adamant in rejecting the truth, said to his followers, "Surely, if you follow Shu'ayb, you will certainly fail." Then, suddenly, an earthquake destroyed them, and they lay buried in their very homes, crushed into the ground—those who had rejected Shu'ayb (were) as if they had never existed: those rejecters of Shu'ayb (the fact is) they were the real failures. Furthermore, he turned away from them and said, "Truly, I represented to you my Lord's messages, and, what's more, my advice was sound. Then, how could I mourn for a people who have deliberately rejected the truth?"

Clearly, We have never sent a prophet to a community without testing its people through misfortune and hardships. This is so that they might humble themselves. Then, We transformed the affliction into ease and comfort, so that they were able to thrive again—so they were able to say (in their rebellion, essentially), "Our fathers (and other predecessors) also had such difficulties." Then, We held them accountable, suddenly, without realizing what was coming.

Yet, if the people of those communities had merely become genuine (in their faith) and mindful of Us, We would have definitely provided them with blessings galore cascading from the heavens and earth. However (instead), they rejected the truth, and, thus, We held them accountable through their own (devious) actions. Thus, can the people of any society ever feel secure from Our punishment—that it will not descend upon them during the night, while they are sound asleep or that it will not strike them, even in broad daylight, while they are engaged (in activities)? Can anyone ever feel (fully) secure from God's profound plots? However, none feels secure from it, except people who are already lost.

Then, for today's residents of the earth who have inherited it from the former generations is it so difficult to understand that, if We desired, We could also destroy them due to their sins, sealing their hearts, so that they are incapable of comprehending the truth? To those earlier societies, some of whose stories We have related to you, there had certainly come their own prophets with complete evidence of the truth. However, they refused to believe in anything which they had previously rejected. This is how God seals the hearts of those who reject the truth. What's more, in most of them We found no true loyalty (to commit to what is right). In fact, We found the majority of them to be totally wicked.

Lessons from Moses and Pharaoh; the escape of the Israelites

After these ancient peoples We sent Moses to represent Our messages to Pharaoh and his high ones. However, they purposely rejected them. Then, realize what ultimately happened to those evil perpetrators.

Moses said to Pharaoh, "Truly, I am a prophet from God almighty, Lord of the vast universe. I am of a nature that all I can say regarding God is the truth. Surely, I am presenting you with obvious evidence from your Lord. Thus, allow the Israelites to go with me." Pharaoh said, "If you are capable, show me proof of your truthfulness." Then, Moses threw down his staff, and, incredibly, it became what was obviously a snake. What's more, he revealed his (formerly hidden) hand, and, actually, it appeared as a brilliant white light, clearly visible to the onlookers. Pharaoh's powerful ones said, "This is, without doubt, a magician of great prowess. Obviously, he seeks to overtake your rule." Pharaoh asked, "What do you advise?" They responded, "Detain them while we gather together our finest magicians."

The magicians came to Pharaoh and said, "If we win, we must receive a great reward." Pharaoh replied, "You truly will, and this will be nearness to my Court." Then, they said to Moses, "Do you wish to begin, or should we begin?" He answered, "You begin." When they threw down their devices, they caused the onlookers to be spellbound, and the mighty magic that they produced left them dazzled. Then, We inspired Moses, "Throw down your staff," and, incredibly, it overpowered all their deceptions— at which time the truth was confirmed, and all that these people were attempting proved inconsequential (and, so,) they were immediately defeated and humiliated. Thus, in fact, the magicians fell down in submission, prostrating themselves and exclaimed, "We now believe in the Lord of all the worlds, the Lord of Moses and Aaron."

However, Pharaoh responded, "What?...Have you done so before receiving my permission? This is surely a plot you have cunningly devised to create dissension. Eventually, you, as well as any who side with you, will understand the scope of my vengeance, because I will cut off your hands and feet in great numbers, all because of your perverseness, and, then, I will crucify you simultaneously in great numbers." However, these believers answered, "It doesn't matter, because to our Lord do we turn. You take vengeance against us only because we have decided to believe in our Lord's messages as soon as we became aware of them." Furthermore, they lovingly prayed, "Our Lord, give us (through Your mercy) patience in difficulty, and make us die as men who have submitted themselves to You."

Then (as time proceeded), Pharaoh's powerful ones said, "Are you going to allow Moses and his followers to incite dissension in our country, causing your subjects to forsake you and your gods?" Pharaoh replied, "We will kill their sons in vast numbers and spare only their women. The fact is it is we who have power over them." In response, Moses told his people, "Ask God for support, and regardless of the circumstances remain patient. Certainly, the entire earth is God's. He gives it as a legacy to whomever He wills of His servants. Remember, the future belongs to those who have God in their hearts." However, the Israelites said, "It is worse here since you came." Moses replied, "It may well be that your Lord will destroy your enemy and put you in power. Then, He will observe how *you* act."

Surely, We overwhelmed Pharaoh's people with (trial through) drought and as a result famine✦—all so they

✦That is because of the patience of Moses and his people and their willingness to place their trust in Him exclusively God responded, afflicting Pharaoh and his people with trials. Yet, this is a parable for all future generations of believers, that is despite the challenges or perceived threats to place all trust with God. This is because, always, the true believers, who are fully patient in adversity, will ultimately win. It was also to demonstrate that Pharoah and his cohorts would never admit that they themselves were the cause of their difficulties, always blaming their strife on others.

might develop a degree of humility. However, whenever good came to them, they claimed, "This is our right," while, whenever they were afflicted with difficulty, they blamed it on Moses and his followers.

By no means was their misfortune decreed by God. However, most of them were unable to understand (the implications of) this. What's more, they said to Moses, "It doesn't matter what miracle you show us, we will never believe." Then (as a result of their obstinate behavior) We afflicted them with the plague of every vile thing: locusts, lice, frogs, and blood, each of them distinct signs. However, they became (even more) obstinate, because they were a people immersed in sin.

What's more, whenever they were stricken by a plague, they would cry, "Moses, use your influence as a prophet,✦ and beg your Lord to relieve us. If

✦That is they recognized him as a prophet only when it suited their desires. Yet, a deeper meaning is that they truly did recognize him and thus almighty God. Even so, despite this they still refused to consciously believe. This was because they were immersed in worldly lusts and refused to abandon them.

you do so, we will definitely believe in you and will allow the Israelites to go free." However, whenever We removed the plague, giving them time to honor their promise, without exception, they broke their word. Thus, We inflicted Our retribution on them and caused them to drown in the sea, all because they rejected Our messages and were heedless of them.✦

✦That is they were repeatedly given opportunities to make amends but refused to do so. This proves the boundless love and mercy of God for His creatures. Obviously, this is true, even for those who reject Him. He truly warned Pharaoh and his associates essentially for years trying to humble them. This was through causing them to suffer numerous tests, all so they would save themselves. Then, they would save themselves merely by humbling themselves to Him.

The salvation is simple. It is merely to recognize the power and authority of almighty God as the only Lord, the only Being to be worshiped. Here, Pharaoh failed miserably. He did so by holding himself as all-powerful instead of the almighty One, the only One truly in power, which even Pharaoh himself ultimately realized.

In contrast, to the people who had been deemed low class, We gave as their legacy the eastern, as well as western, parts of that region We blessed. Thus, your Lord's honored promise to the Children of Israel was fulfilled, this as a result of their being patient in adversity. In contrast, We completely destroyed all that Pharaoh and his people had produced as well as all that they had built.

The rebellion of the Israelites: Moses on the Mount

(As it was) We ushered the Children of Israel across the sea (bed), when, eventually, they encountered people who were devoted to the worship of their idols (and incredibly), they said, "Moses, create for us a god like theirs." He replied, "Obviously, you have no sense. Regarding these, clearly, their way of life is bound to lead to destruction. Their achievements will hold no value." Furthermore, he said, "Do you expect me to find you a god other than God almighty, even though He favored you above all other people?" (Then, how could you be so ungrateful)? Surely, We saved you from Pharaoh's henchmen, who afflicted you with unmerciful suffering, killing vast numbers of your sons and sparing only your women. Surely, this was an awesome trial from your Lord.

Then, We appointed for Moses a total of forty nights✦ on the Mount, a number determined by his

✦That is in one last attempt to guide the Israelites and to on their behalf seek the guidance of God. The Israelites had proven that they couldn't live in pure gratitude to their Lord, and at the slightest temptation they would descend into evil. So, almighty God deemed it necessary to establish a code of conduct. The remnants of this is the so-called Ten Commandments, a system of life for the benefit of His humans. He brought Moses before Him to establish this system in order to prevent the tyrannical tendencies of the former's followers.

Lord. Moses told his brother Aaron, "In my absence act as their leader. Do what is right, and never follow the way of those who spread evil."

When Moses came to the Mount at a time determined by Us and his Lord spoke to him, he said, "My Lord, show Yourself to me, so that I might see what You are like." God said, "You could never see Me." Instead, look at this mountain. If it remains firm in place, only then will you see Me. However, as soon as his Lord revealed His glory upon the mountain, it was crushed to smithereens. As a result, Moses collapsed (overwhelmed), fainting.✦

✦That is as if he was pressed downward by an overpowering weight due to the massive power of the presence of almighty God. The mere energy from His presence is sufficient to crush entire mountain ranges. Moses collapsed in a swoon due to the gravitational/magnetic power and concussive force of this energy. He was literally pressed to the ground due to the massive forces in God's presence.

He said, "You are unlimited in your glory. I turn to You in repentance, and I will always serve you." God said, "Moses, I have certainly elevated you above all others by virtue of the message which I have entrusted to you and also by virtue of My speaking directly to you. Thus, remain firmly committed to what I have given you. In addition, always be grateful."

In the tablets We made clear through (sound) revelation all issues. Plus, We said (metaphorically), "Remain committed (to your Lord) with all your strength, and charge your (fellow humans) to also remain committed to their rules. I will show you the path of those who pursue evil. I will cause them to reject My messages, that is all those who, without any basis, behave arrogantly on earth. This is because although they may realize every evidence of the truth, they refuse to believe in it and though they may perceive the way for correcting their behavior, they refuse to follow it. In contrast, if they perceive a way to error, they immerse themselves in it wholeheartedly. This is because they have already rejected Our messages and have remained totally aloof of them. All who reject Our messages and the truth of the next life will find that whatever they achieve will be in vain. They will, after all, only be rewarded for the caliber of their actions."

Yet, in his absence Moses' people worshiped a golden calf, made from their own jewelry, which (when wind blew through it) produced a lowing sound. Were they unaware that it could never on its own power speak or guide them? Yet, they ritually worshiped it, because they were perpetrators of evil✦—although they would later

---

✦They did this so they could feel no responsibility to a greater power—so that is they could do as they pleased and immerse themselves in worldly lusts. Homage to such man-made beings has a derogatory influence, that is to a person's psyche, in fact, soul. It creates only internal confusion. In contrast, sacrifice for almighty God raises the soul to its pinnacle. This sacrifice includes active performance of good deeds to earn God's pleasure and to gain His rewards. Thus, for those who reject God other powers and forces serve as a distraction. In fact, through this they attempt to escape any thought of God. This is so such people can continue to commit vile deeds without feeling any consequences for their acts. This was why they lowered themselves to worship a mere idol. By doing so all that can result is corruption, whereas belief in the one God causes a person to reach the greatest heights conceivable.

lament in remorse, because they perceived that they had done wrong. (Thus,) they would (eventually) say, "Unless your Lord has mercy upon us and also forgives us we will certainly lose all."

Moreover, when Moses returned to his people, scornful but also saddened, he exclaimed, "In my absence the direction you have taken is vile. Have you achieved anything by your acts other than abasement, abandoning your Lord's commands?" Then, he threw the tablets to the ground and grabbed his brother by the head, dragging him towards him. Aaron cried, "My own brother, the people defiled me and nearly killed me. Therefore, never allow my adversaries to celebrate at my expense, and never equate me as wicked." Moses said, "My Lord, forgive me and my brother, and cause us to gain the benefit of Your unlimited mercy. You are truly the (Source of) all loving mercy." Turning to Aaron, he said, "Clearly, those who worshiped the calf have earned their Lord's condemnation. Furthermore, they will (also) be disgraced◆ in this life."

◆That is the disgrace due to ingratitude. This is a permanent curse. This discrace is because the Israelites actually fabricated God's way. Even so, this is a general warning against any who would purposely alter

God's system. Incredibly, for instance, in modern Judaism, as well as Christianity, much of the ritual is based upon man-made laws, the original divine principles being lost. So, the condemnation to which this Qur'aan alludes consumes them in this life because they knowingly follow valueless ritual but also because at the time of judgement they will endure only loss. Of course, those who follow the original principles of this faith will be protected, while those who purposely defy it will suffer only torment.

This is how We punish all who invent lies. However, regarding those who commit evil but then repent and afterwards truly believe, the fact is after such repentance (they will find) your Lord exceptionally forgiving, full of mercy.

When Moses' fury was quelled, he gathered up the tablets—whose writing was full of merciful loving guidance for any who are awed by God— and selected from his people several dozen men as a group of worshippers. Then, when violent trembling overcame them, he prayed, "My Lord, if You had willed, You would have destroyed us for what the fools among us did. We know that this is only a trial from you through which you allow to err whomever You will and correctly guide whomever You will. You are certainly near us (and always looking after us). So, forgive us, and have mercy upon us. You are the best One to give forgiveness. What's more, give us the good things of this world, as well as those of the next life, because no doubt we turn only to You in repentance."

God responded, "I inflict chastisement upon whomever I will. However, My immense mercy overshadows all else. Thus, I will provide it to whomever does good, that is those who are charitable, believe in all My messages, follow the last Prophet, that is the illiterate one, who was *predicted in the Old Testament and also in the Gospel,*✦ the Prophet who will make lawful for

✦That is the Prophet Muhammad, who was specifically selected by God to guide not only the Arabs but, actually, all humankind. This includes people of established religions, particularly Jews and Christians. The Qur'aan makes it clear that it is the duty of all followers of the previous scriptures to now follow it. This is because it is pure revelation from precisely the same God, who revealed the previous books. So, this more modern book, God commands, is the only one to reliably adhere to, since it is unaltered. This applies to Christians, Jews, and Muslims as well as all others who deeply search for the truth.

In fact, this is a test of the truthfulness of the Christians' and Jews' beliefs. Then, when they are commanded by God to follow his new prophet, who happens to be from a slightly different region than the other messengers and of a slightly different race, will they do so? Or, will they cling to racial pride and thus reject him? Incredibly, according to the Qur'aan the majority will reject him, even though it is obvious that his message is true and that he bears real revelations. Yet, even so, Jesus himself was of a unique race and color. Surely, he was Palestinian, plus recent research indicates that he was from a mixture of races.

them the good things and prohibit the foul, who will free them from their burdens and oppression that were (imposed) upon them from past (tyranny). Therefore, those who will believe in, honor, respect, and uphold him, while following the inspiration given to him from the heavens: these are the ones who will attain ultimate happiness."

Tell them, O Muhammad, "You human race, truly, I am a Prophet of God for all of you, sent by the One who is the owner of all that exists in this

Universe. He is the only divine power. In addition, He alone gives life and deems death." ✦

✦That is for those who dispute God this is obvious evidence. Here, He commands people to stop the dispute. Can any human give life? Can any human decide upon death, that is precisely when and where a person will die?

Can any human give to anyone a new life? Is it possible for a human or even all of humanity to produce a new species? Obviously, no humans have such powers. What's more, only He can save a person from dire crisis. Plus, when a person is faced with life and death circumstances, only He is called upon for salvation. Then, this is why God says, essentially, "just believe," as follows:

Thus, believe in God, as well as (the message of) His Prophet, the illiterate Prophet, who believes in God and His revelation. What's more, follow him, so you might find the ultimate guidance. ✦

✦In fact, this is a call for all people to follow this man. In particular, it is directed to Christians and Jews, who already admit to essentially following him. This is because of their admission to be followers of the way of Abraham and even the claim that this man was a Christian or Jew. Then, the Prophet Muhammad is a direct descendant of Abraham. Plus, he brought an updated version of the original scriptures. Furthermore, the city in which the Prophet originally preached was founded by Abraham. His purpose was to merely revive the original way of this man.

Clearly, it was the One God, precisely the God of Abraham, who selected him to represent this newer scripture. Then, what other decision could there be for the people of scripture other than to follow him?

Moses and the Israelites: lessons regarding gratitude

(Over the ages) among the people of Moses there have been people who would guide others in the way of God, speak the truth, and act justly. Ultimately, We divided them into numerous communities. When his people asked Moses for water, We inspired him, "Strike the rock with your staff," after which numerous springs spurted from the rock, so that the people all knew when to drink. What's more, We caused the clouds to shade them from the heat, plus, We delivered to them manna and quails, saying, essentially, "Make use of the good things of life, which We provide to sustain you."

Yet, alas, through all their sinning they could never harm Us, rather, they only harm themselves. Remember, too, when you were told, "Live bountifully in this new land, and freely take advantage of its blessings. However, do pray, 'Remove by Your hand the burden of our sins.' What's more, enter this (new) world in humility. If you do this, We will forgive you and amply reward those who are truly good." However, certain of them (of the later followers of Moses) who were insistent on evil fabricated their divine words. As a result, We unleashed against them a plague from the heavens, all as a punishment for their wickedness.

Also, ask them about that coastal city—how its people violated the Sabbath. Whenever their fish came to them, breaking the water's surface when they were supposed to keep Sabbath—because they stayed away on non-Sabbath days—this was how We tried them through their own wretched devices.

Then, there was the time when some of these same people asked those who were against this (practice of violating the Sabbath), "Why do you preach to people whom God is about to destroy or punish (that is if your claim of judgement against us is true)?" The believers would say, "So that we will be free from blame from your Lord and also that you could possibly reevaluate your position and therefore become mindful of Him." Then, when those sinners had completely forgotten their responsibilities, We saved those who tried to warn them against their committing evil acts and destroyed the perpetrators of evil with dreadful torment.

Yet, when (in still other generations) they persisted in their arrogance, continuing to do what they had been forbidden to do, We said, "Be as if decadent apes." Thus, your Lord made known that, certainly, He would raise against them people who will, until resurrection, afflict them with cruel torment. Surely, your Lord is efficient in His punishment. Yet, He also forgives much and is absolutely kind, truly compassionate, in how He dispenses His love.

Ultimately, We scattered them throughout the earth as numerous tribes. Some of them were good (in conduct), while others were of lesser status. Regarding the latter We tested them with both blessings and difficulties✦ in order that they might mend their ways.

✦That is due to His love for them He tests them, attempting to humble those who reject Him. This is so they would mend their ways—for their own benefit. This demonstrates His vast love for His creatures, a proof that He desires only good for all humans. The fact is God is constantly pursuing His creation in an attempt to guide them. He is constantly giving them chances. However, most people never realize this. Instead, they follow their own passions, while refusing to submit to His commands. It is as if they have their own inherent system, their own right, to do as they will, without consequences. Then, it is precisely this Qur'aan which makes it clear that this life is more than merely a game, in other words, there is a serious component to it. That component is the duty to serve almighty God.

In God's way there is no allowance for the mere pursuit of personal passions. In this regard many people claim that is is righteous to merely follow whatever the 'conscience' allows. Such a claim is simply a proof that the person rejects any duty to God and rather follows only his own erroneous ideas.

They have been succeeded by generations who in spite of inheriting the divine word cling only to the temporary good of this (lower) life. They claim, "We will be forgiven," even though they would readily pursue yet another temporary gain and thus repeat their sin. Are they not obligated through their own scriptures, which they have so thoroughly studied, to attribute to God only the truth? Have they not read repeatedly their entire contents?

Since the hereafter is superior to the present life, for all who truly believe in God, will you not, then, use your common sense?✦ This is because regarding

✦That is, essentially, since these Israelites admit to following scripture and also proclaim the power of God 'why won't you truly follow what is right in order to save yourselves?' This demonstrates the love of God, that He continually attempts to guide His creation, so they can avoid ultimate harm—so they can earn the blessing of receiving His love.

those who resolutely adhere to the scriptures and are constant in their dedication (to their Lord) the fact is We will give them their reward. ✦

✦That is regardless of their denomination and as long as they truly believe in God they will gain their ultimate reward. This demonstrates the mercy of their Lord and how he will never neglect to reward the good. Anyone who says harsh things about this grand Lord is at such a loss, because He is truly the most generous, absolutely compassionate in how He deals with His creation.

What's more, did We not say when We caused Mount Sinai to quake above them as if it were a mere shadow, and they thought it would crumble down upon them (as if to say), "Hold devoutly to what God has revealed to you. Plus, keep in mind its entire content in order to always remember Him."✦

✦This is a metaphor aimed mainly at the modern Jews to remind them of the consequences of rebelling against God. It is a warning that under the risk of God's punishment they must not violate Him and rather must hold to the entire revelation they were given. In other words, they must be just or ultimately suffer God's condemnation.

Whenever your Lord brings before Him any humans He asks them to testify about themselves as follows, "Am I not your Lord?" to which they answer, "You most certainly are." We remind you of this in case during resurrection you might say, "We were completely unaware of this." Or, in case you might proclaim, "It wasn't us, but, rather, it was our previous relatives—our ancestors—who in the past began to make as divine other (powers) besides God. We simply were their later children. Will You, then, destroy us for their lies?"✦ This is

✦That is, essentially, admitting that they realized all along that the way of the ancestors was fraudulent. However, they adhered to it regardless. What's more, they did so only because of false pride. It was a pride which made them oblivious to any real guidance and which prevented them from accepting anything new as revelation.

how We clarify these messages: We do so with the objective that those who have previously sinned might return to Us.✦

✦That is instead of holding exclusively to the pride of ancestors, the latter being fruitless, only the most sincere submission to the almighty creator can result in measurable gain. This gain is in the form of the love and pleasure of God, which is both infinite and permanent. God wishes humans to gain these benefits, which are denied to them through the worship of the ancestors or any other fraudulent way. This is because the ancestors themselves were completely lost. So, to rely on them is the epitome of folly.

Yet, despite their seeming reliance upon those ancestors they themselves deny their status by their attack upon this book. This is because they make light of them by calling the Qur'aan "fables of the ancients." Yet, again, incredibly they claim these same ancients as their guide. Through this they reveal their hypocrisy.

Explain to them the consequences for the person to whom We entrusted Our messages and then discards them—Satan overtakes him and he strays, like so many others, becoming completely debased. Had We desired, We could have elevated him through those messages. However (such a person), consistently clung to this earthly life, following only his own desires. Thus, parabolically, he is like a dog. If you approach him threateningly, he will pant. If you leave him alone, he will pant. Such is the parable of those who are determined to reject Our messages. Then, explain this to them in order that they might consider (its implications). Evil is the representation of those who reject Our messages and because of this have harmed (through these sins) their own selves.

Whoever is guided by God—he alone is truly guided. In contrast, whoever God allows to err, surely, such a person is deeply lost.

There is no doubt about it: We have destined for hell vast numbers of the invisible beings, as well as humans, whose hearts failed to grasp the truth—who despite the fact that they are capable were unable to perceive or sense it in any way. The fact is they are like cattle, rather, they are even less aware of the right way. These are the ones who are truly heedless, unable to respond.

The attributes of perfection belong exclusively to almighty God. Thus, implore Him by these. What's more, disregard those who attempt to corrupt His attributes. They will be punished for their misdeeds.

Some of Our creation truly guide others towards the truth and are, as well, just in their behavior. However, regarding those who work hard *against* Our messages, We will diminish them, gradually, without them realizing it. Surely, though I may give them power temporarily My (mighty) strategy is exceedingly unrelenting.

Have they ever considered that madness could never exist in this fellow man of theirs, this Prophet preaching to them? He is only a warner, who represents the obvious truth.

Have they ever considered God's mighty control over the vast universe, as well as the high heavens—as well as all the things God has created? Have they ever even considered whether, possibly, their own demise might be near? Then, what other message will they, after this, consider?✦

✦That is if this statement fails to awaken a soul to the responsibility to God, what will? Plus, where else can any human find such a vast revelation, teeming with wisdom and guidance? Obviously, the book contains true guidance for the human soul. Where else can this guidance be found?

Regarding those who God allows to err there is no (way) to guide or warn (them). (Rather,) without doubt, He will leave them blindly stumbling in their arrogance, wherever they go.

They will ask you regarding that final time (of judgement, that is) "When will it occur?" Tell them, "Only God knows (its precise time). He alone will tell us when it is." However, it will weigh heavily—even on the heavens and the earth—and furthermore it will strike you suddenly.✦

✦That is it will be a catastrophic event, which will affect the entire earth and all its inhabitants. This most likely indicates a celestial disaster such as the striking of this earth by a massive interstellar fragment, like an asteroid or comet.

They will repeatedly ask you (regarding the time of judgment), as if their constant harassment would make you more knowledgeable. Tell them, "Only the Lord knows," yet, most people are unable to understand this. Tell them also, "I am unable to bring you any help or prevent you from any disaster except as God pleases. What's more, if I knew the unknown, I would become incredibly successful. However, I am only here to warn and to (disseminate) good news, that is to people who (have the desire to) truly believe."

He is the One who created you from a single living essence.✦ From it, He created its mate—so that man

✦Now, it is confirmed that just as the Qur'aan proclaims, all people arose from a single human. The evidence is found deep within the genetic code. That fact, fully elaborated by the Qur'aan, was recently documented in the *National Geographic*, March 2006. It is the fact that, somehow, all humankind arose from a single genetic pool. In other words, all human beings are directly related. It means that all people in the human race have developed from a single male-female pair. Ultimately, it means that all humans beings are brothers and sisters.

might incline in love towards woman, so that when he embraces her in love, she conceives, first as a light load, continuing to bear it, then, eventually, when her load is heavy and she nears term, they both beg the Lord God, "If you would only give us a healthy child, we would surely be grateful." However, as soon as He has granted their request, they begin to give other powers besides Him a share in what He has created for them. High and mighty is God, far beyond all their idolatry. Then, will they idolize, along with Him, entities which are impotent in their ability to create, they themselves being created? What's more, such beings are unable to help even themselves. So, then, if you pray to them (that is these beings or entities that you hold so dear), they never respond.✦

✦That is regardless of whatever a person holds high such a power must be able to respond. Otherwise, it is useless. This is true even of Jesus. It is also true of Mary. Such beings have no divine powers. Nor can they intervene on anyone's behalf. Nor can anyone demand anything of them. They have no ability to help a person in need. Only God can do so. What's more, if anyone directly prays to them for help, they are unable to respond. They don't even know if such a person is calling. Only God can respond to the pleadings of His servants, which He does constantly. This is why He alone must be held dear.

The ludicrous nature of false gods

Whether you actively seek their help or say nothing as far as you are concerned it is the same. Those who you ask for help besides God are, like yourselves, merely created beings. If you are truly correct (in this belief of yours, that is that there are other gods besides Me), ask them for help, and let them answer your prayers.

Do these objects of worship have (functional) feet on which they could walk? Or, do they have (actual) hands with which they could grasp? Or, do they have (functional) eyes through which they see? Or, do they have (functional) ears with which they could hear?

So, tell them, "Bring to your assistance all who you claim share powers with God. Then, make any plot you wish against me, and give me no quarter. No doubt, God is my protector. He is the One who has provided the divine revelation. He is also the One who protects the God-fearing. In contrast, all who you infer power besides God are incapable of helping you. In fact, they are unable to even help themselves. What's more, if you pray to (such supposed benefactors), seeking their assistance, they are unable to hear, even though you might imagine that they do so: they are unable to comprehend."

Give humans the benefit of the doubt (and never be too harsh or unforgiving). Furthermore, mandate only the good. Additionally, disregard all who choose to remain ignorant. Furthermore, if Satan tries to provoke you (to blind anger), seek countenance with God. No doubt, God is aware and also knows everything.

Surely, those who hold God in awe—who truly fear Him—think of Him whenever any dark prompting arises from the devil. Immediately (as a result of invoking Him), they begin to understand things clearly, while in contrast *their (godless) fellow men would like to draw them into error.*✦ Thus, as a result (of this propensity) they cannot fail.

✦That is by causing the true believers to succumb to anger. The godless continuously provoke the believers in God, so they will act rashly. Here, God tells all believers never to do so and, rather, remain patient. The purpose of this patience is never servitude to the godless. Rather, it is to do the duty to God with clarity and without emotion. In other words, it is to act based upon wisdom and justice rather than senseless emotion. It is also to allow the divine justice to unfold.

Anger causes only blindness. Then, to act upon it is a sin. When acting upon anger, there can never be any positive result. In contrast, actions based upon love are a prescription for success. These are actions based upon the will of God, and what's more it is God's will that no harm comes to His creation. Therefore, the believer is urged to let the will of God evolve and to hold tightly to His way. He is to follow all that He commands. What's more, he is to remain patient and never succumb to blind anger. Then, he is never to be apathetic and rather to always be positive regarding the ultimate result.

Yet, if you are unable to satisfy their demands for proof, some (people) say, "(If you really are God's Prophet) ask God for it." Respond to them, "I only follow whatever God reveals to me."

This is meant as an insight from your Lord and as a guidance, as well as mercy, for people who (make the effort to) believe. Therefore, when you hear these divine words, adopt (the essence of) its message within your heart. What's more, remember your Lord in silence (in the peace of your hearts), so that you may be blessed with God's mercy. Additionally, think about your Lord with humility, but also (definitely) hold Him in awe. Think of Him constantly (whether by morning or by night), without raising your voice. Also, never distance yourself from Him.

Surely, those who are close to their Lord are never too proud to worship Him. What's more, they glorify Him and humble themselves completely (in adoration) before Him alone.

Section 8
Captured Treasures

In the previous section God systematically describes the consequences of godlessness. He demonstrates how due to their heinous practices the ancient societies caused their own destruction. Now, in sections 8 and 9 God describes the establishment of justice through the divine code. This includes rules of warfare regarding those who fight in His way, that is those who fight against aggression, oppression, and tyranny.

Today, there is vast tyranny on the earth. Its basis is mere lies. These lies are fomented by the powerful ones, who seek to maintain control of their power. Much of this is due to financial monopolies. Since Islaam is a threat to these interests it is continuously attacked. It is these arrogant powers, built upon mere fraud, that the Qur'aan weighs against. The fact is according to it the believer is obligated to fight against such arrogance or else risk the condemnation, rather, punishment of God.

In the name of the most merciful
and compassionate God

They will ask you regarding the booty you capture in warfare. Tell them, "Whatever war treasures are captured belong to God and the Messenger." Therefore, if you truly believe, be in awe of God. What's more, never make disputes about it.

The ones who truly believe are only those whose hearts tremble with awe at the mention of God and the consequences of defying (Him), whose faith is strengthened whenever they hear His messages—who trust in their Lord implicitly, worship constantly, and are (in humility) charitable to whatever degree possible. This is the nature of the true believers. In their Lord's view their status will be great. What's more, they will have earned complete forgiveness of their sins and the best possible provision (in the future for their souls).

Your Lord required that you leave the security (of your homes) and *fight for justice*. However, some of the true believers hesitated. So, too, they would argue with you regarding the truth itself, as though they were being led to certain death and could see it happening.

Yet, you (O Prophet), were deeply praying for your Lord's help,✦ when He responded with, "The

---

✦That is the gaining of his monumental help against the hostile Arabs. The pagan Arabs planned an attack against the Prophet and his movement, attempting to crush it. So, against great odds he fought back and ultimately prevailed. This section explains some of the principles which are derived from this event. Yet, his victory was strictly due to the mercy of God. Even so, this is true of any future believer(s) who for His sake fight against the perpetrators of evil.

No true believer can 'engineer' a victory. Rather, any victory can only occur at the hand of God. This is especially true when facing overwhelming odds. Any victory by the believers against their enemies is precisely due to the direct intervention of almighty God. Thus, regardless of the event the Muslims require an act of God to succeed. This is proven by the Prophet himself who always sought God's intervention, praying to Him repeatedly and sincerely, for any crisis.

---

fact is I will assist you with a thousand angels, rank upon rank." In truth, your Lord ordained this purely as a mercy, so that your hearts would be assured, since only God can provide (effective) support, because, without doubt, God is almighty, truly wise.

Also, remember when He caused inner calmness to permeate you—as an assurance from Him—and sent from the skies rain, so that He might cleanse you from Satan's corrupt insinuations—so He might strengthen your hearts and thus empower your resolve. What's more, the Lord inspired the angels to tell the believers, "Have no doubt—I am with you." Plus, He commanded them, "Strengthen the resolve of the believers with the following: 'I will put fear into the hearts of those who commit evil. (So,) attack them and destroy them completely (that is destroy all their power sources), and *cut off every one of their supports.*'"✦This is because they have

✦That is 'completely destroy their ability to wage war.' This entire section relates to the original battle fought by the Muslims, when they were attacked by the pagan Arabs. The Prophet sought peace, but the pagans refused to allow it. Therefore, when in a position of strength, although outnumbered, the Prophet fought back valiantly, defeating his enemies. To do so he used every legitimate means possible, sanctioned directly by God. What's more, in contrast to modern powers or conquerers he became victorious without killing the innocent and destroying infrastructure.

cut themselves off from God and His Messenger. What's more, regarding whoever cuts himself off from God and his Messenger—and there is no doubt about this—(such a person should realize that) God punishes severely. This suffering (in the eternal torment) is for you, O enemies of God. So, experience it, because for any who reject God's truths all that results is torment.

You true believers, when you fight against those obstinate ones, who reject the truth, advancing as they do in great force, be stalwart and firm: never run away (that is God is with you). In fact, with the exception of strategic reasons or in order to join force with another group of believers whoever, then, runs from the fight will have incurred God's condemnation. What's more, He will go directly to hell, the vilest of all destinations.

It was never you but rather God Himself who killed them. What's more, you didn't cause them to be terrified: it was God who did so.✦ In fact, this

✦That is God abhors people who fight against the truth and who attempt to kill His beloved servants. Thus, He will use these servants as a means to establish justice. This may mean fighting to kill any who fight against God. Under these circumstances God makes it clear that any deaths due to the hands of such believers are, rather, inflicted by God Himself. Thus, the believers are merely agents of God to achieve His will.

entire design was to test the believers with His own particular test. (This is because, surely,) God is completely aware of all (events). This was God's purpose and also to show that God (renders) powerless the vile schemes of the godless.

If you were praying for victory, then, now you have it. If you now stop yourselves from sinning, it would be to your benefit. However, if you revert to it, We will stop Our aid. As a result, regardless of its size your community of believers will be powerless. Make no mistake about it *God is only with the true believers.*✦ Thus, you who truly believe,

✦That is those who are completely dedicated to His cause and never falter in it. These are the ones who are completely sincere in their faith and prove it through their actions. They are also the ones who never compromise their beliefs for mere material gain. They are only the ones who are fearless in the face of all evil and rather are in awe of God. This means they fight such evil directly, without compromise. Then, with any such group of believers God gives them His full support.

obey God and His Messenger. Furthermore, never act like those who say, "We understand," while in fact they are not listening. Certainly, in God's view the vilest of all creatures are those foolish ones (behaving as if deaf and dumb), who refuse to use their reason. Yet, if God had found any good in them, He would have made them understand (the truth). However, even if He would have done so they would have still obstinately turned away.

You true believers, when he (that is the Prophet) calls you to that which will gain you immortality, respond to the requests of God and the Messenger. Also, realize that God intervenes between a man and his heart. Realize, too, that you will indisputably return to Him.

Even so, beware of the temptation to evil. Rather than mere people who (actively) commit evil, all people are subject to it.✦ In this respect never take

✦That is no one is immune to dark forces. A person must be constantly aware of this and ask for protection. This is by seeking the protection of God against all evil. The prayer is, essentially, 'O God—protect me from the evil machinations of that satanic one, who is a definite vile force, a true enemy bent upon destroying me. What's more, always guide me, so I never succumb to any such wicked force.'

lightly the fact that God is stern in punishment.

Furthermore, remember when you were such a small group and you were persecuted wherever you went. You constantly feared the attacks of your enemies—*how He protected you and through His support strengthened you.* Plus, He provided for you the good things of life (expressly for the purpose), that you might become grateful. Thus, you (dedicated) believers, remain loyal. What's more, regarding God and the Messenger never betray your trust. In this respect realize that your material possessions, as well as children, are merely a trial, as well as a source of temptation, while what is preserved with God✦is infinitely greater.

✦That is in the form of the future rewards held in trust by God for any sincere efforts. Whatever the believer achieves for God is recorded and placed to his credit. It will all be returned to him, greatly multiplied. Even if he gives his life it is of no consequence: he will gain a new life and this one will last forever. That is the divine guarantee, and God never fails in His promise.

You true believers, if you always (and deeply) think of God, He will give you the ability to perceive the good from the evil. Plus, He will cleanse your errors from you and will also forgive all your sins. In fact, in His giving God is vast, unlimited in generosity.

Remember, too, how the people who reject the truth, who are devoid of any godliness, schemed against you to stop you from spreading the message, to kill you, and drive you away. This has always been their tendency. However, God caused all their scheming to be of no consequence, because God is superior to all schemers. Furthermore, whenever Our messages were presented to them they would say, "This is nothing new. If we desired, we could produce a similar (book). It is merely fables of the ancients."

They would also say, "God, if this is truly from You, then, go ahead—send us Your punishment." However, God did not choose to chastise them while you (O Prophet), are still among them. Nor would

God chastise them if there was even the slightest chance that they would eventually ask forgiveness.

Even so, why wouldn't God chastise them, since they prevent the believers from going to the Sacred Mosque,✦ despite the fact they are not its rightful

✦This relates to the pagan Meccans (seventh century A.D.), who deliberately prevented the early Muslims from worshipping at Mecca. Then, it wasn't their house but was, rather, the House of God. So, then, their attack was also directed at God Himself. The folly of their aggression is also demonstrated by the fact that these original Muslims were followers of Abraham, and the pagans recognized the latter as legitimate. More contemporarily, it also applies to those who attempt to denigrate the Islaamic rite or call for the invasion of these Muslim centers. God says, essentially, 'How would it benefit the adversaries to block Muslims from their holy rites?' The answer is obvious, that is such an act is based merely upon hate and intolerance.

guardians? Rather, its only guardians are those who tremble (in awe) at the thought of God, though most of them refuse to comprehend this. What's more, their attempted prayers before the Temple are mere show. Then (for any such people who do so, worshipping only for superficial gain), experience this scourge, all because you refused to believe.✦

✦That is demonstrating that the only real faith is that which is in the heart. Only the most sincere and pure prayers from the depths of the heart are accepted as true. Worship merely as a ritual, merely because it is ordained, is of little if any significance. Regarding the adoration of God a person must put his heart and soul into it. That is the means to gain the ultimate benefits of any worship service.

No doubt, the godless spend their riches to prevent others from the way of God. Thus, they wastefully squander their own wealth. However, they will regret it. Yet, they will be absolutely defeated. What's more (as part of this ultimate defeat), the godless will be gathered into hell. This is so that God might separate the wicked from the good and join all the wicked together, so that He might, in fact, bind them as a unit and then place them all in hell. Certainly, they are completely lost.

So, tell the godless that if they mend their behavior, their previous sins will be forgiven. However, if they persist in (their wickedness), let them consider the consequences endured by those previous nations.

Then, fight against them (these godless rejecters of the truth), until oppression is eradicated and all worship is dedicated to God alone. However, if they desist, it is God who is aware of all their actions. What's more, if they reject doing what is right, then, realize that almighty God is your exclusive source of protection (and that) He is the noblest protector and helper (conceivable).✦

✦This is a reminder to the believers in God that regardless of the circumstances they are to rely upon Him alone. If a person is in a difficulty, like a life-threatening natural disaster, no human can guarantee help—no human has the power to do so. Only God has the ability to help.

By trusting exclusively in Him the believer is truly empowered. Then, ultimately, due to the direct help from God he is invincible. Thus, obviously, when called to fight, the true believers must do so. They must engage any enemy fearlessly. Any lesser effort is proof of failure to believe.

Realize, too, that regarding anything you acquire during conquest one-fifth belongs to God and the Messenger, as well as the close relatives, orphans, needy, and needy strangers, that is if you truly believe in God and Our provisions from the heavens for Our servant—on the day when the truth was isolated from the false, when the two armies met in battle. What's more, God has the power to will anything.

The power of belief: the Battle of Badr

Remember the way God designed it, that when you were at the near end of the valley (of Badr) and they were at its farthest end, while the convoy was below you: if you had known that a battle of such a magnitude was to occur, you would have refused to accept the challenge. However, it happened regardless, so that God might accomplish His will and so that whomever was destined to die might do so in full view of the truth, while whomever would survive might live in clear evidence of it. Most certainly, God is aware of all (that occurs) and has complete knowledge (of it all).✦

✦During the time of the Prophet this was the decisive battle. This battle prevented the destruction of the early Muslims. Fighting was the only option. Had he failed to fight vigorously this system would never have been established. As a result, the world would be consumed by barbarism.

The way of the Prophet, based upon absolute submission to God, was precisely that force which defeated oppression. Here, in a true divine miracle the ill-equipped and outnumbered Muslim army defeated the well-equipped and larger pagan army.

Of note, it must be remembered that the Bible also mandates warfare. So, for those who deem Islaam as aggressive or hostile consider the fact that the dictates of the Old Testament are far more aggressive than any similar passages in the Qur'aan. Plus, before engaging in warfare the Prophet and his people were tyrannized. They were attacked first. He was never the aggressor. Thus, this is no different than any other war fought by the people against oppressors.

These early Muslims deeply believed in their mission. Thus, God placed His power with them. This was so that true belief in God would become decisively established versus the corruption of godlessness. The Prophet's wise recognition of the need for fighting and his bravery led to a vast result: the elimination of pagan rites, which were replaced by the worship of the one almighty God. This led to a social revolution of such a profound degree that humankind still flourishes in it.

The people of Islaam then created the largest civilization in history. Here, people of all cultures and religions were safe, far safer than in their own countries. The borders were free. Economic conditions were sound. No passports or visas were required. What's more, there was no racial or religious discrimination. The Prophet's movement was revolutionary. It led to the advancement of civilization. The entire world was positively impacted. This is the consequence of his efforts. The actual fighting was comparitively insignificant.

It is important to note that, globally, the Prophet's war against tyranny had a vast impact. By crushing barbarism civilization flourished. This led to the Renaissance. Thus, the civilized world today relishes in the benefits due exclusively to this man. It was he who gave his all to end all barbarism and tyranny. It was also he alone who ended tyranny based upon race, color, and class. What, then, were his wars? They were battles against the established tyranny of the time. Once the tyrannical powers were overwhelmed the fighting stopped. Peace and prosperity were the norm. The Islaamic Empire became the largest and most powerful empire of all time, even greater than the Roman Empire.

It was God who made them appear in a dream as few. This is because if He demonstrated them to you as numerous, you might have felt weak and thus would surely have argued internally regarding any course of action. However, God saved you from this. Without doubt, He has full knowledge of what is in human hearts.

Thus, when you met in battle, He made them appear (in your minds) as insignificant, just as He made you appear of little consequence to them. This was so that God might accomplish what He desired and because, ultimately, it all returns to God. Thus, you believers, when you engage an enemy in warfare, be resolute. What's more, remember God frequently, so that you will be happy. Furthermore, heed the dictates of God and His Prophet. Thus, never allow dissension to occur in your ranks due to the concern that you lose heart and that your moral strength is depleted. What's more, be patient despite any difficulty. Without doubt, God is with those who are patient. Thus, never be like those who left their homelands full of conceit and a desire to be seen and praised. They were attempting to cause others to reject the way of God, even though God has complete power over their actions.

(Regarding the godless) it was Satan himself who made all their activities seem appropriate to them. He insinuated (to them), "Today, you will be invincible, because I am definitely your protector." However, as soon as the two groups came within view of each other, he abandoned them and said, "Surely, I am not responsible for you. Without doubt, I perceive what you cannot: the fact is I fear God, because God's punishment is extreme." Simultaneously, the false believers and those who vacillate in their faith were saying, "These believers are deluded by their faith." Yet, whoever trusts in God alone realizes that, without question, God is the exclusive source of strength and power, completely wise.✦

In this example there is a deep message. It is that for those who reject God their claim is weak. Any hopes they have held in their hearts will be dashed. Despite insinuations otherwise they will never be supported. At the last minute and during any crises they will be abandoned. They have no supporters of any kind. Then, too, the supporters they have always relied upon will suddenly abandon them. Not so with the true believer. He has his Lord for support. Thus, regardless of the crisis his Lord is with him, guiding him and strengthening him. The message is that for the believer who deeply trusts in his Lord he will never be abandoned, while all who claim to support the godless will under the slightest strain withdraw their support.

Yet, if you could only experience it when He causes the godless to die. The angels will slap them on their faces and backs and will say, "Experience agonizing despair due to your own actions, because God never harms in the least His creatures." They will suffer the same consequences endured by Pharaoh's people as well as even more ancient civilizations. Such people obstinately rejected the truth of God's messages. As a result, God held them entirely responsible for their sins. God is absolutely powerful, severe in punishment. This is the inevitable result, because God never improves a people's condition *unless they change their inner selves*. In this respect realize that God is fully aware of your actions.

The same consequences will occur to (today's) sinners as happened to Pharaoh's people as well as their predecessors. They rejected their Lord's messages, and, thus, We destroyed them. Also, We drowned Pharaoh's people, because the entirety were of the propensity to commit evil. The fact is the most hideous creatures in God's view are those who belligerently refuse to believe.✦

✦That is because regardless of any attempts to guide them "they will refuse to believe." Yet, these people are creations of God, who are beholden to Him. Can anyone imagine, for instance, an infant human rejecting its mother and father? What if a newborn bird were to reject all nurturing from its parents? All that would result is catastrophe. In this life no one would accept this behavior. Then, how can anyone even consider the rejection of God as 'right' or legitimate? In fact, since He is the only guide and provider this is the greatest rebellion conceivable. This is why God deems such a rebel as hideous. Then, so do all other heavenly beings as well as all good and decent people, who make it their goal to please Him.

Regarding those with whom you have a treaty and who, afterwards, repeatedly violate it, not giving any credence to God's laws, if you wage war against them, make them a fearsome example for those who follow them, so that they might take it to heart. Or, if you fear their treachery, that is from your supposed allies, strike them with a similar treachery. However, always be just. Without doubt, God despises the treacherous.

Then, give them no hope, that is those who reject the truth, that they will ever escape (God's design). Truly, they can never frustrate (His purpose). What's more, prepare to wage war against them by any means possible (that is with whatever resources you can muster). This is so that you destroy the enemies of God, who are your enemies as well—and others you are unaware of but of whom God is aware. What's more, whatever you spend in God's cause will be fully repaid. You will never be wronged. However, if they incline to peace, you do so as well. Too, place your trust exclusively in God. Absolutely, He alone hears all and knows all. Should they seek to deceive you by their show of peace be aware that God is all you need.

God is the One who strengthened you with His support and through giving you sincere followers, people whose hearts He unified (making them powerful). If you had expended all the most extreme of efforts, you could never have joined their hearts. However, God did it. Surely, He is the almighty One, absolutely wise.

You Prophet, God is all you need, both for you and your true followers. You Prophet, when fighting, inspire the believers to overcome all fear of death. (What are the results of this fearlessness?) If there are twenty of you, fully patient regardless of any (supposed) challenges, they might defeat two hundred. Or, if there are one hundred of you, they might (due to this fearlessness) defeat one thousand of the faithless. This is because they are people incapable of grasping it (that is the absolute certainty of resurrection). However, for now God has reduced your burden, because He realizes that you are spiritually weak. Thus, if there are one hundred of you *who are completely patient*,✦ they should readily

---

✦Patience equals trust. Without trust, no one can be patient. Whenever a person panics due to a lack of trust, this is when failure begins. With deep trust in God there is nothing to fear. This is reminiscent of the Qur'aanic phrase that, essentially, 'If you put your full trust in God, you are invincible.' In contrast, a lack of trust leads to loss, even defeat. Thus, if a person truly believes in God's existence, then he must completely trust in Him. This creates a power that cannot be resisted.

The degree of trust a person has in Him is a measure of faith. When a person truly trusts in Him, nothing can overcome him. Again, anyone with such a deep trust is impossible to defeat. Such a person knows that the only power to fear is almighty God. This is the epitome of success. In contrast, the fear of human elements, government, or power circles is tantamount to a lack of faith and may even be regarded as a type of disbelief. This disbelief is known in Arabic as *kufr*, which means darkness. Then, what could be more dark than to submit to useless powers, while rejecting the divine light? Thus, the Qur'aan preaches that the believer must in order to truly please God exclusively hold Him as the only source of might. Then, he is never to submit to fear of any humans. As a result, the believer is perpetually at peace. This is the patience of which the referenced passage alludes.

defeat two hundred. If there are one thousand of you, they should readily defeat two thousand, that is by God's allowance. There is no doubt about it: God is with those who are patient despite any challenge.✦

✦That is even if faced with overwhelming odds even here there are major demands on the believers. They are to ignore any fears. They are to willingly sacrifice themselves. Even so, in warfare they are to use the most adept strategy possible.

God demands that the true believers wage war against those who reject God. They are also to fight against all who tyrannize them.

It is the Muslims' duty to battle all groups who wildly kill and torment the good. This war is against any group which maliciously imprisons them, tortures them, and torments them. Thus, God's true servants are commanded to fight against any source of tyranny with all means possible. This may include physical combat.

The Qur'aan stipulates that this war is against all godless people, who attempt to crush the faith. These are the ones who foment horror and tyranny upon the earth. They are also the ones who brutalize others, all for greedy gains. However, if they desire peace and cause no harm, they are to be left alone. Yet, as described throughout the Qur'aan every effort must be pursued to create peace: war is absolutely the last option. In contrast, in the Western system if it creates material gain, war is the first option. These are wars of aggression. Islaam bands them.

It does not behoove a prophet to take (or hold) captives (and particularly hostages)—unless he has (been forced to) wage much war.✦ You may desire

✦In Islaam, taking hostages, common citizens, as political pawns is prohibited. This only occurs as a consequence of legitimate battles, that is the capture of so-called prisoners of war. However, to purposely hold people for political gain is never sanctioned by this faith. Even so, obviously, capturing them during an act of war is acceptable.

the temporary (and unimportant) rewards here. In contrast, God desires for you the good of the next

life. What's more, God is almighty, completely wise. Even so, if it were not for the (decision) that had already been made, you would have, without doubt, been stricken by a immense punishment, that is due to all (the prisoners) that you took.✦

✦Again, this makes it clear that according to the Qur'aan hostage taking is prohibited. In other words, the deliberate attempt to take people against their will and hold or imprison them—all for some supposed financial gain, with the intent of gaining via ransom—all such acts are banned. In fact, it is punishable as a criminal act, condemned by God Himself. Even so, if during actual war, where fighters encounter other fighters, such capture is allowed. Also, if a plain-clothed person is acting as a warrior in disguise, such as a spy, he, too, is subject to the rules of warfare.

Then, take advantage of all the lawful and good things which you have obtained through war. Yet (in all instances), make (your duties to) God the priority. Surely, God forgives greatly and is great in His giving. Thus (O Prophet), tell the captives who you hold, "If God determines any decency in you, He will give you (something) far superior to what you have lost. What's more, He will forgive you (any past sins)." Surely, again, God's forgiveness is great, and so is His generosity.

Even so, if they attempt to deceive you, they were, no doubt, attempting to deceive God previously. However, He gave (the true believers) power over them. What's more, God has complete knowledge (of all that humans do) and is truly wise.

Also, regarding those believers in God's way who have abandoned their former way (of life) and give their all, as well as those who support and protect them in God's cause: these are the only real friends of each other. However, regarding other such true believers from other regions (distant from you) you are not responsible for their protection, that is unless they ask for your help against religious persecution (the exception being if you have a prior treaty with the people who are persecuting them, which you are not allowed to breach). Even so, have no doubt about it the godless are allies of each other.

Then, unless you take the same tact (as they do) of developing strong bonds with each other and fully supporting each other, only oppression, in fact, corruption will rule on the earth.✦

✦The purpose of God's system is to maintain peace on this earth. To do so a war is waged against corruption. Thus, Islaam wages a constant war against oppression, a duty of every Muslim. What's more, when under tyranny, each true believer is obligated to assist his fellow true believer, regardless of denomination. As the Prophet made clear regardless of religion or race the believer must help the fellow human.

Yet, regarding those who truly believe (in God) and have abandoned all their formerly evil ways— who are working with all their might and assets in God's way, together with you—they are (spiritually) yours, as if truly your blood brothers (as if from the same mother and to be treated this way) and who, thus, have the greatest claims on each other regarding whatever God ordains. Yet, surely (above all), realize that God is fully aware and that He has complete knowledge, absolute awareness (of all issues).

Section 9
Repentance

This section deals almost exclusively with war. This is an ultimate consequence when the forces of good are confronted with the realm of evil. This is why it does not begin with the standard phrase found at the beginning of other all Qur'aanic sections. The Muslims are obligated to fight against all tyrants, who attempt to crush their faith. Since God loves peace, He chose not to use the words "merciful and compassionate" to initiate a chapter that directly calls for war. Yet, this war is an absolute requirement for all Muslims. This is in order to prevent raw tyranny from corrupting this earth.

The point is Islaam is a buttress against oppression. This war against tyranny is the precise purpose of the submission to God. Thus, as a result, it is the divine law which holds precedence rather than human laws, where people serve their own petty desires. The latter is a source of great oppression throughout the earth. Through the divine law peace is brought to the earth. Thus, oppression is halted.

The Qur'aan has two sections specifically on warfare. It is to raise up the believers to fight against all oppressors. In this fight the believers may be forced to give their lives. Yet, they are urged to do so, but only against the aggressors.

This is a proclamation of the freedom from obligation from God and His Messenger, that is regarding the godless ones with whom you have a treaty. (Tell them:) "Then, do what you will for four months, however, realize that regarding those who reject Him (such persons) will never escape (His overwhelming grasp) and will only experience disgrace. This is also a proclamation from God and His Prophet *to all humankind* on this day of the

Greatest Pilgrimage, that is "God rejects all who give others power besides Him, and so does His Prophet." Thus, if (after this realization), you are truly sorrowful and make amends, it will be for your own benefit. However, if you reject it, realize that you can never escape God. What's more, regarding those godless ones who are determined to reject (God's messages), give them the news of (due to their refusal to believe in Him) extreme punishment.

The exceptions (from the godless) are whomever you have made an agreement and who abide by these commitments—who never aid anyone against you. Then, abide by your agreement with them. Make no mistake about it God loves, truly loves, those who are deeply conscious of Him.✦

✦That is those who always keep God in the forefront, this is how a person can avoid critical errors. These errors are based upon emotional reactions, while the dictates of God are based upon the laws of justice.

The laws in this book are obviously divine. Thus, He rejects those who attempt to corrupt, even destroy, it. Yet, He truly loves those who always think about Him and make His way their life. This includes fighting against all who attempt to destroy His system. In order to fight for God against the agents of tyranny great faith is required. This is the deep consciousness of which the Qur'aan speaks.

Therefore, when the sacred months have ended, attack and destroy (the basis of) the godless (who are at war with you and who have systematically violated all agreements). What's more, take (this enemy) hostage,✦ besiege them, and prepare to

✦That is as legitimate prisoners of wars. Thus, if the true believers are engaged in warfare, in the foray if they capture people, of course they may be taken prisoner. Surely, Western powers do so. Yet, any taking hostage of *innocent people strictly for political gain* is, as demonstrated in Section 8, banned. Thus, clearly, the Qur'aan only mandates the capture of those who are actively fighting against the Islaamic system. All other hostage taking is banned. Put simply, innocent people are never to be harmed. In contrast, in modern warfare innocent people are routinely harmed, even brutally killed, and are listed as so-called collateral damage.

ambush them at every conceivable place. However, if they truly seek forgiveness and amend (their behavior), adopt prayer, and pay the appropriate charity, leave them alone. This is because, certainly, God forgives greatly and gives vastly of His mercy.

Moreover, if any of the godless seeks your protection, give it to them—so that (such individuals) might be able to hear the word of God from you. Thus, if this happens, make sure they are protected (from any harm or attack). This is because the godless may sin only because they are unaware of the truth.

How could the godless be granted a treaty by God and His Prophet unless it relates to those who have made a treaty with you (that is in the vicinity of the sacred House of Worship)? Regarding the latter as long as they hold true to (any such agreement) be true to them. God loves those who (always) hold Him deeply in their hearts.

How else could it be?—because if those who are (inherently) hostile to you had power over you, they would never respect any previous agreement or relationship nor would they uphold any obligation to protect you. They seek to merely please you superficially, while in their hearts they hold only hostility (towards you). Moreover, most of them are terminally immoral to an extreme. They have exchanged God's messages for a temporary gain and have, thus, rejected His way. Their only objective is vile, and with regard to a (true believer) they respect no agreement, relationship, or obligation. Furthermore, they violate all common decency. Yet, if they repent and adopt true worship, as well as perform charitable acts, they become your fellows in faith. This is how We clarify these messages for those who use their innate knowledge.

However, if they break their promises after having entered into an agreement and also revile your way of life, fight these (godless) rejecters of the truth, who clearly disregard their promises. Do this, so they might stop their aggression.

Then, would you neglect to fight against those who have violated their commitments and have done all that is conceivable to drive the Prophet away and who, what's more, *initiated* the conflicts? Are you in awe of them? Truly, if you really do believe in Him, you should only be in awe of God.

So, fight against them. Through your efforts God will chastise and disgrace them. What's more, He will (fully) support you against them. Plus, He will soothe the hearts of the true believers and will cleanse their hearts of any anger.✦

✦Regardless of the circumstances anger is destructive. It is the emotion of the devil. The believer can be strong, even adamant. Yet, he can never be angry. The fact is anger leads to injustice. In contrast, there is great power in love—the love of God and the love for humanity. What's more, as a part of that love the fight for justice *for the sake of humankind* is ordained.

In fact, God will turn in His mercy to whomever He wills, because He has full knowledge of (who is deserving) and is completely wise. Do you think that you will be spared, unless God determines (which of you are willing to) work hard in His cause—without seeking help from any, except God and His Prophet as well as other fellow believers? There is no doubt about it: God is fully aware of all your actions.

As long as they are in a state of rejection the godless are disallowed from visiting or attending God's houses of worship.✦ Plus, they are the ones whose

✦Only the Prophet's followers, confessed Muslims, are allowed entrance to Mecca. Christians, then, raise this argument as evidence of 'bias.' This is done as a form of hostility in attempt to prove that Islaam is restrictive. Yet, the only reason such Christians wish to gain access to this site is to cause corruption. They seek to cause discord among the Muslims. They do so by attempting to 'convert' the Muslims to a way contaminated by paganism.

Rather than any sincere effort in worship they desire to corrupt the oneness of God, all to make Christianity dominant. Then, this Christianity is based upon certain pagan rites, such as the crucifixion and the trinity, all of which are diametrically opposed to Islaam. Thus, Christians are banned from this region, because God wishes to keep it purified and in peace. The purification is the absolute worship of God as a single Being devoid of any associates.

Historically, Christians and Jews have attempted to corrupt the Muslim faith. What's more, they continue to do so and thus publish many falsehoods against it. In contrast, Muslims do not publish falsehoods regarding Christianity. Nor do they do so regarding Judaism.

Today, there is a war against Islaam. There is an aggressive campaign in the West to falsely portray it. What's more, many Christians are confused regarding the oneness of God. Somehow, they hold mere humans—the Christ and certain saints—as divine. The Kaaba is the house of the single God. Therefore, professed Christians and Jews, as well as atheists, are banned from entering the Sanctuary. The only way they can enter it is to publically and sincerely adopt the faith of Abraham.

Yet, what is this faith? It is merely testifying that there truly is only one almighty God, that He has no other associates, and that, surely, the Prophet Muhammad is His Messenger.

accomplishments are of no consequence. Moreover, they will be the residents of the fire. Ultimately, the only (legitimate) visitor or attendant to God's houses of worship is the believer, that is the one who believes in God and resurrection, is constant in prayer, is charitable, and remains in awe only of God. Without doubt, such people may expect to be rightly guided.

Do you possibly regard the mere giving of water to pilgrims and the tending of the Sacred House as being equal to those who believe in God and resurrection and who work with their fullest capacity for God? (How could they be equal)—in God's view the fact is they are far from equal. What's more, God never blesses with His guidance people who deliberately commit evil.

Those who believe in God and also work hard in His cause and do so with all that they possess, as well as their lives, these are the ones who in His view have the highest status. Surely, these are the true winners. Their Lord gives them the good news of the mercy that results from (the pleasure of earning) His acceptance, as well as the prearranged paradise, full of permanent happiness, as well as gardens, a paradise where they will live forever. Certainly, with God is a mighty, magnificent reward.

You true believers, if a rejection of the truth is dearer to them than true belief, never associate yourself with your brothers and even fathers. Those who do so after becoming aware of this are, without doubt, perpetrators of evil.✦

That is because the only real relatives of the true believers are fellow believers. Mere blood ties are irrelevant and mean nothing unless such persons are dedicated in their worship of God. In fact, to associate with people who reject God, merely because they are genetic relatives, violates the divine code. This association is an example of racial pride. Furthermore, it is tantamount to the rejection of faith.

Tell them, "If your fathers, sons, brothers, spouses, tribes/clans (that is your relatives and close associates) and even your worldly possessions, even the commerce in which you fear a decline, as well as the homes in which you take pleasure, if all these are dearer to you than the service of God and His Prophet and the struggle in His cause, then, wait until God manifests His will. What's more, realize that God never graces with His (merciful) guidance people determined to commit evil.

Certainly, God has supported you intensively on many battlefronts when you were outnumbered. (This includes) the Day of Hunayn, when you became overconfident, because of your increased numbers, which proved of no use to you because the earth, despite all its breadth, became narrow (making you vulnerable to enemy attack), and, thus (in fear) you retreated. Then, God infused from the high heavens His gift of inner peace upon His Prophet and the believers and provided for you from the heavens invisible forces and thus thoroughly chastised the godless. For all who reject the truth this is the appropriate result.

Yet, even so, God turns in is mercy to whomever He deems. This is because (as He desires) God forgives greatly and gives abundantly of His mercy.

You true believers (realize that), those who associate other powers with God are by definition impure. Thus, from now on they are prohibited from approaching the Sacred House. What's more, if you fear poverty, realize that, eventually, God will, if He desires, enrich you through His generosity—because, certainly, God knows all and is completely wise.

Furthermore, fight against those (Christians, Jews, or any others) who despite having been provided with revelation previously do not believe either in God or resurrection, who refuse to abide by what God and (his various prophets) have forbidden, who have abandoned the truthful way of life commanded upon them by God. Fight them until they agree to willing pay the exemption tax, that is after being defeated in war.✦

✦That is fight all rebellious people regardless of denomination, who attempt to destroy the way of God. These are the hostile Christians and Jews, who conspire against the Muslims and do everything possible to destroy them. They are an enemy of equal status to the outright rejecters of God. In contrast, God-loving Christians or Jews are never to be attacked. Rather, the Muslims are obligated to protect them as well as their religious shrines. Even so, the Qur'aan makes it clear that God Himself has obligated the people of scriptures to be just but that due to their failure in this regard they have become, in fact, *His enemies*.

Son of God: pagan origins

The Jews claim that Ezra✦ is God's son, while the

✦No one knows for certain who is Ezra. He is presumed to be an early Israelite Prophet, perhaps after Moses, who was sent to revive the original teachings. Thus, this tradition of attributing to God's men 'divine' powers is a fabrication. Such attributions were common in ancient Egypt, Phonecia, Greece, and Rome. Yet, obviously, no such men were documented to have inherently any God-like powers. Rather, in speech they proclaimed themselves as servants of God.

Christians claim that Christ is God's son. They say this without giving it any thought, following the same assertions made previously by (what were, essentially,) godless people. They deserve the curse, "May God destroy them."

How perverted is their thinking. Rather than God they have (essentially) taken their rabbis, priests, and monks, as well as the Christ, Mary's son, himself, as their lords. This is despite the fact that they had been commanded to worship exclusively the one God,✦ the only known power

✦Abraham preached the oneness of God, as did Jesus and Mary. In fact, all the Israelite prophets were his relatives. Thus, it makes no sense that Jesus and Mary would preach any other message besides the way of Abraham. Then, this is the belief in the one universal God who has no associates.

and even though He is so far beyond in His magnificence anything that can be comprehended, that is from anything they may regard as sharing in His power.

Through these statements they wish to extinguish God's guiding light. However, God disallows this, because regardless of how much they hate it He has determined to completely spread His guidance. Thus, He sent His Prophet with the task of spreading guidance in order to demonstrate the way of life based upon (a system of) truth, so that regardless of how hateful it may be to the godless He may cause it to prevail over all (other) false ways.✦

✦That is all other ways which are applied today, which lead to the oppression of common people, are man-made. This includes democracy, which is nothing more than a tool to create, as well as maintain, global tyranny. Rather than democratic this system is demonic. This is because all it has created is global strife. Of note, consider how Iraq was forcibly 'democratized,' all to gain control over its oil wealth and strategic position, rather, to further the agenda of powerful Zionist elements. This aggression has led to destruction of this country. It is these powerful ones, seeking their own wicked agenda, which perpetrated the invasion.

You true believers, realize that many of the rabbis, monks, and priests wrongfully consume other peoples' assets, and (as a result) turn others away from the way of God. However, regarding all who hoard treasures (of gold, silver, money, and more) and neglect to spend it for the service of God, remind them about an awesome affliction—when all that hoarded wealth will be heated in the fires of hell and used to brand their foreheads, sides, and backs, while being told, "Experience the vile result of your hoarded treasures."

Clearly, the number of months in God's view is twelve, established in God's (astronomical) decree, when He created the universe as well as the earth.✦Of these, four are sacred. This is the eternal

✦That is the concept of 12 months based originally upon a lunar system is, in fact, a divine creation. Humans gain voluminous advantages of this and rarely give thought to its Source. This was to give human beings a system, which allows them to structure, as well as predict, their lives. This is an immense mercy from the completely loving and merciful Lord. It was all thought out by Him with the benefits of human creation in mind. Thus, humans owe their Lord in a way which is beyond imagination. This is why ingratitude to Him is such a crime.

law of God. Thus, never sin against yourselves regarding these. Furthermore, fight as a solid team—

---

one uncompromising unit—against all who give powers to others besides God, just as they fight against you as a team. What's more, realize that God is with those who hold Him in awe.

The intercalation, that is the insertion of additional day(s) in the calendar of months, is merely another example of their refusal to accept the truth, merely a means by which the godless deviate. They declare this intercalation to be permissible in one year, while forbidden in another. They do so merely to superficially conform to the number of months which God has deemed hallowed. Thus, they attempt to make legal for themselves what God has forbidden,✦because

✦In the Prophet's time God established the lunar calender, setting aside sacred months. The pagans developed a modification of it to avoid this duty. However, the lesson is universal and applies to all those who attempt to escape any duty to God by making up their own laws.

they believe that the evil they commit will, somehow, benefit them. What's more, God never favors with His (merciful) guidance people who refuse to acknowledge the truth.

You true believers, what is the defect in your commitment that when you are urged to proceed to wage war in God's cause you instead cling firmly to (worldly) attachments? Are you content with the comforts of this transitory life (to such a degree) that you prefer it to the next life? However, the pleasures of this life are of no consequence compared with the (benefits of the) final one.

(You are being told this, because) if you shirk your obligation to wage war in God's service, He will punish you with an incomprehensible punishment. Furthermore, He will replace you with another people, while through your behavior you will by no means have harmed God—because it is a fact that God can do anything.

If you refuse to support the Prophet's cause, then, realize that God will take care of it, just as God supported him when the godless drove him away and he was alone with only one other (man), that is when these two were in the cave, and the Prophet said to his companion, "Have no fear, God is with us." Then, from the heavens God gave him His inner peace and debased the purpose of the godless, while in contrast the purpose of God remained supreme. This is because with God is all the power and wisdom. Thus, proceed to war, whether it is easy or difficult for you. What's more, work hard in God's cause with all that you possess, including your lives. If you only realized it, this is for your own good.

(Regarding the waging of war) had there been the opportunity for immediate gain and a easy path, they would definitely have followed you. However (in their view), the struggle was too great for them. Yet, after returning (victorious) they will swear by God, "If we had only been able to help, we would surely have gone with you." So, by this false oath they merely add to their doom. This is because God knows they are liars.

Hypocrites: behavior and tendencies

May God pardon you (O Prophet): Why did you allow them to remain home before it had become obvious to you✦regarding who was really telling the

✦That is before God made it clear to him through divine revelation. The Prophet may have accepted their excuses as legitimate, while God realized their true nature, that is that they were frauds. Through this they proved that they had no awe of God but were fearful instead of fellow humans. Yet, these humans had no power over them, a fact which is undeniable, since Islaam prevailed despite the fears of those hypocrites.

truth versus who was lying? Those who truly believe in God and in the resurrection never request exemption from struggling with their fullest capacity (and with all they own), even their lives, in God's service. Furthermore, God is fully aware of who is truly in awe of Him.

The only ones who ask to be exempted are those who fail to believe in God and resurrection and whose hearts have become open to doubt, so that through this doubt they constantly vacillate. Yet, if they truly wanted to go with you, surely, they would have prepared for it. However, God was averse to their going (to battle), so He caused them to be held back (as if to say), "Stay at home with the rest of those who do so."

Had the false believers gone with you, they would have merely added the vileness of corruption. Furthermore, without doubt, they would have gone from one person to the other, seeking to cause dissension within your ranks, since in your ranks there are those who would have responded to them. However, God is fully aware of those who are wicked. In fact, even before this they attempted to incite dissension and devised a wide variety of plots against you until the truth was revealed and God's will became manifest, regardless of how much they despise it. Moreover, some of them requested, "Give me permission to remain home, and don't make my life too difficult." Yet, surely, by making such a request they had already failed their test and had succumbed to a temptation to evil. Furthermore, hell will surely overwhelm all who refuse to acknowledge the truth.

If you become successful, they will be miserable, while if you suffer harm, they will (delight in it), saying, essentially, "We have already taken the appropriate precautions" and will, in fact, reject (you) and rejoice. Tell them, "No harm can come to us, except what God has already decided. He is our Supreme Lord, and in God let the believers place their trust."

Also, tell them, "Are you hoping that we will be harmed, while nothing can happen to us, except the two finest results (that is death and paradise)? Yet, regarding you we are, hopefully, waiting for God to inflict punishment upon you, either from Himself or through us. Then, wait, hopefully, we, too, will wait." Tell them, "Regardless of what you do, consciously or unconsciously, it will never be accepted, because truly your whole purpose is wicked." This is because all that prevents their efforts from being accepted is that they deliberately refuse to acknowledge God and His Prophet. Furthermore, they never worship without reluctance and never spend on the truly good without resentment.

Thus, never be overwhelmed by their worldly success or apparent pleasure they derive from it or from their pride of lineage. God only seeks to torment them through these means in this material life, so their souls will depart while in a state of rejection.

Furthermore, they swear in God's name that they are with you, but it is not true: they are merely a people consumed by fear. If they could only find a hiding place—anywhere—they would immediately run for it. (The fact is) they are completely afraid.

Also, some (of these false believers) find fault with you (O Prophet,) concerning how you distribute the offerings given for the service of God. If they receive a portion of it, they are pleased. Yet, if they are denied any of it, the fact is they are consumed with rage. Yet, if they could only be happy with whatever God and His Prophet provides them and would say, "God is sufficient for us. God will provide us with whatever He deems from His generous disposal and (will cause) His Prophet to give us (our appropriate share), too. In fact, we exclusively turn to God with our hopes."

The charity given for God's service is meant only for the poor and destitute as well as for those engaged in its distribution. It is also for those whose hearts are to be won over, as well as for the freeing of a human (in prison or wrongly held) and also for those who are in debt. It is also for every effort in God's cause as well as for the traveler/stranger in need. This is a duty from God. Moreover, God has the complete spectrum of knowledge and is absolutely wise.

Yet, some of them imply derogatory things about the Prophet, saying, "He says so little (and seems to only listen)." Tell them, "If he talks minimally and listens much, it is because he is listening to (precisely) what will benefit you. He believes in God and trusts implicitly in the believers." Moreover, he is a manifestation of God's generosity towards those who truly believe (in their hearts). Regarding those who malign God's Messenger they will be (in the next life) severely punished.

The people who claim to believe (but are, in fact, hypocrites) swear to you in God's name that they are acting on your behalf. (They do so) merely to appease you, while if they truly understood (the nature of belief they would realize that), above all, it is God and His Prophet whose pleasure they should seek. Are they unaware that the consequences of fighting against God and His Prophet are dire, that is to live in the fires of hell, the greatest (conceivable) disgrace?

Some of these false/hypocritical believers dread that a new Qur'aanic section would be revealed, which proves them wrong and thus makes them realize their true nature. Tell them, "Go ahead and belittle us. The fact is God will bring to fruition precisely what you are dreading." Yet, if you questioned them, they would surely answer, "We were only joking and didn't mean it." Tell them, "Then, were you belittling God, His revelations, and His Prophet? Make no excuses for your (behavior). Obviously, after committing yourself to it...you have denied the truth." While We may pardon some of you others will be punished, because they are lost in sin.

Whether male or female the believers who are false in their beliefs are all the same. They recommend wicked acts and forbid goodness. They also prevent themselves from doing good. They are oblivious of God, and, thus, He is oblivious of them. In fact, it is only the false believers who are truly consumed by evil.

Whether male or female God has assured the (hypocritical) believers, as well as the godless, the same consequence: the burning (torment) of hell. They will live there forever, which is appropriate. What's more, God has rejected them, and their future only consists of great and prolonged torment. Tell them, "You are like the false/hypocritical believers who existed previously. They were far more powerful than you and far richer too. Moreover, they reveled in their share of worldly happiness. You, too, have been enjoying your share, just like those who preceded you. Plus, you have been abusive (in your speech and actions), just like them." It is (such individuals) whose achievements have become of no consequence in this world as well as in the next life. What's more (rather than the believers in God), these are the ones who are truly lost.✦

✦That is in permanent despair. The loss they will experience is that instead of giving their lives to God they wasted them in self-centered pursuits. Thus, such people consume their entire lives in trivial pursuits. They give nothing to God. By this, they gain the greatest loss of all—the loss of His compassion and love.

Are you aware of the histories of those previous extinct civilizations: Noah's people, the people of Thamood and 'Aad, Abraham's people, and the people of Midian as well as those of the lawless cities? All received prophets, who represented the obvious truth. However, since they rejected them it was not God who wronged them, but, rather, it was they who wronged themselves.

Regarding the male and/or female believers they are essentially the same. They all prescribe good and forbid evil. They are constant in prayer and give charitably. They pay heed to God and His Prophet. They are the ones who God will give His generosity. In truth, God is almighty and totally wise.

God has promised both believing men and women paradise as well as beautiful homes in gardens of eternal happiness. However, God's sought-after acceptance is the greatest peace and happiness of all. Surely, this is the greatest of all achievements.✦

✦That is rather than merely desiring paradise because of its 'fruits' the highest achievement is to desire the loving acceptance of God—to, in fact, earn His approval. In fact, it is to desire His wondrous presence. This is the most grand achievement possible, the earning of the peace that results from being in His presence, nourished by His love. It is the peace of earning His favor for a job well done.

You Prophet, exert yourself (with all your might) against the godless as well as the false/hypocritical believers. What's more, be adamant with them. However, if they refuse to repent, their goal will be hell, and what a vile ending that is.

(The false, that is) hypocritical believers swear in God's name that they have said nothing wrong. However, they certainly have done so, making statements that are tantamount to a rejection of the truth. Also, by their statements they have, essentially, denied (their faith of submission), even after their original profession to God. This is because (in their self-centeredness) they were attempting to achieve the impossible.✦

✦That is to, somehow, benefit by serving two masters, God and themselves. This is through neglecting their commitment to God, merely to serve their own selfish desires. Yet, still, they attest to His worship, even though it is superficial. In other words, it is merely empty words. In any crisis such people will desert any former obligation and instead seek to serve only themselves. Thus, while they appear to hold to the truth they are the most unreliable of all people.

Moreover, they could find no fault with this (new religion) except that God has enriched (the hearts of) those who follow it and caused His Prophet through His generosity to also enrich them.

Thus, if they make amends, it will be for their own benefit. However, if they reject it, God will make them suffer, both in this world and in the next life. Furthermore, they will find no recourse on earth and no support anywhere.

In addition, some of them swear to God, "If only God was (first) generous to us, we would, then, be generous for (His cause) and would surely do what is right." However, as soon as He gives them some of His generosity, they cling to it (that is these worldly gains), greedily and (then) obstinately reject (all that they promised). As a result, He causes their false beliefs to become imbedded within them, to remain there until they meet Him— all because they refused to fulfill the promises they made to God and because their only desire was to disguise the truth from their own selves.

Don't they realize that God knows all the most deeply hidden secrets in their hearts, as well as their secret plotting and planning, and that God is fully aware of all that human beings are unable to perceive? In fact, those 'believers' who find fault with the (true) believers who give generously for the sake of God beyond their obligation, as well as with those who find nothing to give beyond what little they have and who also mock them—these are the real hypocrites. Yet, God will cause their mockery to become a source of great regret. What's more, a wicked torment is their consequence.

Whether you pray to God on their behalf or fail to do so it doesn't matter—because even if you were to pray for them endlessly, God will never forgive them, since they deliberately refused to accept God and His Prophet. What's more, God never guides those who deliberately persist in spreading evil.

After the departure of God's Prophet (to wage war) those false ones, who were slackers, were thrilled at staying behind (from the conflict), because they hated the thought of giving of themselves with their lives and assets in God's way. What's more, they even said to the others, "It is foolish to go to war in this heat." Tell them, "The fire of hell is far hotter."

If they just understood this. So, let them mock (it) for now, because ultimately they will cry a great deal—all as a result of their own actions.

If, then, God causes you to again engage them where they ask you to allow them to join you in war, tell them, "You will never be allowed to join me. Nor will you be allowed to fight on my side." No doubt, initially, you were satisfied to stay home. So, stay there, along with the others who (are obligated) to do so. Furthermore, at their deaths never pray for them, nor attend their funerals. This is because, no doubt, they purposely rejected God and His Prophet and remained sinners to the bitter end. Moreover, never be confused by their material success and the apparent happiness they derive from it. God merely wants to torment them by these means in this world as well as to cause their souls to leave this planet while still in a state of rejection.

(Their condition is obvious) because when they are requested through revelation to believe in God and give their all on His behalf, along with His Prophet, those armies✦ that were fully capable of

---

✦That is, originally, those armies arising in Medina to fight the threat of godlessness, although this would apply to Godly movements in any era. It is the attitude of holding personal desires over the obligation before God and thus due to the fear of loss abandoning the duty to Him.

going to war asked you for exemption, saying, "Let us stay behind with the others."✦ They were fully

✦That is "the others" in this case signifying those who were legitimately given exemption by the Prophet due to sickness or obligations—the lame, teachers, caretakers, women, etc.

satisfied to remain with those (women and others) who were left behind and as a result their hearts have been sealed, so they are incapable of comprehending the truth.

Even so, the Messenger of (God) and all who share his faith work with their fullest effort in God's cause with all that they possess, even their lives. They are the ones who will (earn major gains in the next life), the most supreme of (all) achievements. They are also the ones who will achieve (the ultimate) happiness. As a permanent residence God has prepared for them a paradise.✦ This is the greatest of all achievements.

✦That is, incredibly, each person gets his own paradise. According to the Prophet a few square feet of paradise is equal to this world and its contents. This demonstrates the vast mercy of almighty God, who is according to His own description merciful beyond comprehension.

A few of the (tribal) people offered feeble excuses, while the godless, who denied God and His Prophet, remained idle at home. A vile punishment will befall those who truly rejected the truth. However, the disabled, the sick, and those lacking the means are exempted (from any punishment), if they are true (in all other respects) to God and His Messenger.

The truly God-fearing will never be blamed. God is loving and merciful. Nor will there be any blame upon those who, when they came to you requesting to be transported to the battlefield and you could find no means to do so, those who left in tears in grief that they were unable to contribute. The true offenders are those who request exemption, even though they are fully capable. They are satisfied to be with the slackers.✦

✦That is, literally, "pleased to sit at home securely with the women." Such people allow their own fears to rule them and by doing so prove their lack of commitment. This is the lack of commitment to sacrifice the person's all for the sake of God, even against seemingly overwhelming odds, even at the risk of death.

This is for the fight against tyranny. It is binding on all Muslims. The real Muslim is one who is willing to sacrifice his entire self, even his life, to God. Then, if called by Him, he does so without hesitation, even if it means he could easily die.

As a result, God has sealed their hearts. Thus, they are unable to use their reason.

What's more, when you return (from the campaign), they will continue to make excuses. Tell them, "Give me no feeble excuses, because we will not believe you. Regarding your true nature God has already enlightened us. What's more, God will take note of your future actions, and so will His Prophet." Further, eventually, you will be returned to Him, the One who knows the unknown—the imperceptible—as well as the obvious. Then, He will cause you to truly understand the real implications of your actions.

When you will have returned to them, they will appeal to you in God's name to leave them (that is the hypocrites,) be. Do so. They are despicable. What's more, the torment is their result, the ultimate compensation for their deeds.

They will swear to you (that they are true) with the objective of making you pleased with them. However, even if you were pleased with them, in fact, God will never be pleased with people who are committed to injustice.

The ignorant tribesmen who accept the faith but have no real belief in their hearts are more tenacious in their antagonism and hypocrisy than the city people.✦ What's more, they are more liable

✦That is the ignorant, illiterate believers of the desert, who failed to understand the depth of this message. Because they lacked any real understanding, when asked to sacrifice themselves for God, they clung heavily to their earthly desires. More contemporarily, this applies to any ignorant people, who act based upon emotions and personal desires rather than common sense or a deep understanding. This is because it is impossible for an ignorant person to gain a true and deep understanding of His nature. Nor can an ignorant person gain a true understanding of His way of life.

to ignore the heavenly ordinances, which God has made (through His Prophet) mandatory. However, God is fully aware (of the implications of this) and is completely wise. Furthermore, some of such tribal people regard all that they might spend in God's service as a loss, while they wait for misfortune to overcome you believers. However, they are the ones who will suffer dire consequences. What's more, realize that God is fully aware and knowledgeable of all that happens.

However, some of the tribal (or primitive) people truly believe in God, as well as the final time, and regard all that they give (in God's cause) as a means of becoming closer to God (also desiring to be), blessed by the Prophet in his prayers. Certainly, their prayers will be answered, and they will be brought closer (to Him). God will admit them to His mercy, because God forgives greatly and is truly merciful.

Regarding those who are foremost, that is those who are leaders in the abandonment of their previously evil ways, as well as those who are the first to uphold the faith, plus any who follow them in the way of goodness, God is absolutely pleased with them, just as they are absolutely pleased with Him. Furthermore, as a permanent home He has prepared for them a paradise. This is the greatest success, beyond comprehension.

Some tribal (that is ignorant/uneducated) people in your region are truly hypocrites. What's more (even), in the Prophet's city✦ there are dedicated

---

✦This applies directly to Medina, but it also applies to a divine movement in any city and in any age. So, in all regions where there are believers there are also hypocrites. This is a kind of system, which God uses in order to test the resolve of the true believers, while also evaluating the true nature of those who merely feign belief.

---

hypocrites. You do not always realize who they are, but We do. We will multiply their suffering in this world, and they will (also) endure unmerciful torment in the future. Moreover, there are others— people who take God to heart (and therefore desire) to make amends regarding their sinning after doing some good as well as bad deeds. In fact, God may accept their repentance. Surely, God forgives greatly and gives vastly of His mercy.

Thus, O Prophet, accept whatever material goods they offer for the sake of God. This is so that you may allow them to cleanse their souls through the offering, so they grow in purity. Thus, pray for them (that is those who sincerely seek to make amends). Certainly, your prayer will comfort them. What's more, God has complete awareness and is fully knowledgeable (regarding all that is).

Are you unable to comprehend that it is God alone who can accept the repentance of His servants—that only God is the true recipient of whatever is offered for His sake—and that God alone is an acceptor of repentance as well as the only One capable of giving mercy? So, tell them, "Do what you will. Regardless, God is aware of your actions, and so is His Messenger✦ as well as

✦The point is it is *His* messenger. No human selected him. He alone chose him, a fact agreed upon by Western historians. Therefore, the rejection of him is the same as the rejection of God.

In the West in particular his message is disregarded. This is despite the fact this message is non-racial. In other words, it is universal. Even so, people continue to deny him despite the fact that it is well known that he was a true Prophet of God.

It is obvious he was true. This is because of his vast influence upon civilization, which is fully documented by Western historians. In all his efforts, even in his war campaigns, he never harmed the innocent. Nor did he, as have Western conquerors, devastate the earth, wildly harming friend and foe. In his whole life he merely supported the people, never taking anything for himself other than his most bare needs. Who, then, could do this other than a Prophet of God?

those who support him." So, eventually, you will be brought before Him—(the One) who knows the unknown and the imperceptible as well as the obvious. Furthermore, then, He will cause you to truly understand (the purpose behind) your actions.

There are yet others who must await God's decision.✦ He may punish them or pardon them.

✦That is during the time of resurrection. Here, there will be people held in limbo, who never clearly demonstrated their beliefs. They are also the ones who neglected to do good works. God will carefully and justly determine their status.

By such a neglect they actually fuel the growth of tyranny. This is because they are indifferent to the tyranny which besets humankind. These are the ones who in their fear blindly follow those in power.

This is because God knows all the circumstances and is completely wise.

There are still others (that is actual hypocrites) who have established a separate facility of worship; (this is) strictly to create mischief as well as to promote the abandonment of the faith (that is apostasy) and dissension among the believers. They establish it as a gathering place for all who from the outset have been fighting against God and His Prophet. What's more, they will surely swear to you, "We only have your (best) interests in mind," while God is fully aware of their lies.

Never enter such a place. Only a house of worship based upon the absolute awe of God is worthy of entering. This is a place where there are people who desire to grow in purity. Moreover, God loves those who purify themselves.

Thus, which is superior—the person who has established his foundation on the basis of the love and awe, in fact, reverence of God, as well as a desire for His love, or the one who has done so (based on falsehood, as if) on the edge of a water-worn, crumbling river bank, which must inevitably crumble, along with him, into the fires of hell? Thus, God never guides those who deliberately do wrong.

The foundation which they have built will remain a source of anxiety in their hearts, until their hearts are disintegrated (into dust). What's more, God knows all and is absolutely wise.

True believers: characteristics and rewards

Surely, God has made a bargain with the true believers: for their lives and assets in exchange for the promise of paradise. For God's sake they will fight. They will kill and be killed. This is the true promise which He made for them in the Old Testament, the Gospels as well as the Qur'aan. Furthermore, who is more true to his promise than God? Then, be thrilled in your bargain. This is the ultimate success.

(It is a success) for those who turn to God in repentance whenever they have sinned and who worship and praise Him. (It is for) those who unceasingly seek His goodly acceptance, who bow down before Him and humble themselves in adoration, enjoining the doing of good, forbidding vile acts, and who adhere to the limits set by God. What's more, give to the believers the promise of this good news (of the ultimate success) from God.

It is not for the Prophet and his faithful adherents to request God's forgiveness for the godless, even if they are close relatives, that is after it has become obvious that those sinners are destined for hellfire. Yet, Abraham's prayer that his father be forgiven was the exception, since he had previously promised him he would do so (and Abraham always kept his promises). Even so, when it was made clear to him that he had always been God's enemy, he disavowed him, although, truly, Abraham was most tender hearted, deeply merciful. Furthermore, after inviting people to His way God would never condemn them (to punishment), unless He (first) made certain that they were properly warned (about the consequences of their acts). The fact is God is fully knowledgeable about all (that is).

Without doubt, the rule over the vast heavens and this earth belongs to God. Only He deems (the timing of and site of) life and death. What's more, only God has the power to protect and/or support you.

Surely, God has turned in His mercy to the Prophet, as well as those who abandoned the domain of evil and those who have supported the faith, as well as anyone else, who followed the Prophet in that difficult time, the time when the hearts of some of the other believers deviated. Even so, He turned to them (that is those who made these errors) in His mercy, because without question He is full of compassion towards them, giving in His mercy. He also turns towards those (groups of true believers), who fell prey unintentionally (in their minds) to corruption until in the end after the earth, despite all its vastness, had become too constricted for them and their souls also had become totally constricted: they ultimately realized in their hearts that there is no refuge from God other than a return to Him, when as a result (of this new realization in their hearts), He again turned to them in His mercy (all) so they might correct themselves. This is because, certainly, only God has the power to accept repentance, and only He is the true giver of mercy.

You true believers, always keep God deeply in mind. In addition, be completely true to your word.

What's more, whenever they suffer any deprivation in the service of God, whenever they make any effort against the godless, or whenever they suffer whatever they may suffer in the battle against the enemy—whenever any issue in which they must struggle in God's cause arises—they are given a credit. Certainly, God never fails to compensate those who do good.

Also, regardless of the extent when they spend anything for God's sake, whether small or large, and whenever they conduct their business to serve God, they are given additional credits. What's more, God will reward them based upon the finest reward, that is the best that they (ever) achieve. Despite this it is inappropriate for all believers to go to battle at once. Some must remain in order to devote themselves to acquiring a more profound knowledge of (God's way), as well as to teach newcomers, so they, too, might protect themselves against evil.

Mandate to fight the godless

You true believers, regarding those godless people who surround you, fight with all your might against them.✦What's more, let them discover that you are

✦That is the war is mandatory, because the entire purpose of Islaam is to eliminate tyranny. According to the Qur'aan the source of all tyranny is the rejection of the truths of God. Thus, it is what a person holds in their heart against God that is the real source of tyranny.

The rejection of God leads to moral deprivation. Then, only vileness reigns. Becasue of this rejection people no longer feel responsible for their actions.

The true believer in God is obligated to resist this. This resistance may take many forms, not necessarily physical war. In many instances fighting with guns is inappropriate, in fact, ludicrous. Tyranny must be fought by any means available, even sincere, loving words. The use of force may ultimately be necessary. Yet, when the real basis of tyranny is exposed, it crumbles. Truly, like all forms of evil it is merely weak, readily destroyed.

adamant in your position. Furthermore, realize that God is with all who deeply revere Him.

Yet, whenever a portion of this Qur'aan is made clear some of the godless act out, saying, "Who is this supposed to help (that is empower)?" In truth, it does empower the believers, and they become pleased (in their hearts) when they hear it. Regarding those whose hearts are diseased it merely adds additional corrupt thinking to their already corrupt minds. What's more, each new message adds further degrees of corruption, and, so, they will die while still godless.

Then, are they unaware that they are being continuously tested? Even so, they never beg for forgiveness. Nor do they have any awe of God or keep Him in mind. Furthermore, whenever a chapter (of this writing) is sent from the heavens, they look at each other and say (essentially), "Is there anyone who can obviously see precisely what is in your hearts?" and then reject it. Yet, God does the same to them, turning their hearts away from the truth—

because they are a people who (stubbornly) refuse to comprehend it.

Now, clearly, there has come to you (O humankind,) one of your own, a Prophet, a guide. He feels great distress at the thought that you might suffer in the next life. He is full of concern for you, full of compassion, love, and mercy towards (those who truly believe in God).✦Yet, if

✦This means that all people are obligated to follow God's Prophet. Ultimately, it means that any argument against this man will be held by God Himself as "groundless." He never decided on his own to be a Prophet. Rather, he was selected by God for this purpose. It was this same God who gave him the Qur'aan. It is also the same Being, who raised up Moses and Jesus. Both these men brought the word of God to humankind. These are progressive words of guidance for this race. Even so, the Qur'aan is even more sophisticated than the existing Bible/Torah, that is in how it guides. This is because it is intact divine revelation. There is no evidence of any human element within it. What's more, for certain it would have been impossible for the Prophet Muhammad to have written it. This book is far beyond his capacity. Also, he was illiterate. So, again, he couldn't have written it.

It is obvious that it is not man-made. Thus, the larger meaning is for all people, Muslims, Christians, Jews, and others, to adhere to him. Men, such as Napolean Bonaparte, Bernard Shaw, and Carlyle made the reason clear. They said that if the people of the world adopted the ways of this man, essentially, the world could be saved. In contrast, without him, there will only be despair. Thus, concludes top Western scholars, only this man can save this world from human destruction. This is why his way must be followed.

they refuse to accept this message, tell them, "God is all I need. He is the only (real) power. I trust in Him exclusively, because He is my almighty Lord, His glorious Highness, His great, almighty self."✦

✦That He is the only One to rely upon and the One in whom to place all trust. To place trust in any other is a loss. Only almighty God has the ability to save anyone, a fact which is surely obvious to anyone who will give it thought.

Section 10
Jonah and the Earlier Prophets

In the name of the most merciful
and compassionate God

A-L-R

These are the revelations of a truly wise, divine book. Do people find it strange that We would inspire a fellow human with, "Warn all humans (of the consequences of their acts)." Thus, give the believers the excellent news that because of their truthfulness in their Lord's view they are the finest of all people. Yet, only the people who lack any concept of the truth (in their hearts) could possibly say, "This man is obviously a fraud."

Yet, in truth your Lord is the one almighty God, who created the universe over six (tremendously long) phases. Now, He rules over it all. No one can plead with Him (for mercy or aid)—unless He allows it. This is God, your almighty Lord. Thus, worship Him exclusively. Are you unable to clearly understand this?

All of you will (ultimately) meet Him. This is the way it is, as God has promised. The fact is He initially creates, then, regenerates them. This is so that He may reward in justice all who make every effort to believe and do good. In contrast, regarding those who fully reject the truth (of God's messages) the result is absolute despair. Surely, because of their refusal to believe they will ultimately experience dire agony.

He made the sun (a source of) radiant energy and the moon (a means of) reflective light. What's more, regarding the latter He has determined (for it) phases, so that you will be able to make calendars and (also) calculate time. Without doubt, it has all been designed by almighty God with a specific purpose.✦ This is how He makes these

✦That is specifically for human benefit and for the survival of all His creation. He did it all for them. This is why the malicious rejection of Him is such a crime.

messages obvious for people who truly have the (innate) ability to understand. Yet, surely, in the natural alternation of the night and day, as well as in all which God has created throughout the universe, there is much evidence for those who are deeply in awe of God.

Regarding those who refuse to believe in the ultimate return to Us, whose focus is merely on this material life and who ignore Our messages, their consequence is the torment, the result of their vile deeds. However, regarding those who truly believe and do good, certainly, their Lord guides them correctly through the (depth of) their faith. Eventually, they will find themselves in (the peaceful gardens of) paradise, living in total happiness. In that state (of happiness) they will exclaim, "You are unlimited in your glory, our God." Then, they will be answered with the greeting, "Peace." What's more, they will conclude their invocation with, "Only God is worthy of praise, the absolute Lord of all the (countless) worlds."

Even so, if because of their vile acts God were to rush to judgement (for human beings) in the same way they rush after material gains, they would all have sealed their fates long ago. However (instead), We give them sufficient time, allowing those who refuse to believe in their return to Us in their arrogance to continue erring. Yet (on what basis does he deny Us, since), regardless of the circumstance if (such) a person endures adverse conditions, he always (in desperation) cries to Us (for help). However, as soon as We have rescued him, he proceeds as if he had never requested it. Thus, their own actions seem appropriate to those who have wasted their own selves.✦

✦That is they take the attitude that they "don't need God." Thus, they believe they can, seemingly, do whatever they want. Yet, when they truly do need Him, they do call upon Him. This is always the case when people experience dire desperation. God points out the hypocrisy of this, because their rejection of Him is obviously baseless, since, always, when confronted with a crisis, it is to God exclusively whom they call.

Yet, there is no doubt about it, previously, We destroyed numerous generations (immersed) in evil, despite the fact that messengers were sent to them with full evidence of the truth. Even so, they refused to believe in them. This is how We compensate those who are lost in sin. Eventually, We made you their successors in order to evaluate how *you* will act.

Even so, whenever Our messages are represented to them despite the fact that they are easy to understand those who refuse to believe they will meet Us—the truly godless—often say, "Bring us a different revelation.✦Or, change it, and then we

✦That is without giving it the slightest thought they reject the existence of God. In other words, despite any warning they won't even investigate it. It is expected that if a person inherently refuses to believe in Him, there will be resistance. Because of pride the person might actually attempt to sabotage the true believer. Then, if God's name is mentioned in any way, only rage and hostility result. This is because such individuals make it their goal to prove that they are righteous, that is that they are correct in their view that there is no divine power. It is also because they refuse to accept even the possibility of their return to Him.

The Messenger and his followers are the opposite, since they fear this return and thus do all they can to please God. What's more, there is resistance, even threats, against the Messenger. This is true even today and largely accounts for the negative press against his system. This is the natural reaction of the person determined to refute God's existence.

may consider it." Tell them, "It is impossible for me to change it. In fact, I only follow what is revealed to me. Surely, I dread the thought of rebelling against my Lord, the agony I will endure on that feared resurrection." Also, tell them, "If God willed, neither God nor I would have brought it to you. Plus, you are well aware that I lived among you for (virtually) a lifetime before I spoke to you in this manner. Are you unable to consider this?"✦

✦That is relating to the speech of the Prophet Muhammad who prior to his commissioning was a quiet, reserved individual. He began his mission at age forty. This mission lasted twenty-three years. Previous to this preaching he said nothing about the divine. It was only after receiving inspiration that he spoke about God. Yet, this could apply to any person who is inspired to preach to the people about their obligations. God causes them to speak His word. Yet, He only does so to good and decent people who are already filled with Him in their hearts.

Yet, who could be more wicked than those who invent their own rules—mere fabrications—as if they are God's or who blatantly reject (what He reveals)? Certainly, those who are lost in sin will never achieve happiness. Neither will those who worship other (impotent) beings or entities in addition to God, as if they are telling themselves, "These are our intermediaries with God." Tell them, "Do you truly think you can inform God regarding an issue in this universe of which He is unaware? He is incomprehensibly vast in His magnificence, far beyond all that you fabricate as His equals."

Humankind was once a single group. Only later did they begin to differ. What's more, if it wasn't for the fact that your Lord had already decided (regarding the evolution of human existence), all their differences would have been resolved long ago.

The real nature of the godless

Those who are godless, who have no God in their hearts, often protest, "Why doesn't his Lord give him obvious miracles?" Tell them, "Only God knows the unknown. Then (you who refuse to believe in it), wait until His will manifests. I, too, will wait."

Thus, whenever such people experience hardship, they scheme against (Our messages).✦ Tell them,

✦That is they use their difficulties as "proof" that there is no God or even that He has 'wronged' them. Then, incredibly, they go to work against Him, seeking every reason to reject Him.

Much of this is due to their own internal emotions, particularly self-pity. This self-pity may even lead them to consider laying blame for their problems on others despite the fact that they alone are responsible for their woes. Even so, in their confusion they become angry, as if life itself has wronged them. They become embittered, rejecting the authority of God, as if, somehow, they have been wronged. Yet, they have fabricated it all, since by no means has He caused them even the slightest harm. It is all merely an excuse, so they can block God from their lives.

"God is more efficient than you in His profound scheming. In fact, Our heavenly scribes record all your plots."

He is the One who makes it possible for you to travel by land or water about the globe. When you travel on ships in good weather, they (that is the travelers), are merry (in that condition)—until (suddenly, when the) waves surge towards them from all sides; then, when they realize that they are hopelessly surrounded and are about to die, they beg God (at that moment) truly believing in Him alone (as if to say) "If You would only save us, we assure you, we will be grateful." Yet, as soon as the threat has passed, they (again) behave outrageously, violating all decency.

You human beings, all your foul deeds will ultimately descend upon your own selves. Unquestionably, you only care about this temporary world. (Yet, then remember,) eventually, you will return to Us, when We will cause you to truly comprehend the consequences of all you achieved.

The (real nature of this) temporary life can be compared to the rain sent from the heavens, which is absorbed by the plants. Humans and other creatures derive nourishment from it.✦Furthermore,

✦That is from the obvious world, rendered here as 'temporary.' The physical nourishment is in the form of food, all through the kindness of the Lord through the heaven-sent rains. Through the effects of this rain there is the growth and nourishment of food—fruit, vegetables, grains, and grasses—for consumption by herbivores and other creatures as well as humankind. In other words, the rain is yet another gift that humans neglect to consider. Even so, when it is lacking, humans beg for its return. Thus, inherently, they know Who is responsible for it.

Yet, the more profound message is that no one is independent. No human has any real power. No one has even the most remote basis to act arrogantly. Without the blessings of this heavenly Being there would be no human life nor any other form of existence. Plus, the lusting only after the pleasures of this life is a waste, since these are transitory, while the pleasures of the next life are permanent. So, God gives people this example in order to cause them to think—so they will reconsider the basis for their rebellion against Him.

when the earth has been fully and lushly embellished and its inhabitants believe that they are in complete control of it, there rains down upon it Our judgment unpredictably. As a result, We cause it to become (barren), as if a pulverized field—as if there was never anything there. Through this (example) We make these messages clear, that is for those who are willing to give it (due) consideration.

What's more, God invites human beings to (through true submission to Him) the realm of peace and internal satisfaction.♦ Furthermore, He

♦That is this is His own personal invitation. This is through peaceful submission to His will. In His kindness He directly urges humans to do what is right and to, what's more, do what is natural. This is to submit to this higher power. For this the human will gain limitless rewards. It is the willingness to accept the fact that He is the all-powerful Lord and each human is merely His servant. This is the only requirement for success in the final life and for, furthermore, avoiding ultimate harm.

This realm is known in Arabic as *dar as-salaam*. Literally, this means the realm of peace. Yet, rather than any country or region it signifies internal peace. It is the peace of knowing that regardless of what happens God is eternally merciful. This is especially for those who bow in servitude to Him.

Belief in the almighty creator results in satisfaction. It results in a feeling of peace. This is the true meaning of dar as-salaam.

guides the person *who allows himself to be guided*, directly to a straight way.

Regarding those who are resolute in doing good the result is ultimate good. Yet, there are additional benefits. They will be free of any torment. Plus, they are destined for paradise, where they will live forever. Yet, regarding those who commit foul deeds they will be compensated only with their equivalent—and since they will be defenseless before God they will be consumed only with the darkest regrets. They are the ones who will live in the torment forever.

Eventually, We will gather them together. Then, We will tell those who worshiped other than God, "Remain where you are, you along with these supposed divinities,"...because by then We will have separated the two. Then, the beings and entities they regarded as (all-powerful) will say, "It wasn't us who you worshiped, without doubt, God knows best what truly transpired between us."✦

✦That is that it was truly this material life that they worshiped, and it was this that they gave ultimate power. Too, they merely used such false powers for their own purposes. This parable implies that it is, then, their own self that they are serving. Those who reject God freely give powers to others, because enamored by this superficial life they give no thought to their return to Him. Thus, they immerse themselves in senseless passions, while giving power to objects or beings that are inconsequential.

Any objects of worship serve merely as wishful distractions in their attempt to remove from themselves any thought of the high and mighty God. These are the people who surely refuse to believe in their ultimate meeting with Him. These are also the ones who refuse to accept that they will be eventually judged by Him.

Without exception, all will be returned to God, the Supreme Master. What's more, then, all their false gods—that is whatever they held as all-powerful besides Him—will abandon them.✦

✦That is they will be alone and without support. All those people or sources, which had previously promised them support or which, somehow, they regarded as all-powerful—all will evaporate into nothingness. The fact is the person who relies upon any power other than the True One will be merely alone, fully isolated, during that overwhelming time.

Ask them, "Who provides you from the universe around you—the heavens as well as the earth—all that you need? Who has full power over your ability to perceive and comprehend? Who also produces life from the non-living✦and then deems

✦That is an allusion to the true origins of humankind from relatively inert substances: hydrogen, helium, oxygen, nitrogen, and the like. It is fully published that these original molecules of this universe gave birth to life. Precisely how this occurred is unknown. Even so, this serves as a test for all humans. Now, how can anyone refute the possibility of resurrection since, as all top scientists attest, in the origin of life the same process occurred. This is the process of causing life to be produced from inert matter.

death? Who rules all that exists?" Moreover, they will (surely) answer, "God." Thus, ask them, "Then (if you know this), what prevents you from becoming completely conscious of Him and from totally bringing Him into your heart, since He is God, your almighty Lord, the source of all truth?" This is because after the truth has been discarded what else remains other than error? Therefore, how could you possibly fail to realize this? Thus, regarding those who sin purposely your Lord's prediction proved true: (no matter what you say) they refuse to believe.

Ask them, "Can whatever you hold high besides God create any (type of) living being, or after such (a being) dies, regenerate it?"✦ Say to them, "Only

---

✦That is there is only one creator. No other being and surely no human has any such powers. The Qur'aan reiterates that only almighty God is worthy of worship. In a most bizarre concept God must actually tell His humans to worship Him. They rarely if ever determine this on their own.

Yet, Abraham did so. That is why he is held so high. All other matters of emphasis, for instance, nation, club, tribe, state, and/or ancestral belief, are forms of idol worship. What's more, during that fateful time before Him these impotent elements will be a source of agonizing regret. God will only accept as true the pure worship of Him. In contrast, the worship of all other powers will be rejected as will those who give obedience to such powers. For instance, to regard the nation-state as if all-powerful, that is blind patriotism, will offer no substance. Nor will claiming Christ as divine serve any benefit. In fact, anyone who holds as mighty any other than almighty God will only endure loss.

God can do this. Are you unable to think correctly?" Ask them, "Regarding what you ascribe as your power (besides God) can any (such power) guide you to the correct way?" Also, tell them, "Obviously, only God can do so. Then, which of these is more worthy of being followed, the One who guides or the one who is unable to guide, that is unless he himself is guided? Then, why are you unable to understand this correctly?"

In fact, the majority of them follow merely their own speculations. What's more, speculation is no substitute for truth. Surely, God is fully aware of all their actions.

The true source of the Qur'aan and the Prophet's mission

Now, without doubt, this Qur'aan could never have been devised by anyone other than God. Surely, it confirms the remaining truths of the previous revelations and also makes clear the purpose of this newer message.✦ Let there be no doubt about

✦That is that the purpose for humans is to submit to God alone as their Lord. The Qur'aan is direct about this, while much of the previous messages have been diluted over the centuries. Originally, these books were purely from God. However, over time certain man-made elements corrupted them, so that only through a careful search are their truths found. Not so with the Qur'aan. It is entirely divine revelation, which is free of corruption.

it—(it is) from the Lord of all the (vast) realms. Yet, those who reject it claim, "Muhammad invented it." Tell them, "If this is true (that is that a human could write it), then, write a chapter of similar value.✦

✦No one has yet taken the Qur'aanic challenge nor achieved it. Its style, as well as content, is impossible to duplicate. Nor is it possible for anyone to accurately write the history of the ancients. Only God knows such precise details. Undoubtedly, the Qur'aan provides an accurate history of the consequences of the ancients, elucidating even the exact details of the interactions.

There is no other source offering such precision. What's more, the latest archeological findings fully confirm its statements. Thus, the claim, "fables of the ancients" is senseless, since even the ancients were never aware of such details. Rather, the ancients left no record of the coming to them of committed prophets and in fact withheld this information. Nor did they have even the slightest clue regarding human nature. Yet, the Qur'aan accurately describes the exact nature of human beings. Then, who, other than His almighty Self, could be its source?

In this regard if what you say is true, get help from whomever you are able, that is other than God.

Undoubtedly, these deniers refuse to accept the rationale of anything they are unable to (superficially) comprehend, anything of which the inner meaning eludes them until the actual meaning becomes obvious. This was the same consequence for those who previously rejected the truth. So, consider what ultimately happened to them.

Even so, some people will eventually believe in this, while (many) others will never do so. Furthermore, your Lord is fully aware of the real spreaders of corruption. Thus, if they reject you, tell them, "I am responsible for my actions, while you are responsible for yours. You are not accountable for my actions, and I am not accountable for yours."

Some of them pretend to listen to you. Yet, do you expect the deaf to hear, even though they refuse to use their reason? Furthermore, some of them pretend to follow you. However, could you (truly) guide those who refuse to recognize the correct way? Unequivocally, God never wrongs His creatures. Rather, human beings only wrong themselves. Yet, when He gathers them to Himself at that fateful time, it will universally seem to them as if they existed (on earth) only briefly, in fact, like an hour, knowing one another. Therefore, they will be completely lost, that is those who refused to believe (in the ultimate) return to God and thus failed to find the correct way.

Even so, whether We demonstrate for you a portion of what the future holds for those who reject the truth or cause you to die before it occurs, realize that, ultimately, they will be (all) returned to Us. What's more, God is well aware of their actions.

Every community has its prophet. What's more, the judgement, which was done in absolute justice, was passed only after its prophet delivered the message. Yet, they are never wronged in the least.

Even so, the godless are inclined to ask, "If, in fact, what you say is true, when will this supposed judgement occur?" Tell them, "I am incapable of protecting and helping (even) myself (from this judgement), except as God wills."

All (humans) have a specified time (for death). When it approaches, they can neither delay it by so much as a fraction (of a second) nor accelerate it. Also, ask them "Have you considered how you would react if His judgement (that is your scheduled demise), happened unexpectedly?"✦

✦That is in the event of sudden death would the person be ready for this judgement? Would he be internally at peace and thus prepared to meet his Lord? Or, would such a person be internally distraught, fearing it absolutely? Those two reactions, either peace and happiness or absolute despair: God asks people to recognize their condition, now, so they might reconsider, so they might make amends and thus come close to Him. These same people who reject Him are repeatedly through various examples and parables asked to think about the consequences of their acts, strictly for their own sakes. Obviously, the love of God for His creation is vast.

Yet, why would the sinners wish to accelerate it? How could they possibly benefit (from it)? Will you regard it true only after you see it directly, when you will be asked, "Now, do you believe?"—at which time the people who refuse to believe will be told, "Experience the agony (of the torment you have brought upon yourselves)—forever. This is the appropriate consequence for your wickedness."

What's more, some people will ask, "Is this really true?" Tell them, "In my Lord's name it most certainly is true. Furthermore, you will be unable to escape the inevitable." Yet (it has always been this way, that is that), all the perpetrators of evil would surely, if it were available to them, offer all that is on earth as a ransom. Plus, when they realize the enormity of the suffering (they will endure), they will be unable to express their remorse. Yet, by then (regarding them) judgment will have already been decided. Even so, they will never be wronged.

Regardless, it all belongs to God—all that exists in the vast universe as well as this earth. Also, clearly, God's promise always comes true. Despite this, most of them are incapable of understanding (the implications of) this. (Yet, the implications should be obvious, since) only He gives life and appoints death. Furthermore, eventually, you will all return to Him.

Humankind, you now have available a means of insight from your Lord. What's more, it is a cure for (all the confusion) that may be in humans' hearts. Plus, it is guidance and mercy to all who (truly) believe.

Inform them, "Be satisfied with the generosity of God and His mercy." This is far superior to the worldly treasures they accumulate. Also, ask them,

"Have you ever considered all that God gives you and which you, eventually, divide into 'the forbidden and the lawful?'" Ask them, "Has God given you the right to do this, or do you (merely) do it yourself (while attributing it to God)?" However, what do they think, these people who invent lies against God—(what do they think) will happen to them during resurrection? God is unlimited in His generosity towards humanity, however, the majority (of human beings) are ungrateful.

We are aware of all your activities regardless of your circumstances, whether preaching the truth (to others), Qur'aanic recitation, or whatever else you achieve, because We are aware of it all. Truly, those who are close to God have nothing to fear. Nor should they feel (even the slightest) remorse. This is because they are the people who have always kept God in their hearts. They are the recipients of the tremendous consequence of happiness, now as well as in the next life. What's more, since nothing could alter the outcome of God's promises this is the ultimate success (which He promises as true, a promise which is absolute).

Furthermore, regarding the statements of the godless there is no reason to be upset. The fact is all (real) power and glory belong to God. What's more, He is fully aware and knowledgeable (about whatever occurs).

Make no mistake about it all that exists (throughout the vast heavens as well as the earth) belongs to God. Thus, what is it that they follow, those who give powers to others besides God, beings whom they regard as His equals? (Without doubt,) they follow merely their own speculations as well as the speculations of others. Surely, they are merely guessing. Yet (if they would only consider the fact that), He is the One who made the night for you, so your bodies can recover and the day, so you could become enlightened. Surely (through) these (examples there) are messages for people who are willing to comprehend it.

The concept of a divine son disputed

Despite this, they claim, "God has established for Himself a son."✦ (Not so,) rather, He is unlimited in

✦A. M. Daryabadi notes in the *Glorious Qur'an* that this entire concept derives from pagan groups, which created such beings as sun-gods. Thus, the idea of a physical son of God is mythological. This ancient pagan tendency is likely the basis for the later belief in Jesus as a divine being. Yet, God rejects any such associations. What's more, how will devout Christians react when brought before God while claiming the concept of a human God? The fact is humans are created beings. They live, eat, and die.

Then, how could they be gods? Truly, how will those who claim humans as divine fare in that divine Court, the very Court where Jesus himself will proclaim the truth against them regarding both himself and his Master? There, he will make it categorically clear that he is nothing more than a human, true servant of God, merely mortal.

His magnificence. He has no need. All that exists is His. You (humans) have no basis for such a claim. Do you claim for God something that you are unable to know? Tell them, "Truly, whoever claims their own fabrications as if divine✦ will never

✦That is on what basis does anyone claim Jesus as divine? Is there even the slightest shred of proof that he had such unusual powers, that he could, somehow, create an object or even a living being? Could he provide sustenance: rain, wind, crops, fruit, and more? Could he possibly live on his own, never requiring food, drink, or shelter? So, on what basis is the claim for his divinity?

achieve happiness." Their enjoyment will be transitory. Afterwards, they will return to Us. Then, We will cause them to experience vile torment due to their persistent rejection of the truth.

Lessons from various prophets and messengers

Tell them also about Noah, when he told his people, "My people, if you find my presence and preaching repugnant, realize that I place my full trust in God. Then, make your decision against me, and, what's more, request the assistance of those beings whom you empower besides God. Also, once you have chosen your course of action, hold to it. Then, act against me in any way you wish, and give me no quarter. However, if you reject this message I have delivered, realize that I have made no demands of you. Rather, compensation (for whatever I do) is from God, because I am obligated to be one of His true servants."

Yet, they rejected him. Thus, We saved him and his (true) followers, all of them, in the Ark. Then, We made them inherit the earth, while causing the people who rejected all evidence of the truth to drown. Then, realize the ultimate consequences for those who were indifferent to the warning (they received).

After him, We inspired other prophets, each for his own people. In all cases they clearly reiterated the truth. However, their people refused to believe (particularly) in anything they previously rejected. As a result, We sealed the hearts of those who violate the bounds of decency.

We (then) sent Moses and Aaron to Pharaoh and his powerful ones. However, they exulted in their arrogance, because they were a people lost in sin. So, when We represented the truth to them, they said, "Obviously, this is merely magic." Moses responded, "So, this is how you react to the revealed word? Does it make sense that this is merely magic when, in fact, magicians never achieve anything (of any substance)?" (Pharaoh's powerful ones) replied, "Have you come to repel us from our ancient ways, that is our ways of living and worship (as practiced by our ancestors), all so you can take rule from us? In fact, we find neither of you believable."

Then, Pharaoh commanded, "Bring before me this country's best magicians." (Eventually,) when the magicians arrived, Moses said to them, "Produce whatever you must produce." Then, they tossed down their spells, but Moses said to them, "You have invented mere magic, which God will make insignificant. Actually, God never furthers the works of those who spread corruption, while in contrast by His words God proves the truth to be absolute, regardless of how hateful it may be to those who are immersed in sin."

· Yet, only a few of his people declared their faith in Moses,✦ while the majority held back due to

✦That is even among the ancient Hebrews. In other words, even with Moses' followers only a modicum demonstrated true belief. While they all followed him in salvation through the Red Sea few of them proved to be sincere, especially during hardship. In fact, the majority proved that under pressure they had no real faith. This is why God tests people. It is the only way to determine their sincerity or lack thereof. This is the divine system. It is based on fairness to all.

fear of Pharaoh and his powerful ones, afraid of persecution. Without doubt (regarding the fear he created), Pharaoh was a powerful figure and was, certainly, given to excesses. Even so, Moses told his people, "If your claim to believe in God is genuine (then), trust in Him implicitly, that is if you have truly become His servants."✦ Then, they said, "We

✦That is, again, reiterating that only truly deep belief can achieve the desired result. In contrast, if belief is shallow, then, under duress the person abandons it, proving his insincerity. Ultimately, due to much rebellion Moses was forced to rely almost exclusively on his brother Aaron and a handful of true followers, since the rest of his followers remained attached exclusively to the passions of materialism.

do place all our trust in our Lord." Thus (they prayed), "Make us not a plaything for the people committed to evil, and through Your kindness save us from the godless." As a result, We inspired Moses and his brother (with), "Reserve for your people some houses in the city, and tell them, 'Turn your houses into places of worship. What's more, be persistent in your worship (services), and encourage and give hope to the believers (that they will gain God's support).'"

Moreover, Moses prayed, "Our Lord, obviously, You have enriched Pharaoh and his associates with incredible grandeur and wealth. The result, Lord, is that they are causing others to deviate from Your way. Our Lord, bankrupt their riches and harden their souls, so that they may never become believers until they see the bitter end." God answered, "I fully accept this prayer. Then, continue, both of you, and remain resolute in your purpose. What's more, never follow the way of those who are unaware of right and wrong."

Thus (eventually), We brought the children of Israel across the sea. Shortly thereafter, Pharaoh and his associates in their hostility maliciously pursued them (fully unrepentant), until when he was ready to drown, he exclaimed, "Now, I believe that there is only the One God, the same God in whom the Israelites believe. Now, I surrender myself to Him."✦ However, God said, "Now (you do

---

✦That is, literally, *Wa anna min al muslimeen,* meaning, essentially, 'I am one of those who truly surrenders to you.' This demonstrates the generic nature of the word Muslim, muslimeen merely being plural. A Muslim is merely one who submits. This could apply to anyone of any culture or race, who gives his all to almighty God. However, as demonstrated here the mere proclamation is insufficient. Real faith is in the heart as represented by the true commitment to God, along with the willingness to sacrifice for His cause. Pharaoh merely proclaimed it to attempt to protect himself from God's wrath. There was no sincerity in his claim.

---

so), when previously you always fought against Us, when you were foremost in spreading corruption? There is no possibility (of saving yourself). Instead, today, We will only save your body, so that you may serve as a representation for further generations. Without doubt, a large number of people are oblivious of Our messages."

Even so, no doubt, We gave the Israelites a fine and secure new life (fully), providing their needs from the good things of life. Yet, it was *only after they received divine revelation that they developed conflicting views.* Even so, regarding these views, surely, during resurrection your Lord will judge between them. So, if you doubt the truth of Our heavenly revelation, ask the previous readers of the divine word.✦

✦That is challenging them to consider the similarities of this Qur'aan with the previous revelations, those held by Christians and Jews. It is also a challenge to the Christians and Jews regarding the accuracy of the Qur'aan's assessments: that this book precisely analyzes the history behind Christianity and Judaism. Even so, it is obvious that its precepts are also in the Old Testament as well as the Gospels. All such books reveal the obligation for humans to worship and adore the one almighty God. This is the basis of these early books. It is also the basis of this Qur'aan.

Surely, you will find that the truth has now come to you from your Lord. Therefore, never doubt it nor reject it obstinately, in case you become lost.

Clearly, those against whom your Lord's dictate has been realized will never accept the truth, even if every proof is demonstrated to them, that is until they directly experience the vile torment that is their consequence in the next life. Yet, regrettably (throughout history) no community has truly believed in its entirety and then gained the (vast) benefits that result, except the community of Jonah. When they became committed to believe, We removed from them the suffering of disgrace in the life of this world and allowed them to enjoy (to the fullest) their life.

Yet, in fact, if your Lord desired, all who existed (and exist) would have believed. Thus, do you really believe that you could compel people to believe despite the fact that no one, not even a single human being, could ever do so unless God willed?—and that He is the One who places the vileness of godlessness (within the hearts of) those who refuse to use their reason?

Methods of preaching

Ask them, "Have you ever considered all the wonderment of this universe as well as the earth?" Even so, how could it be of any consequence, all the messages, revelations, and warnings, to people who refuse to believe? Then, can such people expect any other result besides the same (dire) catastrophe that happened to the now extinct former deniers of the truth? Tell them, "Then, wait for the final result. I, too, will wait."

In fact, it is always the same: We seal the fate of all who reject Our messages. Then, We save Our prophets and their fellow believers. This is what We have willed upon Ourselves: We (make it Our responsibility to) always save all who believe in Us.

Tell the entire human race, "If you doubt the nature of my faith, then, realize that I could never worship what you worship, but, instead, I worship the One God, the same God who, in fact, causes your demise. What's more, I have been commanded to believe in Him exclusively."

Thus, set your heart resolutely towards the true way of life (of submission to God). Furthermore, reject all that is false. Moreover, never equate other powers with God. Thus, *never make as if divine any entity (or being) that is powerless*✦to help or harm

✦This includes patriotic attachment to the state/country. It also includes the 'obedience' to blood ties. Here, according to the Qur'aan obedience to the powers of state, tribe, or clan is a form of idol worship.

you. The fact is if you do—and there is no question about this—(in God's view) you will be one of the godless.✦

✦That is He is the maker of human beings. Thus, He regards this issue of creating false gods or powers seriously, just as a father would regard it seriously if his child rebuffed him, relying, instead, on complete strangers, who have no interest in the child's welfare.

Parents, as well as other authorities, discipline rebellious and violent children. God loves His creatures. He wants them to find the right way. However, like a strong and responsible parent, who due to love wants what is best for his children, God will not tolerate rebellion. What's more, the greatest rebellion—the greatest ingratitude—is to worship beings or powers other than Him.

Even so, realize that if God should afflict you with difficulty, He is the only One who could remove it, while if He intends good for you, no one could restrain His generosity. He causes (that goodness and generosity) to descend upon whomever He wills of His servants. Moreover, He alone is truly able to forgive, the true provider of mercy.

Tell the entire human race, "The truth from your Lord has now arrived. Therefore, whoever chooses to follow it does so only for his own benefit. In contrast, whoever chooses to reject it does so to his own detriment. What's more, I am not responsible for your actions."

Regarding you (O believer), follow exclusively the revelations you are receiving. Also, regardless of any hardships remain patient, that is until God passes His judgement. Moreover, He is the best One to make any assessments, the most wise—and the most accurate—of all judges.

Section 11
Hood and Other Early Prophets

In the name of the most merciful
and compassionate God

A-L-R

This is a divine book manifested by messages which are easy to understand—which have been carefully described (as well as protected)—all as a result of the mercy of the One who is completely wise and aware. (Its purpose:) that you worship exclusively the one, universal God.

Tell them, "Clearly, my purpose (as sent by God) is to merely warn you as well as bring you encouragement of (gaining God's merciful blessings). Thus, ask your Lord to forgive you. Turn, then, to Him for His forgiveness. As a result, He will give you fulfillment, here, until the term set by Him expires.✦ Plus, in

---

✦That is the time-span of each person's life. Here, the Qur'aan directly speaks to the individual regarding his or her salvation. Only God can determine the length of a person's life. People have no control over when or where they will die. So, here, God gives due warning for people to come to Him now, before it is too late.

---

the next life He will give all who are deserving his appropriate reward. However, if you reject this, I dread the agony you will endure during that overpowering time."

Ultimately, you will all return to God. Moreover, He is fully capable of (making this happen).✦

✦That is He truly has the power to resurrect but also has the power to correctly judge. Singlehandedly, He will handle the judgement of all who have ever existed. All people will be held to account. Clearly, He who originally created has the power to cause the return of all humans, even those scattered into mere dust.

He made each person's blueprint originally. He alone designed the mold. He also created the concept of the soul and then produced it. Yet, He made all people ultimately from stellar dust, the most primitive matter conceivable. This itself is a miracle. Thus, He can easily reproduce humans, a relatively minor task compared to the creation of the human originally. While it is beyond human comprehension for God resurrection of the dead is a minor issue.

Even so, surely, the fact is (regarding Him) the evil people are (attempting to) disguise their feelings. This in order to seemingly hide from Him. Yet, even when in their darkness they attempt to disguise from themselves the perception of this (ultimate return), He knows their innermost secrets as well as their obvious acts. In fact, He knows in detail what is in peoples' hearts.

(Yet, are they unaware of the fact that) every living being on earth is dependent upon God for its survival? He (in advance) knows (the breadth of) each being's earthly term. Plus, He knows where it will reside after it dies.✦ All this is memorialized in a clear (heavenly) document.

✦That is proving, again, that in this section God is directly talking to the human being as an individual. It also demonstrates that He knows precisely what each person deserves. He knows whether the person has earned His love and thus paradise or deserves His rejection and thus hell. Surely, He is fully prepared for the final event, because He alone has the ability to know what humans deserve. Plus, He has the precognition, that is the knowledge in advance, of any person's goals.

He created all that exists, and so it all must return to its Source. He is directly connected to all humans through a kind of vibration. Plus, He is physically close to them. He is so close that He may be regarded as within each human, as confirmed in the Qur'aan, "closer...than the jugular vein." This means He is a part of each person. Since He made humans from nothing to regenerate them from nothingness, mere bones and dust, is a minor issue. He knows even the location of every molecule of all humans. Then, obviously, for Him the maintenance of a heavenly record for all humans is also insignificant.

Even so (it is obvious that He has such powers, since), He exclusively created the heavens and the entire universe, including the earth, in numerous (prolonged) phases.✦ What's more, regarding the

✦That is in eons or vast phases, amounting to hundreds of millions, rather, billions of years. Here, it is indicated that each phase was fully planned by God as a systematic act of creation. This disputes the theory that beings exist due to chance evolution. From the Qur'aanic point of view any evolution is merely an additional creative phase. Yet, there is little evidence for the theory of evolution as an actual cause for creation.

Darwin himself deferred to an almighty creator. His so-called theory of evolution was only later promoted by secularists. This was in order to deny the divine role. Again, there is no evidence that natural beings develop on their own. In other words, there is no proof for mindless or chance evolution. There are also no known missing links. In contrast, there is vast proof for deliberate creation based upon organized laws. The point is nothing happens on its own. Rather, it is all under a highly deliberate control. This proves there truly is an almighty God to which humans are beholden.

creation of life (His system) was established on the basis of water. (This is a reminder) to test you. This is so He may determine who is best in conduct. In this regard if you say, "There truly is a life after death," the people who are devoid of faith in God (in their hearts) will respond, "This is merely wishful thinking." Yet, if We defer their punishment (for their ingratitude until a specified period),✦ they will, without doubt, say "(If it is true,) what is preventing it from coming now?"

✦That is by giving them a chance to reconsider and essentially by giving all humans an opportunity to come to Him. Here, God in His mercy is allowing them extra time to beseech His forgiveness. Yet, incredibly, instead of pursuing Him in love and a desire to please Him they taunt Him. They do so by demanding proof of His powers. Yet, He doesn't need them. Rather, they need Him, which is demonstrated by the following:

Certainly, when it happens, there is no way to stop it. Then, they will be overwhelmed by precisely the subject of their ridicule. Even so, if He allows the human to experience Our generosity and then removes it, he abandons all hope, completely forgetting Our favors. Then, if after that period of difficulty We return him to the good life, he is certain to say, "I am free of all troubles." This is because he is by nature vain. Thus, he thinks only of himself. This is the way it is for the majority of people, with the exception of those who are patient and do good. For them, there will be forgiveness of sins and a mighty reward.✦

✦That is most humans will fail to gain the rewards from God—the blessings of His love and compassion—because they never escape their own vanity. Then, how could a person be vain? Can such a person rise high, like a mountain, or create so much as a lowly fly? Humans are powerless. Thus, to be humble before God is the only sensible solution. If anyone should be proud, it is God, since He alone holds absolute power, and, what's more, no one can compete with Him. Then, He is mighty enough to remind humans regarding an issue which is incredible: that they must bow to Him exclusively.

So, would you purposely (because those who reject the truth dislike it) omit any part of this revelation, because your heart is distressed by statements such as, "Why hasn't he been given a treasure from heaven?" or "Why isn't he accompanied by an (obvious) angel?" Yet, your only purpose is to warn, while it is God alone who has all under His command.

They also claim, "He invented it." Tell them, "If this is true (then, you should be able to), write ten chapters of similar value, exclusively your own invention.✦ (To do

✦That is to write a similar document not containing portions or imitations of any existing divine books. This would be an independent effort. Yet, no one has ever achieved it. Nor would God allow it, that is any such vain attempt to counter Him. After all, He is closer to the human than a human's own soul and so can decide all that may be. So, now, 1400 years since its inception no one has produced any such guide, which provides all that humans need to grow their souls. Nor has anyone produced a book such as this Qur'aan, which directly speaks to the human soul.

so) gather all (the forces) conceivable to assist you, that is other than God. However, if these cohorts of yours are unable to do so, this is proof that God revealed it and that He is the only divine power. Now, will you submit to Him?"✦

✦That is, once again, attempting to give humans the opportunity to make the correct decision and bow to Him. He continually pursues humans to cause them to use their reason. He does so by challenging them to think, the latter being the entire basis of this book. It is to cause humans to realize that this truly is a divine revelation sent to them for their own benefit in fact salvation.

Regarding those who are enamored only with this material life and all its pleasures We will compensate them appropriately. They will certainly be given their appropriate (worldly) share. Yet, in the next life all they gain is agony. What's more (because of their refusal to believe in the truth), all their actions will be in vain, totally worthless. Thus, is the person who merely cares for this life the same as the one who commits himself completely on the basis of clear evidence

from His Lord, that is via this divine testimony—a
divine book given as a guidance and mercy for the
entire human race? Definitely and absolutely, *only
those who truly understand and comply with the
purpose of this message fully believe in it*. In
contrast, regarding all who work against it (these
are the ones who) will be consumed by agonizing
torment.✦ Thus, have no doubt about it, that is

✦That is demonstrating those who really deserve permanent torment.
These are only those who actively distort God's messages as well as those
who do their utmost to fight against it. This demonstrates the absolute
mercy of almighty God—that He will be lenient on all others. It also
proves that He is pure love. Here, He says, essentially, that the only
people who will earn His chastisement—who will be permanently and
severely punished—are those who deliberately fight Him, who purposely
work to destroy God's message. In other words, all others may receive
His boundless mercy.

---

what is the real source of this revelation—that it is
genuinely divine despite the fact that relatively
few people will believe in it.

The most wicked of all are those who make their
own ideas as if God's. Such will (ultimately) be
arraigned before their Master. What's more, those
who will be called to testify against them will say,
"people lied about their Lord."

No doubt, the wicked deserve God's rejection.
(These are the ones) who turn others away from God's
way and attempt to distort it—because they have
convinced themselves that there is no future life.

Yet, they will be unable to escape their final
judgement, even though they might (temporarily)
remain secure on earth. Nor will they find anyone
to protect them from God. Their punishment will

be multiplied, because they lost their ability to comprehend the truth—(since) they have wasted their own souls, because on resurrection all their false representations—all that they imagined to have power or authority besides God—will abandon them. Truly, in the next life they will be total losers.

Yet, clearly, those who make every effort to truly believe (in their hearts) and who do good—who humble themselves (in submission) before their Lord—are destined for paradise, where they will live permanently. These two kinds of people (the believers and those who are devoid of any degree of God in their hearts), may be compared respectively to a blind and deaf person versus someone who can (actually) see and hear. Are they the same? Then, will you give this serious consideration?

The people of Noah: lessons for humankind

Previously, We inspired Noah (for the sake of) his people with a similar message, that is "I have come to warn you of the obvious—that you must worship exclusively the one God. Surely, I dread the thought of the consequences (of refusing to do so) *for your sake.*" However, the powerful ones of his people, who had already (made up their minds to reject) the truth, said, "Obviously, you are merely a regular man—a mere mortal—like the rest of us. What's more, the only people who seem to follow you are the low class. We see no evidence that you are superior to us. Rather, we believe you—all of you—are frauds." Noah responded, "Would you consider that if it is truly God who guides me and provides me with His mercy, to which you have chosen to remain oblivious, even if it is true, could we force you to believe in something you despise?"

(He continued,) "My people, I am not asking anything of you—I seek no personal reward. Rather, my reward rests with God alone. What's more (regardless of their social status), I am not about to repulse any of the believers. They are sure they will meet their Lord, while in contrast you are obviously completely unaware of (the reality of) it. Furthermore, my people, who would protect me from God were I to reject them? You should give this some thought."✦ (He continued,)

✦Notice the constant emphasis of the use of reason. This is true, even for the ancients. These ancients were surely sufficiently intelligent; they built vast civilizations. This use of reason is the Qur'aan's method of establishing the truth. Notice also the lack of relying on miracles. Obviously, here, Noah attempts to cause his resistant fellow men to truly consider the consequences of their acts. However, it is to no avail, and, rather, their rejection of God became more profound over time.

"Plus, I don't claim to own God's treasures. Nor do I say I know the unknown. Nor do I claim to be an angel. Nor do I say regarding those who you find contemptible, 'Never will God give them any good,' since God alone is aware of what is in their hearts. What's more, if I took such a position, surely, I would be regarded by God as a perpetrator of evil."✦

✦That is Noah's entire purpose was to was help them. Noah was speaking, in fact, to his adversaries parabolically. This showed his wisdom. It was they who were saying the aforementioned, taunting him. So, rather than telling them directly the wrong they were committing, he warned them instead by using himself as an example, hoping to jar their thinking indirectly—a matter of human nature.

However, the powerful ones of his tribe said, "You, Noah, have needlessly argued with us long enough. So, if you speak the truth, then, cause to occur the disaster with which you threaten us." He answered, "Only God can do so, if He wills, and, if He does, you will be unable to escape. In fact, regardless of how much I want to help you if God decides that you will remain lost in sin, my advice is of no consequence to you. He is your Lord, and you will return to Him (alone)."

Do some, possibly, claim that Muhammad invented this (ancient story)? Tell them, O Prophet, "If I invented it, then, I am responsible for that sin. However, far be if from me to commit the sin for which *you* are responsible."

So it was that We revealed to Noah, "Your people will never believe, that is except those who have already done so. Thus, regardless of their actions never be distressed for them. However, under Our direction build the Ark.✦ What's more,

✦That is a hand-made vessel which was, essentially, according to the Qur'aan little more than a large crude raft. This was very ancient times, possibly 10,000 to 15,000 B.C. The technology for more sophisticated ships had not yet been developed. The raft held at best a few dozen people plus whatever domesticated animals they could collect.

never appeal to Me on behalf of those who commit evil. Truly, they are destined to be drowned."

Thus, Noah proceeded to build the Ark. However, whenever the people in power from his community passed by him, they ridiculed him. In response, he said (in his heart), "If you are ridiculing us, in fact, we are also ridiculing you in your ignorance. Yet, eventually, you will realize who will truly suffer in total humiliation and who will experience intense, as well as prolonged, agony." So, it continued this way, until the time arrived, and torrential waters gushed over the earth's surface. Then, We said, "Place on board (of this raft) one pair of each kind of animal of either sex,✦ as well as

✦That is primarily domesticated animals. These would have been animals of use to the survivors. Only creatures from their locale would have been on board. In fact, it would have been impractical to have placed wild beasts on this Ark, a mere unstable raft. Surely, no giraffes or elephants were on board. Noah lived in Asia Minor, now known as Turkey. The flood was localized. Animals would have been collected only from this region.

your family, except those upon whom the sentence (of doom) has already been decreed, and all (other) believers." Yet, only a minority of Noah's people shared his belief. So, he said to his followers, "Embark in this ship. Let both its voyage and landing be in God's name, certainly, my Lord forgives much and is exceedingly giving of His grace."

Moreover, it moved onward with them among mountain-like waves. Then, Noah yelled to his son, who was isolated (that is surrounded by water), "My son, come with us, and never remain with the godless." However, his son answered, "I will take my chances here by moving to higher ground."

Noah responded, "Today, no one can escape God's judgement, except those who have earned His mercy." Then, a wave arose between them, and the son was drowned with the others.

Ultimately, the word was spoken, "Earth, drain off your waters. Sky, halt all rain." As a result, the waters seeped into the earth, and God's will was done, while the Ark landed on Mount Joodee. Then, the final word was spoken, "Begone with these perpetrators of evil."

Then, Noah beseeched his Lord, saying, "My Lord, surely, my son was one of mine, and, no doubt, your promise always comes true: You are the best of judges." God answered, "Didn't I tell you, Noah, that he was not of you, because, the fact is he was guilty of foul conduct? What's more, never again ask Me regarding those issues which are beyond your comprehension. Through this I reprimand you due to concern that you become one of the ignorant." Noah said, "My Lord, I seek your protection from ever again violating that of which I have no knowledge. Certainly, unless You have mercy upon Me, I will be lost."

Then, it was said, "O Noah, go ashore in peace from Us and with Our full blessings upon both you and some of your sincere followers, as well as the truly good ones, who will arise from you and from those who are with you. However, regarding the godless people of your progeny We will allow them to enjoy life for a brief interlude. Moreover, then (suddenly), it will happen—and they will suffer a vile torment from Us. "

These representations of previous events We now reveal to you. Prior to this neither you nor your people knew about them.✦ Thus, be like Noah,

✦That is prior to the Qur'aan no one knew these details regarding the preaching of Noah. Nor was it known how Noah's son drowned. Nor was it published that Noah was reprimanded for neglecting his promise to God, that is to never ask for mercy on those who reject Him. All that was known was that there was a flood, and Noah and various followers escaped. Thus, regarding these details only God could be its source. There was no way anyone else could have known about it. Also, no Christian or Jewish scholars were aware of these details.

It will be noticed that, here, the Qur'aan begins with the story of Noah. Then, it mentions that after destroying the godless that some of Noah's descendants became godless. Next, it describes these rebellious descendants, first the tribe of 'Aad, and then Thamood. After this, events from Abraham's life, as well as the events surrounding Lot's community, are described. Then, Shu'ayb, who preached to the people of Midian, is mentioned, followed, finally, by Moses and Pharaoh. This adheres precisely to the archaeological record. In other words, it is precisely historically correct.

that is patient in adversity. Surely, the future belongs to those who always keep God in mind.

The destruction of the ancient Arabian tribe, 'Aad: Prophet Hood's warnings

We sent Hood, their fellow man, to the (ancient) Arabian tribe of Aad. He told them, "Worship God exclusively. He is the only divine power. What you have invented is a fabrication. What's more, realize that (regarding my preaching) My purpose is never to seek a reward. Rather, I await my reward from my Lord. Are you unable to make sense of this? Thus, my people, ask your Lord to forgive you for your sins. Then, turn to Him in penitence. If you do so, He will bless you abundantly and will give you great strength. Above all, never reject me as a people immersed in sin."

They said, "You have failed to demonstrate to us sufficient proof, Hood, that you are truly from God. Furthermore, on your recommendation alone we will never abandon our gods—the more so, since we find you unbelievable. The only explanation we have for your behavior is that our gods have bewitched you."

Hood responded, "Surely, God is my witness, and you, too, will witness, that is that it is impossible for me to worship what you worship. So, plot against me in any way you desire, and give me no quarter. The fact is I trust completely in God, the Lord of all of us. He has a powerful grasp over every living being. Certainly, my Lord's way is correct. However, if you choose to reject this, realize that I have delivered the message with which I was entrusted for you. Also, realize that my Lord may replace you with another people, while in contrast there is no way you can harm Him. Surely, my Lord is always watching (and is therefore aware of all your actions)."

Thus, eventually, Our judgement arrived. Through Our merciful love We rescued Hood and his fellow people. Too, more importantly, We saved them from the agony of the next life.

That was the culmination for the tribe of 'Aad. They had rejected their Lord's messages and rebelled against His representatives. Instead (of accepting that message) they followed the bidding of every vile enemy of the truth. Furthermore, they were also pursued in this world by God's condemnation,✦ plus they will ultimately be

✦That is even in their graves, where they will experience only terminal regret, all because they purposely rejected the revelations of God. Yet, this was precisely why God sent them these revelations, so they would have a means to ease their souls and to prevent this agony by sincerely coming to Him.

These descendants of the rightly guided Noah returned directly to their hedonistic ways. To God this is particularly vile. Therefore, they will be punished severely for their rebellion and ingratitude.

overcome (by it) when they will be raised from the dead (to face God). That tribe, 'Aad, certainly, they were extreme rejecters of their Lord. Begone with that tribe.

The destruction of the rebellious Arabian tribe, Thamood: warnings by the Prophet Saalih

We also sent Saalih (another), local man for (the benefit of), the (Arabian) tribe of Thamood. He told them, "My people, worship only the one God: He is the exclusive divine power. He created you from the (the mere dust of the) earth and caused you to flourish on it. Thus, ask Him for forgiveness, and turn towards Him, sincerely remorseful (for your sins). Surely, my Lord is always close and (always) responds to whomever requests Him."

They answered, "Saalih, we had such high hopes for you. (Why) are you attempting to prevent us from worshipping what our ancestors worshiped? Because of your behavior, we have serious doubts about your intentions, in fact, we are suspicious of you." He responded, "My people, will you consider this: If I am truly basing my position upon irrefutable evidence from my Lord, the same Lord who has showered His mercy upon me, if my position is true, who would protect me from God were I to rebel against Him? Thus, your offer to me would be tantamount to my absolute ruin." (Further, he said,) "My people, this female camel, which is of God, is a symbol for you. Thus, leave her to graze on God's earth, and never hurt her or else you will be overwhelmed by a sudden punishment." Despite this, they cruelly butchered her. As a result, We told Saalih, "You have only three days to escape. This is a final position, which is unalterable." Thus, when Our judgement was finalized, by Our mercy We saved Saalih and his followers. What's more, ultimately, We saved them from the greatest failure of all: the disgrace during resurrection.

Certainly, your Lord is completely powerful, almighty. Thus, the blast overpowered the perpetrators of evil, and as a result they lay dead on the ground, precisely in their homes, as if they had never existed. Oh, certainly, the people of Thamood refused their Lord. Away with the people of Thamood.

Abraham and the warners: angels dressed as men

To Abraham there came Our special heavenly messengers, bearing helpful insight. They greeted him with "peace," and he answered, "and peace be on you," and he prepared a feast, serving them a roasted calf. Then, when he saw that they did not indulge in it, he regarded their conduct as strange and so became apprehensive. However, they said, "There is no reason to fear. We are sent as messengers to the people of Lot."✦

✦That is they were heavenly beings sent directly from the distant universe disguised as men. Such beings, apparently, never eat flesh. They are spirits and are beyond such material needs.

Furthermore, his wife, standing nearby, laughed with happiness, when We gave her the news of the birth of Isaac and, after Isaac, of Jacob. She said, "For me, I am now an old woman and my husband is also very old, so how could I withstand a pregnancy: this is bizarre." They answered, "Do you regard it bizarre that God should mandate whatever He wills? The mercy of God and His blessings be upon you, O people of this house. Clearly, He is always to be praised, a majesty of the highest degree."

When Abraham was no longer afraid and was fully appraised of the news, he began to plead with Us for Lot's people—because Abraham was most clement, tender-hearted, intent upon turning to God repeatedly. However, God's messengers replied, "Abraham, stop this pleading. In fact, your Lord's judgement has already been initiated. Clearly, there will fall upon them a punishment that no one can stop."

So, it was mandated, and, what's more, when Our agents came to Lot, he was deeply distressed on their behalf, since he was powerless to protect them. Thus, he exclaimed, "This is a horrible day."

When his people came running to him, impelled by their passion—because they were consumed in their desire to commit such abominations—Lot said, "My people, take instead my daughters. They are purer for you than men. Then, always keep God in mind, and never disgrace me by assaulting my guests. Is there not even a single decent person among you?" They answered, "You have always known that we have no use for your daughters. You know what we want." Lot exclaimed, "If I only had the strength to defeat (you) or that I could rely upon some mightier support."

Then, the angels inspired him, "Lot, We are agents from your Lord. Your enemies will never be able to overpower you. Then, leave with your household under the protection of night, and let none of you reconsider. Take with you all your family, except your wife, since certainly she will suffer the same consequences as they. In fact, their appointed time is in the morning, and the morning is coming quickly."

Thus, when Our judgement was implemented, We turned those sinful towns upside down and rained upon them a punishing rain as hard as stones, one (punishing, pulverizing rain) after the other,✦ all fully established in Your Lord's view as

✦That is because of their own internal rebellion they destroyed themselves. It was not God who was brutal to them. Rather, He showed them love by repeatedly warning them of the consequences of their acts.

The biblical turning of people into "pillars of salt" may now be explained. A natural disaster, for instance, a volcanic eruption could cause mass extermination and could fossilize people. Yet, the fact that these towns were turned upside down would also indicate a massive earthquake perhaps combined with a volcanic eruption.

(the appropriate) punishment for *their own sinful acts*. In fact, such punishments are always near those who (deliberately) commit evil.

The wealthy people of Midian: warned to no avail by their messenger, Shuʿayb

We also selected Shuʿayb, a local man, to guide the people of Midian. He said, "My people, worship only God—He is the only divine power. What's more, never cheat people by failing to give proper measurement or weight. Prosperous though you are, beware of the torment of that fateful time. Thus, my people, be honest in all your dealings. Furthermore, never deprive people of their rights. Also, never in your wickedness spread corruption. That which is held in trust with God is superior for you (than mere material accumulations), if you truly believe. Yet, realize that I am free of responsibility for all your actions."

They said, "Shuʿayb, does your communication with God compel you to demand that we abandon the ways of our ancestors, the way we have always worshiped, which our previous fathers✦ and our

✦This proves the error of Shuʿayb's antagonists. This is because Noah was their original ancestor. Then, ancestrally, instead of paganism, to which they, incredibly, tightly held, the worship of the one God was their true way. In other words, through their rebellion they precisely disobeyed their original ancestral way, because it was due to the mercy of almighty God that they were safely settled there, that is after the flood. This proves the fallacious nature of their arguments. Their purpose was merely to serve their own 'interests,' by attempting to maintain their perceived power structure, which they regarded as being threatened by Shuʿayb's message. They simply refused to relinquish any of their material lusts, which ultimately resulted in their self-destruction.

ancestors worshiped, or that we refrain from doing whatever we desire with our material possessions? Definitely, you would have us believe that we are all wrong, and you are the only one who is right." He answered, "My people, consider this: if it is true that my position is based upon deliberate facts revealed from my Lord, facts which He has provided me with through His loving mercy (how else could I possibly speak to you)? What's more, I have no interest in taking from you anything. I only desire to establish what is right as best as possible."

He continued, "Even so, my capacity to achieve this is dependent on God alone. I place my full trust in Him, and I always turn only to Him for help. What's more, my people, never allow your disagreements with me to drive you into the sin of disobedience in concern that you may suffer the same disaster that struck the people of Noah, Hood, or Saalih.✦What's more, remember that the

---

✦Again, this demonstrates the correct sequence. First, there was Noah, then Hood and then Saalih. Finally, Shuʻayb came to that same general region in order to guide yet another pagan group into the magnificence of God's oneness. All such pagan groups were descendants of Noah, whose story initiates this section.

---

people of Lot lived close to where you now live. Thus, ask your Lord to forgive you, and, then, seek His repentance; your Lord is full of love and kindness."

However (despite this), his people told him, "Shuʻayb, we are unable to understand the purpose of your message. Furthermore, it is obvious that only the most low level people follow you. The fact is if your family wasn't so influential,✦ we would

✦It is noteworthy that God selects the most prominent people, men and women of the highest nobility and status, as His messengers. The common idea that the prophets were often poor and down-trodden is false. Bhudda is another example, as is Moses. Regarding Moses he was raised in Pharaoh's household, the domain of one of the wealthiest and most powerful people of all time. This means that Moses was a Pharaoh. Jesus and Muhammad also arose from prominent families. These men were always of noble lineage. They were among the most dignified people of society known.

have stoned you to death long ago, since you have no power over us." He responded, "My people, do you regard my family to be more influential than God? (Incredibly,) you treat Him as insignificant. Without question, regardless of your actions my Lord is fully aware of it. Thus, my people, do whatever you wish to me within your power, while I, surely, will work hard with all my powers in God's way. Eventually, you will realize which of us will experience torment, as well as disgrace, and which of us truly is the liar. Watch, then, for what is coming. I, too, will watch."

Thus, when Our judgement was finalized We saved through Our love Shu'ayb and his fellow followers, whereas the blast✦ overtook the godless.

✦That is most likely due to the concussive force of an intra-atmospheric explosion of a celestial fragment. A massive volcanic eruption could also have been responsible for this cataclysm.

So, they lay dead on the ground in their homes, as if they had never existed. Like Thamood, they were obliterated.

Moses and the lesson of Pharaoh

We also sent Moses armed with clear signs from us to Pharaoh and his powerful ones. Yet, despite this they continued to abide by Pharaoh's authority, even though whatever Pharaoh commanded was corrupt. In the same way he will lead his people during the time when all will be raised from the dead (and then arraigned before God), having already (while they were on this earth) led them in life towards hell. What's more, the only result they achieved was merely wicked, truly odious.

Ancient communities, modern lessons

This description of the fate of those (ancient) civilizations, the remnants some of which still exist, with others being more completely obliterated, We represent to you (O humankind), as a lesson. Even so, We never harmed them in the least, but rather they harmed themselves. What's more, when your Lord's judgment ultimately occurred, their false gods, which they invoked instead of God, proved inconsequential. Rather, they brought them merely eternal damnation. Such is the relentless grip of your Lord's punishment, that is whenever He holds accountable an evil community for its (continuous) crimes. Truly, the grip of His punishment is tremendously extreme.

This represents a definite warning for any who fear the agony they may endure in the next life, those who are aware of the existence of the time when humankind will be gathered together, when it will be witnessed by all who ever existed—a time which We will not delay even a moment beyond the (predestined) date.

When it arrives, no one will speak, unless God allows it. What's more, some will be wretched, while others will be thrilled. Regarding those who inflicted misery upon themselves they will live in agony. There, for relief they will only experience moans and sobs. They will reside there for eternity, unless the Lord deems otherwise. Let there be no doubt about it your Lord is the One, the Universal Ruler, who does whatever He deems.

In contrast, there are those who as a result of their past deeds will have been blessed with happiness (a permanent gift from Us). They will live in paradise, remaining there for eternity, unless your Lord deems otherwise. Thus, have no doubts about whatever the (misguided) people worship. They only worship what their ancestors (and recently deceased relatives) previously worshiped. Furthermore, We will definitely compensate them in full for all that they have earned.

Yet, truly (the same situation occurred, when) We delivered the divine words to Moses, although some of his people resisted it. What's more, were it not for a decree already established from your Lord, judgement would have (already) been administered precisely at the moment of their rebellion. This is because for certain they were gravely in doubt, even suspicious, regarding the truth of his mission.✦

✦That is not just Pharaoh but also the Israelites resisted Moses' message. They never completely surrendered to the authority of the revelations he presented and constantly argued among themselves about this. Thus, Moses died at best with only a handful of true believers.

(Yet, based upon their actions) without doubt, all people will be given what they deserve by their Lord. Surely, He is fully aware of all that they accomplish.

Thus, as you have been instructed pursue the right course, together with the other believers (who do so). Plus, never allow yourself to be arrogant. Certainly, He is aware of all your actions. Also, never associate with or rely upon the obstinate ones, who purposely commit evil. If you do so, you will have no one to protect you from God. Nor will you ever be supported by Him. What's more, establish (within yourself a constant state of) worship, morning, noon, and night and also (late) in the night. Truly, good deeds drive away hateful ones; this is a reminder for all who truly keep God in mind.

So, despite adversity be patient. Certainly, God always rewards those who work with their fullest effort to do good.

Yet, unfortunately, among those previous civilizations there were no people endowed with any virtue—people who would speak out against corruption—except the few whom We saved because of their goodness. In contrast, the people who purposely commit evil pursued only their own prurient pleasures and thus lost themselves in sinning.

Even so, in truth your Lord would never destroy a civilization for errant beliefs alone, that is as long as its people treated each other decently. What's more, if your Lord desired, He could have surely made all humans one affable community. However (He allowed free will to reign and so), they continue to differ with each other, all of them, except those upon whom your Lord has showered His mercy.✦

✦That is in-fighting and bickering are a sign of weakness. This is also a sign of a lack of deep belief in God. In contrast, those graced by Him seek always a peaceful solution to any ordeal and reject all conflict. This is the deeper meaning of this passage.

Concerning this issue (of the attribute of free choice) He has created (all of) them.✦ However

✦That is 'and, so, He knows their nature.' He also knows their potential. From the Qur'aanic point of view God knows in advance the choices people will make and how they will respond to guidance. This is because He knows precisely what is in a person's heart. So, He will directly guide any who truly believe in Him, while He will allow to degenerate those who obstinately reject Him. Regarding the borderline people, who only superficially believe, he will also guide them, if they allow Him to do so and if they truly open their hearts to Him.

(despite this freedom of theirs for those who disregard the truth), that ultimatum of your Lord will be fulfilled: "I will certainly fill hell with invisible beings, as well as humans, all together."

Regarding the earlier messengers We relate to you only whatever strengthens your belief. Through these accounts you receive the truth, as well as a deliberate reminder, that is for those who (truly strive to) believe.

So, tell the godless, "Do whatever you will (in your desire to harm us), we will continue to work (towards Our meeting with God). Wait, the fact is we, too, are waiting."

Only God comprehends the secrets of the universe and the earth.✦ All that exists ultimately

✦That is including the nature of the ancients. This section is an accurate summary of ancient civilizations of which no modern people were aware, in terms of the actual details. These are definite secrets, known only to the almighty Lord. Thus, it would be impossible for any human or group of humans to have known these details. Incredibly, all the archeologists in the world have been unable to reveal these factors. Then, this same pattern by the Qur'aan of revealing historical secrets is continued in the forthcoming section regarding the story of Joseph.

returns to Him, which is indisputable.

Then, worship Him alone, and place your trust exclusively in Him. Furthermore, your Lord is fully aware of all your actions.

Section 12
The Parable of Joseph

In the name of the most merciful
and compassionate God

A-L-R

These are the messages from a revelation which clearly demonstrates the truth. We have sent this Qur'aanic book, which is, without doubt, divine in origin in Arabic, so that you will comprehend it (through the use of your reason). What's more, We reveal it to you in stages, explaining its contents in the finest possible way, since obviously before this you were unaware.

It was Joseph who told his father, "My father, clearly, I saw (in my dream what appeared to be) eleven stars, as well as the sun and moon, all submit themselves to me." Jacob responded, "Never tell your brothers about this for fear they will plot against you. Surely, Satan is man's sworn enemy. This is because as your dream demonstrates your Lord will select you above all others and will give you the ability to interpret the deeper meaning of things. What's more, He will fully bless you, as well as the family of Jacob, in the same way He blessed your ancestors, Abraham and Isaac. In fact, your Lord is completely knowledgeable and is truly wise."

Surely, in this description regarding Joseph and his genetic brothers there are messages for all who search for the truth (for instance), when (these brothers) conversed together, "Truly, our father loves Joseph and his brother (Benjamin) more than us, even though we are a bigger family. Our father is obviously deranged."✦

✦That is the lesson is to never be jealous. God gives two examples of the destructive nature of this emotion through the parable of Cain and Abel, and now the story of Joseph. Then, He demonstrates that the only result of this jealousy is hardship, mainly for the person who is so consumed. From the Qur'aanic point of view this is a vile tendency, which no true believer must portray. Thus, again, no true believer can harbor it. Then, to gain God's pleasure it must be eliminated.

This entire chapter is dedicated to this lesson, that is to remind humankind that jealousy is a low emotion. It is also to remind people to be grateful for whatever they are given and to never jealously seek to harm others. It is also to demonstrate that jealousy is synonymous with selfishness. Then, this selfishness is due to a lack of trust in God. Then, the true believer is one who realizes that regardless of events it is all under God's mighty control. Such a person also realizes that in any crisis He is the only One in whom to trust. These are the deeper messages of this parable.

One of them suggested, "Let us kill Joseph or perhaps exile him, so that your father will focus his love on you instead. Afterwards, we could (repent) and do what is right." However, another of the group said, "Why kill him? If you must do something, dump him into the dark depths of this well. Eventually, someone will retrieve him, taking him far away."

They (approached their father and) said, "Our father, allow us to take Joseph with us. We only wish him well. Let him go with us tomorrow for enjoyment and sport. We promise, we will protect him." Jacob answered, "I feel saddened at the thought of your taking him, since I fear that as soon as you are negligent of him he could be eaten by a wolf." They said, "Surely, if the wolf were to eat him, we are such a large group, then, we, too, will die (defending him)." Thus, they took him away, resolved to throw him into the darkness of the well. However, We revealed thus to him, "You will eventually remind them of what they did at a time when they won't even realize it."

Then, during the night they approached their father, as if weeping, and said, "Father, you must believe us, we were distracted while playing sports and left Joseph behind with our things. Then, the wolf ate him. However, we knew that you would never believe us, even though we are telling the truth." So, they provided him (as evidence) a blood-stained shirt, the blood being fabricated. Jacob exclaimed, "Not at all, it is only your own delusional thinking that causes something so vile to be (in your minds) insignificant. However, my patience during such difficulty is the best in God's view. What's more, I seek only God for the strength to withstand this loss."

Then (eventually), a caravan arrived and lowered a receptacle into the well: when they saw Joseph, they exclaimed, "What a lucky find," their thought being to sell him. However, God was fully aware of their intentions. Thus, they sold him for a pittance, a mere few coins, demonstrating how little they valued him. The man from Egypt, who bought him, said to his wife, "Make his stay with us respectable. He may well be of value to us, or we may adopt him as a son." By this means We firmly established Joseph on the earth. We did so in order that We might inculcate within him the ability to comprehend the inner meaning of events. No doubt, God always prevails in His purpose. Yet, this is beyond the comprehension of the majority of people.

Ultimately, when he reached maturity, We endowed him with the capacity to judge correctly. We also gave him instinctive powers. This is how (in Our mercy) We reward those who pursue good.

Attempted seduction; Joseph's resistance

Eventually (when he reached maturity), the lady of the house became passionate for him and attempted to seduce him. So, she locked the doors and said, "Come to me, love me." Joseph answered, "God forbid—my host has been extremely kind to me. What a waste it would be to do such wrong." Yet, she certainly desired him, and for a moment he felt a passion for her. In fact, he would have succumbed had he not realized in this temptation an evidence of His Lord's wisdom. Thus, We willed it to be in order that We might protect him from all evil and vile deeds, because surely he was one of Our dedicated servants.

Moreover, they both rushed to the door; and she grabbed him, ripping the back of his shirt—and, then, they met her lord at the door. She cried, "Shouldn't the man who had evil designs on your wife be punished, put in prison,✦ or something

✦That is now, again, Joseph was the victim of intrigue. Either people were attempting to kill him or control him. This demonstrates how vulnerable are the truly good to evil plots. Without God's protection, surely, Joseph would never have survived. Only He took care of him, ensuring his future. Too, he would have never achieved his ultimate high status without the immense mercy of almighty God.

even more extreme?" Joseph exclaimed, "She was the one who tried to seduce me." Now, there was a servant (or family member) present who suggested, "If his shirt was torn from the front, then, she is telling the truth. However, if it is torn from behind, then, she is lying." Then, when her husband saw that the shirt was torn from the back, he said, "You, woman—it is you who are wicked in your guile. Joseph, forget this. You, wife, beg forgiveness for your sin, because you are certainly at fault."

Gossip spread among the women of the city that (essentially) "The nobleman's wife attempted to seduce her servant, falling in love with him. Obviously, she is deranged." However, when she heard of their slander, she invited them to a banquet. There, she handed each of them a sharp knife and then said, "Come forth and show yourself to them." Then, when the women saw him, they were so enamored that they all sliced their hands, exclaiming, "God excuse us, this is no regular human: he is but a pure angel." Then, she told them, "So, you blamed me for this (—for becoming passionate over this extraordinarily handsome man)? True, I attempted to seduce him, but he could not be tempted. So, if he refuses to succumb to my demands, he will go to prison and live with the degenerates." He replied (in his heart), "My

Lord, prison is more desirable to me than to submit to their demands. In fact, unless you protect me from their wickedness, I might yet succumb to their enticement. Then, I would certainly have lost all and thus become confused regarding right and wrong."

(Thus,) His Lord responded to his prayer and released him from the threat of their deceit. Surely, He has complete awareness and knowledge. This is because, as the nobleman and his household realized, at least for now, their only option was to imprison him.

Stint in prison—preaching and patience

On his way to prison Joseph encountered two young men, also being imprisoned. One of them told him, "I clearly saw in a dream myself pressing wine," while the other said, "I clearly saw myself in a dream carrying bread on my head, and birds were eating from it." Then, they both requested of Joseph, "Tell us the true meaning of this, since you, obviously, have this (instinctive) capacity." Joseph answered, "I will inform you within the day of the true meaning, so that you are prepared for the consequences"...(and already Joseph knew in his heart and said to himself,) "Truly, I have removed myself from the ways of people who refuse to believe in God and who categorically reject the existence of the next life. What's more, I follow the faith of my previous fathers, Abraham, Isaac, and Jacob. It is inconceivable that we humans could make other powers or things as God's equals. This is the result of God's overwhelming generosity to us and to the rest of humankind. However, despite this the majority of people are devoid of gratitude."

Then (he said), "My prison mates, which makes more sense: belief in various minor lords, each with different characteristics and/or powers, or belief in the One (true) God, the absolute Master of the Universe? Whatever you worship instead of God is of no value to you and is merely empty names. All are invented by you and your ancestors: God never authorized you to do it. Yet, God alone is the true judge. In this regard He has made it clear that you must worship Him alone. This is the true religion. However, most people are unable to comprehend this."

"My fellow prisoners regarding your dreams one of you will survive and give his lord, the King, wine to drink. However, the other will be killed, crucified, and (vultures) will peck at his head. Even so, regardless of your future the matter on which you have asked me to enlighten you has already been decided." Then, Joseph said to the man whom he considered saved, "Once you are free mention me to your lord." However (after he was freed), Satan caused him to forget, and, thus, he remained in prison a few more years.

The King's dream and Joseph's rescue

Then, one day the King said, "I had a dream in which I clearly saw seven fat cows being devoured by seven starving ones and seven ripe ears (of wheat) next to seven withered ones. If you are capable, you wise assistants, explain to me the meaning of such a dream." They responded, "This is one of the most convoluted dreams we have ever heard: we have no ability to interpret such dreams." Then, suddenly, after all that time the (surviving) ex-prisoner remembered and said, "I can find the true meaning. Thus, allow me to search for it."

(So, when he came to Joseph in the prison,) he said, "Joseph, you truthful one, explain to me the meaning of this dream: seven fat cows are devoured by seven starving ones, and seven ripe ears (of wheat) are next to seven withered ones. Tell me its meaning, so that I can return to the people—so that they will know you speak the truth." Joseph replied, "You will raise crops for seven years and all will proceed normally. However, reserve most of your grain in its ear, only preparing a small portion for food. This is because after that there will come seven years of poor harvest, resulting in the consumption of most of your reserve. After that, the harvest will return to normal."

When thusly informed, the King said, "Bring him before me." However, when the agent of the court came to him (Joseph) said, "Return to your ruler, and ask him to first determine the truth about the women, who cut their hands. Surely, my Lord alone has full knowledge of their vile plots." So, the King questioned the women, asking: "Why did you attempt to seduce Joseph?" They answered, "God forbid, we never suspected the least evil intent on his part." Then, the wife of Joseph's former lord exclaimed, "The truth has become evident. In fact, I was the one who sought to seduce him. Joseph speaks the truth." When Joseph heard what had transpired, he said, "I did this so that my former lord (and caretaker) would know that I never betrayed his trust. What's more, God never guides those treacherous ones, who betray (their trust). Even so, there is no attempt to absolve myself, *since the inner self surely incites to evil deeds*. Only those upon whom God provides His mercy have any hope of being saved from it. This is because my Lord forgives greatly and is truly generous (in His mercy)."

The King proceeded, "Bring him to me, so that I may make him my trusted assistant." Moreover, when he was brought before the King and he had spoken to him he said, "Clearly, from now on you will be placed in a high position with us, given all trust."

Joseph instructed him, "Give me control of the granaries. Certainly, I will do an excellent job."

This was how We established Joseph securely in the land. In fact, he had total control over it, doing whatever he deemed appropriate.

This is how We shower Our mercy on whomever We will. As a result, the truly good will always achieve their reward. Even so, from the perspective of those who truly believe in Us and have always kept Us in awe the reward in the next life is far more significant than anything this world can offer.

Arrival in Egypt of Joseph's brothers

Then (years later), Joseph's brothers arrived, presenting themselves before his Court. He knew them immediately, however, they failed to recognize him. Then, when he had filled their grain sacks with the requested provisions, he said: "On your next trip bring to me your other brother, the one from your father's side.✦ You can see I am

✦This is regarding Joseph's only pure brother, Benjamin. The purpose behind his efforts was to secure his brother due to concerns for his safety. This was the concern that his half-brothers, in yet another fit of jealousy, might harm him. This plot by Joseph—which was actually inspired by God—led to the return of his entire family.

exceedingly generous, that is I am a good host. However, if you decide against bringing him, you will never again receive a full quota of grain. Nor will I allow you to see me." They answered, "We will attempt to persuade his father to part with him; we will do our best." Then, Joseph said to one of his assistants, "Return to them their merchandise (that is bury it in their packs), so they might discover it after arriving home. This will make them more eager to return."

Thus, when they returned to their father, they said, "Father, we will be unable to procure grain in the future unless we bring Benjamin with us. Thus, send him with us, so we can obtain our needs. We will certainly guard him well." Jacob replied, "Should I entrust you with him just like I did with his brother? By no means; rather, trust in God's protective power is completely superior to whatever you offer. He is truly the most merciful of all." Then, they opened their packs, discovering that their original merchandise (for barter) had been returned. They said, "Father, what more could we desire? We even were returned our merchandise. Obviously, if you send Benjamin with us, we will be able to bring much food for our families. We promise, we will protect our brother, plus we will return with an additional load of grain, because in reality this first batch we received was insufficient." Jacob told them, "I will send him with you only on one condition; that you swear to me in God's name that you will return him to me (barring some unforeseen catastrophe)." Then, when they had solemnly sworn to him, Jacob finalized it with, "God is the witness to all that we say." He added, "My sons, when you enter the city, do so with caution, choosing different entrance points. Yet, even so, I am incapable of protecting you against anything willed by God. The decision regarding the ultimate result is His. Thus, I place my trust exclusively with God. This is because all who truly trust (in His existence) must place their trust in Him alone."

Yet, even though they entered the city in the manner their father instructed them this proved of no avail against the plan of God. Such a request only served Jacob's sincere feelings, that is his desire to protect them. Definitely, thanks to what We had imbued within him he was a man completely aware that God's will must always prevail. Yet, most people are unaware of this.

The plot to retain Benjamin

Then, when Jacob's sons came (before Joseph), he brought his brother near him, whispering, "I am your (lost) brother. So, have no grief over what they have done previously." Later, when he had filled their quota, he placed the King's (jeweled) drinking vessel in his brother's pack. Then, as they were leaving the city they were pursued by agents of the court, and a herald called out to them "You departing travelers, you are thieves." The brothers asked, "What are you missing?" They answered, "The King's (jeweled) goblet. Whoever produces it will be rewarded with a camel-load of grain." They said, "God knows, we have no intention of doing anything wrong here. Certainly, we are not thieves." However, the Egyptians said, "If you are proven liars, what is the appropriate punishment for this act?" They replied, "Whoever did it should be enslaved by your court. This is how we ourselves punish the guilty." Then, they returned them to Joseph. He first searched the bags of his half-brothers and finally the bag of Benjamin. From it he produced the cup.

This was how We contrived for Joseph the attainment of his heart's desire. Under the King's law if it were not for the will of God, he would have been unable to detain his brother. Thus, We raise to greater heights of knowledge whomever We will. However, beyond everyone gifted with knowledge there is the One who knows all.

What's more (as soon as the cup was found in Benjamin's bag), the brothers exclaimed, "If he has stolen it (it is no surprise), because in the past he had a brother used to steal." Then, Joseph said (to himself), "You are far worse in this respect—but God is fully aware of your statements."

Then, they said, "You great one✦—his (Benjamin's)

✦That is, incredibly, this person, who they now deem the "Great One," is the same one they just deemed a liar. This was because they were still blinded by their envy of Joseph. This demonstrates that jealousy, particularly between close relatives, is highly destructive. What's more, it is obviously banned by God, a prohibition specifically detailed in Section 16. The Qur'aan, then, demonstrates that it is a low emotion, which causes only self-destruction. Thus, it is an emotion unbefitting of a true believer.

Then, what was the main difference between Joseph and his brothers? Joseph focused on God, making Him the priority, while his brothers focused on themselves. So, this was why Joseph was elevated to such a high position, while his brothers remained, relatively, mere beggers.

father is very old and frail. Detain instead one of us, because obviously you are a just man." He answered, "God forbid, since we are unable to detain anyone other than the one upon whom we have found our property. If we did, we would be guilty of a crime."

Thus, they lost all hope of convincing him, and they went aside to privately discuss it. The oldest son said, "Remember that your father made you swear to keep your commitment in God's name. Plus, with regard to Joseph you failed miserably. Regarding myself, I will not leave this region until my father gives me permission or until God passes judgement in my favor. He is the best One to judge. You others, return to your father and tell him, 'Father, your son has stolen.' However, we can only explain to you what we experienced. Although we swore to you, this was an event we could never have foreseen. For confirmation (of the truth of our story) ask the others in town, who traveled with us. In fact, you will find that we speak only the truth."

Yet, when they returned to their father and explained to him what happened, he exclaimed, "It is not true; you have only convinced yourself as such. Yet, regarding me I will remain patient in this time of trial. Perhaps God will bring them all back to me. Certainly, He truly knows (all) and is truly wise." Then, he turned away from them and (secretly) said to himself, "Woe is me for Joseph." And his eyes became dim from the grief with which he was filled. His sons responded, "God knows you will never cease to remember Joseph until you ruin your health or die." He answered, "It is only to God whom I turn for my grief. The fact is I am aware from Him of an insight which you are unable to comprehend. Thus, my sons, go again and attempt to obtain some information regarding Joseph and Benjamin. What's more, never lose heart regarding God's life-sustaining mercy. Certainly, only people who in fact reject (Him) lose hope of His life-sustaining mercy."

Eventually, Jacob's sons returned to Egypt, saying (to Joseph), "*You noble sir✦, we beg your*

✦Here, again, they demonstrate that they were wholly dependent on precisely the person they had previously abandoned "to the wolves." The same man who they sought to kill or exile—this is the one before whom they now submit? Yet, incredibly, had they succeeded in their plot to destroy him they, too, would have suffered, since it was Joseph alone who managed the food of that empire to prevent starvation. This may surely explain the phrase "blind jealousy." Better to be happy within whatever God provides and to, what's more, bless others rather than to be consumed with envy.

This story is obviously divine in source. No human could conceive of it. No one could reasonably justify any other source, that is other than almighty God. It is the parable that for those who are patient, always, goodness and decency will win, even over familial jealousy. This shows that God is mysterious in His ways of revealing His will. It also demonstrates that He is the only real Power behind all events.

help as we have again suffered hard times, and, thus, we have brought little of value. Even so, give us a full quota, that is give us due consideration. We know that, surely, God rewards those who are considerate."

He replied, "Do you remember what you did to Joseph and his brother when you were morally unaware?" In (shock) they exclaimed, "Why, are you Joseph?" He answered, "I truly am Joseph, and this is my brother (of like faith). God has truly been kind to us. Surely, whoever restrains themselves from evil deeds and endures all with patience, God will reward them." The brothers said, "In God's name, certainly, God has raised you high above us: we were surely sinners." He replied, "There will be no reprimand against you today. May God forgive your sins. This is because of all who offer mercy He is the most merciful. Now, go. Take this shirt, lay it over my father's face, and he will recover his sight. Afterwards, bring them all back to me."

It happened that as soon as the caravan was on its way their father said to the people around him, "Surely, if it were not for the fact that you might call me an old fool, I would tell you that I truly sense the presence of Joseph." They answered, "By God, you (really) are still lost in your aberration." However, when the messenger in excitement brought Joseph's shirt, he laid it on his face (as it were) at which time he regained his "sight" and said, "Haven't I informed you that I am certain from God of something which you are unable to comprehend?" His sons answered, "Our father, ask God to forgive us, because the fact is we were sinners." He said, "I will ask my Lord to forgive you. He alone is the One who truly forgives and grants mercy."

Eventually, when they (all) came before Joseph, he embraced his parents and said, "You are now in my jurisdiction, if God so wills, secure from all danger." Moreover, he raised his parents to the highest stature: and they all fell down before the Almighty, prostrating themselves in adoration. Then, Joseph said to his father, "This is the real meaning of my original dream, which, now, my Lord has made true. Certainly, He was kind to me when he freed me from prison and when He brought you all from the desert after Satan disrupted the unity between us brothers. My Lord is mysterious beyond comprehension in how He (achieves whatever He) wills. He alone has the full spectrum of knowledge and understands all. So, I pray, "My Lord, You have surely given to me an allotment of Your power and have inspired in me the ability to understand the inner meaning of things. The maker of the vast universe and this earth, You are near me in this world as well as in the life after death. (Then,) let me die as one who has submitted himself to You, what's more, make me one of those who are truly good."

This previously unknown description is what We now reveal to you.✦ In fact, you were not present

✦That is, again, proving the divine nature of the Qur'aan. This is because this is the first complete summary of the life of Joseph.

While deemed by its detractors "fables of the ancients," obviously, this is impossible. When the Qur'aan was revealed, these ancients were long ago dead. What's more, the ancients believed in multiple gods and would never promote the concept of the universal Lord. Plus, these ancients never left a single document describing, as does this Qur'aan, their faults and failures. Nor do documents written by them give even a hint of the lives of God's messengers, accurately describing the stories of Abraham, Jacob, Joseph, Moses, Jesus, and Muhammad. Rather, these were their adversaries; why would they memorialize them? Nor could Jewish or Christian writings be the source. This is because, for instance, the Qur'aanic story of Joseph contains information in addition to the biblical description. The Qur'aan illustrates in detail the story of a man who lived nearly 5,000 years previously. Who else could do so besides almighty God?

then, when Joseph's brothers conspired against him. Yet, however strongly you may desire it most people will never believe, despite the fact that you ask nothing of them.

This is merely God's reminder to the human race. Yet, how numerous are the signs in this universe and on the earth which they ignore and which they (summarily) reject.

In fact, the majority of them fail to even believe in God without (simultaneously) believing in other (supposed) powers. Are they oblivious to the consequences, that is that there might descend (upon them) God's terrifying punishment or that the Final Event might strike them by surprise?

Tell them, "This is my way of believing—*this use of reason to gain an understanding of the truth*. By this, I am calling you all to God, I and those who also believe in this way." What's more (tell them), "God's magnificence is unlimited. As a result, I would never associate others as having divine powers with God." Yet, even before your era only regular humans were sent as apostles (never spirits or angels). Plus, they were people from the local communities.

Regarding those who reject this have they never traveled to and observed those previous societies? Then, isn't it obvious (to them) that regarding those who deeply consider God the next life is the superior of the two? Are they unable to use their common sense? ✦

✦This describes the fact that, obviously, a person who heeds the call of God and works in his service is infinitely superior to the one who only follows his own passions, while rejecting any call from God. One works hard for God—to whom he realizes he is obligated to submit—and the other works fiercely against Him. One helps good and decent people, and the other torments them. One will be rewarded and placed at peace, and the other will be destroyed and demoted. Obviously, there is a vast difference between these two types of people.

All the previous messengers suffered prolonged persecution. However, finally, when those messengers lost all hope—when they were completely rejected—Our mercy descended upon them. Then, everyone whom We willed to be saved was saved (while those who were immersed in sin were destroyed). This is because regarding those who are immersed in sin, truly, there is no escape from Our punishment.

Clearly, in the representations of these men there is a lesson for those endowed with true insight. Regarding this writing this could never be a human invention. Instead, obviously, it is a divine exposition, which confirms whatever remains of the earlier scriptures (and) which makes clear all that is (needed spiritually by humankind). Furthermore, it is an offering of guidance, as well as loving mercy, to those who (have the desire to) truly believe.

Section 13
Thunder and Other Universal Powers

In the name of the most merciful
and compassionate God

A-L-M-R

These are the messages of a book revealed to you
(directly by God). This—the revelation by your
Lord—is the absolute truth. Yet, the majority of
people refuse to believe (in it).

God is the One who built the universe without
any perceptible supports. What's more, He is
firmly established in His almighty authority.
Furthermore, He has made the sun and moon to
adhere to His laws, each proceeding on its
pathway for a period determined by Him. Let there
be no doubt about it He has absolute authority—
complete control—over all that exists.

Without doubt, He makes these directives clear.
This is so that you might be absolutely certain in
the deepest recesses of your heart that *you will
ultimately meet your Lord.*

Too, He is the One who has made this earth a
vast expanse, placing on it firmly established
mountain ranges as well as rivers. He is also the One
who created on it two sexes of every type of plant and
causes (for the proper biological cycle) the night to
welcome the day.◆Through this, without doubt, there

✦That is such statements by the Qur'aan are symbolic. They symbolize His powers of creation and also His loving mercy. There are the mountains, which give rise to rivers. Then, the mineral-rich water, cascading from the mountains, denudes the earth, leading to soils. The soils cause the creation of plants based upon the two sexual types. The latter produce repeated generations of vibrant growth, fed by mountain springs and run-off, while nourished by solar rays. All such blessings are the inventions of almighty God.

Regarding plant development these sexual types require the darkness of night for rest plus during the day protons from sunshine for activity. God gives these signs as a test—to determine who has the insight to feel gratitude. Yet, prior to this book no other writing espoused such statements. These are the statements which demonstrate natural phenomena and then urge human beings to feel gratitude. This method is unique to the Qur'aan. Again, of the tens of millions of books in existence only the Qur'aan does this. No such statements are found in the bible.

are messages for people (willing to) use their reason.

On this earth there are numerous acreages of land near each other but yet so very different. On (this same earth) there are fields of grains, clusters of (date) trees, originally from one root or standing alone, all nourished by the same water. Yet, We have favored some more highly than others, that is regarding the quality of the nourishment (they provide man or animals). Certainly, through this there are signs (of His creative powers) for people who would deeply consider it.

Yet, if you are astounded by the marvels of creation, astounding, too, is their statement, "What—after we have decayed into mere dust will we truly be recreated?" These are the ones who (through such a statement) prove their determination to reject their providing and generous Lord, the ones who, therefore, carry burdens of their own making around their necks, who have earned a permanent residence in the fire.

Yet (since they are determined to prove the truth as false), they ask you to speed up the arrival of disaster instead of expecting good, although they should realize that prior civilizations met a similar fate (of what they are now deriding). Even so, certainly, despite all their wickedness your Lord is full of forgiveness, free of wants. Yet, make no mistake about it your Lord is also extreme in punishment (as a consequence of rejecting Him). Even so, those who refuse to believe say, "Why hasn't his Lord given him an obvious miracle?" Yet, your only purpose is to warn (because ultimately), only God can truly guide people.

God is aware of (the nature of) all developing offspring. He knows the exact timing for any premature birth. He also knows the extent of the length of time by which they might be overdue. Moreover, everything that is created is monitored by Him in its degree as well as purpose.

He alone knows the imperceptible as well as whatever the mind can perceive: the Great One, the One far superior to anything imaginable.

(As far as God is concerned) it makes no difference whether you hide your thoughts or make them evident or whether anyone attempts to disguise his wicked designs or does (his vile deed) brazenly, believing he has countless associates, both those he can perceive and those which are hidden from him, that could (somehow) protect him from whatever God may have deemed.

Truly, God never changes human beings' conditions unless they (first) change (what is within their inner selves). Moreover, when God determines a people to endure agony, none can stop it. This is because they have none who could protect them from Him.

He is the One who unleashes the lightning before you to inspire both fear and hope. Then, He commands into production the dense clouds, at which time the thunder by its roar praises His magnificence. What's more, He unleashes lightning bolts and strikes with them whom He wills. Yet, they stubbornly argue about God despite the fact that all evidence demonstrates that He alone has the power to do whatever He wills.

To Him alone is due all praise, since it is obvious that all that human beings worship besides God are incapable of responding to any degree. Thus, the one who relies on them is like a person who stretches his gaping hands toward water, hoping he can bring it to his mouth, but it never reaches him. Thus, the prayers (made to such other deities or powers) of those who refuse to believe are of no consequence and in fact drive them deeper into ruin.

All that exists submits itself before God—whether willingly or unwillingly—as do the morning and evening shadows. (Then,) ask (those who refuse to believe), "Who is the Lord of all?" They will say, "God." Ask them, "Then, why do you make others as your lords instead of Him, such beings which are impotent—incapable of helping you and are unable to even help themselves?" Furthermore, ask them "Are the (spiritually) blind and those who can see equal—or are (deep) darkness and (bright) light the same?" Or, do they truly believe that there are, along with God, other power (sources), who can create like God creates, that is powers (which have) created similar to His creation, so that this (other) act of creation appears similar to them? Tell them, "God is the One who is the creator of all that exists. Plus, He has complete command over it."

Whenever He causes rain to descend from the sky and the previously dry riverbeds fill to their capacity, the stream carries scum on its surface. Likewise, scum rises from the metal, which is smelted to make jewelry or utensils. Through this, God establishes the parable of truth versus falsehood. This is because scum, like all dross, dissipates. In contrast, whatever benefits humankind remains established on the earth. Through this God establishes a comparison between those who have accepted their Lord's call with a desirable acceptance and those who refuse to respond to Him. Regarding the latter if (at resurrection) they possessed all the riches of the earth, in fact, twice the amount, they would definitely offer it as ransom. A most vile punishment is their due, and their destination is hell, the most wicked of all results.

Thus, is the person who understands, as well as perceives, the truth revealed to him by his Lord the same as the one who is oblivious (to that truth)? Truly, only those who are endowed with insight keep this in mind, that is those who are true to their commitment with God and never violate it, who maintain the sanctity of what God has ordained to be joined, who are in awe of their Lord, and who fear the most vile of all reckoning. (They are also those) who are patient regardless of (the degree of) difficulty due to a desire to gain their Lord's pleasure, who are constant in maintaining their (prayerful) connection to Him and are generous to others to the best of their capacity, both privately and openly—and who combat wickedness with good. These are the ones who will achieve satisfaction in the next life: Paradise, which they will enter, along with the good and decent people from their parental ancestors, parents, spouses, and children. The angels will come to them from all directions and will say, "Peace be on (your souls), because you have remained firm in your faith." Thus, how excellent is this satisfaction in the next life.

However, regarding those who violate their (instinctive) commitment with God despite it being naturally within them and tear apart what God has commanded to be joined, spreading corruption on earth, their consequence is rejection by God. What's more, their destiny is truly vile.

God provides abundantly to whomever He wills, while withholding from whomever He wills. What's more, those who are given (His abundance) delight in this temporary life, even though compared with the next life this is an illusion, completely transitory.

Regarding those who reject the truth they tend to say, "Why hasn't his Lord given him an obvious miracle from heaven?" Tell them, "God allows to err whomever allows himself to err, just as He guides to Himself all who turn to Him. Those who believe sincerely and whose hearts find comfort in the remembrance of God. surely, human beings' hearts do find comfort in the remembrance of God. Thus, the true believers are destined for happiness in this life plus the most spectacular of all destinations in the next one.

So, We have elevated you to the status of Our Messenger among a community of (essentially) godless people, who were preceded by other similar communities. This is so that you might enlighten them regarding Our revelations, because in their ignorance they reject the truth regarding their most merciful Lord. Thus, tell them, "He is my Lord and He is also the only Lord. Besides Him, there are no other divine powers. (Thus,) I place my trust fully in Him. What's more, regardless of my circumstances I turn to Him for all my needs."

Yet, even if they should listen to a presentation from the divinity, one so powerful that mountain ranges are displaced (powerful enough), that it (tears) open the earth, those obstinate deniers of the truth will still reject it. In truth, God alone has the power to decide all events. Then, are the true believers still unaware that had God desired He would have certainly guided all humankind correctly?

However, regarding those who commit evil as a consequence of their vile deeds sudden catastrophes will continuously befall them or will strike close to their homes. This will continue until God's promise is fulfilled. Unquestionably, God always keeps His promises. Yet, certainly, prior to you men of God have been ridiculed. Furthermore, for a time I gave rein to those godless ones. However, eventually, I punished them. What's more, My retribution was extreme.

Then, is He—this Being who deals with each on the basis of what it deserves—comparable to any other, this One who has every living being under His (mighty) care? Yet (despite this obvious nature of His power), they make other powers as if they are equals with God. Tell them, "Give (these earthly powers) any name you desire. However, do you attempt to inform Him of anything on earth that He is unaware of, or are you merely jesting?"

Surely, regarding these rejecters of the truth their fabrications seem correct to them. Thus (due to their own fabrications), they are hindered from (following) the way of God. What's more, whoever God allows to deviate will never find any (other) guide. Such individuals will receive agony in this temporary life, however, the agony they will endure in the next life will be even more extreme. Plus, they will have no one to protect them from God.

Symbolically, the paradise promised to those who hold God in awe is like a (lush) garden under which running water flows. ✦ Its fruits will last forever,

---

✦Running water represents eternal life, a fact which is confirmed in the forthcoming statements. Water is required for all life. Without it, nothing can survive. Running water is the purest type. This creates a sense of peace. The waters of paradise are cleansing and soothing for the soul—eternally. Yet, it is a mere parable making it clear that, like the soothing effects of a gently running brook, paradise is a place of absolute peace.

There is a place that all people should seek. This is the realm of God's generous mercy. It is a realm achieved by anyone who truly believes in

Him, while performing good deeds from the goodness of the heart, a mandate by almighty God.

and so will its shade. This is the destination for those who remain in awe of God, just as the destination for those who reject (Him) is the agonizing fire.

Thus, those who truly believe in whatever We have revealed gain satisfaction (from it). However, certain followers of scripture reject parts of it.✦

✦That is merely because the Qur'aan brought the obvious truth to them that their revelations were in error. For instance, it makes clear that Jesus was, like the previous messengers, merely a servant of God. It also makes clear that the Jews could never truly follow God unless they abandon corrupt practices, including the taking of usury. Because of these novel views many people of scripture attack the Qur'aan and attempt to dispute it. They may attest to certain portions and then attempt to contradict others, all because they wish to maintain their own power and control. Thus, they have no legitimate or historical basis for such a dispute but rather do so because of their own hostile intentions.

In the time of the Prophet this is precisely what occurred. After he attempted to make peace with the various Arabian, Christian, and Jewish societies leaders within these groups plotted against him. They did all in their power to disparage both him and his message, directly disputing certain passages in the Qur'aan. Then, when they failed to dissuade the people from following it, they plotted against him, breaking any treaties and essentially declaring war against him. They sided with the pagans in an attempt to destroy him and therefore halt the advance of his mission. Yet, obviously, they failed miserably and in fact only proved that their claim to worship God was merely superficial. Even so, the Prophet maintained his composure and never attacked them until they viscously attacked him.

Tell them, "My only responsibility is to bow myself in worship (before) God and never make others His equals. I ask all of you to humble yourselves (in worship) before Him alone. Furthermore, my (only) goal is to serve Him." For this reason We have revealed this divine book✦

✦That is to clarify the truths of the older revelations, purging any falsehoods. This was also to halt arrogance and self-righteousness within the peoples of the former scriptures. It is also to correct any human errors, which would be the cause of disputes. The Qur'aan is exact divine revelation, and, so, it disputes some of the contents of the previous revelations as man-made. However, it also confirms their origin—as writings by almighty God.

(as a means of enlightenment), produced in beautiful Arabic. Moreover, without doubt, if you were to follow the whims of man, despite the fact that you have this evidence from God, no one will be able to protect or save you (from Him).

Yet, surely, a wide range of prophets were sent by Us previously. Such (messengers)✦ were provided

✦That is these people, men and women, who represented God, were mere regular humans. They ate food, drank water, married, and bore or fathered children. Plus, all of them eventually died. Thus, again, they were normal humans. In addition, none of them practiced monasticism but were, rather, actively involved in this world. This is also true of Jesus who, like Muhammad, carried a weapon.

with spouses and children. What's more, the prophets were unable to produce a miracle, that is unless God willed.

Every human era has had its revelation. God annuls or reestablishes whatever He wills of these prior books. This is because He is, in fact, the source of all revelation.

Yet, whether We allow you to experience in your lifetime a portion of (the punishment) We have promised them or whether We remove you prior, your obligation is only to deliver the message. What's more, the final judgement is Our responsibility.

Then, are those (who reject Us) unaware of how We inflict upon the earth Our punishment, systematically depriving it of all its finest features?✦ Surely, when God passes judgement no

✦That is, for instance, the creation of a barrier region, like the Sahara desert. Can anyone stop its oppressive encroachment? Or, the erosion of a riverbank or shoreline due to massive movements of water, for instance, the Grand Canyon or the destruction of shorelines due to hurricanes. Can anyone recreate it? Again, no one can rebuild such shorelines, tighten such canyons, or halt desertification. Only He has the power to systematically deprive blessings—and only He can dispense them thoroughly, based upon each person's achievements, as confirmed in the remaining part of this section (as below):

one can alter the course (of that) judgement. What's more, He is efficient in how He achieves it.

These previous rejecters of the truth also plotted many a vile deed. However, even more subtle is the plotting of God, *the One who knows* (precisely) *what each person deserves*. What's more, eventually, those who reject (His messages) will discover who really owns the future.

If those who refuse to believe say, "We don't believe you represent God," tell them, "God is sufficient witness between us, and so are those who truly understand scripture."

Section 14
Abraham's Prayer

In the name of the most merciful
and compassionate God

A-L-R

We have sent this book from the heavens (so you can) elevate humankind from the darkness (of human error) into the light (of divine guidance)—to the way which leads directly to the almighty, the only One worthy of praise, to God, who owns all that exists.

Yet, any who reject the truth are doomed. (This is because) they are destined to endure extreme punishment, that is those who exclusively love this life, who choose it completely over the future life, and who (purposely) attempt to prevent people from (discovering) the way of God. (They do so) by attempting to distort (and corrupt) it. These are the ones who have certainly deviated vastly from the correct way.

Even so, We have always sent Our messengers to (the human race) to represent messages in the languages of their own people. This is so they might clarify (for them) the truth in a language easy to understand. However, God allows to err whomever He wills. Furthermore, He guides whomever He wills, because He alone is truly almighty, wise (beyond comprehension).

Messages delivered by various prophets

In fact, this was the reason We sent Moses to represent Our messages, that is "Lead your people from the dark despair (of their former condition) into the light of divine inspiration. What's more, remind them of the inevitable judgement of God." Surely, in this description there are obvious truths—clear signals—for every truly patient and deeply steadfast, as well as grateful, person.

It was Moses who told his people, "Remember how God blessed you by saving you from Pharaoh's people (since the latter) afflicted you with brutality, killing your sons and sparing only your women: an awesome trial from your Lord." Remember, too, when your Lord made known, "If you are grateful to me, I will cause you to flourish. However, if you are thankless, My punishment is extreme." Moses added, "If you deviate in the least from the truth, you and any other human, the full compliment of you: God has no need for anyone or anything, while He deserves all praise."

Are you aware of what happened to the previous rejecters of the truth, that is the people of Noah, the (Arabian) tribes, 'Aad and Thamood, and those generations after them? God alone knows the details regarding them. Prophets were sent to them with full evidence of the truth. However, without giving it the least bit of consideration they said, "We reject your claim to have a divine message. What's more, actually, we doubt you to such a degree that we are suspicious of (even) your intentions." The prophets said to them (essentially), "Is there any doubt (in your minds) regarding the existence of God, the almighty creator? God is the One who is asking you to submit to Him, only so He may forgive you of your past and give you the opportunity to make amends, that is until a (well established) term." Despite this they said, "You are merely a mortal human like us. You only want to cause us to abandon our old religion. If you are truly from God, then, bring us real evidence." Their prophets answered them, "It is true that we are humans like you. However, it is God's decision whom He will favor. Thus, we are powerless to prove to you the truth (of our mission), that is unless God wills. So, we believers trust exclusively in God." They continued, "What other choice could we have, since He is the One who originally guided us? Thus, we will endure with patience whatever you afflict upon us. This is because all who trust must place their trust exclusively in God."

The consequences of rejection

Even so, the godless told their prophets, "Unless you return to our ways, we will exile you." Then, their Lord revealed this to them, "Know that, certainly, We will destroy these evil people and replace them with you. Let him (internalize this fact, the one) who is in awe of Me and fears My warnings—(let him) take heed." Moreover, they prayed that, ultimately, the truth would win.

(Then, their prayers were made true:) because every arrogant enemy of the truth will truly be disappointed, destined (as he is) for hell. (There,) he will be forced to drink the beverage of bitter disappointment, gulping it down unceasingly, little by little, and yet hardly able to swallow. What's more, death will besiege him from all directions. However, he will never die, and he will, ultimately, endure excruciating pain. Thus, the following is, parabolically, the description of those who deliberately reject their Lord: all their efforts are like ashes, blown away in a violent storm. Likewise, in the next life they can never achieve any benefit from *any* of their (seemingly good) accomplishments. This is because to reject God is the most extreme anyone can deviate.

Are you unaware of the fact that God has created the entire universe, as well as this earth, in perfect balance?✦ If He desires, He can eliminate you and instead create a new human race.❖ This is easy for God.

✦❖Notice the first statement (perfectl balance). It means peaceful submission. Nothing in the universe defies His command, that is except humans. It is all obedient, every heavenly body, every solar system, each galaxy—every universe—all of it summarily submits. The animals also obey Him, as do the plants. Only humans purposely violate Him and therefore disrupt the universal balance. This is a warning that unless humans disavow violent and hateful acts, acts of corruption, they will be eliminated. Then, as this Qur'aan makes clear this has already occurred numerous times previously. So, if humankind follows the same trend, it will occur again.

Other prominent societies disrupted the balance of nature and thus were eliminated: the people of Atlantis, Pharaoh, and Babylon. It could also bring evidence for the extinction of other beings, that is by sudden catastrophe, for instance, the dinosaurs. After this catastrophe God reestablished on this earth entirely different species, which were adapted to the new environment. Thus, He creates in whatever way He wills.

There is certainly no evidence that any other creatures evolved from the dinosaurs. Rather, they were merely exterminated. Then, they were replaced with entirely different creatures. Also, there is no evidence that lesser creatures evolved into dinosaurs. Regardless, the fact that the human race is vulnerable to extinction is alluded to, as follows:

> In addition, all in existence will appear before God, when the weak will say to those who were blatantly arrogant, "We were actually following you. Then, can you ease some of God's punishment?" These others will respond, "Had God guided us, we would have guided you, too. Regardless, it is the same, that is whether we grieve impatiently or patiently endure this pain, because, obviously, their is no escape." What's more, when the full scope of judgement has been finalized, the devil will say, "As you can see God's promise has come true. I, too, promised you. However, I deceived you. Yet, I have no control over you. All I did was (make the suggestion to) you, and you responded to me (on your own). So, never blame me, rather, blame yourselves. Furthermore, I am unable to respond to your pleas. Nor are you able to respond to mine. The fact is I have always refused to admit that there was any justification in your former beliefs, that is that I, the devil,could share with God in His powers✦."

✦That is rather than a physical or external entity this evil force is *within the individual*. All evil is within. There are no outside evil forces, like a physical Satan. Rather, it is an internal element, a kind of internal temptation.

These thoughts are within all people. All hateful acts are produced within; they are never created by God. Thus, there can be no excuse based upon some supposedly uncontrollable or outside force. In fact, the Qur'aan repeatedly alludes to the fact that the devil has no real control over anyone. It is the person who listens to devilish insinuations and then acts upon them—who succumbs to his own self-centered lusts—this is the one who is Satan's partisan.

All people experience the urge for vileness. The actual source of the temptation is unknown. Even so, there is a natural sense in each person for recognizing evil. Yet, for those who feel no moral responsibility for their acts whatever wicked urge they sense they pursue. In fact, they recklessly surge into such wickedness.

Yet, regardless, as the Qur'aan makes it clear there is nothing independent in this universe. It is all His creation. This means that even the concept of temptation is His. This is a part of the earthly test. Then, the greatest protection against such urges is to bring God into the heart and therefore think of Him. To always think of Him and in fact be continuously grateful to Him is the secret to success. This is the person who is deeply reverent of God at all times. This is the person who is guaranteed his protection from wickedness. This person does good, because he is inherently good. Yet, it is this turning to God that is responsible for his success. So, even in such success he is beholden to Him. So, if he does gain paradise and therefore escape the torment, it is strictly due to God's mercy.

Yet, in fact, regarding all who commit evil they will endure extreme torment. However, in contrast (for), those true believers, who have achieved goodness on earth, they will be placed in paradise, to live there forever by their Lord's permission. "Peace" will be their greeting.

Are you unaware of God's parable regarding a productive, good word? It is like a healthy, well-rooted tree, branching out vigorously towards the sky, continuously producing fruit with God's permission. God speaks to human beings in parables, so they might be mindful of the truth. However, a vile word—the dark word—is like a rotten tree, uprooted and thus wholly unable to survive. This is how through the clear truth of this book God grants firmness in faith to the believers in this life as well as in the future life. However, He allows the sinners to deviate, because He can do anything.

Are you aware regarding those who preferred the rejection of the truth to God's blessings and through this drove their people into a destination of total desolation, bringing them to hell, which they must endure, the most vile of destinations? This is because they claimed that God has equals,✦ and,

✦That is, for instance, the giving of power to today's rulers, who demand the submission of their subjects to the authority of the state or to the leaders themselves. They demand this only for their own gain. While they claim the need for patriotism, they are busy pursuing their own selfish agendas for wealth, fame, and power. Mere glory seekers, they lead people only to ultimate loss. To regard a nation all-powerful does nothing for the individual, while in contrast the submission to God brings permanent rewards. Blind patriotism is yet another example of the rejection of the authority of God.

When all people are before God, how could patriotism to such a country serve them? There is no security in bowing to the power of state. Rather, all real power is held by God alone. This is why obedience is only His. Thus, rulers who demand obedience never have the peoples' interests in mind, but, rather, seek to oppress them for their own wicked gains. So, by demanding that they hold the power of state high all they do is lead their people into loss.

thus, they deviated from His way. Tell them, "Consume yourselves (now) in worldly pleasures, however, your consequence will be the fire."

What's more, tell My servants, that is those who truly believe, to remain constant in worship and to be generous in God's name to whatever degree they are capable (both privately and publicly), before it is too late.

Blessings of God: need for gratitude

God is the One who created the (entire) universe (as well as earth), who sends for your benefit the rain from the skies and through it makes all manner of nourishment for your needs. He is also the One who has created (the process of) shipping to serve you to cross the oceans and what's more has made the rivers to serve you. He has also made the sun and the moon, continuously revolving in their orbits,✦

✦In all history this is the first reference to the fact that the sun and moon are spinning balls. The ancients never made this discovery. Nor did they relate the continuous rotation of these spheres as "beneficial" to humans. The gravitational effects of these revolving balls are now well established as essential to the health and stability of the solar system. What's more, the tides are directly related to the gravitational influence of the moon.

The Qur'aan is the first document to describe such phenomena in an accurate and scientific way. The purpose of this representation is to cause humans to reflect over the mercy of God. This is so they will more deeply believe in Him and also feel gratitude for His favors.

for your benefit. Too, He made the night and day for your benefit, so that you might utilize this (pattern). Additionally, He always satisfies your desire (that you request of Him) to some degree. Yet, the blessings (of God) are so vast you could never count them.✦ Certainly, humankind

✦That is for His creation the almighty Lord has nothing but love in His heart. Thus, with a deliberate plan He plots His giving for humankind. He provides the earth, a fine and secure place to live. He creates the rotation of night and day; one for rest and the other for work. He answers in some fashion all prayers. He is truly merciful in all that He gives. That is why He holds ingratitude as a crime. Yet, it is so simple. All that a person must do to gain God's pleasure is to be grateful. This is the simplest and most effective method for success. This is also the only requirement for gaining

His help and protection. In contrast, the loss of God's love due to ingratitude is the greatest failure conceivable, that is if people only realized it.

is most persistent in wrongdoing, completely ungrateful.

Abraham as an example of gratitude

Also, remember when Abraham said, "My Lord, secure this region (from all evil). What's more, prevent me and my children from ever worshipping false gods, because such false representations have certainly caused many to err. Thus, after this whoever follows me in this (monotheistic) way is truly of me. Furthermore, whoever rejects my way You are, certainly, much forgiving and a giver of mercy."

He continued, "My Lord, I have settled some of my children here in a valley where the land is desolate, near Your sanctified Temple. This is so that, My Lord, they might devote themselves to Your worship. Thus, cause the peoples' hearts to incline toward You, and give them a productive life, so they might have reason to become grateful."

"Our Lord, You know our deepest thoughts that we may disguise in our hearts as well as all that we reveal." Certainly, nothing in this entire universe remains hidden from God.

(Abraham continued,) "All praise belongs to God, the God who has blessed me in my old age with Ishmael and Isaac. He (my Lord), is the One who hears all prayer. Thus, my Lord, make me and my future generations of those who remain always devoted to You. Also, my Lord, accept this prayer of mine: 'Forgive me and my parents— forgive all the believers during the time of final judgement.'"

Yet, never think that God is unaware of the actions of the wicked. He simply allows them sufficient recourse until the time when they will stare in horror, while running wildly back and forth in mass confusion, their heads raised (in realization) towards heaven yet unable to look away from the home they will see. Moreover, there will be nothing but emptiness in their hearts.

Thus, warn the human race regarding the time when they will be overwhelmed with agony, when those who are immersed in sin will cry, "Our Lord, give us another chance, so we might respond to Your message and follow (Your true messengers)." However, they will be told, "Why (should We)? Didn't you swear previously that there would be no resurrection or punishment? Yet, you lived in the same region as those previous errant souls—and We made obvious the consequences of such peoples' actions." This is because We have established for you numerous examples (of the consequences of divine retribution).

Moreover, because of their deceit this retribution will be dealt upon all such terminal sinners, since God is fully aware of this deceit. Yet, despite their fabrications the godless will never be able to prevail, even if these fabrications were so well designed and so powerful that (through them) they could displace mountain ranges. Thus, never be despondent regarding what God will fulfill, that is The Promise He gave to His prophets. The fact is God is almighty. Furthermore, He (is the true) *avenger of evil.*

(Then, this promise will be realized) at the time when the earth will be completely transformed, as will be the heavens, a time when all who have existed will appear before God, the One who is truly in control: then, you will see those who were immersed in sin bound together in chains, wearing clothes of black soot, with fire arching over their faces. What's more, then, all will be judged, so that God may reveal the real nature of all human beings based upon their actions. Truly, God is efficient (and accurate) in judgement.

This is a mandate to all human beings. So, be forewarned. He is the exclusive God. Let those who are endowed with insight give this deep consideration.

Section 15
The Active Creator

In the name of the most merciful
and compassionate God

A-L-R

These are the revelations of a divine book that is easy to understand. Eventually, those who reject this truth will wish they had surrendered themselves to God. However, disregard them, as they engage in fanciful pursuits. Eventually, they will comprehend the consequences (of their actions).

Even so, We never eliminated a society unless it had previously become aware of the message (of the divine way). However, regardless of the civilization the ultimate result could never be prevented. Nor can it be delayed.

Despite this the godless say, "You who God has given this supposed warning of doom, obviously, you are irrational. However, if what you are saying is true, then, make the angels appear before us." Yet, We only send the angels if it conforms with the truth. In fact, if they achieved what they asked for, the end (of humankind) would come precipitously. Undeniably, We Ourselves methodically revealed from the heavens this warning.✦ What's more, We definitely guard it against any form of corruption.

✦That is rather than the Prophet Muhammad or anyone else these are the messages of God. No human wrote them. This is obvious, since, revealed in the seventh century, it would have been impossible for humans to produce such a document. It is too vast. Plus, in contrast to all other ancient books it is historically and scientifically accurate. Furthermore, it directly guides humans, soothing their hearts.

No man-made document can do so. It even brings humans to tears. Plus, it causes humans to find happiness and peace. Thus, it would be impossible for humans to produce it.

Even so, We truly did inspire prophets for the previous (ancient) civilizations. However, without exception, when the prophet approached them, they scorned him. In the same way We cause this message to pervade the hearts of those immersed in sin, those who refuse to believe in it, despite the fact that the example We made of these previous communities is obvious to them.

Yet, even if We (performed a miracle, for instance,) created an opening for them in heaven, then, they ascended toward it, higher and higher, until they reached it, along the way they would still have said, "Its an illusion—a trick."✦

✦That is they would refuse to believe in it due to their own false pride. Here, they refuse to accept that they are wrong. Nor will they accept anything of which they are unfamiliar. Nor are they willing to make amends. Nor will they in any way lower themselves in humility before a higher Being. They are merely too proud to admit their loss. Then, to truly make amends they would have to admit that they had squandered their lives on mindless pursuits, while neglecting the worship of God. For most people such an admission is impossible.

The divine mercy: evidence

(Yet, even so, Our mighty presence is obvious:) We established in the universe magnificent constellations. Plus, We endowed them with incredible beauty, clearly visible. What's more, We secured them against every wicked, vile force. This is so that anyone who seeks to learn the imperceptible by deception is pursued by what is clearly raw frustration.

Regarding the earth We have made it a vast expanse, with firmly placed mountain ranges (arising from within it).✦What's more, We caused the growth

✦That is due to the forces of compression. Vast pressure was required to raise the mountains. The necessary internal forces are unfathomable. Here, the Qur'aan makes it clear that the mountains have an internal geological origin within the earth and that due to powerful forces they were raised upwards. This precisely coincides with the latest geological models.

Today, the mountains are still rising, the Himalayas, for instance, moving upwards a foot or more per year. Yet, the point is God almighty specifically did this for human benefit. As a result of these mountains *firmly and strategically established* there are the weather patterns, which lead to the formation of rain and snow. Then, this leads to the creation of soils and food as well as fresh water to drink: all obviously due to God's mercy. Therefore, He is testing humans to determine if they are truly grateful for these blessings.

of every (conceivable) type of life, all in a balance. Through it you are provided a livelihood, as are all other domestic and wild beings. In truth, We hold the future deposits needed for the survival of all that exists. Furthermore, We provide it from the heavens based upon a specific, deliberate plan.✦

✦That is it is all by design. Otherwise, without His guiding power chaos would reign. No one in this life can work without a plan. Every businessman, builder, and architect—every specialist of any kind—requires one. The same is true for the heavenly power, though unfathomable—God almighty—who always operates by specific plans.

Additionally (as an example of Our mercy), We unleash the winds (in order to) fertilize (the plants) and also to deliver rain, so you can drink. However, you are incapable of arranging its arrival. Furthermore, no doubt, We alone can give life and also deem death. Plus, once everything is dead, We alone will remain.

How thoroughly We realize (the inner thoughts as well as actions), regarding both those who lived prior to you and those who will arise after you. There is no doubt about it your Lord will unite them, because He is full of wisdom and is completely aware of all (that men do).

Yet, truly, We created humankind from mere wet mineral matter—slimy (organic) muck transmuted. In contrast, long before We had created the invisible forces from hot (radioactive) winds.✦

✦That is the swirling, radioactive winds of the early universe—the dust of interstellar space. Just how almighty God created these beings from this material is unknown. Yet, what is known is that this is the source of all life.

This is now confirmed by modern science. Top astronomers, such as Smoot and Hawking, clearly state that radioactive stellar dust is the precursor of life. This fact is confirmed by the Qur'aan, a document revealed some 1400 years ago. Again, this proves that it is strictly a divine document. Thus, the Qur'aan gives numerous types of evidence proving its extraterrestrial source.

Even so, people will continue to dispute it as a man-made writing. Here, they cling to the senseless assessment that it was, somehow, written by the Prophet Muhammad. Merely to be argumentative they call it "his writings." Yet, they do so without even investigating it.

As stated elsewhere in this Qur'aan, essentially, 'Then, after this (revelation) in what else could they possibly believe?' In other words, nothing God can do will enlighten them. Even if God sent another revelation to, for instance, a different person—even if in this new revelation He brought forward similar scientific examples and historical facts about other obliterated societies, for instance, information about the destruction of the Atlantian, Mayan, Celtic, or Oriental dynasties, would anyone really believe?

No human could have written the historical, social, or scientific facts encoded in the Qur'aan. Isn't this sufficient proof to cause people to directly acknowledge it? Then, if they dispute these obvious proofs, what would cause them to recognize Him? A new revelation? Thus, obviously, the rejection of this Qur'aan is merely an excuse, rather, an evidence of the desire to reject Him as well as any liability at resurrection.

The humble origins of humanity

It was in this vein that your Lord told the angels, "I am going to create mortal man from wet earthen matter and organic muck. Furthermore, when I have finished forming him and have breathed My essence into him, I ask you to submit yourselves to him." Then, all they did so, except Iblees, who refused. He said, "Iblees, why do you refuse to submit?" (He) responded, "Why should I? You created these (mortals) from mere transmuted mineral matter, that is organic muck." He said, "Leave this (angelic state), because from now on you are one of the accursed—in fact, you deserve only My rejection—until the end of time."

Iblees responded, "My Lord, if this is the case, give me recourse until I am resurrected." He answered, "So it will be. You are given recourse until a predestined time of judgment." Then, Iblees said, "My Lord, since you have thwarted me, I will (due to jealousy) tempt humankind, seducing them into error. (As a result,) only Your deeply believing servants will be saved."

He responded, "What is with Me is a perfectly straight way. Certainly, My creatures will be immune to you, except those who are already immersed in sin and thus (choose to) follow you.

Moreover, hell is the ultimate goal for such people, with its multiple entrances, each receiving its preordained quota of sinners."

Surely, those who are deeply in awe of God will be surrounded by lush gardens (and will be told): "You are now secure. Enter here in peace." By then, We will have cleansed them of any unworthy thoughts or feelings that may have been lingering in their hearts. There, they will be as brethren, facing each other in love on thrones of happiness.

They will never tire of this. Moreover, they will never be forced to leave.

Tell my servants that I alone am the true forgiver of sins, the true giver of mercy. Tell them also that the enormity of the suffering I will inflict upon the sinners will be beyond comprehension.

The story of Abraham, Lot, and the vile cities

Also, tell them, once again, about Abraham's guests, who came to him with the offer of "Peace." He answered, "The fact is we are concerned of your intentions." They said, "There is no need for concern. Certainly, we have brought you the news that you will soon have a son, who will be blessed with great wisdom." He said, "I am an old man: why do you tell me this?" They responded, "This omen is so you will never lose hope of the ultimate truth. Thus, be not of those who lose hope of the Lord's ever-present mercy." Abraham exclaimed, "And who, other than the completely depraved, could ever lose hope of the Lord's mercy?" He added, "What else do you have in view, you divine messengers?" They answered, "We have been sent to a people immersed in sin and who, therefore, will soon be destroyed, except Lot's household, all of whom we will rescue, that is other than his wife, because God has deemed that she will remain."

When God's messengers came to Lot's house, he said, "You have no idea what you are encountering here." They answered, "It is of no consequence. We have come to you with precisely the objective of their derision, that is The Certainty. We know of what we speak. Thus, leave, now, you and your household, and do so under the protection of darkness. Follow them yourself at the rear, and let none of you reconsider. Thus, proceed as you are ordered." These messengers inferred to Lot that the last vestige of those sinners will be eliminated by the morning.

The residents (of the city) came to Lot, thrilled at the news (of his visitors). He said, "These are my guests, so never shame me. Instead, give consideration (to the authority of) God, and free me from this disgrace." They answered, "Didn't we warn you of the consequences of housing strangers?" Lot said, "It would be better if you must do whatever you intend to do to take instead my daughter." However, secretly, the angels inspired him, "No matter how long or hard you preach, they will never listen. Truly, in their unbridled passion they are completely oblivious of what is right."

Then, at sunrise the screaming blast overtook them, and We obliterated their city, pounding (the inhabitants) from the skies with rock-hard blows (of chastisement), predestined. Surely, this serves as a message (for any who are capable of understanding its significance). No doubt, the road which passes those (now extinct) towns still exists. This is a clear sign for all who truly believe (in the ultimate meeting with God).

Other sinful cities and their consequences

The people living in the forested town (of Midian) were also committed to evil. Thus, We also destroyed them. Like the Sodomites, these people lived by a highway, still visible today.

The people of al-Hijr (an old Arabian tribe) rejected their prophets. We produced for them Our signs. However, they obstinately refused to heed them. This was despite the fact that they greatly benefited from Our blessings, carving out homes in the mountainsides, where they lived securely. Thus, early in the morning the howling blast obliterated them. So, all their accomplishments were of no consequence.

Yet, We never created this entire universe, every aspect of it, as well as the earth, except with a specific purpose. Then (never neglect this fact and), beware of the inevitable time, when everyone will understand (the real purpose for this life). So, be gracious in your forgiveness (of peoples' inadequacies).✦ After all, He is the absolute creator of all that exits.

✦That is why pass judgement upon people, since it will all return to God? He will deal with all who exist. Then, no human must judge. What's more, there is no reason to become frustrated over the doings of anyone else, including any who reject this, since it is all under His almighty control. Rather, by exerting patience and mercy, perhaps, people may find this way to God attractive and may, therefore, submit to it. This is precisely the method of the dedicated Prophets, including Moses, Jacob, and Jesus, including the Prophet Muhammad. All exerted patience at God's command and thus brought peace to impetuous humanity.

In addition, We have provide you (with a system of divine revelation)—that is the seven often-repeated (points of fact)✦ plus the grand and

✦That is the first chapter of the Qur'aan, known in Arabic as *al-Faatiha*. This is a powerful invocation asking for God's blessings and guidance, while praising Him. It is simple and basic. In fact, it is a summary of the true nature of the relationship with God. It is also protection. Its purpose is to prevent the believers from faltering by reminding them to rely exclusively on God. It is also a reminder of His infinite mercy as well as loving forgiveness.

glorious Qur'aan. Thus, never allow yourselves to desire the material benefits which We have provided to others. Nor have any grief over those (who reject your message), but, rather, be generous in forgiveness (of human failings), and overwhelm the believers with love and compassion.✦ What's

✦That is concentrate only on the positive, plus focus only on those who are deserving. It is to them that the believer must share his love. The believer is commanded to pay no attention to the pompous rejecters of God, people who despite obvious material success are, spiritually, feeble. The believer is instructed to waste no energy fretting over the godless but rather put all energy into the love and compassion for his fellows, who sincerely believe in His almighty Self. He is also obligated to share the message of God with others, but always in a compassionate way. Furthermore, it is his obligation to never be abusive with others regardless of their beliefs or behaviors. Thus, he must retain his dignity at all times. This is the true believer in almighty God, who truly follows the refined ways of the Prophet Muhammad.

more, tell them that you are merely here to give clear warning (promised by God)—(bearing) the same (warning) We have previously revealed but was dissected into pieces, the same (kind of) people who now insist that the Qur'aan is a fraud. However, in God's name We will certainly hold them responsible, every one of them, for all their acts. Thus, tell them exactly what you have been ordered to say. Furthermore, ignore all who associate other powers with God. Certainly, We will fully support you against all who deride this message, who claim that there are other 'powers' besides God. This is because, eventually, they will realize the truth (regarding this).

Furthermore, We are fully aware that your heart is oppressed by their vile statements. However, instead praise God for His unlimited magnificence—and what's more submit yourself to Him in adoration. Furthermore, worship your Lord in absolute worship—until your last breath.

Section 16
The Bees: Servants of God

In the name of the most merciful
and compassionate God

God's judgement is inevitable. So, never demand
for it to be accelerated. What's more, He is
unlimited in His magnificence, far beyond
anything which men attempt to attribute to Him.✦

✦That is including statements such as 'the gods will be angry,' or 'if the
gods will,' as if there is a different divine being for every function. Or, the
claim that God bears children or has even the need to do so. Ultimately,
He will disavow all such proclamations as nonsense, rather, destructive.
The fact is, obviously, such statements are merely human inventions and
have never been sanctioned by Him. Their purpose is to prevent humans
from devoutly submitting to Him.

He causes the angels to deliver this divine
inspiration, done at His choosing upon whomever
He wills of His servants—filling their souls with
this command, "Warn everyone that there is only
one divine power. Thus, always give Me due
consideration."

Blessings galore

He created the earth and the rest of the universe
through a deliberate system. High beyond
comprehension is He, far above anything to which
human beings may fabricate as sharing in His
power.✦

✦That is humans create impressions of God based upon their own feeble understanding. Since such humans refuse to consider themselves as created beings, who are responsible to their creator, they produce their own confabulated understanding of the universe. Thus, they invent for themselves power sources, which suit their passions.

The entire emphasis of this section is to warn against this dire propensity—the invention of other powers as if divine. In God's view this is the worst of all crimes. It is also unforgivable. This is because it violates all sense and is even a violation of the obvious nature of this universe. The extent of this violation is made clear by the fact that the universe is one, completely organized. In other words, obviously, it is operated by one sole Being.

Consider how people operate on this planet. Consider the functions of a nation or even an organization. No one would allow there to be numerous heads of state or presidents. For an organization there can never be two chiefs, nor can there be for a corporation two CEOs. This would result in absolute chaos. Then, why would anyone attribute to the universes multiple powers, unless such a person's objective is corrupt? In fact, such an attribution is obviously the most ludicrous claim of all, purely fraudulent.

He creates humans originally from a mere (lowly) drop of sperm. Yet, incredibly, this same being proves contentious. Too, He creates for you cattle, which provide you with warmth, food, and other benefits. You find beauty in them when you drive them home in the evening and back to pasture in the morning. Also, they transport your burdens to places throughout the earth, which you would have, otherwise, been unable to reach without great difficulty. The fact is your Lord is completely compassionate, truly merciful.

(We have also created for you) horses and other equine species for you to ride as well as to admire (for their beauty). Also, He will create (futuristic) methods of transport of which you are now unaware.✦Furthermore, God alone has the power

♦That is in His wisdom He created the various species that would help humans—horses, donkeys, camels, and others. This is because He knew humans would need them. Plus, He provides iron, titanium, and other metals, as well as coal and oil, so humans could create modern devices. All that can be said is "Glory to God, the great" for all His merciful love and for this elegant plan for the human race. Yet, how rarely do human beings show gratitude for this.

to show you the right way. Even so, many deviate from it. Yet, if He desired, He would have guided every one of you.

He is the One who delivers rain from the heavens from which you (gain water to) drink and also the pasture (needed for) your animals. Through it, He produces crops, olive trees, date palms, and grapes, plus all other types of produce.♦

♦That is as is found in other areas about the globe. As the Qur'aan was originally revealed in Arabia it emphasizes local produce, although the emphasis is on the entire Mediterranean region. Even so, these are among the most nutritious and medicinal fruit known. The powers of these foods are demonstrated by the fact that they are now used throughout the world. Thus, the very life blood of humanity, powerful food substances, such as olives, olive oil, sesame, dates, figs, and pomegranate, all derive from the Mediterranean and Middle East. This is that blessed land blessed by almighty God Himself: for all times to come.

Surely, this serves as an obvious message for people who use their reason.

Additionally, He created the night and the day, as well as the sun and the moon, all for your benefit. The abundance of the (countless) stars are (also) subservient to His command. Surely, these are signs for people willing to use their ability to think. What's more, notice all the variations in contrast♦ He has created for you on earth. This is

✦That is as represented by colors, land formations, strata, rock formations, mountain ranges, and pathways, all prepared for human benefit. It is also represented by the fact that no two things are alike, whether living, such as human beings, or 'dead' such as mountains, rocks, lakes, rivers, and more. A deeper meaning is the variations in species and races of humans and other Godly creatures and the various paths which can be taken to serve almighty God.

a certain sign for people willing to accept it in their hearts. Furthermore, He made the oceans conform to His laws, so that you can eat protein from it, as well as extract valuables from it, which you may wear. Plus, on precisely that ocean you see ships ploughing through the waves, so that you can proceed in search of His plentiful blessings and thus have reason to be grateful. He is also the One who firmly placed mountain ranges (arising from) within the earth, so that it wouldn't wobble✦ and

✦That is due to a lack of friction as it orbits. As the globe rotates on its axis the mountains create much needed friction to stabilize the orbit. A smooth ball would have a relatively unstable orbit. Thus, if it were not for the mountains, the earth would shake uncontrollably. This would make it impossible to inhabit. This, again, proves the incomprehensible mercy of the divine source. In other words, God is the most loving Being conceivable. Yet, how rarely do humans consider this.

The message is due to His love; God ensured this instability wouldn't occur. This was by systematically producing a plethora of mountain ranges found on every continent. He did so because of His love for humankind to provide for them a peaceful and productive home. The purpose was all to determine which of His humans are truly grateful for this blessing.

rivers acting as natural pathways, so you can find your way as well as various other means of orientation. The fact is it is by the stars (which We have Ourselves created for this very purpose) that humans orient themselves.

Then, how can you compare the One who creates to that which is incapable of creating? Are you unable, then, to make sense of this? In truth, if you were to attempt to calculate the blessings of God, you could never do so.✦ Then, surely, God

✦That is, as mentioned in this section up to this point: the actual birth of each human, the creation of substances, which provide warmth, the production of cattle as a species for food, the creation of vast and multiple species of fish for protein, the making of means for transportation, including modern means, the sending of rain to provide drink and also for buoyancy (for transport), the creation of seed crops for mass production of food but also fruit and items of relish, such as olives, the making of the night-day system for rest and activity, the spinning globe balanced by mountains to 'slow its spin', and the creation of the distant stars in the perfect formation in orderly constellations for human navigation.

These are all mentioned on pages 463 to 465. Then, these are merely a modicum of the countless blessings of which He speaks. The making of the visible stars itself is an unfathomable miracle. How did God do it so long ago, so humans could know them? It is all so incomprehensible, that is His incredible design. Thus, in absolute truth there is no way humans could ever determine the degree and scope of His blessings. Truly, they are beyond count.

forgives much and gives vastly of His mercy. What's more, God is fully aware of all you hide (in your hearts) as well as whatever you reveal.

Now, these other beings that people adore besides God are they capable of creating anything?✦Certainly,

✦That is only God can create the life force within a living body. No human nor any team of humans can do so. Humans are unable to create even a single gene, let alone a living being. The chromosomes are exclusively a divine creation. In fact, despite the most intense efforts of modern science it has proven impossible to create from nothing any living being. Humans are unable to even create a mere molecule, and they could never create a single vital gene, let alone an entire species.

they themselves are created. Far from alive, they are dead. What's more, they are unaware of when they will be resurrected.

This God of yours is the only divine power. However, because they are so full of false pride, the godless refuse to admit this.

Without doubt, God is fully aware of all that they keep secret as well as whatever they reveal. In fact, He has no love for the arrogant. What's more, whenever they are asked (to consider it, that is this revelation We have revealed, they say), "This revelation that you claim is from your Lord is merely fables of the ancients."✦ Thus (during

✦That is they summarily reject it, without even giving it the slightest thought: without taking the time to investigate it. Thus, their purpose is to disprove the existence of a divine authority as well as resurrection. Regardless of the message delivered they will never believe.

resurrection), they will bear the full burden of their own vile deeds and also some of the burdens of those ignorant ones whom they misguided. Oh, what a vile load it is with which they will be burdened.

Consequences of rejection

The previous rejecters of the truth also schemed against (the divine way). As a result, ultimately, God obliterated their civilizations, caving in their roofs and burying them alive. What's more, they were taken completely by surprise by that punishment.

As well, during resurrection He will surely humiliate (these same rejecters of the truth), saying, "Now, where are these false gods which you worshiped? Where are they now, the ones who in order to serve them you rejected Me?" Then, those who were given of knowledge will say, "Today, those who rejected the truth are disgraced, totally miserable, the ones whom the angels took from life while they were still sinning." Then, they will profess their servitude, saying, "We didn't mean to do bad things." However, the answer will be, "Without question, God knows the basis of all your actions. Thus, go directly to hell, your permanent residence." What's more, absolutely, the condition of any who tend towards arrogance is vile. However, those who keep God in their hearts are asked, "What is it that your Lord revealed to you?"—and their answer, "The very finest of everything."

Obstinance versus true belief

Good fortune is the consequence in this life for all who persevere in doing good. However, their ultimate result will be far superior. Certainly, in the next life the condition of the God-fearing will be excellent: entrance into Gardens of never-ending satisfaction fed by pure springs, receiving all that they desire.

This is how God rewards His dedicated servants, those whom the angels take (when they die) while they are spiritually pure, greeting them with, "Let your souls be at peace. Enter paradise: you earned it."

Are these others merely waiting for the angels to appear in their presence or for their Lord's judgment to be realized? Yet, the obstinate sinners of the previous civilizations acted in the same way. Upon their destruction God never wronged them. Rather, they only wronged themselves. In fact, all the evil they had achieved returned to haunt them. What's more, they were completely overpowered by precisely the subject of their mockery.

The godless say, "If God wanted, He could have made us worship the right way instead of our own ways and the ways of our ancestors. He could have stopped us from making our own rules attributed to Him." This is precisely what the previous sinners said. Yet, the duty of the messengers is merely to warn.

Even so, without doubt, within every civilization We have elevated a prophet, with this message, "Give yourselves fully to God, worshipping only Him. Plus, shun all wickedness, all corruption." However, in such previous civilizations there were people whom God graciously guided, just as there were many others who inevitably fell prey to the allure of evil. Thus, go about the earth and determine for yourself the ultimate consequences of those who defied the truth.

(Regarding the deliberate rejecters of the truth) while you are eager to show them the true way, yet, God withholds His guidance from any whom He deems derelict. What's more, during resurrection such people will be devoid of all support. (Even so, for them there could be no other consequence:) they make it their objective to swear in God's name that

"There is no life after death." There most certainly is: a promise which He has willed upon Himself. However, the majority of people have no clue regarding it. Yet, He will (resurrect them to) expose their differences, so those who refuse to believe might realize that they were lying to themselves regarding (this act of) resurrection. (This is easy for Us:) whenever We decide a thing, We simply say, "Be"—and then it is.

Regarding those who in God's service abandon all evil after suffering harm We will, certainly, give them an excellent status in this life. However, the benefits (they will accrue) in the next life are infinitely greater. If they only knew—if the godless could only understand, that is it is those who having remained fully patient despite any difficulty, in their Lord do they place their trust.✦

✦That is because instead of false pride they trust exclusively in God. This is why these truly patient and believing ones will be the true winners. Their earnings will be so vast that it is inconceivable. In contrast, those who belittle them and maliciously fight against them will suffer only horrifying loss. If they only realized this and accepted true belief—and followed the way of the true believers—how easy it would be for them, too, to gain the supreme benefits.

Regardless of the era We always sent inspired humans. So, if you are still unable to comprehend this, ask the followers of scripture. They will tell you that their prophets were also divinely inspired humans, who were given (clearly understandable) truths and scripture. Upon you, too (O believer,) We have provided from the heavens this reminder. This is so that you might clarify before the people all the moral values that have been (already) revealed to them, so they might use their wisdom.

Then, can the plotters of evil ever be certain that God will not cause an earthquake to consume them or that (any other type of) punishment will not overtake them by surprise, (or do they regard themselves immune to Our power)?...or, that they are immune from being suddenly afflicted by God while they are in transit and therefore unable to escape?...or, that He might afflict them through a slow (methodical) decay? Despite this, certainly, your Lord is tender in His love for His creatures, a giver of love and mercy.

Then, have the godless ever considered all that God has created—how their shadows must bow down, right or left, before God, completely submitting to His will? This is because all that exists in this universe, as well as the earth, submits to Him: every living creature, the angels: even the latter never act arrogantly.✦Furthermore, God has

---

✦That is despite the fact that they are near Him and favored by Him. The angels are exceedingly powerful. They send inspirations on behalf of God directly to humans. They have monstrous strength but also are delicate, loving. Apparently, they are quite huge. Yet, despite their powers and their close association with God they never descend into arrogance and what's more as truly humble servants of God never brag.

said, "You will not attempt to serve more than one God. God is God. Thus, I am the only One of whom to be in awe." Furthermore, the universe is His. Obedience is His. Thus, would you worship anything else? This is because if you are graced by good, it is from God. Plus, whenever you suffer harm, it is to Him that you plead for help. However, as soon as He rescues you (from that danger) the fact is some of you give power to others, as if to blatantly prove your ingratitude. Then, go ahead, indulge in the pleasures of life, because eventually you will realize the truth.

Yet, they revere as if divine precisely those things that We created for their benefit, even though they have no basis for it. By God, you will definitely be held responsible for your fabrications. They also claim God has daughters. Far beyond (such an association) is His glorious Self. This is despite the fact that they would never make such a choice themselves.

Surely, when (such a one) is told the news (of a female newborn), he becomes filled with (hidden) rage, avoiding any contact with people, because of (what he regards as) bad news. What's more, he contemplates, "Should I keep this (despite the contempt he feels for it)?" Or, will he bury it in the earth? Regardless, it is corrupt. Thus, anyone who refuses to believe in the final meeting with God becomes, characteristically (and unavoidably), corrupt in nature. In contrast, the characteristics of God are of the purest and noblest degree. This is because He is the only almighty One, the truly wise.

It is such that if God were to immediately hold men accountable for their various wicked acts, no one would remain on the face of the earth. However, He gives them an abundance of opportunities, that is until the preordained time.✦Yet, when their time is

✦That is, again, demonstrating His incredibly, vast love and mercy for human beings, that He would repeatedly and endlessly give such humans the opportunity to find Him. Then, He also gives them the chance to redeem themselves for any wrong they have committed.

Obviously, He wants no harm to befall His creation, just as a parent would desire no harm for his or her children. Rather, He wishes them only peace and happiness. So, He gives them countless opportunities to make amends: for their own sakes. This is why He usually allows people a full lifespan, despite the fact that they rebel against Him.

up, they will be unable to delay it by a single moment, nor can they accelerate it.

Yet, they attribute to God something they would dislike for themselves, and while they are making these fabrications they believe it will bring them great success. Instead, all they earn is torment—and (as a result of their refusal to believe) they will be abandoned of God's mercy.

God swears that the exact circumstances occurred previously. We raised prophets within various civilizations. However, those who (inherently) reject the truth refused to listen, because Satan deceived them by making the traditions (of these people) seem so correct. Similarly, he is the associate of today's sinners. Thus, they (too,) will suffer enormously. Moreover, the only reason We revealed this divine guidance to you was so that you would clarify all issues of belief in which they differ so greatly and also to offer guidance and mercy for people who are willing to believe.

Also, God sends water from the sky and as a result gives life to the land after it was lifeless. Without doubt, this is a message for those who are willing to consider it.

Vast blessings: domesticated animals, milk, fruit, and the parable of the bee

In the various livestock there is also an insight. We provide you with a drink, which is derived from their abdominal cavities, a selected portion between the waste products and the blood products—pure milk, a pleasant beverage. This, again, is a message for any willing to consider it.

The various fruit trees and vines from which you derive (potentially damaging) alcoholic beverages, as well as nourishing foods; this, too, is a message for any willing to give it thought.

Consider also how your Lord created instincts in the bee, telling it, essentially, "Make homes for yourselves in mountains, trees, and (man-made) devices. Then, gather the essence of every type of fruit. As well, humbly perform whatever responsibilities your Lord requires of you." From within them various types of extracts are produced, which is a medicine for humankind. Through all this there is a message (profound in its meaning) for those who are willing to consider it.

God created you. Then, eventually, He will cause you to die. What's more, many of you will succumb to gradual decay—aging—to a most decrepit state, unable to remember anything that you previously knew so well. Without doubt, God knows all and is unlimited in His power (to achieve whatever He wills).

More blessings: division of human talents, loving spouses, progeny, and housing

Furthermore, God has favored some individuals above others. Yet, those who as a result of God's blessings are given greater favors often refuse to share with its rightful recipients, that is (for instance) those under their care, so that they might be equal in this respect. Will they, then (by their refusal to be grateful) demonstrate their rejection of God's blessings?

It is God who has given you a correctly matched spouse and through (such spouses) children and grandchildren. What's more, He has provided for you all that you need to survive. Thus, will human beings relentlessly put their trust in the false and (purely) self-serving, violating the blessings of God? Moreover, will they persist in the worship of all that is powerless, none of which can even remotely help them and which are completely useless? Thus, make no comparisons with God. God knows, but you are incapable of knowing.

God gives you the example of two men, one who is enslaved and thus dependent on others and a free man gifted from Us with vast abundance that he takes advantage of it at will in any way he chooses. Are these two equal? *God is the only One to be praised*. However, few of them comprehend this.✦

✦Yet, as this parable indicates the person who deeply believes in Him is given by God every conceivable blessing, including freedom to live with gusto. It is also the freedom of knowing he is free of sin, because of his complete trust in God. Then, because of this trust and the sincere goodness he generates he has earned absolute forgiveness, a vast reward.

Despite this the majority of people give no thought to Him, even though, truly, only God holds all power, even though He is great in His love and forgiveness. If people only realized the degree of His forgiveness, they would all turn to Him immediately and fully. The human being is enslaved by his own erroneous thinking, while God seeks to free him from this. So, the message is anyone who He relieves of the burden of sin is free, while anyone who refuses Him is, essentially, a slave to his own desires.

No other being or element has any real power. This is why only God deserves praise. To praise any other is not only a crime but also an absolute waste. So, as deemed by the Qur'aan it makes sense to praise Him alone. In this parable the one who is free is the person who chooses God as His master, while the one who is bound, locked to this earth, is the person who rejects Him.

Yet, there is an even more profound element to these statements. It is the fact that, incredibly, God must remind humans to whom they are responsible and Who alone deserves praise. He must clearly tell humans to worship Him. If He doesn't remind humans of His powers, they fall into corruption. So, any such reminders He provides are strictly for human benefit. His words benefit the human race. This includes the reminder to be grateful for which God never benefits. Only humans benefit from this gratitude. Then, anyone who accepts this reminder and acts upon it becomes free, in fact, cleansed. This is the freedom to which this parable alludes. It is the permanent freedom from the burden of sins, which can only be ensured by almighty God.

> **God provides another example regarding two other men, one who is unable to hear, as if deaf and thus is dependent on others—a sheer burden on his Master. Regardless of how the Master directs him he fails completely.♦ Then, can such a**

♦This describes the one who refuses to believe in or respond to God. It means that despite being called, the person refuses to listen. God sends messages. He delivers all manner of insights, and still, the person fails to recognize it. He even sends human messengers, real people, often from the local region, to awaken him. He may even send divine spirits, actual angels, disguised as humans, with the goal of reviving him. Yet, despite this monumental effort such a person rejects every attempt by his merciful Lord to guide him.

This is the greatest failure of all. This is why He gives numerous examples, all to cause humans to think correctly, all so they will come to Him.

In God's view the praise of any other is a crime beyond comprehension, in fact, unforgivable. Humans, somehow, believe they will benefit from these insignificant powers, so they seek them for their own gain. Yet, they never gain benefits. Rather, they only gain harm. This they must know—that only their high Lord God can help them. Even so, the formula for success is simple. By merely truly believing in Him and avoiding all major sins they gain His mercy as well as His much desired love. Then, too, His true religion is easy, a fact confirmed on page 480, as well as page 484. This is the most monumental success anyone can achieve.

person be equated to the man who (because he hears and responds to the truth) promotes the doing of good and himself does good?

Only God comprehends all the deep truths within the universe. Thus, regarding the final meeting with God—that appointed time of resurrection—it will happen suddenly and unpredictably. Without doubt, God can will anything.

When God caused you to be born, you were devoid of knowledge. However, He endowed you with the ability to hear, see, and think, all so that you might have reason to be grateful.

Have they never considered the birds, how We have enabled them to fly, reliant on only divine power to keep them airborne? Through this there is evidence for any who is willing to believe.✦

✦That is without His great creative genius there is no way birds could fly. This is because flight is dependent upon the existence of an atmosphere. If there were no atmosphere, all flying creatures would immediately drop to the earth and summarily die. Thus, it is exclusively by God's mighty power that such beings survive.

Then, like the bees, the birds are His humble servants. They are always grateful for His blessings. So, again, this is an example for people to consider: is the individual human grateful for all these blessings, or does the person summarily reject the divine role?

God has also made houses for you, so you can rest. He has provided you with dwellings from animal hides, easy to handle, when you travel and when you camp as well as furnishings and goods for temporary use (derived from) their rough wool, soft furry wool, and hair.✦ Also, throughout His

✦That is He created all such creatures in advance to serve the human race. He made the hide, so humans could easily prepare it for their use—for their protection. He also designed wool, so it would be a protection against the elements. Thus, all that exists in the entire earth was created for the benefit of humans. Now, God challenges humans to recognize this and to feel gratitude for these blessings, for their own sakes.

creation God has established (specifically for your benefit) various means of protection. Thus, He provided you with the mountains as a means of shelter,✦ clothing to protect you from extremes of

✦Mountains offer many degrees of shelter. Here, valleys are created, for which the mountains modify the weather. Too, these mountains provide numerous caves, used as housing by primitive man or even today for temporary shelter. The mountains also provide marble and stone used to create dwellings. Thus, the meaning of this seemingly basic statement becomes profound. Too, metal is extracted from them and used to make buildings, homes, and vehicles, all of which serve as divinely-provided shelter. They are also the main source of trees, which are harvested and again used for buildings. Thus, the meaning of this single statement is profound.

weather, and also clothing that might protect you from violence. This is how God gives you the full measure of His blessings—all so that you might submit to Him in absolute servitude.

However, if they reject you, realize that your only role is to clarify the truth. Those who reject it are fully aware of God's (numerous) blessings. Yet, despite this they refuse to accept them as such, since most of them are inclined to obstinately reject it.

Yet, ultimately, We will provide every civilization with a person of truth. As a result, those who deliberately reject it will be unable to plead ignorance. Nor will they be allowed to correct their behavior. What's more, when those who commit evil comprehend the punishment that they must endure, they will beg for mercy. However, it will be to no avail. Nor will they be given another opportunity. Furthermore, when those who upheld idolatrous beliefs encounter their former objects of worship instead of God, they will say, "Lord, this is what we adored instead of you." However (these false gods), will yell at them, retorting, "You have only been misleading your own selves." In addition, during resurrection such people will present themselves in full submission to God. Furthermore, their false objects of worship will be nowhere to be found.

We heap layer upon layer of suffering upon all who reject the truth, those who purposely discourage others from the way of God. This is in compensation for their corruption. The fact is, eventually, We will produce within every civilization a witness against them from among themselves.

We will also bring you as a witness (regarding) your own people. This is because We have exposed you to this divine book, revealed systematically in order to clarify all issues and to provide guidance, as well as loving mercy and good news, for those who are willing to serve God.

God's way: basic requirements; the prohibition of jealousy

In fact, God requires the following: doing justice to the fellow man, the doing of good and (productive) deeds, and generosity (both in spirit and materially), towards the fellow person. Plus, *He prohibits all acts which are morally reprehensible as well as jealousy. In addition, He urges you repeatedly to adhere to this.*

Then, remain committed to your agreement with God, that is in the pledges and promises you make. Never break your promises after having made proper, binding agreements in God's name. Without question, God is aware of all your actions.

Thus, never be like this, that is the woman who unwinds and breaks apart the yarn, which she herself has worked (so arduously) to spin and strengthen. Don't be like this by using your promises to create deception, simply because you may be in a higher position than another. Through this God is testing you. This is so that during resurrection He will make clear the real causes for your malice against each other.

Without doubt, if God willed, He could have made you all into one affable community. However, He allows whom He wills to deviate and guides correctly *whomever is willing.* What's more, unquestionably, you will be held responsible for whatever you achieved (in this life).

Therefore, beware of abusing your commitments to others for selfish gains, because, if you do so, you will violate the trust you have established with God. As a result, harm will befall you in this life, plus you will be caused to suffer in the next life. Thus, never abandon your commitment with God for an insignificant gain. In truth, having console with God is sufficient for you, if you only realized it.

Everything you possess will ultimately be of no consequence. In contrast, whatever is (held in trust) with God is permanent. In addition, realize that, certainly, for those who despite their hardships remain patient We will deposit their reward in accordance with the best of their deeds.

Regarding the recitation of this Qur'aan when you do so, seek God's protection from the accursed devil. Clearly, he is powerless over the true believers, who trust fully in their Lord. Rather, he has power only over those who choose to follow him and as a result pay homage to lesser gods.✦

✦This refers to the act of actually giving authority to others. This includes the power of selfish desires. Thus, a person makes his/her own passions and desires the object of worship, essentially admiring the self above all else. Then, since this person does only what he sees fit there is no allowance for submission to God. Thus, selfishness is a kind of idol worship, where the individual places his own desires above any duty to God. Or, the person may submit to impotent elements such as the power of government or state, even the authority of other humans. These are the modern idols—the trendy Satans—of which the Qur'aan warns.

The Qur'aan as a modern revelation

Now that We have updated (these older) revelations, displacing the previously orthodox (works)—for which God best realizes (what needed to be displaced)—now that we have purified revelation, those who refuse to believe say "You invented it." In no way is this the case, yet most of them are unable to comprehend it. Tell them, "It is a heavenly (script) from God, revealed systematically by your Lord. Its purpose is to establish the truth to create confidence for the true believers, while providing guidance and good news to all who fully dedicate themselves to God."✦

✦The Qur'aan distinguishes two types of believers: those who believe deeply in Him and then regular believers. The latter never quite reach this depth. Even so, both are offered the glory of paradise plus another prize: the power of real confidence for their success. It is the power of knowing in advance that they will ultimately win. Plus, it is the knowledge that regardless of their difficulties God is supporting them. Yet, this support is particularly acute for those who deeply believe in Him and sacrifice their entire selves for Him. These are the ones whom God surrounds with His love.

We are fully aware that they maliciously claim, "He (that is Muhammad), learned it all (not from God but, rather,) from another person." Yet, this is despite the fact that this supposed teacher speaks a different language. This is Arabic, itself obviously demonstrating the truth (of its source). In fact, those who refuse to believe in God's messages are devoid of His guidance, and they will (as a result) eventually endure extreme torment. It is merely those who reject (the existence of) God who are responsible for these lies. Yet, they are only lying to themselves.

After becoming a believer anyone who rejects God, and this, without doubt, never applies to anyone forced to do so under duress, while his heart remains true, but rather only regarding the person who purposely opens his heart to a rejection of the truth: upon all such descends God's condemnation. Thus, as a result of their deeds they will endure immense suffering. Their rejection is due to the fact that they regard their (earthly) life as superior to the next one. What's more, God never guides those who reject the truth.✦

✦This relates to the natural truth that is within all people. It is that element which tells them to be good, honest, and kind. It is also the element which reminds them that there truly is a higher power to whom they owe homage.

Even so, despite this native intelligence God still makes a special effort to guide them. He does so from His love. This is in order to prevent them from degenerating into errant ways. Yet, if they deliberately choose to revert to rejecting Him, ultimately, they will find themselves abandoned. This is because they will be devoid of His loving kindness and mercy, and this is the worst loss conceivable.

(Those who reject the eternal truths within them): they are the ones whose ability to comprehend has been sealed by God Himself. They are also the ones who are derelict (in their duty before God). Certainly, in the next life they will be the true losers. Even so, your Lord is a granter of forgiveness, that is to those who abandon their evil tendencies after having fallen prey to it, who from now on work hard (in God's cause) and who remain patient despite any trials. In fact, after such sincere repentance by them they will discover their Lord (to be) much forgiving, truly merciful. Thus, beware of the time when every human being will plead for himself alone, when every soul will be fully compensated for whatever he has done, and when everyone will be treated fairly.

Also, God provides you the following example: there exists a town, totally peaceful and secure, flourishing with every conceivable exotic pleasure, which then refused to be grateful for God's blessings. As a result, God caused it to experience a comprehensive misery—hunger, famine, and fear—as a result of its peoples' evil deeds. They had undoubtedly been provided with their own prophet. However, they refused to accept his message and therefore were consumed by punishment, while they were still sinning (against themselves).

Thus, regarding all the good things of life take full advantage from My provisions to you.✦ What's

✦That is it is perfectly acceptable to live a brilliant, beautiful life, enjoying and relishing all its wondrous aspects—like the aforementioned town. The only caveat is for people to never deliberately violate His truths.

This command to "enjoy" is a Qur'aanic vote against fundamentalism and extremism. This means that the true religion of God is highly liberal. In other words, in the Qur'aan there is no justification for extremist or 'strict' views. Rather, this book commands its followers to be liberal and to, in particular, never impose their own views as if God's. In fact, the attribution of rules as if God's—that is either making prohibitions or allowances that God never sanctions—is a crime. Thus, for a true believer all the healthy exotic pleasures of this world are for the taking, minus the exceptions listed throughout the Qur'aan, as follows:

more, thank God for what He has given you, that is if it is He that you truly hold high.

His prohibitions are minimal:

- the consumption of animal blood
- the consumption of meat (from animals which

have died) from unknown causes or carcasses of fallen prey (unless killed by your own hands while hunting)

- swine flesh

- anything killed under a name other than God

Yet, if the aforementioned is done as a consequence of desperation, neither purposely coveting it nor exceeding the immediate need, God forgives much and is merciful beyond comprehension.

So, after understanding this beware of creating your own laws, proclaiming, "This or that is lawful or forbidden," in essence, representing your own ideas as God's. In fact, anyone who creates their own laws and attributes them to God will never prosper. Rather (such persons), may gain merely temporary benefit. However, in the final realm the torment they will suffer will be extreme.

Even so, it was only for the adherents of Judaism that We legislated all the previous prohibitions. However, We weren't the Ones who wronged them, rather, in their persistent arrogance they wronged themselves. Yet, once again, your Lord responds in forgiveness to those who do wrong due to ignorance and afterward amend (their ways), living decently. Truly, after such (asking for forgiveness and new behavior) your Lord will be found to be thoroughly forgiving, totally merciful.

Abraham: universal role model

In Abraham, you have an example of a man who combined within himself all the finest virtues. A devotee of God's will, he always rejected anything that was false. Continuously grateful for God's favors (he was) grateful to Him who selected him and guided him to a way that leads to Us. Thus, We honored him with greatness in this life, as well as in the next one, where he will reside among the finest of God's servants.

In culmination, We have inspired you with the command: "Adhere to the ways of Abraham, the one who rejected all that is false, the one who refused to believe in any other gods or powers besides (the true) God." Realize, too, that the Sabbath was ordained only for those who began creating their own religions based upon him.◆

◆That is by creating burdensome rituals and concepts and then attributing them to God. This is proven by the fact that within this Qur'aan, for instance, the prohibitions, as well as requirements, are minimal. Then, incredibly, God emphasizes the liberal nature of His way. This is to prevent people from descending into schisms due to excessive rules and regulations. It is to prevent people from creating their own religion, focusing on only the legal and illegal.

Throughout this chapter God makes it clear that His way of life is liberal, that is that His servants are to enjoy this life with relatively few restrictions. These restrictions are heinous acts and dangerous foods or beverages. He hereby deems modern religions or sects, with their onerous rituals, as man-made.

True, the Qur'aan mandates a few commands, notably daily worship, charity, and the yearly fast. Yet, these are a kind of atonement, which, when performed, act to the individual's credit. Thus, this simple way of believing, that is the way of Abraham, is the faith of choice. This is the belief in God and complete obedience to Him, regardless of the consequences. This is the crux of the Qur'aan's message. This way, known in Arabic as Islaam, is submission to almighty God.

Yet, regarding their differences during resurrection God will make clear all issues between them.

Responsibility to share God's message

Then, call to your Lord's way with every type of wisdom and intelligent persuasion. What's more, make discussions with them in a gentle manner. The fact is your Lord fully understands who deviates from His way as well as who remains steadfastly on it. Thus, if you must respond to hostility in an argument, do so only to the degree of the attack against you. Yet, it is better to remain patient: God is with you.

(Thus,) patiently endure (whatever is your affliction). Remember, God is the One from whom you gain (all) strength. What's more, feel no grief regarding them. Nor be distressed by their intrigues. Surely, God is with those who always keep Him in mind and who, furthermore, always do good.

Section 17
The Prophet's Night Journey

In the name of the most merciful
and compassionate God

He is praiseworthy, who transported His servant during the night from the Sacred House of Worship (at Mecca) to the blessed Distant House of Worship (of Jerusalem), so that We might demonstrate for him some of Our powers. This is because, without question, He alone has complete awareness and understanding.

In a similar manner We provided Moses with revelation, making it guidance for the Israelites, commanding them, "Regarding the ability to determine your destiny take no other power as God besides Me." You progeny of the survivors of Noah on the Ark, realize that, certainly, he was a truly thankful servant (of Ours). Furthermore, We made the (following) abundantly clear to the Israelites in their own revelation, in fact, twice (that is): "You will definitely commit great evil throughout the earth and will spread corruption, while you gloat (in it)." What's more, when the punishment predicted against you for the first of those two periods (of excesses) was executed, We sent against you powerful warriors. Furthermore, they devastated the region, and, thus, the prediction (of Our retribution) was realized.

Even so, eventually, We allowed you another opportunity, strengthening you with (material) wealth and children (for your lineage) and caused you to increase in population, saying (essentially), "If you continue to do good, you will gain only good. However, if you do evil, you will bring only evil upon yourselves." So, when the second period of your vileness was realized, We raised a new group of enemies against you and allowed them to completely disgrace you—to enter the Temple like the previous one and devastate it. This was so that (by humbling you and giving you another chance) your Lord might have mercy upon you. However, if you return to sinning,✦ We will as a consequence

✦That is if the Israelites revert to sinning a third time, after the first two episodes in antiquity. This is precisely what has occurred. These rebellious Israelites were at first destroyed by the Assyrians and then later by the Babylonians. Now, in modern times they have reverted to vileness, abandoning all that their scriptures demand. So, as predicted in the Qur'aan by the hand of God they will be completely destroyed. Yet, this destruction will, in fact, serve to help them: to give them a final chance to realize their sins and hopefully bring themselves in humility before God.

punish you. Furthermore, remember this: those who reject the truth will be imprisoned in hell.

Without question, this Qur'aan guides to all that is decent and ethically sound. What's more, it promises the believers that for the good they do they will receive a great reward. It announces, too, that We have prepared a vile torment for those who refuse to believe (in the next life).

Invariably, the human being prays for whatever is wretched, believing he is praying for what might benefit him. This is because the human being is prone to be impatient (in judgement).

What's more, We have appointed the night and day as two key evidences. In this regard We cause the night to be transformed into the day through (the power of) light—so you might seek to gain the plentiful bounties of your Lord. It is also so you know to calculate time but also realize (the reality of) the final judgement. This is because, certainly, We have made everything obvious. Furthermore, We have wrapped the destiny of every human being around his neck. Plus, during resurrection We will produce a record, which (each person) will find fully clarified and will be told, "Read your own record. (For what you have done) you are your own best witness."

Whoever decides to adhere to the correct way of life only benefits himself. What's more, whoever refuses to do so only hurts himself. Furthermore, no soul will bear another's burden.✦

✦That is this nullifies the modern concept that the sins of the 'father' are bore by the children. It also refutes the Christian dictate of so-called original sin. Here, the Qur'aan makes it clear that each person is solely responsible for his/her actions. There is no savior—except the self. That is the Qur'aanic system of justice. What's more, God can only save those who make the effort to do what is right, while believing in Him. Plus, God has no harshness in Him. Rather, He is ready and willing to give profusely of His kindness. This is demonstrated by the fact that He only judges people based upon their intentions. Mere innocent mistakes are not the source of punishment. Furthermore, only real wickedness, done maliciously, is punishable.

Also, no community will ever be punished before We send them a messenger. However, once this is done and it is Our decision to destroy a community, We transmit Our final warning, that is to those consumed in prurient desires. Then, if they continue to act wickedly, the doomsday sentence is enacted, and We obliterate them.

Even so (for those who would doubt the seriousness of this warning), consider it: how numerous were the generations We similarly destroyed since Noah's time? This is because only your Lord has (the ability to know) and does know the real truth regarding the violations of His creatures.

Regarding whoever only cares about (the pleasures of) this transitory life, We freely give it as much as We please—to whomever We choose. However, ultimately, We send (such a person) to (the agony of) hell, which he must endure, abandoned and disgraced. Yet, regarding those who truly believe and who are serious about the responsibility for the next life, who strive for it in the way that it should be striven for, they are the ones whose effort God truly respects. Yet, for both types (the ones who reject Us) and also those who (truly) believe, We freely give some of your Lord's gifts, since your Lord's giving is never restricted (to only one group).

Notice, too, how We give more generously to certain individuals. Yet, always remember that the future life is far greater in degree and far more significant in merit and magnificence (than the earthly one).

Thus, never make other beings as gods besides God, in order to avoid being dishonored and abandoned; because your Lord has made it an obligation, rather, preordained, that you (O humans) exclusively worship Him. He has also ordained that you be good to your parents.✦ If they are under your

✦Interestingly, the dictate to love the biological parents is a mere parable. The deeper meaning is to have *gratitude to anyone responsible for a person's welfare*. This surely includes the biological parents but also includes the One who truly provides all. Then, who is the Ultimate Parent? Is it other than almighty God? Thus, the same love, even more so, must be shown to Him.

Yet, when God tells people to give of their love lavishly to their parents, do they give it any thought? Do they realize it also means to give love to the Supreme Parent? This is the hidden message of this parable.

care in their old age, never treat them with the slightest disrespect nor scold them. Rather, speak to them with dignity, and overwhelm them with love and kindness. What's more, pray, "My Lord, have mercy upon them, just as, when I was young, they were merciful in their caring for me."

Your Lord knows best what is in your hearts. If you are decent, he will forgive your errors. This is because surely He forgives overwhelmingly, that is those who repeatedly turn to Him for forgiveness.

Also, give what is appropriate to the close relatives as well as to the poor and the stranger/traveler in need. However, never squander your assets. The fact is those who foolishly squander are associates of the devil in respect to the fact that the devil has certainly proven to be completely ungrateful to his Lord.

Now, if you must turn aside the needy due to the fact that you are yourself attempting to please God, at least be kind to them. What's more, neither be miserly nor wasteful to avoid (due to your squandering) being blamed by your dependents or even bankrupt. Truly, your Lord gives generously or minimally to whomever He deems. This is because He is fully aware of His creature's (needs), and He cares for them all.✦

✦That is almighty God has an awareness of all people—as well as all other living beings. Also, He sees to it that the true needs of all such beings are fulfilled. How He can simultaneously do so is unfathomable. This demonstrates how truly great God is and how, in contrast, absolutely limited are human powers. In fact, there is no way to compare the two. Human 'powers' are truly feeble. In contrast, God is infinitely powerful. Incredibly, despite His awesome nature by this statement God establishes that He is constant in His love for attending to His creation.

Thus, never murder your children due to fear of poverty. I am the One who will provide for them as well as for you. To kill them is truly an enormous crime. Also, never commit (nor even consider committing) adultery. This is an abomination, truly wicked. Also, never kill another human, the life of which God has deemed sacred, except in the pursuit of justice.✦ In fact, if anyone has been unjustly killed,

✦That is in a just war or in a civil legal action or, for instance, if threatened by a criminal and acting in self defense. The point is God is just, and in this justice all acts of harm must be resisted.

There is no allowance in this faith for the slaughter of the innocent. For instance, in Islaam there is a code of war. Here, only legitimate fighters are to be targeted. Yet, if they surrender, they are never to be tortured or killed.

According to the Qur'aan believers are obligated to fight oppression. They are to resist all aggression against them. This is the only legitimate fight in the cause of God. Yet, this is precisely the war fought by the famous historical figures: Moses, Jesus, and Muhammad. So, then, killing is only allowed in the heat of battle, in self-defense, and as a result of the penal code, as follows:

We have allowed the one in defense of the deceased's rights to exact a just retribution. However, let him not exceed the bounds of equity in retribution. Even so, regarding the wrongfully killed, no doubt, such a person is under God's loving mercy.

Also, leave the orphan's belongings intact, unless your objective is to enhance it before he matures. Furthermore, truly honor all your promises. You will absolutely be made responsible for them. Also, be honest and fair in all your dealings, and weigh with a balance that is accurate. This will be for your own benefit and is ultimately for the best.

Furthermore, never pursue whatever doesn't pertain to you. Truly, you will be questioned about what you hear and see—even what you feel. What's more, never act arrogantly—because (you don't have any true power)—without doubt, you are not so powerful that you could rip open a part of the earth. Nor can you ever rival the mountains in height. All this is loathed by your Lord. This is part of the knowledge of right and wrong, which your Lord has instilled within you. Thus, make no other power—no other authority—equal in status with God (the concern being), that you be thrown into hell, blamed by your own self and rejected by your own God.

Then, do you truly believe that your Lord honors you with sons, while He has adopted for Himself (merely) daughters (that is), in the form of angels? Truly, what you say is vile.

Certainly, We have given the message in this Qur'aan numerous dimensions, all so that those who reject it might reconsider. However, all this merely increases their aversion. Tell them, "If there were, as some people attest, other divine powers besides Him, surely they themselves would make every effort to seek Him—the One who has absolute ownership of all that exists. He is unlimited in His magnificence, infinitely beyond anything the human mind can conceive regarding Him".

All that exists in the countless heavens, as well as the earth, glorify Him. In fact, everything (that exists) sings and glorifies His praise. However, you humans are unable to even perceive this. Despite this, clearly, He always leans towards restraint, always tends towards forgiveness.

Also, whenever you mention (the message of) this Qur'aan We place an invisible barrier between you and those who refuse to believe. This is because their hearts have been obstructed (in order to) prevent them from grasping its true meaning, and their ears have been made as if deaf. Thus, whenever while representing to them this divine writing you mention (the name of) your Lord as the only God, they categorically reject you.

Even so, We are also well aware of what they allow themselves to think when they listen to you. This is because when they are in private, they tell each other, "The man you follow is insane." See what they (themselves) associate you with (O Prophet), because they have erred and are now incapable of determining the truth. Thus, too, they say, "After we die and are mere dried up dust and bones are we really to believe we will be recreated?" Tell them, "(It is true) regardless of whether your remains are petrified, mineral, dust, or any other substance which your minds find so remote"—and if, then, they ask, "Then, who will recreate us?" Tell them, "The One who originally made you." Then, if at that time they shake their heads in disbelief and ask, "When?" Tell them, "It could be very soon—at a time when He will call you and you will from your grave answer by praising Him, while you, in fact, believe that you only existed a short time."

Tell My servants that they should speak in the kindest way possible to any who do not share their beliefs. Surely, the devil is always ready to incite strife between people. This is because, certainly, the devil is human beings' avowed enemy.

The inner self: known only by God

No one knows what is in your heart like your Lord. If He desires, He will be generous to you, and, what's more, if He chooses, He will punish you. Thus, the purpose of the men whom We have sent is never to determine their fate,✦ because

✦That is to 'change' their ways. Rather, it is merely to warn, regarding the consequences of rejecting His rule.

In the next life all rule belongs to God. No one else will have any power. Thus, unless a person has earned His favor he/she will be lost. He wants to give people the opportunity to recognize this, so at that dire time they will be free of regrets.

your Lord already knows what is in the minds of all beings. Even so, We clearly have made some of them of greater significance than others (the high status of) David (being an example), who We graced with a special book of divine wisdom.

Tell them (in rebuttal), "Seek assistance from those who you consider equal to Him; you will find that they are incapable of relieving or displacing your distress." Actually, those (saintly beings) whom they seek are themselves determined to benefit from their Lord's favor. Even those who are closest to Him desire His mercy, while they dread His punishment. This is because your Lord's punishment is something to (truly) fear.

There is no doubt about it: without exception, prior to resurrection We will destroy every community—or, if it proves sinful, We may punish it earlier with extreme torment. This is all established in Our decree. What's more, there was nothing to prevent Us from delivering this message accompanied by miracles, except the fact that We knew that the ancients rejected (even) these. So (as an example), the Arabian tribe of Thamood was given a female camel as a sign. Yet, they violated it. However, the signs were provided exclusively to warn. Plus, recall that We said to you (O Muhammad), "Your Lord has complete authority over humankind. (In this regard) the vision We showed you and also the accursed forces of hell are merely a trial." Yet, such a warning only increases their aversion.

The parable of Adam reiterated: Iblees' rebellion

Consider the fact that We said to the angels, "Submit yourselves before Adam." They all did so, except Iblees. He said, "Do you really expect me to bow before one whom You have created from mere (organic matter)? What's more, he said, "Tell me, is this (foolish) creature the one whom You have placed higher than me?" (Out of spite) he said, "In fact, if you would allow me the capacity (of deception) until resurrection, without doubt—and with rare exceptions—I will cause his descendants to blindly follow me." God answered, "Proceed (with your plan). However, regarding those who follow you, certainly, you will all end up in hell, the most appropriate consequence. Then, tempt whomever (you will) with all the capacities at your disposal. Furthermore, use all the power (and tactics) you can muster. What's more, offer every conceivable promise to them, despite the fact that they will be unaware that whatever Satan promises is a delusion. Even so, you will be powerless over My (true) servants, who fully place their trust in Me, because your Lord is the most worthy of trust."

Human dependency upon God and their ingratitude

Your Lord is the One who makes ships move onward on your behalf through the seas, so that you might pursue some of His generous gifts. Truly, He distributes His kindness to you profusely. Even so, if danger strikes while you are at sea, all those that you tend to invoke, in fact, forsake you. Only He remains. Even so, as soon as He has rescued you, safe at shore, you forget Him, because without doubt (as a rule) the human race is devoid of gratitude. Then, can you ever feel secure, that is that He will not cause a tract of land to consume you or pummel you with a deadly wind storm, in which case you will find no one to help you? Or, could you possibly feel secure that He will not return you to that circumstance (at sea) and then strike you with a violent storm, drowning you as a consequence of your ingratitude, when you would be helpless against Us?

Now, certainly, We honored the human race (in a high status).✦ In this respect We gave them

✦That is by creating an entire part of the universe for their use. Here, He systematically converted the originally cold and barren earth into a form functionally adequate for humanity. This took hundreds of millions, perhaps, billions of years, but it was all done with the human in mind. This was done as a test, to determine which humans would be truly grateful to Him.

The purpose of humans is easy to understand. It is memorialized by the ritual of Abraham, that is the hajj. Here, the masses of humanity commemorate Abraham's finding: that there is only one God and that all worship is due exclusively to Him. This is what this man professed on his own. He came to a realization through his own thinking that there must be a universal God and that all obedience is due to Him. Then, God tested him, demanding that he sacrifice all that was dear to him. Yet, he passed this test brilliantly, giving all that he loved to God. This is why God holds him, that is his effort, so high.

full access to the land and seas,✦ providing them

✦This reference to the land and seas really means the "surface of the earth." It means that God gradually and systematically created the earth's surface, its oceans, lakes, rivers, mountains, and continents, exclusively with humans in mind. It is strictly made for human use. It demonstrates His vast love and mercy for humans. Yet, all He asks is that they give thought to Him and be grateful for this wondrous blessing—for their own sake.

with every type of bounty from the good things of life. What's more, We favored them above most of

Our creation. ✦ Yet, eventually, We will summon all

✦This is an incredible statement. This confirms that throughout the universe there are other beings, some of which are superior to humans. It may also refer to heavenly beings in God's personal realm of even a superior nature to humans. Regardless, it is a clear proof that within this universe there are other intelligent beings, which are novel creations of almighty God.

People are fascinated by this fact. However, isn't it far more fascinating to know that there exists a creator capable of making numerous forms of intelligent life? It is He that people should truly find fascinating, this Being who creates endlessly, if they would only give it thought.

human beings and evaluate them according to their true intentions. Then, those whose record is rich in goodness will read it with joy. None will be wronged in the least, because whoever is now oblivious to the truth will also be oblivious to it in the next life and therefore be even more distant than ever (from it).

Incredibly, they seek to tempt you away from your religion to make you to invent a different divine way, in which case they would have surely befriended you. Had We not made you firm you might have had the inclination to do so, in which case We would have, without doubt, punished you with extra punishment in this life and additional punishment after death. What's more, there would be no one to defend you against Us. Plus, since they realize that they are unable to persuade you (to reject your faith), they attempt to isolate you from your own country to exile you. Yet, then, even after they have done so, even they themselves will not remain there much longer. This has been Our way with all Our previous messengers. Furthermore, Our ways never change.

Thus, remain constant in your worship from the time when the sun passes noon until the darkness of night. What's more, be ever mindful of its recitation at dawn, because there is no doubt about it this recitation is witnessed.

Furthermore, arise from your sleep, and worship during part of the late night as an offering from you. As a result, your Lord may well raise you to a glorious station (now and in the next life). When doing so, pray, "My Lord, make me begin whatever I do in truth and sincerity, plus cause me to end it in truth and sincerity. Plus, so I can remain resolute give me of Your tremendous strength."

Tell the people that the truth has arrived, and, thus, falsehood will dissipate. Without question, all that is false will eventually become dissoluted.

Thus, We have methodically revealed through this writing all that gives spiritual health, that is all which is a mercy to those who believe. Even so, it only accelerates the ruin of the godless. This is because when We give human beings Our blessings, they reject (any sense of gratitude) and in their arrogance remain aloof. Despite this, the human tendency is that when evil strikes, he abandons all hope. Tell them, "Everyone selects his own course in life. Yet, your Lord is completely aware regarding who has truly chosen the correct path (versus whoever allows himself to deviate)."

Also, they will ask you regarding the nature of divine inspiration. Tell them, "Inspiration comes exclusively from my Lord, although you are unable to fathom it, since you have been given only a modicum of real knowledge."

If We had desired, We could have unquestionably taken away your revelation. What's more, in that needy condition you would find no one to plead on your behalf before Us. You are only spared because of your Lord's merciful (love). The fact is His favors upon you are vast. Thus, tell them, "If the entire human race, as well as all invisible beings, would together attempt to produce this book, regardless of the effort they would be unable to do so." This is because We have given in this book components which are dimensional, that is to provide (merciful guidance) for the benefit of humankind.

The night journey: rejected by those who oppose the Prophet's message

Even so, most people are unwilling to accept anything, except blasphemy. Thus, they say, "We will refuse to believe until you produce a miracle, like a spring, which suddenly opens up for us from the earth, or a garden of palm trees and grape vines, with running waters suddenly gushing among them, or until you cause the skies to descend upon us in smithereens, as you threaten, or until you bring God and the angels for us to see directly, or until you have a house made of gold— or until you yourself ascend to heaven. However, even if you did all this, still, we would not believe that you (really did) rise up to the heavens, unless you return with a book specifically for us." Tell them, "My Lord is infinite in His glory. I am only a mortal, a mere messenger."

Yet, whenever guidance came to them nothing has prevented the people from believing, except (the following objection), "Why would God send a mere mortal man as His messenger?" Tell them, "If angels were the natural inhabitants of the earth, We would have certainly sent them." What's more, explain to them, "God knows best what is being transacted between us, because He is absolutely and fully aware of what is in the hearts of His creatures."

Resurrection: the real miracle

Moreover, only the person who God guides has truly found the correct way. In contrast, regarding those who (due to their own actions) He allows to deviate, you could never find anyone to protect them from Him. Thus, during resurrection when We gather them together, they will lie prone on their faces, unable to speak, see, or hear, with hell as their ultimate consequence. Every time the fire abates, We will on their behalf accelerate its flames. This is how they will be compensated, because they rejected Our messages and proclaim, "Are we really to believe that after we die—mere dust and bones—that we will, then, be recreated?"

Then, are they unaware that God, the creator of the entire universe, as well as the earth, has the power to re-create them in their own exact form, having already decided beyond any doubt to schedule their resurrection? However, all such perpetrators of evil refuse to believe in anything, except blasphemy. Tell them, "If you owned all my Lord's vast treasures, still, you would be stingy." This is because human beings have always been greedy, whereas God gives freely.

Moses and the ingratitude of the Israelites

Moses was also given definite signs, a number of them, all obvious. Then, ask the descendants of Israel to explain what happened when he first appeared among them, appealing to Pharaoh, when Pharaoh responded, "Surely, you, Moses, are possessed (by evil)." Moses replied, "You know fully well that only the Lord of the worlds Himself is responsible for these miraculous signs. The fact is, Pharaoh, you are the one who I believe is truly lost." As a result, Pharaoh resolved to eliminate them, but, instead, We drowned him and all who were with him. Afterwards, We told the Israelites to live in their new land, but be sure to keep in mind that when the promised resurrection happens, "We will return you to Us in the midst of the teeming masses (of all other humans to be judged)."

Responsibility of the messenger: methods of preaching

So (like the former truths), We have revealed this in truth (directly) from the heavens (in an unaltered state). Even so, your only role is to give good news (of the consequences of true belief) as well as to warn (of the consequences of rejection). Moreover (for that precise purpose), We have revealed it little by litle, so you would, then, present it to humankind in a similar way, since We have provided it from heaven a little at a time (ultimately culminating as one large revelation). At this, tell them, "Believe in it or refuse to do so: (it is your choice)."

Yet, those who naturally (within their hearts) understand (its truth)—who have the wisdom to appreciate its truths—as soon as this is represented to them, fall down upon their faces in prostration, saying, "Our Lord, You are unlimited in your magnificence. Certainly, our Lord's promise has come true." Thus, they fall down on their faces, weeping, and this understanding of God increases their humility. Tell them, "Call Him by the name God or by the name the Lord Merciful or whatever name, He is always the One, because all the names of perfection belong to Him." When you do pray to Him, follow a middle path, being not too boisterous or meek. What's more, realize that all praise belongs to God, who never has children and never has associates in His lordship. He is devoid of any weakness and thus never requires aid. Furthermore, praise Him (this magnificent One), for His unlimited greatness.

Section 18
The Parable of the Cave

This section introduces the concept of the will of God. It is the fact that this will overcomes all events, thus the origin of the phrase *insha Allah*. To demonstrate this principle of divine control it describes three legends which were known by the original recipients of this revelation. The legends are the Youths of the Cave, the story of Moses and God's Special Agent, known in Arabic as *Khider*, and the parable of the Two-Horned One, known in Arabic as *Dhul Qarnayn*. God relates these stories to clarify any misunderstanding regarding them, since these events occurred in antiquity.

In the name of the most merciful and compassionate God

All praise is due to God, who revealed (from the heavens) this divine book to His servant, while making sure that it is free of contradictions. Devoid of all errors, it is direct. Its purpose is to warn the godless of His overwhelming punishment, as well as to give good news to the good-acting believers, that they will achieve a tremendous reward, a state of happiness, where they will permanently reside.

It is also meant to warn those who say that God has bred a son. They are completely unaware of any such event with Him. They have no evidence (for such a claim), neither they nor their ancestors. Their statement is vile, purely false. Yet, if they refused to believe, would you torment yourself?

Clearly, We have willed that all the magnificence on this earth is merely a means to test humans, that is to demonstrate which is best in conduct. What's more, eventually, We will reduce all that exists to lifeless dust.

God's love for His believers: special protection

Since this life is merely a test do you consider the parable of the men of the cave, those who were *devoted to scripture*, as particularly significant? When those youths hid in the cave, they prayed, "Our Lord, have mercy on us and help us regardless of our circumstances to have the consciousness, that is the ability, to do what is right."✦ Thus, We distanced

✦Notice the way of belief of these youths. These were most likely early followers of the old testament. They believed in one almighty God. These believers gave no credence to false powers. In other words, they rejected all man-made modes of worship. Rather, as this parable demonstrates they fully submitted to only their Lord and emigrated from their hostile community in order to continue their mission for their Lord. This is why He granted them protection.

them from all contact for many years. Then, We awakened them to distinguish which of the two viewpoints was more correct in comprehending how long they remained in this state. So, now, We will demonstrate the truth regarding their story.

No doubt, these were young men, who deeply believed in their Lord. So, We deepened their faith and strengthened their hearts. This is so that they resisted together the great tyranny of the time and told each other, "Our Lord is the Lord of all.

(Despite the demands of our people) we will never worship any other power (besides Him). If we did, we would have committed a vile act. Our people are adoring false Gods, even though they have no basis for it. Thus, who could be more depraved than the person who invents lies about God." (What's more, they continued to remind themselves,) "Now that you have separated yourselves from the idolatry (of those pagans) hide in that cave. God will have mercy on us and regardless of our apparent situation will provide everything your soul may need."

For years you might have noticed the sun as it was rising, inclining away from their cave on the right and during its setting turning aside from them on the left, while they continued to exist in that roomy cave (a representation of the truth) of God's message. (It is the truth that) whoever God guides is the only one who has found the right way, whereas, in contrast, whomever He allows to err, you will never find anyone who could direct (them) to the right way.

From their appearance you would have thought they were awake. However, they were asleep. (To prevent damage to them) We caused them to turn over repeatedly, to the right and then to the left. What's more, their dog lay at the opening, forepaws outstretched. If you would have unexpectedly encountered them, surely, you would have been frightened and would have run away scared, completely in awe.✦

*That is God made them appear ominous in order to protect them. Since they gave their whole selves to God—since they refused to submit to the arrogance of the time—they were greatly loved by Him. So, He took special care of them. He made a specific plot to keep them away from all tyrants, so they could escape and ultimately lead a decent life. Thus, He kept them in a state of 'hibernation' until circumstances changed, so they could escape and/or live safely.

Eventually, We awakened them, and, then, they began to ask each other what happened. One of them answered, "We have remained in this state for a day or less." However, the one with a deeper insight said, "Your Lord alone knows how long we have been like this. Why doesn't one of you go into town with these silver coins, and get some food and other necessities. However, let him (approach the situation) cautiously, and try not to draw attention. Definitely, if they should recognize you, they might beat you to death or alternatively force you to follow their religion in which case you would never achieve anything constructive."*

*That is by being forced into a life of tyranny. In such an instance there can be no real good. In such a life of spiritual enslavement all that results is despair, that is the agony of enslavement. Then, the human potential is wasted on fruitless efforts, and the person becomes nothing more than a pawn for the system, imprisoned both physically and spiritually. God loved these youths too greatly to allow them to endure this. From the point of view of almighty God this is a waste, a fact proven by the statement that nothing of any substance will result when His servants are consigned to oppression.

Thus, in this manner We have drawn attention to their story, so people might comprehend a degree of it, that is whenever they debate about what they presume happened to those (men of the cave), in order that they realize that, without doubt, the promise of resurrection—this final meeting before God, where all will be held accountable for their actions—is true.

Over the generations some people suggested, "Create a monument in their memory: God knows best their status." Yet, it was said by others, whose opinion prevailed, "Build, instead, a place of worship." Over time speculation continued (with comments such as) "If the dog were included, they numbered four," while others said, "Including the dog they numbered six," thus making blind presumptions regarding an issue of which they had no knowledge and so on until some claimed, "If the dog is included, there were seven." Tell them simply that "Only the Lord God knows the precise details. Those who really know about them are very few." Thus, never argue regarding them, unless it is for the purpose of edification. What's more, never probe into it whimsically with storytellers.

Thus, never say about anything, "I will do it tomorrow" without also saying, "God willing." If you forget to do something and later remember it, think about your Lord, praying, "My Lord, guide me, rather, bring me nearer to the truth than even this."✦

✦This is a command with a deep meaning. It means, essentially, 'Make it so that I will automatically follow the truth' that is without even asking for guidance. This is the person who is so close to God that he realizes His desires immediately. This is easy to do, because all that is required is to always deeply consider Him. This is the person whose entire life is given to God, the one who is a manifestation of His will.

Some people claimed, "They remained in the cave for three hundred years," and others believed it somewhat longer. Tell them, "Only God knows the precise time."✦ He knows all which you are

✦That is, again, reiterating the lessons of this section. It is that humans have no real knowledge, and, rather, all deep truths are held by God. Instead of speculating it is better to leave it with Him and say, "Only God really knows. In fact, our understanding is limited. So, we merely trust in Him. Too, we rely upon Him for guidance. We are merely His servants."

incapable of knowing. How well does He comprehend. He is the only Helper for humans, because no one else is allowed a share in His rule.

Furthermore, whatever has been revealed to you from your Lord, tell it. There is nothing that could alter His words—and (so, like the youths of the cave) you will find no protection other than His. Also, console yourself in patience, along with all who continuously call upon their Lord, seeking His acceptance. In this respect never allow yourself to ignore (the true believers) in pursuit of the distractions of material desires. Nor reject in neglect the sincere ones, instead (concentrating on) the heedless, those whom We ourselves have prevented from achieving any remembrance of Us. This is because (such godless ones) have always followed only their vain desires, abandoning all that is decent.

Belief: a choice

In addition, tell them, "This is truthful revelation (now available to you) from your Lord. Whoever wishes to believe in it will do so, and whoever wishes to reject it will do so." (Yet, the consequences of this rejection are dire, because) certainly for those who sin against themselves there has been prepared a fire, which completely surrounds them. If they plead to quench their thirst, all they will be given is (a kind of) water, hot, like molten lead, which will scald their faces. How dreadful a drink, and how rotten a place to live. Yet, without doubt, the true believers who do good deeds—and (keep in mind that) We never neglect to reward those who do good—will achieve paradise, where they will happily live forever. There, they will be adorned with bracelets of gold and wear green garments of silk and brocade, where in absolute comfort they will rest in happiness. How excellent a reward and how wonderful a place to live.

Disregard for God's will: consequences

Tell them also about the story of two men, one of which We gave two vineyards surrounded by lush date palms and in-between a field of grain. Consistently, each of the gardens was productive, because We had caused a stream to flow out within each of them. Thus, the man had abundant produce.

Then, one day he said to his friend, bragging, "I am much wealthier than you and more powerful, too, in regard to my followers." So, thus, in this state of sin he entered his garden, saying, "I believe this will last forever: nothing will ever hurt it. Nor do I believe that there will even be a return to God, where I will be regenerated. However, if it did occur, I am sure that if I were returned to my Lord, I will find an even better one than this." However, during their discussion his friend✦ said

✦That is, in fact, his other self. This is an allegory—because the actual friend is God, who speaks to him through inspiration. It is God almighty who constantly reminds humans of their humble nature. He is the One who tells them never to act arrogantly. Thus, it was this man's own internal warners who were speaking to Him through his best friend, almighty God.

to him, "Are you willing to violate against the One who created you from nothing, mere dust particles, who from a drop of sperm ultimately fashioned you into a complete man? However, regarding myself I am certain He is God, my Lord. Furthermore, I cannot conceive of giving power to anything else."

He also told him, "If you only would have said upon entering your garden, 'Whatever God wills is acceptable to me—He is the only (true) power.'" He continued, "Although I am poorer than you materially, yet it may well be that my Lord will give me something far superior than your garden, just as He may blast your garden into oblivion or exhaust its water to such an extent that you won't even recognize it." Thus, it happened—his productive gardens were overcome, and there he was, agonizing over all that he had spent on what was now wasteland, with its walls and vines collapsed to the ground. All he could say was, "If I had only avoided giving godly powers to others besides my Lord..." because now since he distanced himself from his Lord he had no one to help him. Nor could he help or protect himself. So it is that all protective power belongs to almighty God alone, the true One. He is the best One to give proper compensation, the best to determine what is to be.

Also, explain to them, parabolically, the life of this world: it is like the water, which We send from the skies and which is absorbed by the plants, from which they thrive. However, eventually, they turn into dry waste, which the winds scatter freely.✦ Furthermore, it is only God who determines all ultimate results.

✦In other words, all that a person materially accumulates in this life will hold no value. Only a person's useful achievements, his or her good actions, will transfer, recorded by God in His sophisticated system. The implications are obvious. It is that each person must leave the earth with goodness, while truly and sincerely believing in Him. According to the Qur'aan that is the highest goal to achieve. What's more, this is the only way to achieve it, this gaining the approval of God through doing good. Then, to gain His loving approval is the ultimate success, one that is beyond imagination.

The insignificance of this material world

Mere material wealth and (the mere lineage of) children are of superficial value. However, achievements of lasting value are regarded more superiorly by your Lord and offer the best opportunity for salvation. Thus, keep in mind the time when We will obliterate the mountains and when you will see the earth absolutely bare, because We will, without exception, gather all people together. They will be arrayed before their Lord with "Now, clearly, you have returned to Us, just as We created you originally, although you claimed that We would never appoint for you this session." Then, the record of everyone's deeds will be revealed. You will, then, see the guilty consumed with horror as a result of what they see therein. They will exclaim, "We are doomed; this is a horrible record. It includes everything, major or minor. Nothing has been excluded." This is because, then, they will find that they will be confronted with all that they ever achieved, plus they will realize that your Lord never wrongs anyone.

The insignificance of this material world

Also (recall the time), when We told the angels, "Submit yourselves before Adam."✦ They all did so,

✦That is the original thinking being, Adam, represents, parabolically, the creation of a being "in God's image." This is the first earthly being who can think for himself—who can judge the difference between right and wrong. So, because of these powers of reason such a being can choose to believe in God as his Lord and also not to fall prey to the plots of Satan. He can use his reason to confirm that the only logical conclusion is that God truly exists and is needed for help and guidance as well as for personal salvation. This is the test God presents before humans. Yet, are they willing to take this challenge and thus succeed?

except Iblees. He (too,) was an invisible being. However, he was rebellious. Then, will you take him and his cohorts for masters (by listening to their evil insinuations) instead of Me, even though they are your avowed enemies? What a vile decision, made by those determined to commit evil.

(These things that you associate with Me:) I never brought them in My presence to witness the universe's creation nor (even) the creation of their own selves. Neither do I have any need to use as My helpers any of those beings (and false powers) which cause humans to deviate.

It will be a time when God will ask them, "Request help from those beings whom you presumed had some of My authority." Then, they will request their aid. However, no one will respond. This is because We will have placed between them a distance too vast to bridge. What's more, those who were immersed in sin will see before them the fire, realizing that they will ultimately descend into it. Furthermore, they will never be able to escape from it.

No doubt, in this divine book We have given humankind numerous ways of self-evaluation via a variety of lessons, all for human benefit. Yet, above all, human beings always tend to be argumentative. Even so, now that they have been exposed to guidance, what is preventing people from becoming believers, that is unless they wish to suffer the same consequences as the ancients or that they (desire to) endure the ultimate torment in the next life?

Yet, We send Our messengers only to deliver good news (of future happiness) as well as to warn. Despite this the godless argue against them with fallacious arguments. (Their goal is) to confuse the truth. Furthermore, they make a mockery of My messages and warnings. Thus, who could be more vile—more completely wicked—than the person to whom his Lord's messages are broadcast and who, then, rejects them, remaining oblivious of all the evil that he may have committed? The fact is (regarding such vile ones) We have darkened their hearts due to the concern that they might recognize the truth. Plus, their ears have been silenced (as if) deaf. Even though you might invite them to the right way they will never allow themselves to be guided. Yet, despite it all your Lord is truly forgiving, merciful.

If He wanted to punish them precisely when they committed their vile deeds, He could have done so. However, this is not the case. Instead, they have (been allotted) a specified time after which redemption is impossible. This was the way it was previously with all those other civilizations We destroyed, those who were committed to doing wrong. This is because We had set a time limit for their destruction.

The story of the divine agent, known in Arabic as Khider

It was during his wanderings that Moses told his servant, "I will persist (in my search) until I reach the confluence of the two seas, even if I have to spend a lifetime searching for it. However, when they reached it, they forgot all about their fish (caught previously), and (as a sign) it wiggled back into the sea and disappeared. Then, after the two walked some distance Moses said to his servant, "Bring us our noon meal. We have certainly had a strenuous day." His servant said, "Can you believe it? When we laid down on that slab of rock to rest, I forgot about it—none but Satan made me do it—and, thus, somehow, it slithered back to sea."

"How strange" Moses exclaimed, "That was the place we were seeking." Then, they went back, retracing their direction, when they encountered one of Our servants, whom We had specially instilled Our knowledge. Moses asked him, "Could I follow you, so I might learn through your wisdom?" He replied, "You will never be able to bear with me, because how could you do so, since what you will see you have never previously experienced?" "Trust me," Moses said, "I will be patient, plus, God willing, I will obey you implicitly." The divine agent replied, "Well, then, if you insist upon following me, you must never question me about anything until I myself tell you about it."

Thus, they journeyed together (until they reached the shoreline) and when they got out of the boat, he made a hole in it, when Moses exclaimed, "How dare you...are you ruining this boat in order to drown (any future) passengers? Certainly, what you are doing is devious." He replied, "Didn't I tell you, that you would never be able to bear with me." Moses said, "Pardon my forgetfulness, and do not be angry with me." So, they continued until they encountered a young man: He (that is the divine representative) killed him. Then, Moses exclaimed, "You have just killed an innocent man, who has (obviously) harmed no one. You have committed a hideous act." He replied, "I told you that you would never be able to remain patient with me." Moses said, "If, after this, I ever question you, make me leave. You have heard enough excuses from me."

They continued until when they encountered some villagers; they asked them for food. However, they refused them all hospitality. Moreover, they saw in that village a wall, which was in disrepair. The divine representative rebuilt it, which, as a result, Moses said, "You could have at least asked for some compensation for your efforts."

He responded "This is the end of our relationship. I will now explain to you the real meaning behind these events, which you were unable to patiently withstand. Regarding that boat it belonged to some poor people, who made their living on the sea and I desired to damage it, because approaching them was a King who tends to seize every boat by brute force. Regarding that young man his parents were kind (sweet) people, true believers, while we had every reason to believe that he would cause them great anguish through his wickedness and godlessness. Thus, we desired that their Lord give them instead a child of greater purity than him, a true son, dear and loving to their hearts. Regarding that wall it belonged to two orphan boys who lived there. Under that wall was a buried treasure. Now, their father was a good and decent man, and thus, your Lord willed it that when they reached maturity, they should uncover their treasure by their Lord's kindness. What's more, there was nothing that I did exclusively on my own. This is the true meaning of that which you were unable to patiently withstand."

The legend of the Two-Horned One, known in Arabic as Dhul Qarnayn

They will also ask you regarding the (legend of the) Two-Horned One. Tell them, "I will provide you with a certain degree of information through which he should be remembered." Certainly, We securely established him in the land, providing him with the capacity to achieve the correct solution for all issues. (For instance,) he marched westward until, when the sun set, it appeared to him as if it was setting in a dark, turbid sea. Nearby, he found a people unable to distinguish right from wrong. We said (in the form of a test) "You Two-Horned One (that is the one who can distinguish the true from the false, that is the two 'horns'): You may either destroy them or treat them kindly. It is your choice." He answered, "Regarding whoever wrongs others we will, eventually, cause such a person to suffer. Then (ultimately), they will be referred to their Lord, who will cause them to be sternly punished. In contrast, regarding the true believer, who does good deeds, his reward will be the ultimate good of the next life. What's more, we will be lenient and understanding with him."

So, once again, he selected the right means to achieve the correct result.

He, then, marched eastward until when he came to the rising sun, he found it rising upon a people who were naked, unprotected from it. This was how he found them, and this was how he left them. So, thus, We surrounded with Our knowledge all that he represented.

Thus, once again, he chose the right means to achieve the correct result.

He marched (further) until when he reached a valley between mountains, he found a primitive people hardly able to communicate. They said, "You man of Two Horns (the force of evil,) Gog and Magog, are corrupting this region. Would you accept a fee on the basis that you will create a protective barrier for us?" He answered, "The strength my Lord has given me is superior to any fee. Instead, help me with your labor, and I will build a barrier between you and them. Come now, give me ingots of iron." So, he filled the gap between the two mountainsides with the (molten) iron. Eventually, when he made it so hot that it glowed, he commanded, "Bring me molten copper, (in order to make bronze) which I may pour upon it." Thus, the barrier was constructed, and their enemies were unable to scale it, nor were they able to penetrate it.

He responded, "This is a mercy from my Lord. Yet, eventually, when the time preordained by my Lord will arrive, He will level this to the ground. Surely, my Lord's promise always comes true."

The frightening nature of resurrection

At that (inevitable) time of judgement We will leave them to surge like waves surging forward, one after the other. What's more, the trumpet of judgement will be sounded, and We will gather them. Then, they will see hell right in front of them, that is those who previously rejected the truth, whose ability to perceive had been veiled against any remembrance of Me, merely because they couldn't bear to listen (to the voice of truth).

Do the godless truly believe that they could (without consequence,) hold My creatures, beings I Myself have created, as (if powerful)? The fact is as their residence We have prepared the torment (of hell) for such godless (ones). Tell them, "Should we tell you who will be the greatest losers as a result of their own efforts? They are those whose efforts are misguided as a consequence of the (sole) pursuit of worldly gain, who despite this, in fact, believe their actions are correct. They are the ones who have *chosen* to reject their Lord's messages and the fact that they will ultimately meet Him. Thus, whatever they do is of no consequence, that is during resurrection (these achievements) will be given no value. The wicked torment is their consequence, because they rejected the truth and made a mockery of My messages as well as messengers. However, surely, regarding those who truly believe and are truly good in their actions, they will be welcomed to lush gardens to reside permanently, desiring no change nor having any dissatisfaction.

Tell the people, "If the entire oceans were ink to write my Lord's words, the sea would be consumed before my Lord's words were exhausted. Thus it is, sea upon (countless) sea." ✦

✦The words of magnificence and mercy arising from the almighty Lord are endless. For humans a single lake full of ink would take untold eons to use. Can anyone imagine the words that could be penned through, for instance, the Atlantic ocean? Truly, this is unfathomable, which demonstrates the insignificance of humans and in contrast the vast knowledge of almighty God. Thus, for guidance in any human adversity, obviously, God is the only source, since He is unlimited in His power and knowledge. It is only this Being who has all knowledge in His possession and who, logically, humans must continuously turn.

> Tell them (also), "I am only a human like the rest of you. It has merely been revealed to me that your Lord is God, the One." Thus, whoever has high hopes for the meeting with his Lord (must) do what is right. What's more, let him worship none other than his almighty Lord God.✦

✦That is categorically rejecting the modern Christian claim of Jesus' divinity as false, a rejection which was reiterated on the first page of Section 18 (page 506). God issues this as a warning never to give others ultimate power. This is so they come before them with a soul true to Him. Then, this worship of only Him is the entire basis of this Qur'aan. This is also reiterated in the following section, called Mary's Family.

Section 19
Mary's Family

Traditionally, this section is named after the virgin Mary, who is its primary subject matter. The basis for her mention is the miraculous birth of Jesus Christ. This man is described in the Qur'aan as a mercy for humankind, sent by God to deliver humanity from its dire state of spiritual loss.

Like many other Qur'aanic sections it begins with several alphabetical sounds, the significance of which is unknown. Like all other chapters/sections this was delivered from almighty God through the medium of a divinely inspired angel, that is the angel Gabriel. It mentions various prophets and personalities related to this devout woman.

Through the patriarch Abraham Mary is related to a number of Prophets, including the Prophet Muhammad. Rather than a light-skinned woman she was most likely dark-complected. Unlike the way she is depicted today, She had no genetic origin to Europeans. Thus, she was a true Middle Easterner.

A Muslim is obligated to believe in the virgin birth and also to hold high Mary as well as her son. To say even the slightest derogatory statement about either of them is an unforgivable sin. Thus, the Muslim is obligated to believe deeply in the mission and revelations of both Mary and Jesus. He is even obligated to believe in the actual return of the Christ and even looks forward to it.

In the name of the most merciful and compassionate God

K-H-Y-A-S

This is regarding the mercy given by your Lord to His slave, Zechariah, when he beseeched his Lord from the secrecy of his heart, praying, "My Lord, I am feeble and weak, old and gray. Yet, when I ask of You, always, You have answered my prayers." (He continued), "I truly fear how my predecessors will behave after I am gone, since my wife has always been infertile. From Your kind mercy provide me with a successor, who will advance the faith in the prestigious status of the descendants of Jacob. What's more, my Lord, make him someone of whom you will be proud."

Then, angels told him, "O Zechariah, We are honored to announce the birth of a son named John."✦ However, in his shock he exclaimed, "My

✦That is John the Baptist. According to biblical scholars he was Mary's cousin. What's more, Mary was directly related to Abraham. Thus, the prophets of Christianity are also the prophets of Islaam. Again, all Christian prophets are held in the highest esteem by Muslims. What's more, Muslims believe in all the original Christian rites and practices. Furthermore, there is no history in Islaamic society of the desecration of Christian shrines. In contrast, in the Middle East Western powers systematically destroy Islaamic holy sites.

The Muslims honor the Christian prophets, because these men are also Prophets of Islaam. The Qur'aan speaks highly of these prophets, emphasizing them in terms of frequency of mention even over the Prophet Muhammad. Thus, for this world to be at peace the Christians must do the same and honor the prophets and practices of Islaam. Thus, it is the intolerance of certain Christian authorities—and their hatred against Islaam— that is the cause of much global strife.

Lord, how could it be? My wife is infertile, and, regarding me, I am feeble." However, your Lord replied, "This is easy for Me—just as I created you (as a human race) previously from nothing." He prayed, "My Lord, make an obvious sign for me." The angel revealed, "Your sign is that for three days you will speak to no one." Then, he left the sanctuary and went to his people, signaling them only with gestures (as if to say) "Praise God continuously for His unlimited glory, day and night."

After the son was born and matured, he was told, "John, hold steadfastly to the teachings of God with all your capacity." This is because, even as a little child, John was given wisdom. In addition, as a result of Our kindness (he was given) the gift of love for his fellow man and purity of intention. Furthermore, he always made Us the priority. He was full of reverence towards his parents. What's more, he would never act arrogantly or stubbornly. Thus, the love of God was upon him from his birth until resurrection.

Virgin birth

Also, remember through this divine writing (the virgin) Mary. She withdrew from her family—going to a place to the East. In addition, she put herself in a state of seclusion and meditation. Then, Our angel arrived, looking like a well-proportioned human. In fear, she exclaimed, "I seek the protection of God: if you believe in Him, do not come near me." The angel answered, "I am only a messenger from your Lord God—His message is, I will provide from My mercy the gift of a son (who will be) blessed with purity.'"

She responded, "This is impossible, I have never been touched by a man, since I have never been a loose woman." The angel answered, "It is already decided. In any case your Lord says, 'This is a minor issue for Me—in fact, you will have a son, so We might make him an everlasting symbol for humankind as well as an act of mercy from Us.'"

So, it was decided. Eventually, she conceived him and went into seclusion far away from her people. What's more, when labor pains drove her to support herself against the trunk of a (palm) tree, she exclaimed, "Oh, I would rather be dead than endure this and become a thing forgotten, totally forgotten." Then, a voice arising from under the palm tree responded to her, saying, "Never grieve. Your Lord has provided a fresh spring-fed stream under you (to cleanse her). What's more, shake the tree towards you, and fresh ripe dates will drop for you. Thus, eat and drink, and your spirits will be revived.✦ Furthermore, if you encounter anyone,

✦That is since she was acting as God's agent in order to achieve His will He directly took care of her. Too, without doubt, during childbirth there is great stress upon the female organs. Plus, there may be significant blood loss and therefore fluid loss. This leads to a loss of strength. Dates are highly nourishing, providing a vast density of minerals, including iron and copper, needed to rebuild blood and thus to revive a woman's strength. The fresh water helps replenish blood volume. It was also needed to cleanse the afterbirth. The point is God is loving to His servants and takes special care of all of them, especially those who dedicate themselves to Him.

represent to them, symbolically: 'know that I have made a vow to the Most Merciful to say nothing today.'"

Jesus speaks from the cradle

Eventually, she returned to her people, carrying the child.✦ They said, "Mary, my, have you done an

✦This disputes the commonly held version of Jesus' birth. That version places Mary and her family on the way to, supposedly, pay taxes. Yet, it is well known that in that era pregnant women went into seclusion, let alone in childbirth. What's more, the birth of a gifted messenger in a relatively 'clean' environment—a palm orchard—is far more plausible than an animal stable. Thus, the statement of Mary giving birth "on the way to pay taxes" is fraudulent. It was surely fabricated by the autocratic authorities to ensure the sense of obligation, that is to secular states.

The Qur'aan then merely indicates that she brought the child back to her people. This child was definitely small but not an infant. What is certain is that no one witnessed Mary's birth and that rather it occurred in seclusion. Any other representation of these events is purely speculative.

> incredible thing. You, the sister of a prophet, Aaron: your father was a decent man and your mother was always decent." Then, she pointed to him. They exclaimed, "How can we talk to such a small child still in the cradle?"✦ However, he said,

✦Rather than a newborn it is likely that at this time Jesus was older, perhaps a year or so. Thus, in his advanced state due to the divine spirit within him, in fact, even as a toddler he was able to speak intelligently. This helped vindicate Mary from the inevitable rumor-mongering that spread within the community.

> "As you can see I am a servant of God. He has given me scripture and made me a prophet. What's more, He made me blessed wherever I may be— for my entire lifetime. He has made it my duty to engage in prayer and charity. In addition, He instilled in me reverence towards my mother. He has also made me completely free of arrogance or ingratitude. Thus, peace was upon me the day I was born and will be upon me when I die—as well as during resurrection." In the words of truth such was (the nature of) Jesus, *son of Mary*, about whose nature they so deeply disagree.

It is inconceivable that God would have made for Himself a son. He is unlimited in His magnificence. For Him in order to cause a thing to happen, He merely says, "Be" and it immediately is. So (as Jesus preached),✦ "The fact is God is my Lord and your

✦That is the real nature of Jesus is that he was God's representative. He was a true servant of almighty God, merely one of His creations. Therefore, he was not His physical or natural son, a fact according to the Qur'aan which will be confirmed for all who hold this erroneous belief.

This confirmation will occur upon their deaths. The Qur'aan is emphatic that the birth of Jesus was no more miraculous than any of the countless other examples of His miracles such as the making of the original human. The latter is an infinitely greater miracle than the virgin birth or even the supposed raising up of Christ. Plus, obviously, rather than of European build or color he was instead of Mediterranean descent. This means he was dark-complected. Regardless, he was a universal messenger and never claimed an exclusive religion. Rather, his entire faith was the true submission of the human being to almighty God. In fact, this is the definition of Islaam.

Lord. Thus, He alone is worthy of worship. This is the correct way."

Yet, regarding the nature of Jesus the various Christian sects vary widely. Thus, for those who reject the truth beware of the onset of that Awesome Time. How readily will they, then, understand the truth, that is when they come before Us.

However, now, these people who commit evil✦

✦This refers to those who continuously maintain that, somehow, Jesus is divine. This makes no sense. Obviously, Jesus was a human being, who lived like all others. According to the Qur'aan this making Jesus as divine is a form of paganism, derived from the godless ancients. Jesus' entire mission was to rectify such beliefs. That is why he called all to the Father.

He always deferred to almighty God. Nowhere did he represent himself as a god. Then, what in his attributes makes him divine? Think about it. Did he even perform a single feat that would qualify him as God? If so, let anyone provide proof to substantiate it.

are lost in error. Thus, make them aware of the coming of the Time of Regrets, when everything will have been decided, because since they are heedless they refuse to believe in it. Yet, We alone will remain after all on the earth has become extinct, a time when to Us, all will be returned.

The youthful Abraham and his bravery before the pagans

Through this divine book also remember Abraham. He was certainly a man of truth, already a prophet when (while using his powers of reason) he told his father, "My father, why do you worship something which is incapable of responding to you and is unable to help you? My father, I have received insightful knowledge of which you are unaware. Thus, follow my suggestions, because as a result I will direct you to a truly excellent way. My father, beware of adoring the ways of any devilish influence, because certainly the devil is a rebel against the merciful Lord. What's more, my father, I truly fear the consequences of your behavior, that is that a punishment be inflicted upon you from the most merciful God at which time you will realize you had succumbed to the influence of Satan."

He responded, "Have you no love for my gods, Abraham? Surely, if you continue this, I will have you killed, in fact, stoned to death. Get out of here, and never come back." Abraham replied, "May God's peace be upon you. I will ask my Lord to forgive you. This is because He has always been so kind to me. However, I will withdraw myself from you and your people and from all that you adore instead of God. Furthermore, I will ask my Lord alone for strength. It may well be that my prayer for you could be answered with good results by my Lord."

Because he abandoned them and their evil ways, We supported him with prophets: his own children and grandchildren (such as) Isaac and Jacob. Plus, from Our mercy We gave them numerous gifts. Finally, We provided them with a majestic power (through their examples)—to (forever) represent (the Godly truths) to others.

Other messengers commissioned by God

This also serves as a reminder regarding Moses. In fact, he was a chosen one, a true messenger and prophet (of almighty God). Moreover (recall how), We commissioned him (to Our service) from the right-sided face of Mount Sinai, bringing him near Us in spiritual communion. Then, recall how We supported him through his brother Aaron, a prophet (to help him). Then, also (recall through this divine message), Ishmael. Surely, he, too, was always true to his promise, another messenger and prophet of God—a man who used to urge his people to be steadfast in their worship and in charitable acts and who, as a result, earned his Lord's favor.

Consider also (through this divine message) Idrees. No doubt, he was a man of truth, a true prophet, who We raised high to a fine consequence.

These were a few of the messengers who God blessed: originating from (the original man, Adam) and the survivors with Noah of the Ark as well as the genetic seed of Abraham and (the later lineage of) Israel. What's more, they were all selected and guided by Us. Moreover, whatever messages their Lord represented to them they would (immediately submit to them), falling down prostrate, crying.

Paganism versus godliness: the consequences

Even so, they were followed by generations (of humanity) who neglected (all consideration) of worship and instead followed merely their own lusts. Moreover, eventually (such individuals) will realize the extent of their absolute ruin. The exceptions are those who (after falling astray) truly beg forgiveness and do good—because these are the ones who will enter the elegant gardens and will never be wronged. For them there will be the peace of permanent happiness, which the gracious Lord has promised for His (true) servants—in a realm (that is beyond comprehension). This is a promise that will definitely be realized.

There, they will hear no vain speech but rather only the finest of speech, truly peaceful. Furthermore, their provisions (in that restful paradise) will be provided for them continuously.

This is the nature of that paradise which We will give as an inheritance to Our servants, those who have always been in awe of (their meeting with) God.

What's more (the angels say), "We never come repeatedly (to you) with revelation, except by the Lord God's permission. He owns all that is obvious (before us) as well as all that we are unable to perceive—and, furthermore, your Lord never forgets an iota (of anything), the Lord God of the high heavens as well as the earth—as well as all that exists between them." Then, worship Him alone, and remain firm and unrelenting in such worship. Are you aware of any other who is even remotely comparable to Him?

Despite this (the human tends to say), "After I die, will I (really) be regenerated?" Has he forgotten that We created him previously—from nothing?

So it will be that by your Lord's authority during (the time of judgment) We will absolutely regenerate them, accompanied by the devilish forces (which urged them towards sin). Then, We will certainly gather them, on their knees, around hell, at which time We will definitely extract from every group the most vile transgressors, who were most belligerent in their hateful rebellion against the Lord merciful. This is because, clearly, We best know which of those most deserves the fires of hell.✦

✦This is an allusion that God may even show mercy on those who neglected Him, that is those who never actively refused Him but rather merely mindlessly followed the authorities of the time. So, regarding dire punishment only those who were malicious in their rebellion will endure it. This is clear proof of the vast mercy of His almighty Self, known in Arabic as *ar-rahmaan*—the incomprehensibly merciful Lord.

Furthermore, you will all see it. With your Lord this is a mandate which is inevitable. Then, We will save from hell those who have truly been in awe of Us and who have kept Us in mind continuously. However, We will leave in it the godless, who did evil acts, *on their knees*.

Yet, routinely, whenever Our message is represented to them—despite its clear and obvious nature—those who are determined to reject the truth tell the true believers, "Which of us is more powerful in status and superior as a civilization?"✦

✦That is as if to say, 'If your God is so powerful and your religion so correct, why do we have power over you and why are you, obviously, so inferior to us, materially?' Yet, the true believer disregards this. He knows that any such power is merely superficial and that, rather, all real power is with God. So, any such pomp and authority—guns, muscle, status, and material wealth—none of it has any effect upon him, because he is absolutely sure that the only true power source, the only One who can truly influence affairs, is the great and powerful almighty God. Thus, such a believer is fearless and in the face of the most overwhelming odds retains his composure. Thus, he fulfills his duty to do God's bidding. This is true, even if it means risking his life.

In God's view anyone who truly submits to Him regardless of his material or social status is infinitely superior to the seemingly powerful ones, that is those who claim control on this earth. Furthermore, God gives these powerful ones an extensive reprieve to amend their ways. He does this for their own sakes. This is why he allows them to remain in power, so that they might make restitution. Then, if they refuse to do so and continue to torment His true servants, ultimately, He destroys them completely, while saving the true believers.

Moreover, We previously destroyed numerous civilizations, people who were *even greater in material achievements and stature* (than these modern ones). Tell them, "Regarding the person who lives in error may the merciful Lord lengthen his life on this earth." What's more (ignore their slander), until the time when they experience precisely what they were warned against, whether it is through torment (now) or at the beginning of the next life. This is because, then, it will become clear to them which of the two types of humans is in the worst position in status as well as support.

Yet, the way it is God provides those who take advantage of His guidance with an even deeper degree of guidance. Also (in your Lord's view), good actions, the benefits of which are permanent, are infinitely greater in value than any material achievements. What's more (such good acts), are far superior (to material possessions) in returns.

Are you aware of the type (of person) who (categorically) rejects Our messages and brags, "The fact is I will be given much material success and (I am wealthy because I have) children." Has he, possibly, been able to gain access to the imperceptible, or has he made a special arrangement with the merciful Lord? In no way (is he correct). We will record (his arrogant claim) and, what's more, We will extend for him the length of his torment. Also, We will take command over all that he claimed (rights to), and, therefore, he will come before Us (fully isolated). These are the consequences for those who have made other (powers or desires) as if gods, anticipating that, somehow, they would be a (source of) greatness (or power) for them. This is erroneous. (At that time of accountability) those (objects they had adored) will reject the (homage that was paid to them) and will regard (those who worshiped them) as the enemy.

Are you unaware (of the fact that) We have disseminated (a wide range) of satanic impulses (within their souls), urging those who reject the truth with strong urging (towards sin)? So, never impatiently (demand God's judgement) regarding them, because it is only a matter of time (before they will come before Us). Then, We will assemble the God-fearing people before the Lord merciful as honored guests, while driving those who are lost in error (into a massive herd) to hell. Then, no one will have (the right to) intercede other than those who (in the previous life) had established a bond with the Lord.

The oneness of God reiterated

Despite this some people claim, "The merciful Lord has bore a son." Without doubt, you have asserted something monstrous, while (when such statements are made), the high heavens might be virtually blasted to pieces and the earth split in half—and the mountains crushed into ruins. That humans would attribute to the Lord merciful a son—however, it is inconceivable that the merciful Lord would do so.✦

✦That is why does He need a son? In fact, He has no spouse. God is the absolute creator. He creates the sexes. Also, the process of reproduction is His. He is eternal. He cannot die. Nor does he require food. Nor does He have any type of physical body. Rather, He is the universal creator. He also created the system of genetics, that is the interconnections of the chromosomes. He made the biological man. Furthermore, He is beyond any need for progeny, because He alone is self-sufficient, eternal. What's more, He is not a sexual being, nor does He need or have a spouse. In fact, He created the sexes. So, why would He, then, produce His mere creation—a true mortal—as His son? This being that people proclaim as if God, he, himself stated clearly his dependence upon the merciful Lord.

Almighty God is obviously beyond any need. In contrast, without doubt, Jesus was a dependent, who walked the earth. The latter ate food, drank fluids, and required shelter. Then, again, how could he be God?

Yet, make no mistake about it—and there are no exceptions—no one exists in this universe, unless he is a slave of the Lord merciful. Without doubt, He is fully aware of them and has, in fact, calculated (the value of) their (existence and actions) with a flawless system. Furthermore, during accountability each of them will appear before Him completely isolated.✦

✦That is without belief, none of a person's achievements will gain him any value, a fact clearly alluded to previously in this section. So, the powers of wealth, material success, and family lineage—children and heritage—none of this is of any consequence. There will be no bribery. No child will be able to help any parent nor any parent his child. Only a person's actions done strictly for God's sake—works of goodness—will protect him.

Surely (the exceptions will be), those who truly believe (in the oneness of God) and do good—(for them) the merciful Lord will attach His love. This was why We made this (divine book) easy to understand, all so that you in your own language could represent through it good news to those who are truly good. (It is) also so you will (use it) to warn those who are contentious (regarding it). (Because it should always be remembered:) how numerous were the civilizations which (due to their wickedness) We previously destroyed. What's more, are you able to now perceive (any aspect of them) or even hear the slightest whisper from them?

Section 20
Ingratitude

In the name of the most merciful
and compassionate God

Traditionally, this section is named after the signifying Arabic letters, *Taa Haa*. However, the term ingratitude thoroughly describes its contents. The theme of humankind's ingratitude for the favors of God permeates it. It begins with the story of Pharaoh and Moses, the former demonstrating the epitome of ingratitude. There is also the story of the Israelites, who God specifically rescued from Pharaoh. Too, they proved thankless, even though God saved them from their dire state. Then, who other than God could gain them release from Pharaoh's tyranny? Thus, obviously, from the divine point of view ingratitude is the greatest of all crimes. This is why the almighty creator dedicated an entire chapter to it. Through these examples God warns humankind, so they won't find themselves "spiritually bankrupt" when during resurrection they ultimately are presented before Him.

T-H

The objective of this revelation is never to cause you distress. Rather, it is merely a means to cause those who have the desire to always consider God. (After all,) it is a divine revelation from the creator of the high heavens as well as this earth—the merciful, loving Lord, the ultimate (and in fact only) authority in the universe.

He owns it all,✦ whatever (exists) in the high

✦That is 'including you, O humans.' Each person is a definite creation. Then, obviously, these creations are owned by the creator. This is why it makes sense that each person is a slave of the merciful Lord. This means that it is each person's obligation to do His bidding. Even the one who neglects Him is, ultimately, His property. Yet, they rarely consider this fact and instead do all in their power to distance themselves from Him. They do so by immersing themselves in mere worldly pleasures and lusts. They also do so by refusing to even think about almighty God. Nor do they consider that they themselves are dependent upon Him for their very existence.

heavens, as well as on this earth—as well as whatever is between them, even all that is beneath the earth.

(To demonstrate the depth of His awareness God relates the following parable:) whether you verbalize your thoughts or keep them secret, even whatever is hidden in the depths of the subconscious mind, *God hears it.*

This is the real God. He is the only divine power. What's more, only He is perfect in every way.

Have you heard of the story of Moses, when he saw that distant glow? He told his family, "Remain here, I perceive a distant fire. Perhaps I can bring from it a brand or even discover (at this compelling glow) some guidance. Then, when he came near it, a (kind of) voice spoke to him, saying, "O Moses, surely, I am your Lord. So, remove your shoes. You are in a very blessed place."✦ (He continued) "I

✦That is because this was the place chosen by God to reveal Himself to humans by unveiling a portion of His light and by drawing Moses to it. It is also blessed, because of the selection of Moses by God to revive the true faith in Him and to return people from the depths of internal despair. God is almighty: that He physically represents Himself before humans is a major issue. Then, this lineage of Moses ultimately led to another great movement for the oneness of God: the movement of the Prophet Jesus.

chose you. Then, listen (and deeply consider) what I will reveal to you. (And) have no doubt about it, I

alone am God. Besides Me, there is no one else—
no other ultimate power. Then, only worship Me,
all so you can remember Me."

Clearly, although I have decided to keep the time
secret the final event is inescapable. Its purpose is
to compensate every person for whatever he
achieved—whatever he has (consciously) worked
towards.✦ So, never allow those who reject this

✦This is the simplest explanation of the nature of resurrection found
in the Qur'aan. It was a representation given to Moses some 26 centuries
ago. God wishes to justly reward all the good and decent people who,
with Him in mind, worked exclusively for good. He does this because of
His love. Therefore, the purpose of resurrection is in order for Him to
share His love with all His creation, those kind and loving servants who
sought to please Him.

(return to God as well as this accountability): never
allow them to cause you to abandon it, due to the
concern that you destroy yourself.

"Now, O Moses, what are you holding (in your
right hand)?" Moses responded, "It is my staff. I
use it for support, and I also use it to beat down
the brush for my sheep—and many other uses."
He said, "Throw it down, O Moses." So, he did,
and, astonishingly, it became as if a (frightening)
snake, slithering away. God said, "Grab it, and
never be afraid. We will make it as before. Now,
place your hand inside your cloak (against your
upper chest), then, remove it. Look: it comes out
beaming a white light, which beams inspiration,
without (any damage:) another major sign. Now,
go to Pharaoh, because He has become arrogant
to the extreme."

Moses said, "My Lord, inspire me (deeply in my heart). What's more, make my effort easy for me. Too, cause me to speak freely (in a convincing manner), that is give me power of speech. Also, strengthen my power (base) through one of my relatives, my brother Aaron, so he can assist me, all so that (as a team) we can pronounce Your glory and always hold You in awe. Truly, You (our dearest Lord), You are the One who is aware of even our deepest intentions."

God said, "O Moses, you have been given all that you asked for."

"Yet, in fact, We (have always been protecting you),✦ and gave you benefits previously, when We

✦That is He is continuously caring for His humans, even when they may fail to realize it, even when they never think of Him. Here, God demonstrates that He is constantly caring for His creation, although he develops a special bond for those who deeply consider Him. Thus, God, the ultimate parent, always cares for his 'offspring.'

inspired your mother in this vein, 'place him on a raft, and put him in the river—and the river will deposit him on the bank. Moreover, then, My enemy—who will ultimately also be your enemy—will adopt him.'"

"Furthermore, I instilled within you a love for Me, in order that you develop as a person destined to do My bidding. Also, you were under My watchful (care) when your sister approached (Pharaoh's household), asking them, 'Shall I direct you to one who will care for (that is nurse and rear) him?' Through this We returned you (miraculously) to your mother, so she could be at peace—so that she would be happy. Furthermore, you killed a man. Even so, We saved you from (any grief), although We tested you through numerous trials. Then, you lived for a number of years with the people of Midian, and, now, you have arrived (for the final phase of your destiny), as ordained by Me."✦

✦This entire section is a parable aimed at all true believers. It is in order to strengthen their faith, so they will never doubt His protective powers. It is as if to say, 'Why would you now doubt Me: why would you need any other besides Me? I always protect you, even in truly precarious circumstances. This is proof that I take care of you and watch over you. Any further doubt is merely evidence of weakness of faith. Be strong, and place your trust in Me alone. I have already proven that I protect all who deeply believe in Me, even though you may be unaware of it. So, trust in Me exclusively. I will support you.'

This is precisely this message. It is that almighty God wishes to teach the believers to realize that His support is permanent. This is so they will win the battle against injustice. Then, as long as they do so—as long as they place in Him the most profound trust—they will win. This is His mandate. What's more, the believer must never second guess it. The power in this, as the following alludes, is to always keep God deeply in mind. This makes a person invincible. This is the parabolic message of Moses and Pharaoh. This explains why God repeatedly emphasizes this story, that is to firmly establish in the believers' minds that with the help of God all things are possible. Yet, that help is gained only by truly and firmly trusting in Him.

"So, now, both of you, go to Pharaoh. What's more, never (allow yourselves to) weaken in your remembrance of Me.✦ (So, again,) go to him, the

✦That is this is the secret: to in all apparent crises trust in Him alone and to consider Him deeply. It is to hold to Him, that rope which binds the believer to Him regardless of the degree of difficulty or trial, as did the Prophet Daniel, when he was thrown into a 'den of lions' and when he remained at peace, thinking only of His Lord, and therefore was never harmed.

fact is he has violated all decency. However, speak to him with compassion—be mild (in your demeanor)—just in case he would give Us consideration or at least be somewhat fearful of Us." The two said, "Our Lord, we are afraid that in his rashness he might act against us and thus prevent us from fully delivering Your message (because our real fear) is that we fail in this message to assist You to prevent him from transgressing against all decency." God responded, "Have no fear. Without doubt, I will be with you, fully alert and aware (to guide you)."✦

✦That is, again, the requirement is to rely exclusively on God. He alone has complete power over all that occurs and is fully aware of all circumstances. If a person just allows it, He will guide him. Thus, for guidance, as well as for ultimate power, He is the only One to rely upon. As proven by the profound example of Moses, pitted solely against one of the most powerful empires of all times, that reliance will result in success. This is true against any odds.

"So, go to him and tell him, 'We are representatives from your Lord, so let the Israelites go with us. What's more, stop persecuting them. Clearly, We have come to you with messages from your Lord. Moreover, let there be peace upon anyone who truly follows them. The fact is we are the warners—it has been revealed to us that those who deny, who completely reject, God's messages suffer only torment.'"

Yet, Pharaoh said, "So, who is this Lord that you speak of, O Moses?" Moses responded, "Our Lord is the Master of all that exists and is also the One who is in command (of His vast creation)."

Pharaoh responded, "Then, what of the ancients?" Moses said, "Only God knows their status—He has it all recorded. My Lord makes no mistakes. Nor does He forget." (And he continued,) "You ask (what kind of Lord He is): He (is the One) who made the earth a comfortable home for you and has given you all the necessary elements for creating various livelihoods and has sent down✦ from the

✦Notice in this section that there is mention simultaneously of the divine gift of water as well as the creation of humans. The water is mentioned first, that is as the progenitor of all life. The original water—ice—arose strictly from interstellar space, made by an unknown mechanism from interstellar gases. This explains the reference here to water instead of rain, which as the Qur'aan indicates arose from outside the earth: from deep space. Though, obviously, Pharaoh could not comprehend it, this alludes to the fact that this water was brought from outer space to earth, perhaps through the impact of a comet or other ice-laden object. This explains the terminology, "sent down." The point is almighty God did all this for the sake of His creation, particularly with humans in mind. Despite this, as Pharaoh demonstrated, much of humanity proves ungrateful for His vast blessings.

high heavens) water and has, as a result, caused the development of a wide range of plants (all), so you can 'eat and pasture your cattle.'" Through these examples there are insights for those willing to use their higher intelligence.

(As another evidence of Our powers) *from this earth*✦ We have also created you, O humans.

✦That is demonstrating the insignificant nature of human origins, truly low. Humans arise, apparently, rather than from the heavens as miraculous or spiritual beings 'descending from the clouds' instead from lowly earthen materials: minerals, salts, organic matter, organic muck, and water. In other words, the true origins of humans is humble. Then, obviously, to be arrogant is a gross violation, whereas humility, surely, is befitting of such origins. The human is as humble as the dust of the earth.

This is why it makes sense to give all real power to almighty God alone. Too, it makes sense to worship Him exclusively and to do so continuously until death. This is because as this Qur'aan makes clear humans originate from God and ultimately return to Him:

Then, We will return you to it. What's more, from it We will (ultimately) regenerate you.

So, We demonstrated for Pharaoh evidence of Our powers—a wide range (of such evidences). Yet, he rejected them. He said, "Moses, is your intention to drive us from power by mystifying our people? You leave us with no option other than to challenge you with our (own) magic. So, let us have (such a challenge): a public display between us at high noon in front of the masses."✦

✦That is even in this circumstance Pharaoh had doubts. He was well aware of Moses' sound character. Inherently, he was also aware that there was a basis for his claims. Previously, he had complete power over any situation. He could call his subjects before him and demand absolute obedience. Now, he was being successfully challenged. Never before was he held to account. Moses represented to him great signs, but he immediately plotted to refute it.

So, in his haughtiness he opted for a public demonstration, knowing that people feared his power and would, regardless of the result, bow to it. Yet, in his pomposity he never expected the actual result, that is that the people closest to this event, the magicians themselves, would be compelled to adopt the faith of Moses. Thus, Pharaoh's own plot rebounded against him, merely accelerating his ruin. Yet, then, so are all plots against Him rendered insignificant.

Then, Pharaoh withdrew with his counselors to plot his strategy. He then came from the session, and Moses (bravely) said to him, "May you be condemned. Do not create lies about God—the fact is He may destroy you at any moment without notice, causing you only anguish. Without doubt, any who purposely attempt to fabricate the truth (such as you, O Pharaoh)—any such person is lost in advance (of any resurrection), in fact, ruined."

Then, they argued among each other in their private counsel, attempting to determine the course of action. They concluded, "Surely these two are obvious magicians, intent on ruining you: (all to) eliminate your ancestral way of life.✦ So,

---

✦That is in their arrogance and complete disregard of the obvious truths they came to the opposite conclusion. Here, God is attempting to save His human race, that is the peoples of Pharaoh, and, yet, they claim His messengers are trying to destroy them? This is the most extreme error possible. The fact is God was attempting to purge them of precisely these ancestral ways, because in their worship of false powers they were only causing themselves harm. He was merely attempting to enlighten them. It is the understanding that only almighty God has the ultimate power and that, therefore, only He is worthy of worship. This is precisely the message that they so arrogantly rejected, a rejection that led to their own destruction. Had they only submitted to God's way they would have gained instead a mighty reward, both in this life and the next.

---

devise a strategy and then come forward fully unified. Today, the winner will truly be fortunate." (So, they gathered before Moses and Aaron and said:) "Either you start, or we will start." They responded, "You start first." Thus, they threw down their various devices and by magic made them appear to move. Moses felt (a degree of) apprehension, but We inspired him with "*Be fearless*. Surely, you will overcome. Now, throw down your staff—it will consume all their devices. All they have devised is mere magic, and whatever a magician does has no substance."

Then (the results were as predicted, and consequently), the magicians fell down, prostrate. "We now believe," they said, "in the almighty

Lord—the Lord of Moses and Aaron." Pharaoh retorted, "What? How dare you believe in Him without my permission? Obviously (the only explanation for your behavior is that), you are merely students of Moses, who himself taught you magic. So, as a punishment (for your disloyalty) I will cut off your hands and feet on opposite sides. What's more, I will certainly crucify you (nailing you) to the trunks of palm trees. Then, you will realize which of us (has the power to) inflict the most extreme, as well as prolonged, punishment."

They said, "(Your threats and torture will never dissuade us from our new faith:) We will in no way prefer (your rule) over what has now been given to us (that is) all evidence of the truth. Nor will we submit to you in preference to the One who has created us. So, do what you desire against us. In truth, you can only (impose such tyranny) in this world. (Yet, regardless of your acts against us,) without doubt, we now believe (exclusively) in our high Lord, that He may forgive us for what we previously engaged in (on our own) as well as the false acts you imposed upon us. What's more, with God is the finest, as well as the most permanent, of all (that anyone can desire)."

In fact, whoever appears before his Lord (fully) immersed in vile acts earns only the torment. There, such a person will neither live nor die. In contrast, whoever appears before His Lord as a believer who has done good acts for (such persons) there will be (in the next life) the highest status. (It will be) a permanent existence in the delightful gardens. That is the consequence for those who have purified (their hearts).

(Ultimately,) We revealed to Moses, "Leave with my servants under the protection of night (which We, without doubt, told him, in case there is any doubt about the fact that this miracle of Moses occurred), and find for them a dry path in the seabed.✦

✦That is, literally, to be "alert to" this dry or waterless seabed. This was advance warning for Moses in order to ensure his success, so he could definitely recognize the sign. Here, the Qur'aan is very specific. He was to find an actual crossing within the bed of the sea, which means that, suddenly, the water was drawn away. Otherwise, the term defining seabed wouldn't have been used. Thus, the use of this terminology would infer a tsunami, where the water was suddenly drawn away and a 'dry' crossing was created.

This tsunami, manifested by a temporary and massive withdrawal of the waters, is a natural consequence of an earthquake. Even with a natural phenomenon this would allow sufficient time for the crossing before the dreadful wave recoiled upon the unsuspecting, mighty armies of Pharaoh. The earthquake, which created this temporary crossing, most likely occurred offshore. This is the only physical phenomenon, which could account for a dry 'path' created within a sea.

What's more, have no fear of being overtaken or regarding (the powers of the sea)."

Then, Pharaoh pursued them, along with his great ones, and as predestined the sea overwhelmed them.✦ Moreover, rather than any 'guidance' all Pharaoh did was lead his nation into ruin.

✦In a pitched battle Moses' people did not have the capacity to defeat Pharaoh's well-equipped army, with its powerful chariots and skilled warriors. Nor did they demonstrate the bravery to do so. Thus, only God could halt their encroachment. Otherwise, the largely unarmed Israelites would have been slaughtered. He apparently did so through a tsunami.

At the select moment an earthquake, common in that region, likely caused a withdrawal of the water. Moses, divinely inspired, took advantage of that interlude and caused his people to cross the region.

The striking of the earth was symbolic and was, in fact, timed by God. However, the real source of the power was the predestined movement of the earth's plates, leading to a powerful change in the seabed. This caused the massive movement of water which resulted in the tsunami. The timing was such that as Pharaoh and his mighty army crossed, the water raged forward in a violent tsunami and drowned them to the man. Pharaoh's body was recovered, embalmed, mummified, and entombed. It is still available to see today as most likely the mummy of Rhamses II.

(Thus,) you children of Israel, We saved you (long ago) from your enemy, and, then, We made an agreement with you on the right side of the blessed mountain. Then, We delivered to you special food, (that is) manna and quails (as if to say), "Take advantage of all the wholesome, good things which God has provided, but never act arrogantly due to the concern that you will be stricken with My (justifiable) condemnation. Moreover, whoever is stricken by My condemnation has caused himself only ruin."

Even so, truly, I am exceedingly forgiving to the one who begs forgiveness and (thereafter) believes as well as does what is right and then allows himself to remain guided.

Moses in seclusion at the Mount: his people's rebellion

(Then, in a reminder to Moses it was said) "So, what caused you, O Moses, to leave your people?"✦

✦Temporarily, Moses left his "saved" people, while seeking God's presence. He probably was tired of all their complaining and begging. Here, he was, in a sense, reprimanded by God for doing so. More profoundly, this serves as a warning for all future generations. The lesson is that merely presuming that people will do what is right is naive, especially if they are long established in old habits and particularly if they are victims of oppression. While Moses' guidance alone may not have prevented their rebellion the point is that unless powerful controls are established people fall prey to temptation. There are too many variables, whims, and wishes. People need guidance from a strong personality, even a strong social constitution such as firm, protective divine rules.

Most people are followers. Thus, for spiritual guidance there have always arose devout, strong personalities. That is truly the way of God. Yet, even so, as strong as Moses was, still, he couldn't control them. Even so, the point is without strong and intelligent leadership, people tend to falter and may even become self-destructive.

Moses said, "Why, they are close by (and I have no reason to be concerned), and so I come (hurriedly) to You, my Lord, that You might be well pleased." However, God responded, "The fact is in your absence We have tempted your people, and the Samaritan has caused them to deviate."✦ As a result,

✦There may well be good samaritans, but according to the Qur'aan there are also wicked ones. In Moses' absence a certain perpetrator took advantage of the peoples' weaknesses and led them into sin. The word samaritan is derived from the Arabic *saamiriyyu*, which means to "talk convincingly late into the night." This is, then, synonymous with mischief-making. The convincing talker causes people to come his way. Yet, he does so merely to gain the advantage *for his own selfish purpose*. Thus, the vast majority of the Israelites fell victim to this plot. Yet, they did so willingly, because they were ultimately enamored only by this worldly life and did not deeply believe in the return to God. This is why God tested them, that is to see if they truly believed in this return or if mere temptation for worldly lusts would cause them to abandon their commitment.

Moses returned to his people, full of indignation as well as sorrow. He told them, "My people, didn't my Lord make you many excellent promises? Moreover, was it that this promise (of a better and permanent life) was seemingly too distant for your patience? Or, did you seek to (purposely) provoke the punishment of your Lord, so that you broke your promise with me?" They said, "We never broke our promise we made (to our Lord) due to our own will, but, rather (our excuse is) we were burdened by the weight of the peoples' possessions—gold objects, jewelry, and more—and so, we merely molded these (under the Samaritan's direction in the fire) into a more usable object."

Moreover, he produced for them this (golden calf), which made a lowing sound. Then, they said, "This is your god and the god of Moses; but (Moses) has forgotten (his pagan roots)." Yet, were they unable to comprehend that it was incapable of responding in the least to their requests and was impotent, that is to help or harm?

What's more, Aaron had already told them (to desist), saying, "My people, you are merely being tempted to (wickedness) through this (false god). Moreover, without doubt, your real Lord truly cares for you. So, follow me, and obey what I command you."

However, they responded, "We will only stop (worshipping this idol) when (or if) Moses returns." What's more, when (finally), Moses did return, He said, "O Aaron, what stopped you when you saw them deviate from (the truth)—from rejecting them and remaining (with my faith)? Have you purposely rejected my commandment?" Aaron replied, "My own brother, do not (continue to) grab me by my beard or head. No doubt, I was concerned for fear that on your return you would say, 'You have caused a division among the Israelites and failed to keep to my orders.'"

Moses then said (to his competitor), "You Samaritan, what was your (real) purpose in all this?" He responded, "I had (my own) insight that the rest of them were unable to comprehend. So, I *seized upon the opportunity* to use my insights, that is of my own view of the correct religion, because I found reason to dispute and even change yours."✦ Moses responded, "Leave our presence.

✦That is due to competition and jealousy people, such as the Samaritan, purposely incite corruption. What's more, they maliciously corrupt God's laws. Then, they do so for their own gain. Thus, they are opportunists, who may act as if they have others' interests in mind but are purely self-centered. In this regard they misguide those of weak mind, while, incredibly, claiming to have their interests in mind. This is the beginning of man-made religion.

What's more, without doubt, in our view you are an outcast. However, the fact is in the next existence you will be faced with a meeting which is inescapable." (Then, Moses turned to his people and said,) "Look at this 'god' to which you have become so devoted: now, we will absolutely burn it and while you watch scatter its remnants into the sea."

There is only the one God. Furthermore, this is indisputable. Other than Him there are no divine powers. Moreover, He has full comprehension—absolute knowledge—of all that is.

This is how We describe for you some of the events of the past. In addition, surely, from Our merciful love We have provided you with a reminder. Then, without doubt, whoever rejects it will at the time of judgement bear a monstrous burden. What's more, they will be forced to live with those burdens, and the weight (they will feel) will, then, be unbearable. Then, when the call is broadcast, because at that time We will gather all who were immersed in sin, their eyes dimmed, muttering to each other (they will say), "We lived on earth (apparently, a very short time): was it any longer than a week or two?" We are well aware of during the time of judgment when the most perceptive of them will say, "(Compared to this new existence) the time you spent there (was very short, like) at most a single day."

Moreover, they ask you regarding the mountains, what will happen to them during that final time. Tell them, "My Lord will pulverize them into dust. Then, He will level it,✦ where you will be unable to

---

✦That is the rest of the earth. Eventually, like other planets, such as Mars, so the Qur'aan makes clear, all will be turned into dust. This final event will be associated with a loss of the atmosphere. This may make the earth a ready target for strikes by meteors as well as comets. So, it is definite. Eventually, the surface of the earth will be nothing more than pulverized dust. What's more, with the exception of good acts nothing else will be of consequence.

The parable is aimed at human souls. This is to cause people to think of their ultimate origins as well as the final result.

Obviously, humans were created from mere dust. Too, clearly, this is the final consequence, that is of crumbled bones. "From dust to dust" is to a degree correct. However, it is incorrect to claim that there is no life after such degeneration, since it is fully proven on this earth that life is produced from barren land, mere dust. For instance, the mere falling of rain on dusty dead soil causes it to teem in life. Then, too, prior to human existence or even the existence of this earth there was only dust in the universe. Ultimately, this was converted into life. So, obviously, this coming alive of dust could only mean that there is an all-powerful creator, who specifically creates the vast species of creatures and also creates the molecular basis of life.

---

see any (topographical variations), not even a curve or (the slightest) ruggedness, and thus, it will be flat and bare." Then, they will follow the Voice, which will summon them and from which there is no escape. What's more, then, all will be subdued, truly humbled, before the truly Merciful—all you will hear is mumbling. It will be a time when no one will be able to help each other, except whomever the Lord Merciful gives permission and of whom He approves. He alone is aware of what their future holds as well as their achievements. What's more, they have no capacity to comprehend it. Then, their faces will be humbled before the Vital, Living, and Eternal Lord. Also, those who hold much wrong in their hearts will be disappointed.

Yet, whoever does what is right and also truly believes (regarding such a person) there is no need for fear or remorse. What's more (it is precisely for this purpose of benefitting you, O humankind, that), We revealed (from the heavens) an Arabic recitation, describing within it a variety of aspects (in order to cause you to think)—all manner of warnings for the purpose that (human beings) will be mindful of God or that (this revelation) may cause them to have a new (and profound) understanding (of Us).

Then, realize that far beyond it all is God (that is any false images of Him that human beings associate with Him), the One who in truth has all rule. (Thus, now that you are aware of this) never make rash judgements regarding this divine writing, that is *until you have thoroughly understood* (its true meaning). What's more (to facilitate this degree of understanding), pray, "Lord, cause me to develop an even more profound understanding (of the divine truths that I have now)."

The origin of ingratitude: the parable of Adam

It was in this vein that, previously, We made an agreement with the original man (Adam).✦

✦This agreement relates to the obligation for people to use their minds. This is in the advancement of the intellect and intelligence. God, the ultimate intelligence, wished to create a being who would base his judgements upon the use of the mind. Through contemplation of the nature of this creation, then, this being would come to the realization that there is only one real Power and that in this Power humankind must trust. Even so, God had ordained the human would be tempted away from this higher thinking through material lusts. This is the human tendency.

Through this parable God warns humans of this, so they will resist the temptations of greed and envy, so that, ultimately, they will follow the way of God. This way is to always give consideration to the consequences before committing any act. It is also to in any circumstance think of God instead always being selfish. In this respect 'Adam' failed. Yet, this is a warning for all future humans to beware of the consequences of their acts, because they will surely be held accountable.

That Adam is described as weak in his commitment is actually a parable. It truly means that humanity is weak. It is yet another warning by God for humans to remain firm in their bond to Him. This will prevent the human from succumbing to the temptation to evil.

So, humans are obligated in this bond. They are a mere minor creation of this Being. Thus, it is the natural way to pay obedience to Him, while it violates nature to reject Him.

However, he neglected it. What's more, We found him weak in commitment. So (We decided to create the means to test him and thus), when We told the angels, "Submit yourselves before (this new creation of Mine), Adam," they all did so, except Iblees (who rejected the idea). Then, We warned

Adam, "Certainly, he is your enemy as well as the enemy of your spouse. So, *never allow him to ruin your opportunity and cause you to be miserable.* Without doubt, you will find all that you need (in this paradise), and you will lack nothing. Nor will you feel vulnerable. Furthermore, you will never suffer from thirst, heat, or any other excesses."✦

✦That is life, here (on this new planet earth), will be moderate and pleasant. The only requirement is that humans be grateful. God makes few demands upon His creation. He only asks them to bow exclusively to Him, to clearly recognize Him as the only true power, and to show gratitude for His vast blessings. This is the entire basis of the message of the Qur'aan.

However (in a jealous attempt to undermine this innocence), Satan tempted them, saying, "You Adam, can I guide you to the secret to immortality and thus a realm that is permanent?" Moreover, they consumed the idea, indulging in it and as a result became aware of their nakedness,✦ which

✦That is vulnerability. In the hearts of the original humans, Adam and Eve, there was only innocence and love. Plus, there was obedience to God as well as gratitude. No sin could be committed, because there was only peace. Then through temptation and lust this peace was corrupted. This caused only loss—this loss of innocence and love between the first humans and their Lord. The lesson is with gratitude to God for all His blessings real peace—a true paradise—is achieved.

By continuously being grateful a person can never defy His Lord. Thus, such a person lives in this state of peace and through this creates his own paradise. Then, he transports that paradise with him when he dies.

The parable of Adam emphasizes the importance of gratitude. God was gracious to him and only made a single demand. Adam defied this. This is the lesson which God attempts to teach, all in order to cause mortal humans to give it thought.

This parable may also signify another example: that of a person's birth. Then, whether male or female, there is pure innocence. In this true, divine-like existence greed and competition are unknown.

Another example is an innocent child. Here, there is no conflict nor any desire for defiance. Nor is there any malicious attempt to cause harm. This state is a kind of paradise. When this is found in adults, it is said the person has "a lot of kid in them." The point is it is healthy to have innocence, as long as it is measured with wisdom. In fact, innocence of heart is a sign of true belief in God, one that should surely be cultivated. People should strive to develop a childlike innocence: that unqualified love for all.

Yet, ultimately, the parable describes the divine system of justice. Humankind, this Qur'aan makes clear, is truly vulnerable. Instinctively, he is supposed to commit to God. However, continuously, he succumbs to temptation, usually in the lust for personal gain. So, God developed a system to test him—the temptations of Iblees. This is so He could evaluate humans to determine their real nature. This nature is best revealed under duress. This is so that at the time of resurrection God shall treat all people in justice. This is because on this planet all people are being tested.

they attempted to disguise (by covering themselves up with pieced-together leaves from the garden). So did Adam disobey his Lord, making a monumental error.

(However,) after this his Lord elected him (for His mercy) and accepted his repentance, giving him His guidance, adding, "Down with you all from this (condition of innocence): from now on you will be enemies of each other. Despite this, clearly, some of you will be recipients of My guidance. Then, whoever follows it will neither deviate nor be unhappy. In contrast, whoever rejects any remembrance of Me will live a marginalized existence, spiritually bankrupt, and what's more during the time of accountability We will regenerate him (completely) blind."

(Such a one will then say:) "My Lord, why have You regenerated me blind, while in contrast when I lived on earth, I could see?" God will respond,

"This is the way it is: (it is due to the fact that) you were exposed to Our messages, but you remained oblivious to them, and as a result, now, you will be consigned to oblivion."

This is how We will deal with the one who squanders his own self and refuses to believe in his Lord's messages. What's more, the fact is the agony endured by such sinners in the next life will be extreme and also permanent.

Then, are the godless unable to learn any lessons from what (obviously) happened previously, that is how numerous were the generations We have destroyed before, people in whose (former) residences—(mere ruins)—they now walk? This is surely a sign, a warning, that is for those willing to use their reason. Yet, except for the fact that God had already decreed it and a term (had already been) established, by now (because of their transgressions) it—(this final event of resurrection)—would have necessarily arrived.

So, endure with patience whatever they say. What's more (make it your focus to), praise the name of your Lord—before sunrise as well as after sunset. Moreover, glorify Him during a part of the nighttime as well as during the day—all so that you might achieve (true) happiness.

Furthermore, never jealously desire whatever splendor We have given to others (mere material goods) that We, in fact, give them merely to test them. What's more, God's gift to you—this promise of ever-lasting happiness—is far superior and more permanent (than any possible worldly gains).

Also, urge your people to the worship of God. Furthermore, remain resolute in this. We never ask you to provide (for Us), rather, *We are your* (exclusive) *provider*. Yet, pleasing is the (ultimate) consequence for those who always regard God deeply (in their hearts, always keeping Him in mind).

They also say, "Why doesn't he manifest a (miracle) from his Lord?" Yet, have they not been made aware of the obvious evidence (of the truth of this message) and in (the contents of) the previous scriptures? Even so, if We would have destroyed them prior to this (exposure to the divine writings), they would surely have reason to say, "Our Lord: if you would have only sent us (guidance) in the form of a true guide, we would have, without doubt, followed your messages rather than endure (at judgment time) all this humiliation and disgrace."

Then, remind them, "Everyone is waiting for what the future holds. So, wait for (that final time), because, then, you will (truly) realize who is correct (in representing true guidance from God) and who has truly allowed himself to be guided.

Bibliography

Arberry, A. J. 1995. *The Koran Interpreted*. New York: Touchstone.

Asad, Muhammad. *The Message of the Qur'an*. Gibralter: Dar-al-Andulus.

Ayoub, M. M. 1983. *The Great Tiding*. Tripoli: Islamic Call Society.

Byng, E. J. 1944. *The World of the Arabs*. Boston: Little, Brown, & Co.

Daryabadi, A. M. 2001. *The Glorious Qur'an*. Leicester, England: Islamic Foundation.

Draper, J. W. 1875. *A History of the Intellectual Development of Europe*. Vol. 1.

Dunlop, D. M . 1971. *Arab Civilization to AD 1500*. New York: Praeger Publishers.

Esack, F. 2002. *The Qur'an: a Short Introduction*. Oxford: One World Publication.

Fakhry, M. 2003. *An Interpretation of the Qur'an*. New York: New York University Press.

Gribbin, J. and M. Gribbin. 1996. *Fire on Earth*. New York: St. Martin's Press.

Hart, M. H. 1978. *The 100: A Ranking of the Most Influential Persons in History*. New York: Hart Publishing Company, Inc.

Khalidi, T. 2001. *The Muslim Jesus*. London: Harvard Univ. Press.

Koning, Hans. 1991. *Columbus: His Enterprise—Exploding the Myth*. New York: Monthly Review Press.

Pasha, S.H. *Personal Communication*. Cortland, New York: Cortland University.

Penrice, J. 2004. *A Dictionary and Glossary of the Koran*. New York: Dover Publications.

Pickthall, M. 1948. *The Meaning of the Glorious Qur'an*. London: George Allen & Unwin, Ltd.

Poole, S. L. 1879. *Selections from the Kur-an*. Boston: Houghton, Osgood, & Co.

Sykes, Christopher. 1965. *Cross Roads to Israel*. London: Collins.

Torres-al-Haneef, Iman. 1993. *The Qur'an in Plain English*. Leicester, United Kingdom: The Islamic Foundation.

Watt, M. 1953. *Mohammad at Mecca*. Oxford.

Weavers, J.W. and D. B. Redford (eds). 1972. *Studies on the Ancient Palestinian World*. Toronto: Toronto Univ. Press.

Index

Israelites, 50, 57, 62-67, 70, 72, 96, 120, 121, 134, 148, 190, 201, 207, 230, 292, 294-297, 302, 305, 382, 383, 408, 489, 490, 505, 540, 545, 550-553

J

Jacob, 11, 28, 34, 65, 66, 114, 127, 128, 192, 250, 402, 412-414, 417, 421-425, 428, 461, 526, 532

Jealousy, ix, 29, 69, 86, 114, 158, 197, 202, 211, 212, 217, 279, 413, 421, 424, 426, 457, 481, 554

Jehovah, 67

Jesus, viii, 11, 19, 26-28, 33, 34, 54, 61, 66, 70, 72, 98, 110, 114, 119-123, 126-128, 173, 189-194, 203, 204, 211, 218-221, 229, 230-232, 236, 250, 283, 301, 310, 338, 361, 378, 379, 406, 428, 439, 440, 461, 494, 508, 524, 525, 528-530, 538, 541

Jews, viii, 49, 51-53, 59-71, 121, 134, 150, 191, 203, 204, 209, 210-217, 221, 222, 267, 268, 301, 302, 306, 334, 337, 361, 383, 439

Jihaad, 17, 58, 159

John the Baptist, 526

Jonah, 192, 250, 363, 384

Joseph, 65, 114, 250, 411-428

Judaism, ix, 46, 66, 136, 190, 191, 210, 218, 299, 334, 383, 486

Judas, 190

K

Katircioglu, 27

Kindness, 64, 78, 117, 143, 144, 229, 235, 269, 369, 381, 405, 461, 484, 491, 493, 499, 520, 527

Knowledge, 20, 43, 49, 60, 62, 92, 96, 98, 99, 114, 117, 123, 124, 157, 161, 170, 172, 180, 196, 243, 249, 257, 267, 277, 278, 279, 290, 321, 322, 328, 329, 333, 334, 345, 359, 388, 397, 417, 419, 423, 427, 469, 478, 483, 495, 503, 511, 512, 519, 521, 524, 531, 554

L

Loans, 106, 107

Lot, 250, 288, 398, 402-405, 458, 459, 559

Lupus, 76

M

Maaroot, 58

Magic, 57, 58, 230, 293, 380, 547-549

Magicians, 292, 293, 380, 547, 548

Marriage, 88, 91, 93, 127, 154, 155, 158-162, 184, 199

Mars, 555

Mary, 54, 118, 119, 120, 190, 194, 203, 204, 211, 219, 220, 229, 310, 338, 524-529

Mary's family, 524, 525

Meat, 76, 198, 259, 266, 486

Mecca, 68, 69, 73, 81, 82, 130, 197, 225, 226, 319, 334, 489

Medina, 350, 354

Message of the Qur'an, 556

Menstrual fluids, 89

Menstruation, 89

Michael, 57

Middle East, 69, 145, 252, 322, 465, 526

Midian, 288, 289, 347, 398, 404, 460, 544

Monotheism, 26, 69, 115

Moon, 249, 253, 254, 283, 364, 412, 431, 449, 465

Mosaic Law, 53, 63, 106, 202

Moses, viii, 11, 19, 26-28, 34, 47-50, 53-56, 59, 65, 66, 70, 95-98, 114, 118, 121, 127, 128, 173, 189, 192, 202-206, 218-221, 250, 251, 269, 292-303, 337, 361, 380-382, 398, 406-409, 428, 443, 461, 489, 494, 505, 507, 518-520, 532, 540-554

Mountain ranges, 297, 437, 452, 466

Mountains, 101, 288, 431, 432, 455, 466, 467, 475, 479, 495, 500, 515, 522, 537, 555

Mt. Sinai, 49, 56, 189, 305, 531

Murder, 21, 44, 51, 55, 85, 115, 149, 184, 207, 268, 494